SUSTRANS'
TRAFFIC-FI CYCLE RIDES
150 GREAT DAYS OUT

sustrans
JOIN THE MOVEMENT

Sustrans' Traffic-free Cycle Rides

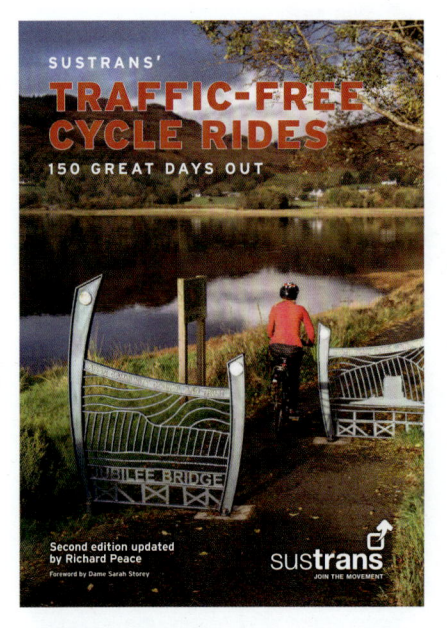

All rights reserved. This publication or any part of it may not be copied or reproduced by any means without the prior permission of the publisher. All enquiries should be directed to the publisher.

We have taken all responsible steps to ensure that the cycle rides in this book are safe and achievable by people with a reasonable level of fitness. However, all outdoor activities involve a degree of risk and the publisher and author accepts no responsibility for any injuries caused to readers while following these routes.

The contents of this book are believed to be correct at the time of printing. Nevertheless, the publisher and author cannot be held responsible for any errors or omissions or for changes in the details given in this book or for the consequences of any reliance on the information provided by the same. This does not affect your statutory rights.

Acknowledgements

Sustrans would like to thank Richard Peace for researching, writing and updating this edition of Traffic-free cycle rides

Commissioning Editor
Kelly Horton

Cartography, Design and Layout
FourPoint Mapping

Copy Editors
Richard Peace and Katie Watson

Published by
Sustrans, 2 Cathedral Square, College Green, Bristol BS1 5DD, United Kingdom
www.sustrans.org.uk

All maps in this publication contain Ordnance Survey data © Crown copyright and database right (2021)

© OpenStreetMap contributors
www.openstreetmap.org/copyright and
www.opendatacommons.org

© Copyright Sustrans 2021
First published 2015

This edition published 2021

ISBN: 978-1-914410-43-7

Registered Charity No. 326550 (England and Wales)
SC039263 (Scotland)

Sustrans' Traffic-free Cycle Rides

CONTENTS

4	Foreword by Dame Sarah Storey
6	Introduction by Xavier Brice
8	National Cycle Network timeline
12	How to use this guide
16	Plan a family ride
17	Good cycling code
18	Get involved
19	Shop with us
22	01 SOUTH WEST
62	02 SOUTH EAST
98	03 WALES
150	04 MIDLANDS
186	05 EAST OF ENGLAND
220	06 NORTH WEST
250	07 YORKSHIRE
278	08 NORTH EAST
300	09 SCOTLAND
332	10 NORTHERN IRELAND
342	Photo credits

Little Haven, South Shields

FOREWORD

BY
DAME SARAH STOREY

Dame Sarah Storey is Great Britain's most successful Paralympian following her sensational road race victory at the delayed Tokyo 2020 Paralympic Games, a victory secured in treacherous conditions at the Fuji International Speedway. In an international sporting career that has spanned more than 30 years, Sarah is also the Active Travel Commissioner in South Yorkshire, working to build a connected network of walking and cycling routes for all purposes.

The simple joy of riding a bike is one of the most inclusive and sociable ways to explore our beautiful corner of the world, and is one of the most fun ways to make short everyday journeys too. Across the UK we are blessed with breathtaking scenery and our lush green countryside is never far from any urban space.

I've been riding a bike since I learned as a child. I used it as a way of commuting whilst doing my A levels. Now I enjoy riding with my children just as much as I enjoy training hard for the opportunity to try and win more medals. I'm fortunate to have some fabulous off-road routes to ride straight from my front door, but I initially bought this book to explore traffic-free routes whilst on holiday with my family.

One of our favourite routes is the Keswick Railway path page 246 which was perfect for our two-year old who learned to ride in the first lockdown. We have also enjoyed the loop of Grafham Water page 206 and had a stopover for lunch on a trip north to ride from Skelton to York and back which proved to be a great way to burn off some road trip energy for the kids!

This latest edition of Sustrans' Traffic-free Cycle Rides has some fantastic new routes to explore. My children have already earmarked the Windemere to Elterwater route for our next trip to the Lake District. We also highly recommend exploring the Taff Trail which is a favourite for when we visit family in Cardiff. In fact it's not a case of which routes you might choose, it's just a case of which route you will choose first!

Every year Sustrans, the custodians of the National Cycle Network, spends in excess of £1 million on route maintenance. By buying this guide you are helping contribute to keeping these paths open for generations to come.

Cycling always brings a huge smile to my face, and I always look forward to my chance to get out in nature and explore the outdoors. So whether you are a veteran of cycling, someone who has just picked up their bike after many years without it, or are keen to experience the benefits that cycling can bring you and your family, this book will give you some great places to explore. It may even introduce you to routes close to home that you can use for other everyday journeys too.

Sustrans' Traffic-free Cycle Rides

"The simple joy of riding a bike is one of the most inclusive and sociable ways to explore our beautiful corner of the world."

The Taff Trail, Cardiff (National Route 8)

Sustrans' Traffic-free Cycle Rides

"More than a Cycle Network, this is a network of paths for everyone, providing space for walkers, scooters, wheelchairs, and horses."

Leeds and Liverpool canal towpath near Foulridge

INTRODUCTION

BY
XAVIER BRICE
CHIEF EXECUTIVE, SUSTRANS

Welcome to the second edition of Sustrans' Traffic-free Cycle Rides. In the pages that follow you will find 150 routes using the National Cycle Network and quiet paths. From short loops of 4 miles to rides of over 30 miles there is a route for everyone. The routes are almost entirely traffic-free, running on bridle-ways, converted railway paths, canal tow paths and quiet lanes.

The routes span the regions, nations and history of the UK, including the Two Palaces ride in central London, to the Great Glen way in the Scottish Highlands. There are a number of new rides for this edition, from a largely flat route pedal along the Leeds to Liverpool Canal to one of the most challenging rides in the book, the 21 miles from Dolgellau to Tywyn in Snowdonia National Park, with spectacular views over Barmouth Bay.

We hope that in cycling these routes you will be inspired to explore more of the National Cycle Network from which they are drawn. Founded over 25 years ago by Sustrans, there are now over 12,500 miles of routes connecting our towns and cities, countryside and communities. The diversity and scale of the Network is impressive but its real success is the impact that it has on people's lives and in the places we live. Every year, 750 million trips are made somewhere on the Network, representing all stages of life; from a child's first cycle ride to a journey to the shops on a mobility scooter in later years. More than a Cycle Network, this is a network of paths for everyone, providing space for walkers, scooters, wheelchairs, and horses.

This Network is made possible by the hundreds of landowners and organisations whose land the routes pass over, and who help maintain it – not least the thousands of dedicated Sustrans volunteers who give their time, and our supporters who provide financial support. As custodians of the Network we are working to grow and improve the routes, and widen access so that more people are able to enjoy it.

In buying this book you too are supporting Sustrans, this Network and the memories it creates. Thank you.

I hope you enjoy creating your own memories from the rides in these pages. Have fun out there, and please share the paths considerately with others. They are special places for everyone.

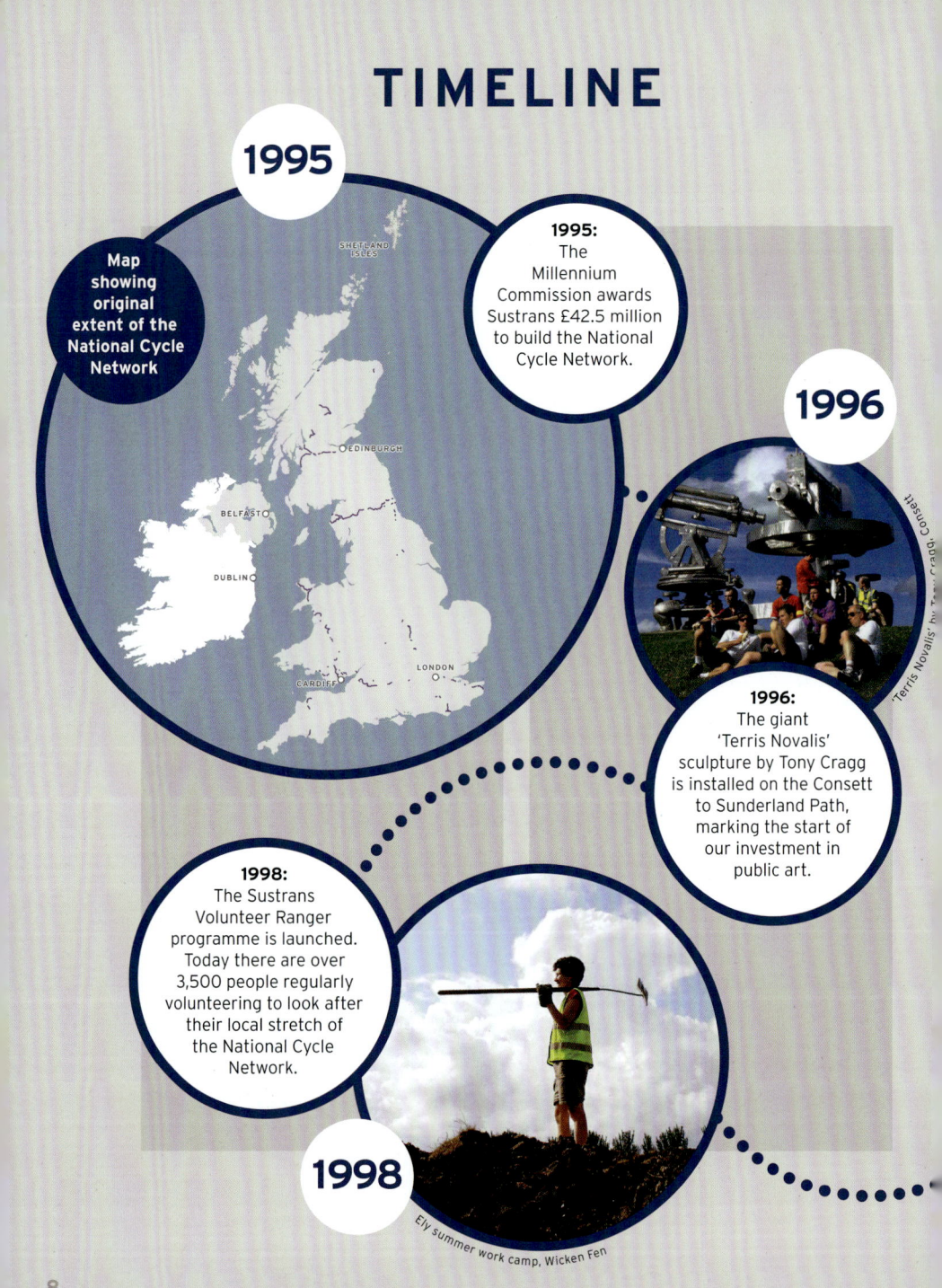

Sustrans' Traffic-free Cycle Rides

TIMELINE

1995

Map showing original extent of the National Cycle Network

1995: The Millennium Commission awards Sustrans £42.5 million to build the National Cycle Network.

1996

'Terris Novalis' by Tony Cragg, Consett

1996: The giant 'Terris Novalis' sculpture by Tony Cragg is installed on the Consett to Sunderland Path, marking the start of our investment in public art.

1998: The Sustrans Volunteer Ranger programme is launched. Today there are over 3,500 people regularly volunteering to look after their local stretch of the National Cycle Network.

1998

Ely summer work camp, Wicken Fen

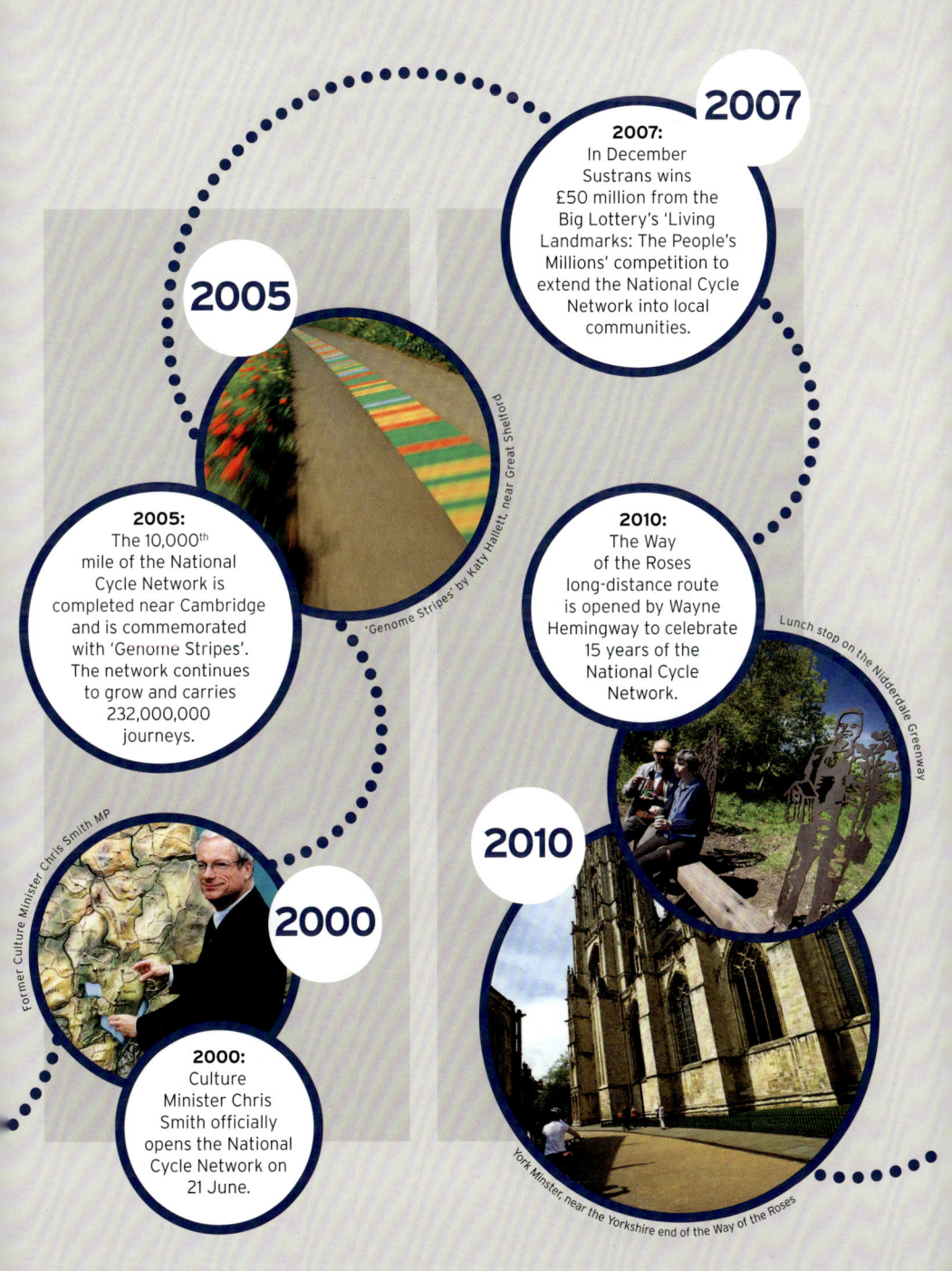

Sustrans' National Cycle Network

2007

2007: In December Sustrans wins £50 million from the Big Lottery's 'Living Landmarks: The People's Millions' competition to extend the National Cycle Network into local communities.

2005

'Genome Stripes' by Katy Hallett, near Great Shelford

2005: The 10,000th mile of the National Cycle Network is completed near Cambridge and is commemorated with 'Genome Stripes'. The network continues to grow and carries 232,000,000 journeys.

2010: The Way of the Roses long-distance route is opened by Wayne Hemingway to celebrate 15 years of the National Cycle Network.

Lunch stop on the Nidderdale Greenway

Former Culture Minister Chris Smith MP

2000

2010

2000: Culture Minister Chris Smith officially opens the National Cycle Network on 21 June.

York Minster, near the Yorkshire end of the Way of the Roses

9

Sustrans' Traffic-free Cycle Rides

2018

2018: Sustrans launches a review of the National Cycle Network and sets a clear vision for its future. The Paths for Everyone programme begins with the goal to deliver 15 key recommendations, including improving route quality and setting out ways to get local communities involved in designing, maintaining and developing the paths.

Paths for Everyone programme begins

2014

Forth & Clyde Canal

2014: The National Cycle Network is crowned the nation's favourite environment project in the National Lottery Awards and carries 4.8 million people.

Malcolm Shepherd receives the award from Kate Humble

2013

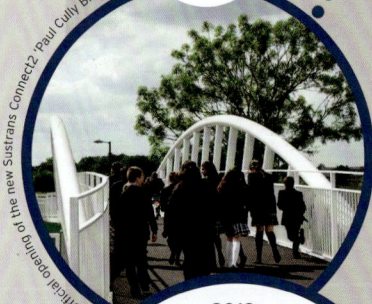

Official opening of the new Sustrans Connect2 'Paul Cully Bridge'

2013: Sustrans celebrates 84 new route links built in towns and cities across the UK, enabling easy access to the Network. Sustrans wins the Ashden Award for Sustainable Travel for the routes, connecting communities to the National Cycle Network across the UK.

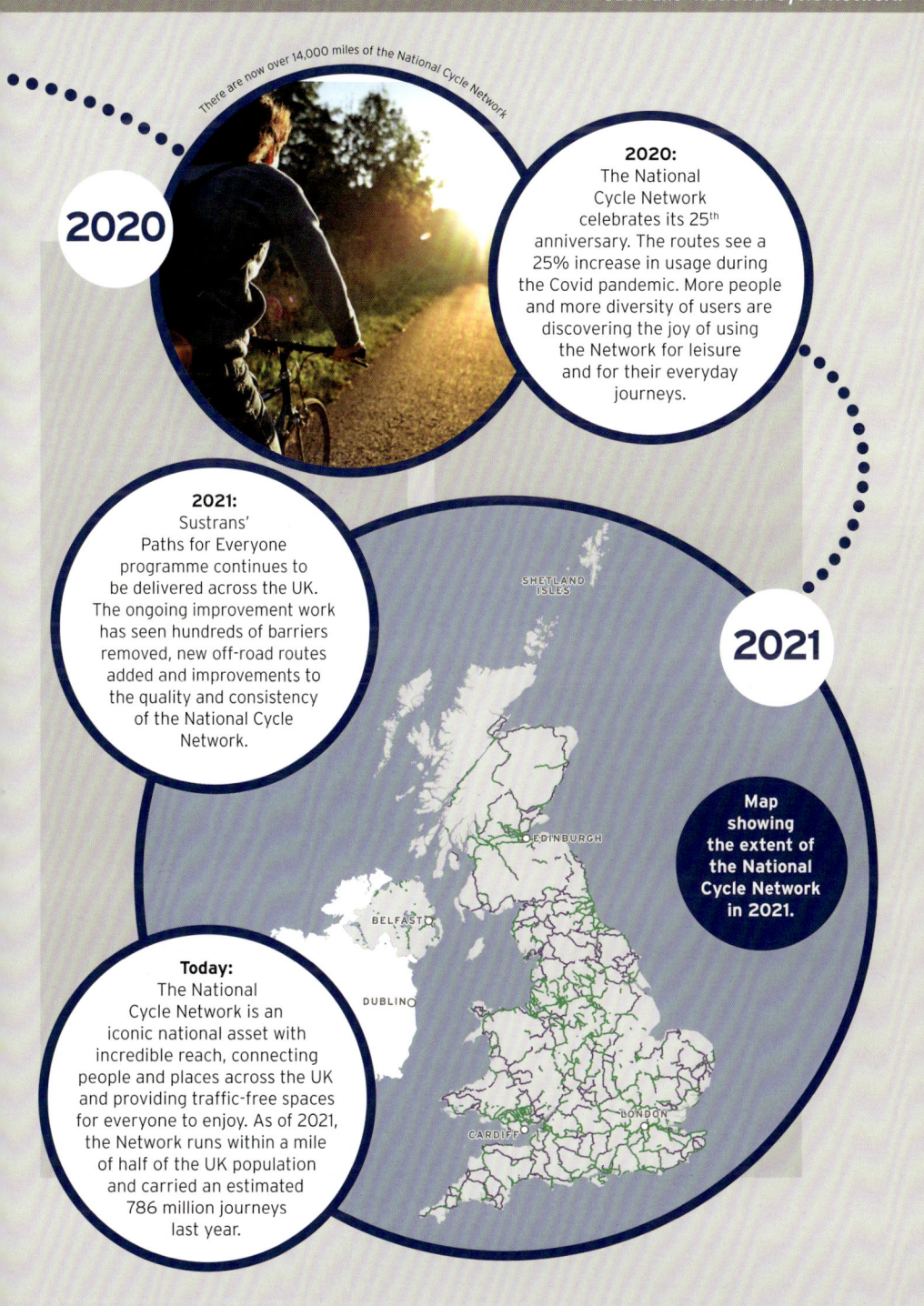

Sustrans' National Cycle Network

There are now over 14,000 miles of the National Cycle Network

2020

2020:
The National Cycle Network celebrates its 25th anniversary. The routes see a 25% increase in usage during the Covid pandemic. More people and more diversity of users are discovering the joy of using the Network for leisure and for their everyday journeys.

2021:
Sustrans' Paths for Everyone programme continues to be delivered across the UK. The ongoing improvement work has seen hundreds of barriers removed, new off-road routes added and improvements to the quality and consistency of the National Cycle Network.

2021

Map showing the extent of the National Cycle Network in 2021.

Today:
The National Cycle Network is an iconic national asset with incredible reach, connecting people and places across the UK and providing traffic-free spaces for everyone to enjoy. As of 2021, the Network runs within a mile of half of the UK population and carried an estimated 786 million journeys last year.

Sustrans' Traffic-free Cycle Rides

HOW TO USE THIS GUIDE

NCN (National Cycle Network) numbers and route names: These blue signs with red and white number patches are listed at the top of the page and you should look out for them as you ride. NCN signs sometimes display the route name, but not always. Many rides have more than one number as they follow more than one route on the Network. There are only a couple of rides in this guide that do not follow NCN routes (e.g. Tamsin Trail in London) and these usually have their own signs.

National Cycle Network signs

Distance: This is listed in miles. For linear routes the mileage refers to a one-way trip only, but for circular routes it refers to the entire ride.

Start and finish: The suggested start and finish points are often at a train station, town or city centre, visitor attraction or other recognisable feature in the area. However, you may want to join the trail at a different point for a shorter ride or to avoid town or city centre cycling. Indeed, alternative start and finish points are included for some of the longer routes to help you plan a shorter ride.

Train stations: In general, only the stations at the start and end of the route are listed, so you may find there are more stations along the way if you want to cut the ride short or start from a different point. Where no station exists along the route, the nearest has been named if possible. In just a few cases (e.g. Kielder Water or North Dorset Trailway) there is no train station on or near the route and other travel arrangements will need to be

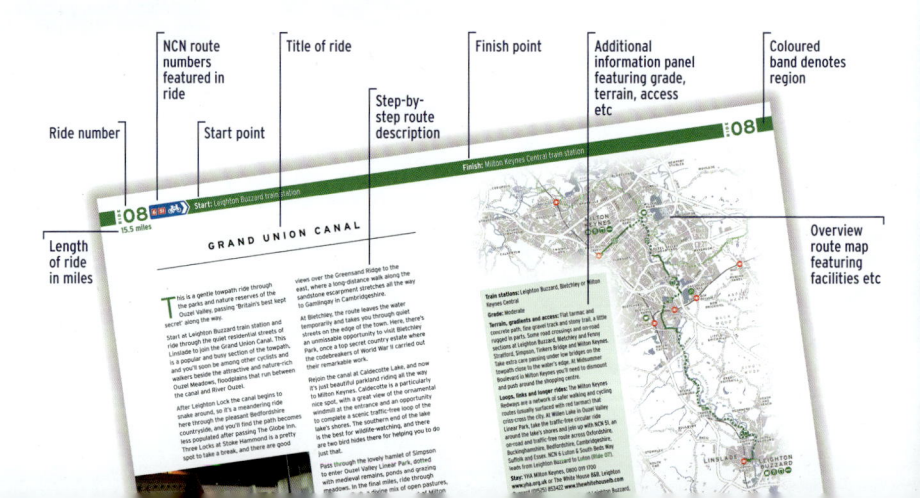

- Ride number
- NCN route numbers featured in ride
- Start point
- Title of ride
- Step-by-step route description
- Finish point
- Additional information panel featuring grade, terrain, access etc
- Coloured band denotes region
- Length of ride in miles
- Overview route map featuring facilities etc

12

How to use this guide

made. Bikes are carried free of charge on most UK trains when accompanied by the passenger, but on-board provisions vary depending on the train operator. Some have bookable spaces, whilst others operate a first-come, first-served policy. Always check when booking your ticket, or contact National Rail for advice on 03457 48 49 50 www.nationalrail.co.uk

Grade: This should help you decide whether the route is for you. Note that the grading only applies to the direction in which the route is written. If you're planning to ride both ways on a route that is graded easy because of a steady descent all the way, then be prepared for a steady climb on the return leg. Easy rides are usually less than 10 miles and are generally flat or descending. Moderate rides are more than 10 miles in length and may include some climbs. Challenging rides are the longest and most difficult in the book, often more than 20 miles in length and containing several hills.

Terrain: Most rides contain a mix of common surface types as described here. Any particularly unusual surfaces, such as where the trail is very rough, have been highlighted individually as appropriate.

On-road: Though the rides are largely traffic-free, most include some sections of on-road riding. These are often at the start and finish, where the paths have been linked to a town or city centre or train station to allow you to

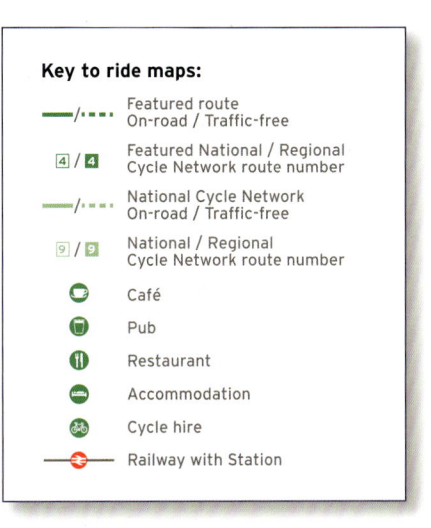

Key to ride maps:

— / ···· Featured route On-road / Traffic-free

4 / 4 Featured National / Regional Cycle Network route number

— / ···· National Cycle Network On-road / Traffic-free

9 / 9 National / Regional Cycle Network route number

☕ Café

🍺 Pub

🍴 Restaurant

🛏 Accommodation

🚲 Cycle hire

🚉 Railway with Station

travel more sustainably. There may also be road crossings and on-road riding mid-route. Every effort has been made to ensure quieter roads are used where possible, but take extra care along all on-road sections and at road crossings. You may prefer to dismount and push along the pavement instead, especially with younger or less experienced cyclists.

Tarmac or other hard path: This type of smooth, sealed surface is suitable for all bike types in all weathers.

Fine gravel track or stony trail: This type of unsealed, hard path may have a 'gritty' coating of whin dust or limestone dust, or be surfaced with larger, looser stones. Usually suitable for most bike types, these surfaces can be more challenging to ride in poor weather and may not suit lightweight road bikes or heavy-laden bikes.

Sustrans' Traffic-free Cycle Rides

Gradients: Many of the routes in this guide follow former railway lines, canal towpaths and riverside paths, so are often flat or include only gentle gradients. Some may have steeper climbs or descents, which are noted here and reflected in the grade of the ride.

Access: If a ride contains steps, or gates that need to be opened and closed behind you, then this is noted here. Narrowed entrances are not mentioned as you can expect to find them on almost all traffic-free paths, usually at the start and end, and at access points along the way. These are in place to prevent motorised traffic from accessing the paths. However, seafront promenade routes are often wider and free of gates or narrowed entrances.

Route description: This should give you a flavour of what you'll see and experience along the way, with some suggestions for interesting detours, attractions and picnic stops. Note that attractions have varied opening times and some are closed off-season. If you're keen to visit a particular place during your ride then check opening times before you set off.

Loops, links and longer rides: To help extend or enhance your trip, a small selection of other routes are listed here. These are a mix of traffic-free and on-road rides that either link directly to the featured ride or can be found nearby. Some are featured elsewhere in this guide and the ride number is then listed here to help you find it. If the featured ride is part of a long-distance route then that may also be included here.

Stay: Just one or two accommodation suggestions have been made for each ride. These are a mix of B&Bs, guesthouses, hotels, campsites and YHAs for various budgets. Most suggestions are on or close to the featured route and have secure cycle storage. Some have extra facilities such as bike wash, maps and guidebooks or even bike hire and repair facilities.

Eat and drink: A selection of places on or close to the featured route have been listed and an extra effort has been made to include places recommended by cyclists or themed 'cycle cafés'. There is only space for a handful of fuel-stops here, so you are likely to find more options on your ride. Opening times vary, so check in advance if there's somewhere you're particularly keen to try.

The Strawberry Line

How to use this guide

The Peregrine Path

Cycle hire: Cycle hire is a great option if you'd prefer not to travel with your own bike. Only one or two suggestions are listed for each ride and they are on or near the route where possible. Where there is no cycle hire locally the nearest has been listed. If you're planning to use a cycle hire centre then contact them in advance to check the location, opening times, bike types and availability. You may need to book or pay a deposit in advance and take ID with you on the day.

Wider area cycle map: This guide is designed to give you a glimpse of what each ride has to offer, but always take a detailed map out with you. The map that covers the featured ride is listed here and is available from the Sustrans shop at **shop.sustrans.org.uk**

Tip: Look out for the Cyclists Welcome logo. Businesses carrying this logo offer services or facilities specifically for cyclists and are assessed by VisitEngland, VisitScotland, Visit Wales or Discover Northern Ireland to ensure they meet certain cycle-friendly standards. Cycling UK also operates a Cyclists Welcome scheme, or some councils and local authorities have their own cycle-friendly schemes for local businesses, usually displayed in their window or on their website.

Note: All businesses are purely suggestions and their inclusion in the guide is not necessarily an endorsement.

PLAN A FAMILY RIDE

Family-friendly cycling

Read up on your chosen ride so that you're aware of what's ahead. Take a look at your planned route on Sustrans' online mapping (www.sustrans.org.uk) and take a map out with you. Getting lost, an unexpected hill or a longer route than you'd anticipated will spoil things if you're unprepared.

Pack food and snacks for a picnic; it's always good to pause to give energy levels a boost and enjoy the views.

Wearing a helmet is currently not compulsory in the UK, so the decision is ultimately a question of individual choice. Although helmets can't prevent accidents from happening they can protect you if an accident does occur, and are especially recommended for children.

Before setting off, check your bike is in good condition. Tyres should be pumped up and the seat and handlebars set to the right position. Also check brakes and lights are in good order and tightly secured, gears are changing smoothly, and gear and brake cables aren't rusty or frayed. Wheel quick release mechanisms should be in the closed position and the chain should be clean and lubricated.

If cycling as a family, remember to keep children in front of you on roads (or in between if there are two of you), and take extra care at crossings and junctions.

You don't need special or expensive equipment to enjoy a family bike ride, but here are some simple items that you'll certainly find useful:

- Puncture repair kit and pump
- Spare inner tubes
- Tyre levers
- Bike 'multi-tool' and/or Allen keys and adjustable spanner
- Bike lights
- Bike lock
- Water bottle
- Bungee cords, panniers or basket to carry luggage
- Waterproofs.

The rides in this guidebook have been suggested by Sustrans to help you enjoy the best traffic-free sections of the National Cycle Network. Cycle routes and road networks change over time, which may affect this collection of rides. Weather conditions may also affect path surfaces. Use this as a guide only, and use your own judgement on the day, based upon the weather, traffic conditions and the ability, experience and confidence levels of riders in your group.

GOOD CYCLING CODE

- Always follow the Highway Code when on-road.
- Cycle at a safe and responsible speed and cycle slowly where there is limited space and when you cannot see clearly ahead.
- On shared-use paths respect others you're sharing the space with and be prepared to slow down. Remember these paths are for sharing not speeding.
- Give priority to people who are moving more slowly than you, including older people, people who are less mobile or have visual and hearing impediments, as well as small children.

The Granite Way

The Millennium Way

- Give way and be courteous to people walking and take care around horse riders leaving them plenty of room.
- Have a bell on your bike and ring it, or call out, well in advance if approaching from behind to avoid surprising people and horses.
- Remember many people are hard of hearing or visually impaired so don't assume they can see or hear you. A bell might not always be enough to alert people you're coming.

- Keep to your side of any dividing line and keep to the left where there isn't one.
- Be particularly careful at junctions, bends, access points and any other blind spots.
- Take extra care going downhill and on loose surfaces.
- Take care when cycling beside rivers or canals and be ready to slow down and give priority to people walking on towpaths.
- In dark or dull conditions make sure you have bike lights and consider wearing brightly coloured reflective clothing.
- Do not cycle whilst using your mobile phone and avoid wearing headphones.
- Do not cycle on pavements unless they are designated for shared-use.

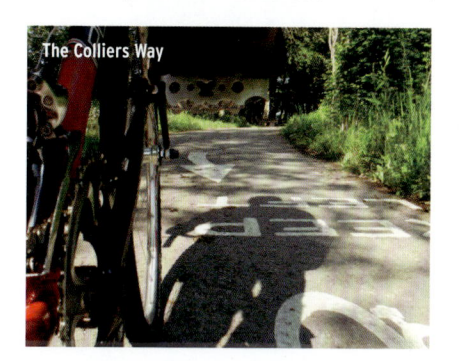

The Colliers Way

Sustrans' Traffic-free Cycle Rides

GET INVOLVED

Signage at Stover Valley Country Park

Volunteers updating signs on the Network

There are lots of ways you can get involved with Sustrans:

- **Make a donation and join our growing community of supporters**

- **Volunteer with us and make a real difference in your local community**

- **Sign up to one of our fundraising challenges or organise your own.**

Visit sustrans.org.uk/get-involved to find out more.

Sustrans' Traffic-free Cycle Rides

SHOP WITH US

- Browse our collection of National Cycle Network maps, guidebooks, cycling accessories and more at the Sustrans shop

- Every purchase helps us to care for and improve the National Cycle Network

- Your support improves walking and cycling for everyone, creating healthier places and happier people.

Visit our shop: shop.sustrans.org.uk

Millennium milepost in Long Newton village near Darlington

SUSTRANS' TRAFFIC-FREE CYCLE RIDES

150 GREAT DAYS OUT

Sustrans' Traffic-free Cycle Rides

Kennet & Avon Canal, near Bath

SOUTH WEST

There has been a special relationship between cycling and the South West ever since one of the original routes on the National Cycle Network was completed – the Bristol & Bath Railway Path. This trailblazing route is still one of the must-do rides in the region, and has a well-deserved place in these pages. However, younger routes around these two handsome cities are rapidly earning a reputation as contemporary classics. The Two Tunnels Greenway, for example, will take you into the beautiful Georgian city of Bath on a memorable and atmospheric ride through the dim depths of the UK's longest cycling tunnel.

Few rides offer such scenic extremes as the Strawberry Line in the Mendip Hills, where the terrain transforms from flat Somerset Levels to the vertical cliffs of Cheddar Gorge within just a few miles. While for mystical otherworldliness there is nothing to rival the lunar landscape of Cornwall's clay pits, where a ride along the Clay Trails is as close as you may ever come to cycling in science fiction.

Ride across the chalk hills of the Marlborough Downs to reach one of the famous Wiltshire white horses, take the Drake's Trail and Granite Way along the wild and remote fringes of the Dartmoor National Park, or visit some of Dorset's chocolate-box towns and villages on the North Dorset Trailway. But, to discover the scenery that the South West is famed for, head for the crystal waters and golden beaches of Devon and Cornwall where you can tackle parts of the popular Devon Coast to Coast ride, the map is available to buy at **shop.sustrans.org.uk**. Ride between two idyllic Cornish villages on the Pentewan Trail, and experience the ethereal beauty of three first-class estuaries on the Exe Estuary Trail, Tarka Trail and Camel Trail.

Glastonbury Tor

Routes overview

- **01** Coast to Coast Trail (part of the Cornish Mineral Tramways) (11.5 miles)
- **02** Pentewan Valley Trail (4 or 6.5 miles)
- **03** Clay Trails (10 miles)
- **04** Camel Trail (5 or 18 miles)
- **05** Drake's Trail (18 miles)
- **06** Stover & Wray Valley Trails (13.5 miles)
- **07** Exe Estuary Trail (17.5 miles)
- **08** The Granite Way (8.5 miles)
- **09** Tarka Trail (30 miles)
- **10** Stop Line Way (4 miles)
- **11** Dorchester to Weymouth (8.5 miles)
- **12** North Dorset Trailway (9.5 miles)
- **13** Colliers Way (18 miles)
- **14** Two Tunnels Greenway (5 miles)
- **15** The Strawberry Line (11 miles)
- **16** Bristol & Bath Railway Path (16.5 miles)
- **17** Kennet & Avon Canal (12 or 22 miles)
- **18** Swindon to Marlborough (11.5 miles)
- **19** Stroud Valleys Trail & Stroudwater Canal (5 miles)
- ▬ Featured ride
- ▬ National Cycle Network (traffic-free and on-road)

RIDE 01
11.5 miles

Start: Portreath Harbour

COAST TO COAST TRAIL

(PART OF THE CORNISH MINERAL TRAMWAYS)

This is one of the few coast to coast routes in the country that can be completed during a leisurely afternoon ride. It crosses the extraordinary landscape of the Cornish Mining World Heritage Site on the old tramroads and railways that served the area's tin and copper mines.

Start at the harbour in Portreath, once one of the busiest and most important ports in Cornwall, and now a popular surf spot with a beautiful little golden beach. The first part of the ride is a steady climb through thick woodland, following the tramroad as it cuts across the steep hillside, before joining hedgerow-lined Cornish country lanes with attractive views over the fields and woods.

The cycle-friendly Elm Farm Café is a good early stop, before riding onwards to reach the gates of the renowned Rodda's Cornish Creamery. Keep a look out for the old stone engine houses of the copper mines that are dotted across the landscape all the way. Their tall chimneys are particularly distinctive, and there's an exceptional example visible from the path near Wheal Rose, almost five miles in, where the old tin mine engine house has been lovingly restored to its former glory and transformed into a cottage.

Some of the ride's best scenery features in the second half as you begin a gentle descent to the coast. It is particularly pleasant to ride through the lush greenery of the ancient woodland at Unity Wood, and this is followed by the vast open heathland of the Poldice Valley. Nature has done a fine job of reclaiming the land here, but the remains of tin and copper works still poke eerily from the thick blanket of purple heather moorland.

A steep and stony descent through the valley leads to the Bike Chain at Bissoe, a trailside cycle café that is perfect for tea and chat with fellow riders of the tramways, before continuing past the crumbling remains of the

Finish: Devoran Quay

RIDE 01

Train stations: Nearest are Redruth and Perranwell

Grade: Moderate

Terrain, gradients and access: Gently ascending in the first half and descending in the second. Tarmac path, fine gravel track and stony trail, with several on-road sections, road crossings and some gates.

Loops, links and longer rides: Cornish Mineral Tramways are a network of mostly traffic-free trails along the tramway and railway routes that used to serve Cornwall's mines. A section of this coast to coast trail is also part of NCN 3 Cornish Way, a mostly on-road route from Land's End to Bude via St Austell.

Stay: Elm Farm Eco Camping and Caravanning, near Porthtowan (01209) 891498 **elmfarm.biz**

Eat and drink: In Portreath, try The Portreath Arms Hotel or The Terrace Restaurant and Bar at Gwel an Mor. Along the route, visit Elm Farm Café near Porthtowan, Etherington's Farm Shop at Scorrier and Bike Chain café at Bissoe. The Old Quay Inn is at the route's end in Devoran.

Cycle hire: Elm Farm Bike Hire, near Porthtowan (01209) 891498 **elmfarm.biz** or Bike Chain, Bissoe (01872) 870341 **bikechainbissoe.co.uk**

Wider area cycle map: Cornwall

Boats moored at Devoran

Point Mills arsenic refinery. From here, pass through the Cornwall Wildlife Trust's Bissoe Valley Nature Reserve, a lovely little haven of open pools, streams, woodland and heathland created on a former mine.

Ride through the beautiful green Carnon Valley, where tin streamers once discovered the largest nugget of gold ever to be found in Cornwall, and you'll spot the huge Carnon Viaduct spanning the river ahead. Pass right beneath the majestic arches of the viaduct, before joining the very quiet road into Devoran to meet the sea on Cornwall's south coast. This is a truly peaceful ending, and there are bike racks here for locking up and walking beside the water. Alternatively, visit The Old Quay Inn for a reviving drink: you have just completed a coast to coast ride after all.

25

RIDE 02

Start: St Austell train station

4 miles to Pentewan Beach or
6.5 miles to Mevagissey Harbour

PENTEWAN VALLEY TRAIL

Mevagissey harbour

From the market town of St Austell, once a cornerstone of the china clay industry, this trail leads to the steep wooded slopes of the Pentewan Valley and two unspoilt Cornish fishing villages. There's also an option to visit the romantically mysterious Lost Gardens of Heligan along the way.

Start at St Austell train station, joining the road to descend out of the town and meet the traffic-free trail near Tregorrick. Here you'll be riding amid rolling green fields, grazing ponies and beside the rippling St Austell River, known as White River because of the clay deposits washed along it.

In the opening miles, enter The Woodland Trust's King's Wood, a simply magical native English woodland which is more than 400 years old. It comes alive with dragonflies and speckled wood butterflies in summer, and is coloured with marsh marigold and bluebells in springtime. At King's Wood there are two options for continuing. For a short, flat ride, continue through the woodland to reach the riverside picnic area at Pentewan Valley Cycle Hire, ending here with a drink or ice cream, or riding on through the village to reach the golden sandy beach.

Alternatively, cross the river in King's Wood to follow the trail all the way to the fishing village of Mevagissey. There are some significant climbs along a steep and stony path on this part of the ride, but the idyllic woodland and far-reaching views from the route's highest point more than justify the effort.

Finish: Pentewan Beach or Mevagissey Harbour

RIDE 02

Train station: St Austell

Grade: St Austell to Pentewan - Easy
St Austell to Mevagissey - Moderate

Terrain, gradients and access: Tarmac path and stony trail. Descending from the train station to the trail then flat between St Austell and Pentewan. Steep and stony sections to the Lost Gardens of Heligan and Mevagissey.

Loops, links and longer rides: At St Austell, join one of the Clay Trails, a series of traffic-free routes around St Austell, Wheal Martyn, the Eden Project and Bugle (**Ride 03**). NCN 3 Cornish Way is a mostly on-road route from Land's End to Bude or St Austell. Follow NCN 2 which terminates in St Austell for the Clay Trails to the Eden Project.

Stay: Travelodge St Austell 0871 9846160 travelodge.co.uk

Eat and drink: In St Austell seek out Cranked Coffee & Bikes and Eden Project Café. The Ship Inn and Pentewan Valley Cycle Hire are both at Pentewan, or visit the Heligan tearooms and Lobbs Farm Shop at The Lost Gardens of Heligan. In Mevagissey, popular waterside fuel-stops include Roskilly's organic Cornish ice cream shop and The Fishermen's Chippy.

Cycle hire: Pentewan Valley Cycle Hire (01726) 844242 pentewanvalleycyclehire.co.uk

Wider area cycle map: Cornwall

A sub-tropical jungle stop at The Lost Gardens of Heligan in the route's second half is an absolute must, and there's a signed, quarter of a mile link path that gently climbs off the Pentewan Trail to the gates of this secretive estate, hidden for almost a century but now lovingly and gloriously restored.

In the final mile, take the steep and stony descent to Mevagissey Activity Centre, before joining the road to ride past gardens of purple bee-filled verbena into Mevagissey village. End among the fishing boats and cottages on the quayside, and take a walk through the delightful maze of narrow streets, lined with tempting cafés, galleries and shops.

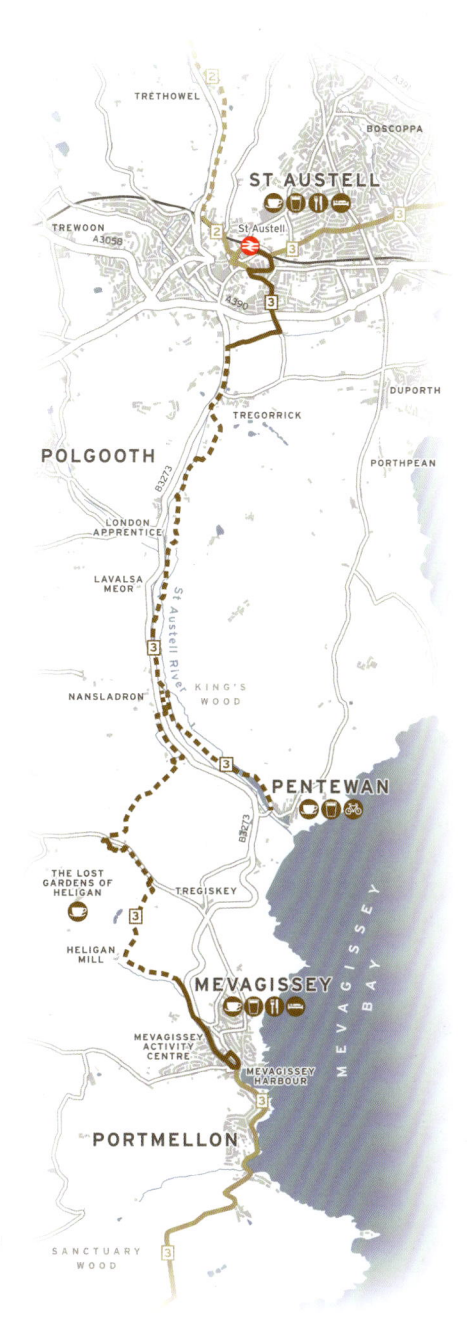

RIDE 03
10 miles — **Start:** St Austell train station

CLAY TRAILS

The ethereal landscape of the 'Cornish Alps', jagged white-tipped mini mountains sculpted by the area's china clay industry, makes this a truly unique ride.

The traffic-free path starts at Tremena Gardens, a quiet little residential area on the west side of St Austell which is just half a mile from the train station. A fabulous mix of forests, coastal vistas, heathland and active mines feature along the way, with a grand view from the very start over the elegant St Austell Viaduct spanning the Trenance Valley. Steep climbs and rugged descents make this quite a challenging ride, particularly in the first half. However, the scenery makes it worthwhile, and you'll ride through dense, dreamy woodland and among the alpine-like peaks and heather moorland of the old clay works. Look out for old clay-drying chimneys poking up in the landscape along the way.

Gliding gently around the top of the large lunar-like craters of Baal pit is like coasting through another world, and you'll be able to see right down the steep pit sides into the cloudy turquoise water at the bottom. Take a rest on the bench around three miles in; it's perfectly positioned for soaking up the scenery of rolling green fields and twinkling sea at St Austell Bay on a bright day.

At the halfway point, a quarter of a-mile link path leads down to the Eden Project, which is well worth a visit (there is discounted entry for visitors arriving by bike). If you don't have time to go inside, just make the short detour to the top of the link path to look down over the giant honeycombed pods that house steamy rainforests, Mediterranean lemon groves and classic Cornish gardens.

A long climb follows, so take a breather at the summit to take a last look back at the sensational sea views, before enjoying a heavenly, smooth descent. With just a few miles to go, pass the pretty Innis fishing lakes before continuing through the craggy mining landscape and woodland to Bugle. It's a very short, on-road ride from the end of the traffic-free trail to The Bugle Inn, or continue a short distance along the road to Bugle train station.

Clay Trail with a 'Cornish Alp'

Finish: Bugle train station

RIDE 03

Train stations: St Austell and Bugle

Grade: Moderate to challenging

Terrain, gradients and access: Undulating along tarmac path, fine gravel track and stony trail. Some gates, road crossings and quiet country lanes.

Loops, links and longer rides: The Clay Trails include a series of other traffic-free routes around St Austell, Wheal Martyn, Par Beach, the Eden Project and Bugle. NCN 3 Pentewan Trail (**Ride 02**). NCN 3 Cornish Way is a mostly on-road route from Land's End to Bude or St Austell. From Bugle, continue to follow NCN 305 along the road to the Goss Moor Trail, a four and a half-mile circular ride around the head of the Fal River.

Stay: Premier Inn St Austell Hotel 0871 5279018 premierinn.com

Eat and drink: The Eden Project has a café, coffee bar, restaurant and juice bar, or try The Innis Inn at Penwithick and The Bugle Inn at the route's end.

Cycle hire: Pentewan Valley Cycle Hire (01726) 844242 pentewanvalleycyclehire.co.uk

Wider area cycle map: Cornwall

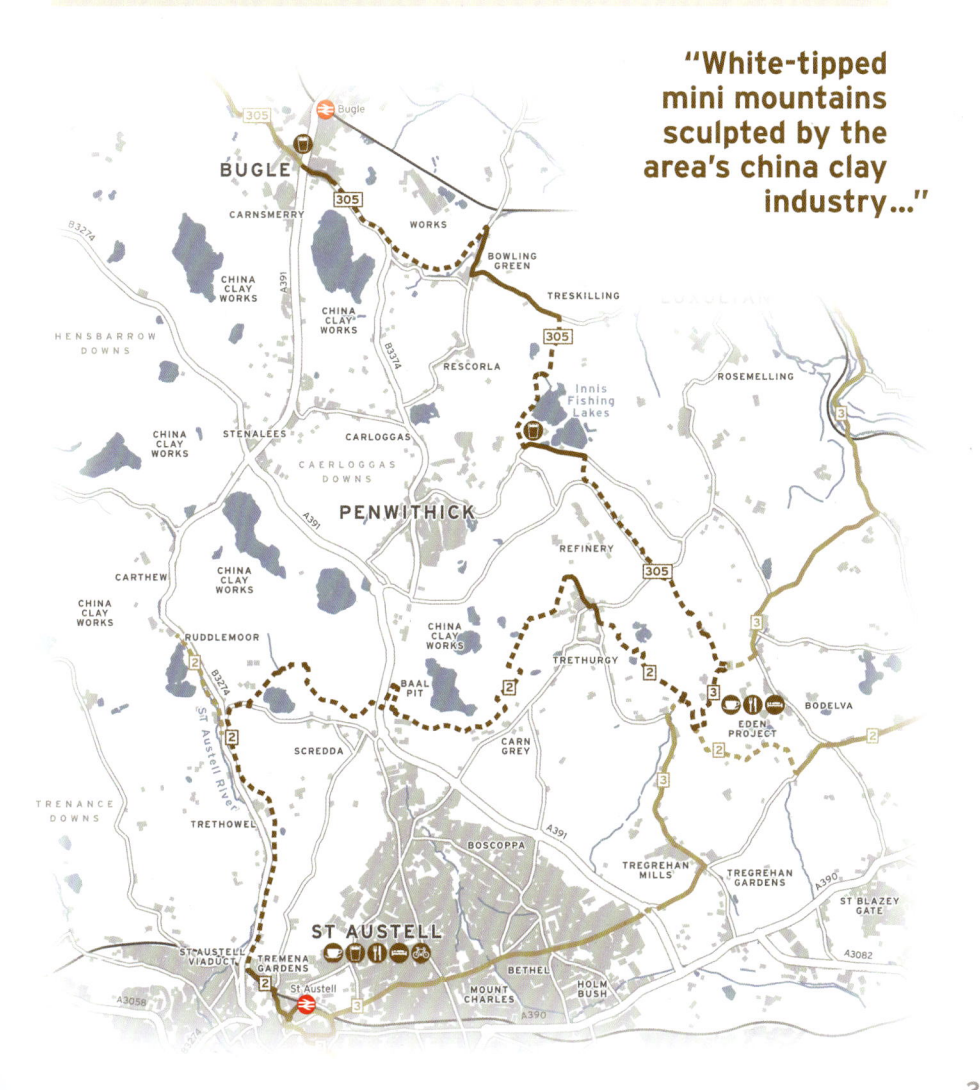

"White-tipped mini mountains sculpted by the area's china clay industry..."

29

RIDE 04

3 **32** 🚴

Start: Snail's Pace Café, Wenfordbridge or Bridge Bike Hire, Wadebridge

18 miles Wenfordbridge to Padstow or
5 miles Wadebridge to Padstow

CAMEL TRAIL

Padstow Harbour

This gentle descent through the Camel Valley is justifiably one of the most popular leisure routes in the country. It follows the meandering course of the River Camel from the edges of the wild and windswept Bodmin Moor to the Cornish Coast, and takes in the celestial beauty of the Camel Estuary along the way.

Start from the doors of the Snail's Pace Café at Wenfordbridge and immediately join the traffic-free path, crossing the De Lank River in the opening miles. Just moments after the river crossing there's an option to take the short, on-road detour to the fringes of the moor, visiting the friendly Blisland Inn in the quaint Cornish village of Blisland. Or simply stay on the trail to enter the thick woodland of the Forestry Commission's Shell Woods, where buzzards can often be spotted circling and calling over the tops of the trees on the far riverbank.

The gently raised position of the route through the trees means there are incredibly pretty views over the river as you approach Dunmere Halt Station, and there's a signed one and a half-mile, traffic-free link near here that leads into the centre of Bodmin, where the underground cells and execution pit of Bodmin Jail are a ghoulishly popular distraction. Alternatively, you'll pass the Camel Trail Tea Garden at Nanstallon a short while later, which makes for a more elegant midway stop, before rolling past the long, trailing rows of vines in the award-winning Camel Valley vineyard.

Scuff along the edges of the ancient woodland and saltwater meadows of Treraven Farm,

Finish: South Quay, Padstow

RIDE 04

Train station: Bodmin Parkway

Grade: Wenfordbridge to Padstow – Moderate
Wadebridge to Padstow – Easy

Terrain, gradients and access: Gently descending along tarmac path, fine gravel track and stony trail. Several gates and road crossings with an on-road section at Wadebridge.

Loops, links and longer rides: NCN 32 Cornish Way leads from Bodmin to Truro via Padstow and Newquay along a mostly on-road route. From Padstow, follow the on-road NCN 323 to Harlyn Bay.

Stay: Premier Inn Wadebridge Hotel (01208) 222066 premierinn.com

Eat and drink: Snail's Pace Café at Wenfordbridge, The Blisland Inn at Blisland and Camel Trail Tea Garden in Nanstallon are all popular. Wadebridge has many good cafés including Relish Food and Drink and Caraways café. Padstow is a real foodie destination: try Rick Stein's renowned Seafood Restaurant, or less formal alternatives such as the excellent Rojano's in the Square, Chough Bakery and Roskilly's ice cream parlour.

Cycle hire: Snail's Pace Café, Wenfordbridge (01208) 851178 snailspacecafe.co.uk, Trail Bike Hire, Padstow (01841) 532594 trailbikehire.co.uk, Bridge Bike Hire, Wadebridge (01208) 813050 bridgebikehire.co.uk or Padstow Cycle Hire (01841) 533533 padstowcyclehire.com

Wider area cycle map: Cornwall

and pause at the perfectly-situated viewing hide near here that overlooks the gradually widening waterway and striking shoreside Egloshayle church. With just five miles to go you'll reach the market town of Wadebridge, a popular start point for many families as it's an easy and entirely traffic-free ride from here into Padstow.

The final miles reveal the best scenery of the entire ride as land and sea begin to merge together in the sandy rivulets and salty creeks of the estuary. Waterside picnic benches on jutting lumps of land are ideally positioned for watching oystercatchers, lapwings and curlews picking their way through the mud and sandflats. Pass through the jagged grey slate piles of the old Penquean Quarry and catch glimpses of Padstow in the distance.

Dennis Hill and its giant obelisk loom ahead as you cross the water on the magnificent old railway bridge, and the little fishing boats in the working port of Padstow can be seen bobbing around in the harbour. End at South Quay and venture into the centre of this enchanting little Cornish village, always bustling with visitors. Take a stroll around the narrow streets and beautiful sandy beaches, or catch the Black Tor ferry over the water to the neighbouring village of Rock.

RIDE 05
18 miles

Start: Laira Bridge, Plymouth

DRAKE'S TRAIL

The scenery across Devon's south coast, woodland and moorland is spectacular as this route climbs through the Plym Valley, beginning in the maritime city of Plymouth and ending on the wild western edges of Dartmoor National Park.

Start the ride at Laira Bridge and cross the Plym Estuary for great views over the sparkling water and marina. The path undulates beside the River Plym in the opening miles, with water and wet meadows stretching out to one side, and beautiful deep woodland to the other. Rolling parkland at the National Trust's Saltram estate makes a great early stop, with Plymouth still visible across the water and a magnificent Georgian mansion house within the grounds.

A mile or so later, the beautiful native trees of Plymbridge Woods take over and you'll join up with Plym Valley Railway to follow the tracks of this little heritage route through the woodland. It's a steady climb from here to Cann Quarry, so take a rest on top of Cann Viaduct and look for the Plym Peregrines, a pair of nesting peregrine falcons on the steep sides of the slate quarry. More views and viaducts follow, with the little Devonshire villages of Bickleigh and Shaugh Prior visible on the hillsides, and the first glimpses of Dartmoor's open moorland beyond.

Around the halfway point, ride through the long and curving Shaugh Tunnel to reach Clearbrook, where the village pub makes an excellent mid-ride rest stop. It's a short but steep climb up the road from the pub, but there is sensational scenery from the top, and here it becomes a classic Dartmoor ride

of exposed gorse and heather moorland, twittering skylarks and semi-wild ponies.

At Yelverton, start a gentle descent that leads all the way to Magpie Viaduct, another magnificent structure where there are raised

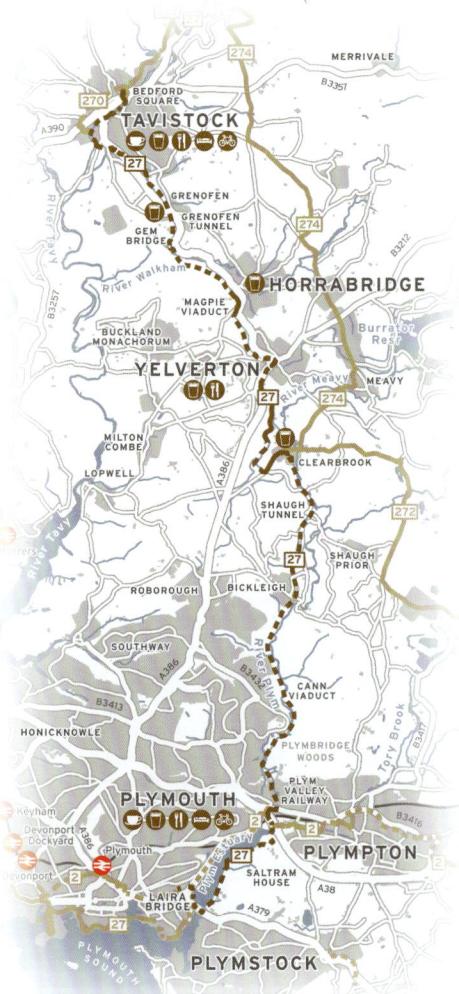

Finish: Bedford Square, Tavistock

RIDE 05

Train station: Plymouth

Grade: Moderate

Terrain, gradients and access: A steady climb for much of the way with a gentle descent in the final five miles. Tarmac path and stony trail with some gates, road crossings and on-road sections at Clearbrook, Horrabridge and Tavistock. Take care passing through Shaugh Tunnel and Grenofen Tunnel.

Loops, links and longer rides: From Laira Bridge at the start, follow the short, on-road section of NCN 27 to Plymouth Hoe, one of the nicest parts of the city which overlooks the incredible Plymouth Sound. The Dartmoor Way is a signed 95-mile circular ride on a mix of roads and traffic-free paths around the perimeter of the Dartmoor National Park. High Moorland Link is a 27-mile on-road route across Dartmoor National Park from Tavistock to Buckfastleigh. Drake's Trail is part of the Devon Coast to Coast, a mostly traffic-free route from Plymouth to Ilfracombe.

Stay: Premier Inn Sutton Harbour, Plymouth 0333 3211593 premierinn.com

Eat and drink: In Plymouth, try Rockets and Rascals cycle café or The Terrace Café on the cliffs of Plymouth Hoe. Mid-route, try The Skylark Inn at Clearbrook or The Halfway House Inn at Grenofen. The Tavistock Inn, Pannier Market café and Dukes Coffee House are among the places to eat in Tavistock.

Cycle hire: Rockets and Rascals, Plymouth (01752) 927555 rocketsandrascals.uk or Plymouth Bike Hire 07577 279589 plymouthbikehire.co.uk

Wider area cycle map: South Devon

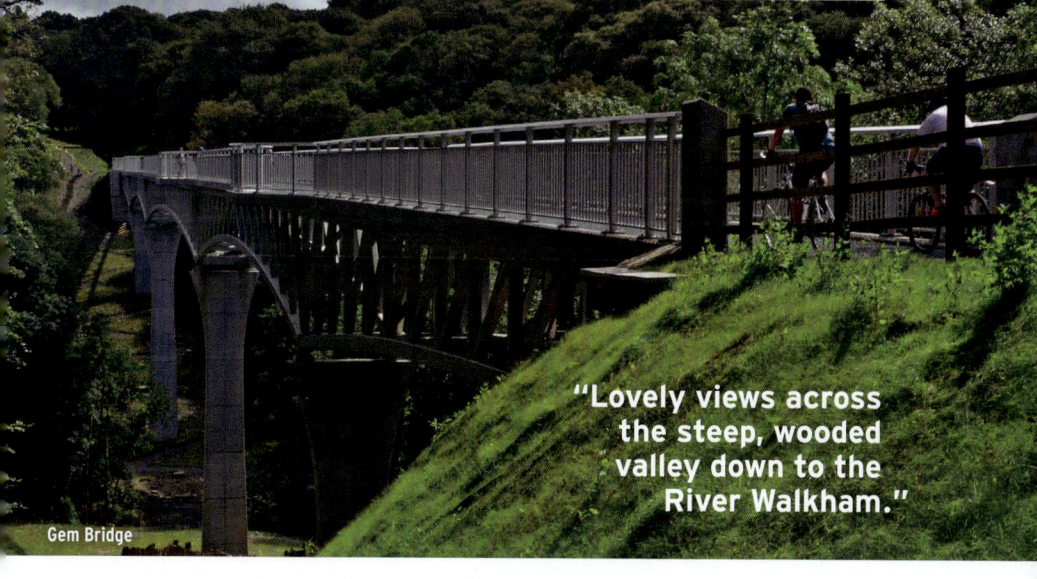

Gem Bridge

"Lovely views across the steep, wooded valley down to the River Walkham."

viewing spots for taking a good look across Dartmoor. From here, descend steadily through thick woodland to reach Gem Bridge, one of the most remarkable features of the ride. From afar it looks like a spider's web spun across the treetops, whilst from the centre there are lovely views across the steep, wooded valley down to the River Walkham.

In the final miles, ride through Grenofen Tunnel and approach Tavistock via the town's pretty riverside meadows. Remains of the old abbey can be seen across the water as you cross Abbey Bridge to the ride's endpoint at Bedford Square. The handsome Town Hall is here in the square, as is Tavistock Pannier Market, which is definitely worth a browse.

RIDE 06

13.5 miles | 28 | Start: Newton Abbot town centre

STOVER & WRAY VALLEY TRAILS

(NEWTON ABBOT TO MORETONHAMPSTEAD)

This route uses a towpath alongside one of the country's oldest and most unusual canals, shady, wooded railpath and some whisper quiet country lanes.

It might be hard to drag yourself away from the colourful and attractive centre of Newton Abbot. Its central landmark of St Leonard's Tower surrounded by pavement cafés and is just a stone's throw from a thriving market hall.

The shared pavement section cycle lane out of the town is the last you'll see of busy traffic, as you are then on country tracks to join the path alongside the Stover Canal that brought granite from Dartmoor to the docks at Teignmouth near Newton Abbot.

There is a signed link to Stover Country Park just before the multi-million pound traffic-free bridge over the arterial A38 before a brief road section leads through Bovey Tracey, a small town that acts as a gateway to the Dartmoor National Park you now enter.

Climbing gradually all the while, don't make the mistake of bypassing Lustleigh village just off the route, one of the most chocolate box pretty villages in the whole of Devon, complete with ancient church and thatched roof pub.

The final section is most obviously a railpath – a gradual uphill pull when it becomes apparent you have climbed over a thousand feet from lowly Newton Abbot, almost at sea level, into the heart of north-east Dartmoor. A short road link takes you to the pretty market town of Moretonhampstead which boasts its own solar-heated outdoor swimming pool and plenty of attractive watering holes and eateries.

Despite the climb gradients are almost always gradual and the return journey is an absolute breeze and downhill nearly all the way.

Countryside views near Lustleigh

Finish: Moretonhampstead village centre

Train Station: Newton Abbot (no train return)
Grade: Moderate
Terrain, gradients and access: Flattish cycle lanes and canal towpath out of Newton Abbot to Bovey Tracey then more gradients, especially around Lustleigh village. There's a very even uphill finale on railpath to Moretonhampstead.
Loops, links and longer rides: These two trails together are part of NCN route 28 which is due to join Okehampton and Plymouth; currently you can continue west on it using minor roads to head over the corner of Dartmoor and join the ever-popular Devon Coast to Coast at Okehampton (NCN 27).

Stay: Newton Abbot Hotel – Premier Inn 0333 321 9234 premierinn.com
Eat and drink: There are some idyllic spots directly on the trail including Mt Tums Café just north of Newton Abbot and the delightful Locksbridge Tea Garden. Bovey Tracey is a small town with a good stock of shops and a supermarket whilst Lustleigh village has the idyllic looking Cleave Inn and Primrose tearooms.
Cycle hire: Animal Crackers pet food just off the trail south of Moretonhampstead has bikes and e-bikes for hire (01647) 440273 animalcrackersdevon.co.uk
Wider area cycle map: South Devon

Railpath near Moretonhampstead

35

RIDE 07
17.5 miles

Start: Dawlish Warren

EXE ESTUARY TRAIL

This exceptionally beautiful ride along both sides of Devon's radiant Exe Estuary is easily one of the best routes in the country for birding by bike.

Start at the little seaside resort of Dawlish Warren, where the sandy beaches and National Nature Reserve are well worth exploring before setting off. After just a couple of miles on the trail you'll reach the lovely little harbour of Cockwood, where the expansive water views across the wide mouth of the estuary are incredible, even stretching as far as the route's endpoint at Exmouth.

Reach the boundary of Powderham Castle's lush green estate, where you might want to detour through the grounds and explore inside the historic home of the Earl of Devon. Alternatively, simply ride along the estate's bottom perimeter and get glimpses of the beautiful ivy-covered castle through the trees, before passing Powderham's gorgeous red sandstone St Clement's church.

From here, the path hugs the estuary all the way to Turf Locks, a wonderful place to picnic whilst looking across the RSPB's Exminster and Powderham Marshes nature reserve. The Turf Hotel is here, too, one of the few pubs in the country that isn't accessible by road, and you can even shortcut to the eastern side of the route at this point by catching the cycle-friendly Turf–Topsham ferry.

Sprawling wild estuary turns to formal waterway following Turf Locks, as you join the banks of the Exeter Canal and ride towards the city. At the midway point there's an option to follow a three and a half-mile path (NCN 34) through Riverside Valley Park

Train stations: Dawlish Warren, Exeter St Thomas and Exmouth

Grade: Moderate

Terrain, gradients and access: Mostly flat tarmac path but on the eastern side of the estuary there are some wooden boardwalks through the marshland and gentle climbs and descents through the villages. Some gates, road crossings and short, quiet, on-road sections at Dawlish Warren, Cockwood, Starcross, Powderham, Countess Wear, Topsham, Exton, Lympstone and Exmouth.

Loops, links and longer rides: From Exmouth, follow NCN 2 along a five-mile, mostly traffic-free route to Budleigh Salterton. This is part of the cross-channel Tour de Manche, almost 750 miles of routes through Dorset and Devon in England, and Normandy and Brittany in France.

Stay: Withall's House B&B, Lympstone (01395) 488123 lympstonebedandbreakfast.co.uk

Eat and drink: Favoured places to eat and drink on the west side include the Farm Shop and Orangery at Powderham Castle or The Turf Hotel at Turf Locks. On the east side, the renowned Darts Farm, Route 2 cycle café and The Salutation Inn are all at Topsham, or try The Puffing Billy at Exton. In Exmouth, Krispies fish and chip shop, Bumble and Bee café in Manor Gardens and Harbour View Café are all lovely, but River Exe Café out on a floating barge is in the most unique setting, only accessible by water taxi.

Cycle hire: Saddles and Paddles, Exeter Quay (01392) 424241 sadpad.com, Darts Farm, Topsham (01392) 878200 dartsfarm.co.uk, Route 2 Bike Shop, Topsham (01392) 879160 route2bikes.co.uk or Exmouth Cycle Hire (01395) 225656 exmouthcyclehire.co.uk

Wider area cycle map: South Devon

Finish: Exmouth seafront

RIDE 07

"One of the best routes in the country for birding by bike."

into Exeter centre, which is a thoroughly recommendable detour and leads through the city's vibrant quayside to its impressive cathedral. Otherwise, cross both the canal and river into Countess Wear to join the eastern edge of the estuary.

This side of the route takes in some of Devon's most handsome waterside villages, starting with Topsham, home to the renowned Route 2 cycle café and the popular Darts Farm. Ride along the wooden boardwalks of the RSPB's Bowling Green Marsh and Goosemoor nature reserves, and over the Clyst Bridge, before passing through the pretty little waterfront villages of Exton and Lympstone.

In the final miles, pass the reed-fringed edges of the National Trust's Lower Halsdon Farm where a one-mile, on-road route leads to A la Ronde, a fanciful 18th Century, sixteen-sided house. Alternatively, simply stay on the path and see the curve of the headland up ahead with Exmouth at its tip, the gateway to the remarkable Jurassic Coast. Cross Exmouth town centre to end on the seafront, where you could catch the Starcross ferry back to the west side of the estuary to turn the ride into a loop, or catch a train on the Avocet Line into Exeter for one of the most picturesque rail journeys imaginable.

37

THE GRANITE WAY

Ride 08 — 8.5 miles — **Start:** Lydford Castle

Lake Viaduct near Sourton

Some of England's most dramatic and ancient landscapes feature on this ride across the north western edge of Dartmoor National Park, unrivalled for wild and rugged beauty. The scenery is remarkable throughout, but never more so than from the middle of the two windswept viaducts mid-route. Before the start, take the very short, on-road descent to the National Trust's Lydford Gorge to explore the deepest gorge in the South West and see the 90 foot-high White Lady Waterfall.

Start the ride at the modest Lydford Castle, actually a notorious medieval prison, and ride past the pretty cottages and gardens of Lydford, a village that oozes Devon charm. Join the traffic-free trail on the edge of the village and head into craggy moorland, lush rolling fields and intoxicatingly pure country air.

In the opening miles you'll be under the silent, watchful gaze of the giant granite Widgery Cross at Brat Tor, before reaching the 19th Century Lake Viaduct where the scenery is spectacular in every direction. The church of St Michael de Rupe on Brent Tor dominates the distant skyline to the left, while brittle brown moorland stretches away to the right, often dotted with hunched hikers creeping their way steadily up the hillside.

At Sourton, pass the doors of the handsome village church and take a mid-ride rest on the grassy banks by its gates, or continue through Prewley Moor for less than a mile to reach Devon Cycle Hire for snacks and drinks.

In the ride's second half, there's a signed link path down to the steep shores of Meldon Reservoir, or simply continue along the trail to roll over the Scheduled Monument of Meldon Viaduct for more extraordinary views. From the middle of the viaduct you can see South Down and Sourton Tors, Meldon Dam, and vast expanses of bleak, dark granite that typify Dartmoor.

RIDE 08

Finish: Okehampton train station

Train station: Nearest are Okehampton and Gunnislake. Services from Okehampton to Exeter due to start by end of 2021 on reopened line. gwr.com

Grade: Easy

Terrain, gradients and access: Tarmac path with a very short unsurfaced section near Sourton. A short and quiet on-road section leaving Lydford and a road crossing at Okehampton.

Loops, links and longer rides: The Granite Way follows a section of The Dartmoor Way, a signed 95-mile circular challenge ride around the perimeter of the Dartmoor National Park. It is also part of the Devon Coast to Coast route, a 99-mile, mostly traffic-free route from Plymouth to Ilfracombe. NCN 27 Drake's Trail (**Ride 05**).

Stay: Meadowlea Guesthouse, Okehampton (01837) 53200 meadowleaguesthouse.co.uk or YHA Okehampton 0345 2602791 yha.org.uk

Eat and drink: The National Trust has a tearoom at Lydford Gorge, whilst The Castle Inn is right beside the route's start at Lydford. Try Riverside Tea Garden and The White Hart pub, both at Bridestowe, or Bearslake Inn close to Lake Viaduct. Devon Cycle Hire at Sourton Down offers snacks and drinks, or try the excellent 2 Rivers restaurant in Okehampton town centre.

Cycle hire: Devon Cycle Hire, Sourton Down (01837) 861141 devoncyclehire.co.uk or Granite Way Cycles Okehampton (01837) 650907 granitewaycycles.co.uk

Wider area cycle map: South Devon

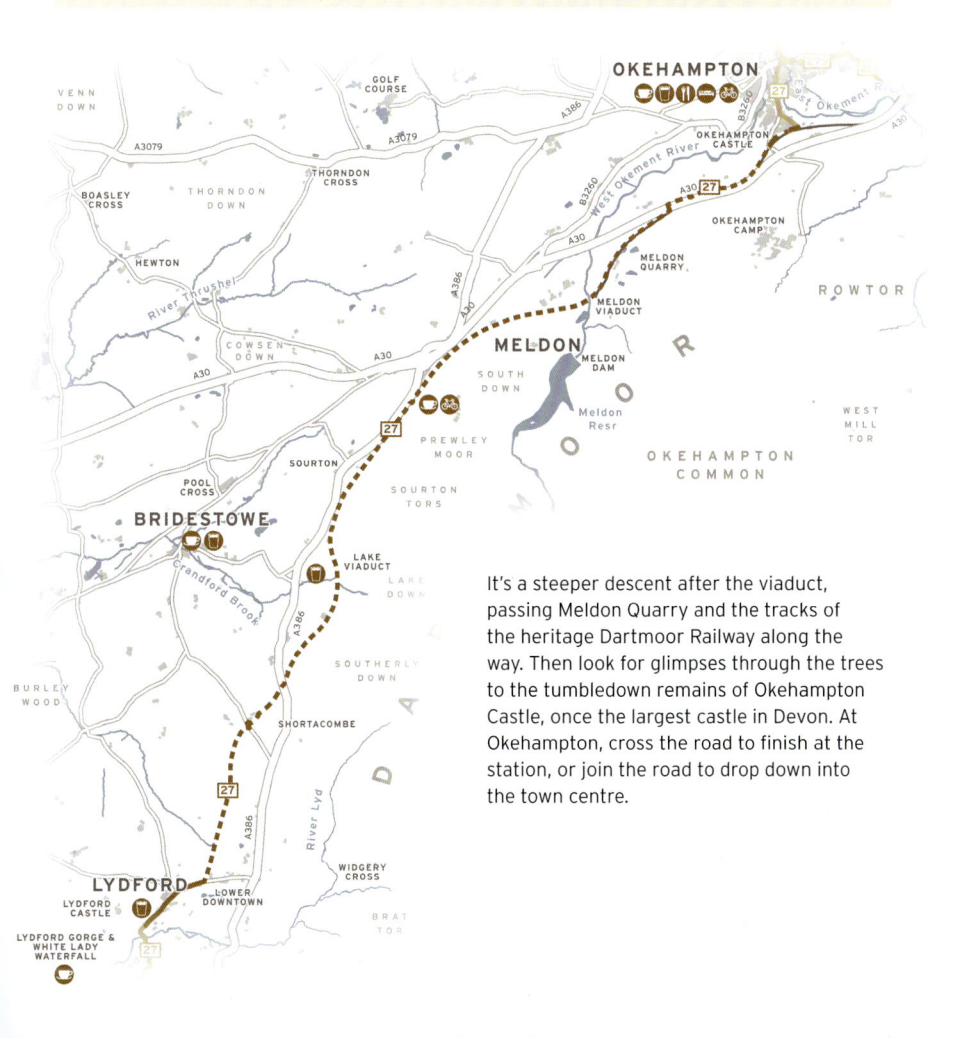

It's a steeper descent after the viaduct, passing Meldon Quarry and the tracks of the heritage Dartmoor Railway along the way. Then look for glimpses through the trees to the tumbledown remains of Okehampton Castle, once the largest castle in Devon. At Okehampton, cross the road to finish at the station, or join the road to drop down into the town centre.

RIDE 09
30 miles | 3 27 | **Start:** Meeth Halt Station

TARKA TRAIL

This popular trail along one of the longest railway paths on the National Cycle Network crosses unspoilt north Devon countryside and follows the magical Taw-Torridge Estuary.

Start at the old platform of Meeth Halt Station and head into the trees of the Devon Wildlife Trust's Meeth Quarry. It's a soothing ride past the enormous lakes and meadows of the old clay quarries and mines here, and you may even spot the reserve's herd of Exmoor ponies. These early miles are easily some of the most peaceful of the entire route, and the twisting trail through the giant oak trees to Devon Wildlife Trust's Ash Moor nature reserve is particularly tranquil. A steady climb leads between open meadows and crop fields to the organic café at Yarde Orchard, arguably the best eatery on the ride and thoroughly recommended for an early break.

It's all easy riding from here, as you descend gently to join the gushing River Torridge and reach the old Victorian station at Great Torrington. The river wriggles and winds here, so you'll find yourself crossing it several times. Look out for the beautiful Beam Aqueduct upstream, ride through the gently curved Landcross Tunnel, and cross the water on the long and impressive railway bridge, where limekiln remains are visible among the greenery on the far riverbank.

The Bideford Railway Heritage Centre is around the halfway point of the ride, and it's worth venturing over the water for a mid-ride break at Bideford's pretty quayside and town centre; the beautiful Pannier Market is particularly interesting.

In the second half of the ride the estuary scenery becomes truly sensational. Pause and look back over your shoulder at the graceful arches of Bideford Long Bridge, before reaching the delightful seafront village of Instow, with its golden sandy beach exposed at low tide and the lush, green Appledore village visible across the water. The short Instow Tunnel and a steep-sided, wooded railway cutting lead to the moody wetlands of RSPB Isley Marsh, and then you'll cross the little inlet of Fremington Pill where the surrounding scenery is astonishing. Fremington Quay Heritage Centre is a popular place to rest, or it's just a further three miles along the trail to Barnstaple, the capital of north Devon.

From Barnstaple, the Taw Bridge takes you across the wide River Taw, and the final miles are a gentle and attractive ride along the north bank of the estuary to Braunton. End at the little Braunton Museum and explore the village, or ride a couple of miles west to reach the long beach at Saunton Sands.

Cyclists on the Tarka Trail

Finish: Braunton Museum

RIDE 09

"One of the longest railway paths on the National Cycle Network…"

Train station: Barnstaple

Grade: Moderate

Terrain, gradients and access: A steady ascent from the start of the trail to East Yarde, then a steady descent to Great Torrington Station and flat for the remainder. Tarmac path, fine gravel track and stony trail with some gates and road crossings. Take care riding through Landcross Tunnel and Instow Tunnel.

Loops, links and longer rides: From Braunton, follow NCN 27 along the road to link up with NCN 278, a beautiful seven-mile ride on quiet roads and traffic-free paths that takes in the award-winning Woolacombe Beach. Tarka Trail is part of the Devon Coast to Coast, a mostly traffic-free route from Plymouth to Ilfracombe.

Stay: Yarde Orchard, East Yarde (01805) 621111 yarde-orchard.co.uk

Eat and drink: Near the start, try The Bull and Dragon in Meeth. Yarde Orchard organic café at East Yarde and The Puffing Billy at Great Torrington Station are directly on the route and in Bideford there is the Café du Parc at the Burton Art Gallery. At Instow village, Johns Bakery and Deli is excellent, and in Braunton there is the lovely Wild Thyme Café.

Cycle hire: Torrington Cycle Hire, Great Torrington (01805) 622633 torringtoncyclehire.co.uk, Tarka Bikes, Barnstaple train station (01271) 324202 tarkabikes.co.uk or Otter Cycle Hire, Braunton (01271) 813339

Wider area cycle map: North Devon

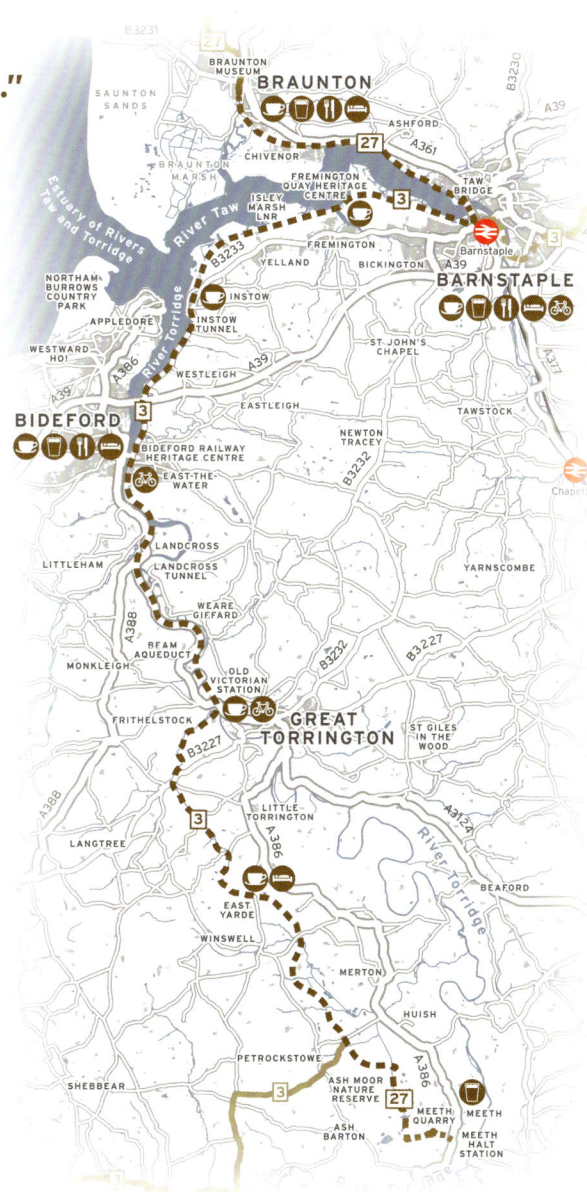

STOP LINE WAY

Ride 10 — 4 miles
Start: Angler's car park, Chard Reservoir

Donyatt Halt

This short ride from Chard Reservoir follows part of the Taunton Stop Line, a system of defences against German invasion during World War II. The peaceful Somerset countryside seems a world away from wartime, particularly on the banks of Chard Reservoir at the ride's start where the surrounding meadows, reedbeds and woodland are abuzz with wildlife.

From the reservoir, ride along a short section of quiet road, before joining the old track of the Great Western Railway. Look out for fascinating reminders of a darker, more turbulent time as you ride; secreted in the landscape are anti-tank obstacles, gun emplacements and pillboxes that are visible from the path. Ride beneath attractive Victorian railway bridges and through the open farmland around the little hamlet of Peasmarsh, before reaching the attractively restored station at Donyatt Halt. It's worth taking a short detour from the path here to ride along the quiet country lane into the thatched village of Donyatt, where the cosy pub is a lovely place to take a mid-ride break.

Back on the trail, ride beneath the oak and ash trees at Donyatt Cutting, looking out for roe deer, badgers, pipistrelle bats and butterflies in the woodland.

In the final mile, the route separates from the railway path and follows Canal Way into Ilminster. End in the town centre at the gates of the 15th Century minster, and take a walk to the lovely colonnaded Market House in the nearby town square.

Finish: The Minster, Ilminster

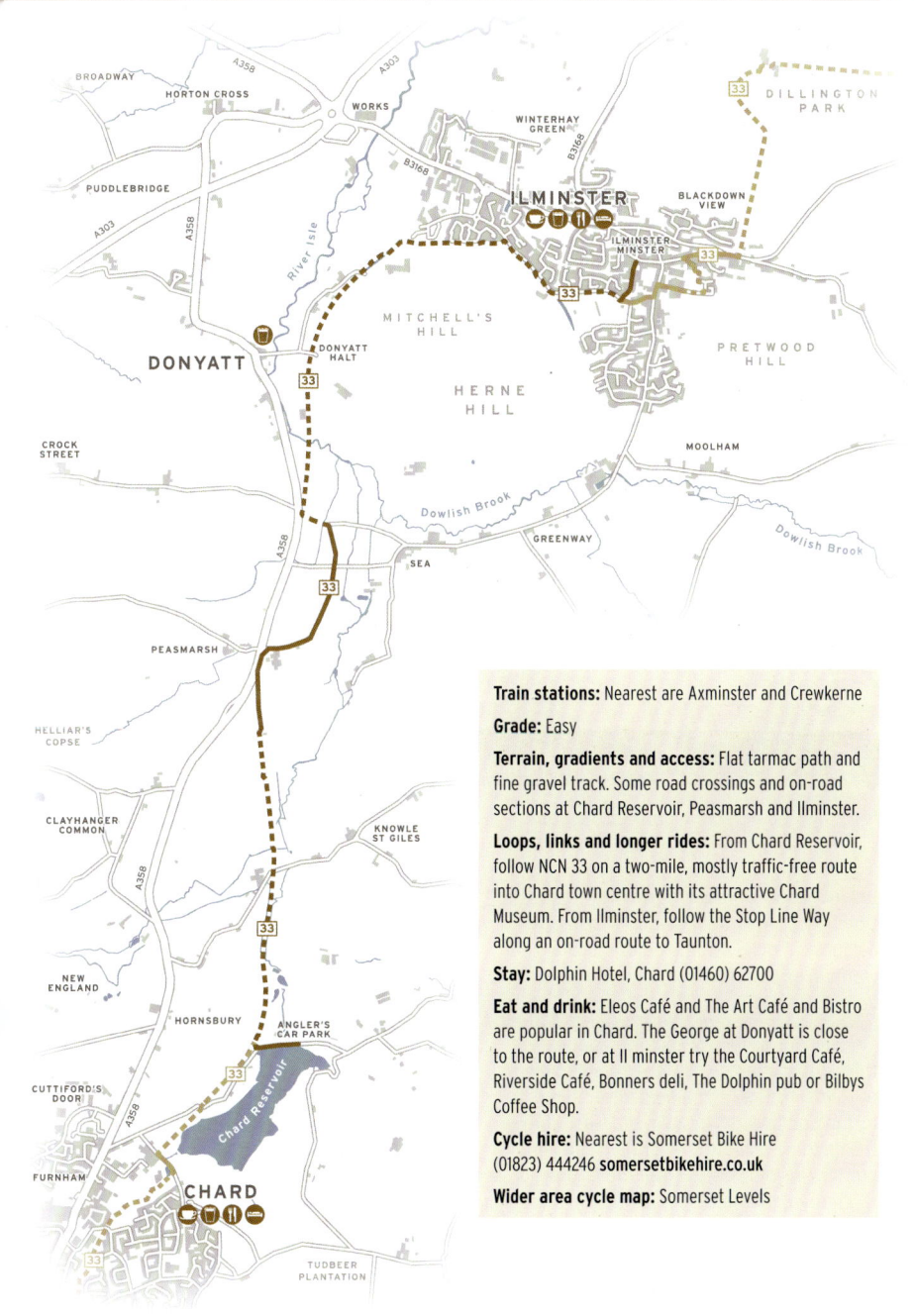

RIDE 10

Train stations: Nearest are Axminster and Crewkerne

Grade: Easy

Terrain, gradients and access: Flat tarmac path and fine gravel track. Some road crossings and on-road sections at Chard Reservoir, Peasmarsh and Ilminster.

Loops, links and longer rides: From Chard Reservoir, follow NCN 33 on a two-mile, mostly traffic-free route into Chard town centre with its attractive Chard Museum. From Ilminster, follow the Stop Line Way along an on-road route to Taunton.

Stay: Dolphin Hotel, Chard (01460) 62700

Eat and drink: Eleos Café and The Art Café and Bistro are popular in Chard. The George at Donyatt is close to the route, or at Ilminster try the Courtyard Café, Riverside Café, Bonners deli, The Dolphin pub or Bilbys Coffee Shop.

Cycle hire: Nearest is Somerset Bike Hire (01823) 444246 **somersetbikehire.co.uk**

Wider area cycle map: Somerset Levels

43

DORCHESTER
TO
WEYMOUTH

Portrait Bench in Weymouth

This delightful ride crosses the South Dorset Ridgeway to reach one of the country's original seaside resorts on the incredible Jurassic Coast. Start from Dorchester West train station and negotiate a couple of quiet streets before joining the traffic-free path at Weymouth Avenue that points you seaward.

The ancient history of the area is apparent throughout the ride, and the rumpled land of Maiden Castle, the biggest Iron Age hill fort in England, is visible in the west during the opening miles. It's a gentle climb initially, but far-reaching views from the bridge across the A-road, followed by a scenic and sweeping half-mile descent through the Dorset country lanes, makes the effort worthwhile. Shortly after the ride's midway point there are long views stretching right down to the sea, where the water is often flecked with boats enjoying the world-class sailing waters of Weymouth Bay. There's also a signed link here to the Dorset Wildlife Trust's Lorton Meadows, just a few minutes' ride away and a thoroughly recommendable detour for a picnic among the orchids and butterflies of the peaceful grassland. Back on the route you'll notice little lumps and bumps starting to appear in the land. These are 'barrows' or prehistoric earthworks that are probably human burial sites.

Ride alongside the broadleaved woodland and wildflowers of Radipole Wood, before joining Weymouth Way and reaching the huge lagoons of RSPB Radipole Lake. The lake is deeply impressive, and the thick purple and amber reedbeds around it move and whisper constantly in the sea air, while wooden pontoons tempt you right to the water's edge. There's direct access from the cycle path to the reserve's visitor centre and viewing hides.

Leave the traffic-free path at Westham Bridge and join the quiet road to reach The Esplanade, ending at the colourful Jubilee Clock. From the seafront there are great views over the sea to the vertical chalk cliffs at White Nothe. Osmington White Horse is visible from the sandy beach, too, a limestone sculpture on the Dorset Downs created in tribute to King George III who had a much-loved seaside home in Weymouth. Indeed, the whole resort is something of a tribute to Georgian elegance and simplicity, with stripy deckchairs, Punch and Judy shows and ornate shelters on the promenade.

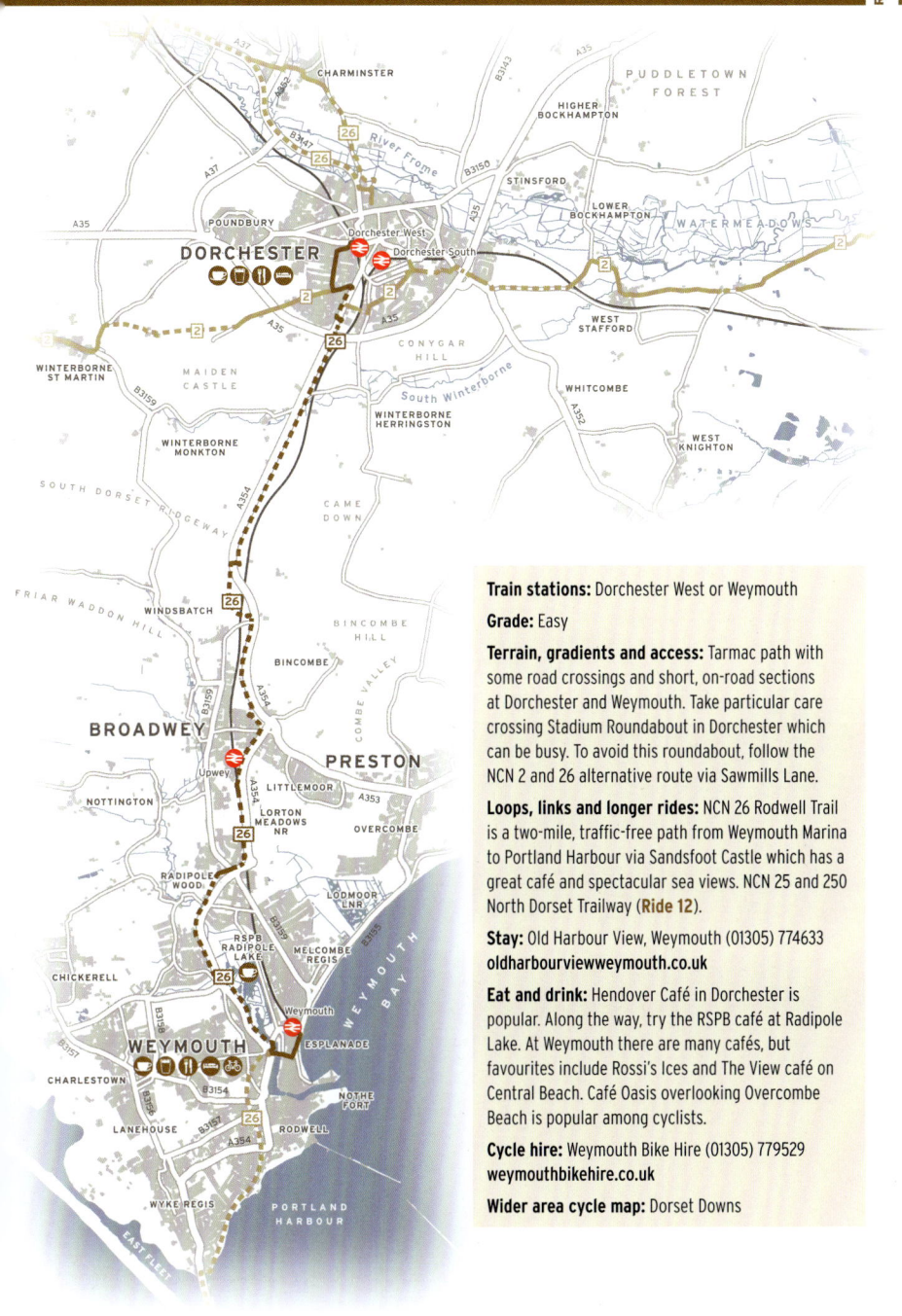

Finish: The Esplanade, Weymouth

RIDE 11

Train stations: Dorchester West or Weymouth

Grade: Easy

Terrain, gradients and access: Tarmac path with some road crossings and short, on-road sections at Dorchester and Weymouth. Take particular care crossing Stadium Roundabout in Dorchester which can be busy. To avoid this roundabout, follow the NCN 2 and 26 alternative route via Sawmills Lane.

Loops, links and longer rides: NCN 26 Rodwell Trail is a two-mile, traffic-free path from Weymouth Marina to Portland Harbour via Sandsfoot Castle which has a great café and spectacular sea views. NCN 25 and 250 North Dorset Trailway (**Ride 12**).

Stay: Old Harbour View, Weymouth (01305) 774633 oldharbourviewweymouth.co.uk

Eat and drink: Hendover Café in Dorchester is popular. Along the way, try the RSPB café at Radipole Lake. At Weymouth there are many cafés, but favourites include Rossi's Ices and The View café on Central Beach. Café Oasis overlooking Overcombe Beach is popular among cyclists.

Cycle hire: Weymouth Bike Hire (01305) 779529 weymouthbikehire.co.uk

Wider area cycle map: Dorset Downs

45

RIDE 12

9.5 miles | 25 | 250 | 🚲 | **Start:** Station Court car park, Blandford Forum

NORTH DORSET TRAILWAY

This is an incredibly scenic ride through the Stour Valley and across the edges of the Dorset Area of Outstanding Natural Beauty. The market town of Blandford Forum is a Georgian jewel on the banks of the River Stour, and a stroll around the exceptional buildings of the Market Place before setting off is an absolute must.

Start the ride from the old railway station at Blandford Forum and immediately join the former line of the Somerset and Dorset Railway. Views over the rich green landscape of the north Dorset countryside are wonderful from the outset and just before reaching Stourpaine Tunnel, after only a couple of miles, you'll see the villages of Durweston and Stourpaine up ahead. Durweston's handsome St Nicholas church is as pretty as a picture amid the surrounding farmland and trees, but the route takes you through Stourpaine, a classically charming Dorset village. The thatched cottages, climbing roses and relaxed rural feel are enchanting, and the traditional country pub leads a double life as the local post office and village shop.

Hod Hill, Dorset's largest enclosed hill fort, dominates the skyline to the north, and you'll get sweeping views across the Blackmore Vale and the thick trees of Blandford Forest as you ride towards Shillingstone. The station at Shillingstone is a real highlight of the ride's second half, as the buildings on the platform here have been tenderly restored to their 1950s glory days. Pause to take tea in the little café, look around the railway heritage centre or just soak up the surroundings. The River Stour flowing through the bottom of the valley and the

46

Finish: Station car park, Sturminster Newton

RIDE 12

Train station: The route is not easily accessible by train.

Grade: Easy

Terrain, gradients and access: Mostly flat tarmac path and fine gravel track with some road crossings and a short, quiet on-road section at Stourpaine.

Loops, links and longer rides: Turn the ride into a much more challenging loop by joining NCN 253 at Sturminster Newton and taking the hillier, on-road route back to Blandford Forum via the pretty villages of Okeford Fitzpaine and Milton Abbas.

Stay: Crown Hotel, Blandford Forum (01258) 456626 crownhotelblandford.co.uk

Eat and drink: Visit the popular Yellow Bicycle Café or The Georgian Tea Room in Blandford Forum. The White Horse pub is at Stourpaine, or at Shillingstone there's a shop and café at the old railway station and Old Ox Inn in the village. In Sturminster Newton, try Comins Tea House or The Bull Tavern.

Cycle hire: Dorset Cycles, Stalbridge (01963) 362476

Wider area cycle map: Dorset Downs

Cyclists on the Trailway

"Views over the rich green landscape of the north Dorset countryside are wonderful from the outset..."

magnificent Hambledon Hill rising up behind, one of Dorset's most iconic sites, gave this station a well-deserved reputation as the most attractive on the whole Somerset and Dorset Railway line.

In the final miles, it's worth taking a little detour from the path at Fiddleford and following the short country lane to Fiddleford Manor, a medieval house built for the Sheriff of Dorset, before re-joining the Trailway into Sturminster Newton.

End at the old railway station, or join the road and ride into the town to the delightful thatched museum building. Alternatively, head down to the river where a visit to the red flour mill is like stepping back in time and is a fitting end to this heavenly ride.

RIDE 13
18 miles

Start: Tourist Information Centre, Frome

COLLIERS WAY

Rolling country lanes and some of Somerset's prettiest villages make this a diverse and wonderful West Country ride.

Start at the pretty Mendip town of Frome and take the wooded trail along the river. This is a gentle warm up but soon the route joins quiet roads that rise and fall steeply in places, making it a testing ride. A climb in the opening mile leads up to the decorative building of the former Selwood Printing Works, followed by a beautiful country lane descent between plump hedgerows to Egford. More long climbs lead up to the pretty village of Great Elm, where there are fantastic views over the Wadbury Valley as the route joins the former Radstock to Frome railway path.

Around a mile and a half later there's a great opportunity for a detour into Mells, one of Somerset's prettiest villages. It's a mile from the route along a quiet country lane, but the ancient St Andrew's church, gorgeous Mells Manor and cosy old coaching inn all enhance the trip beyond measure.

Back on the trail there are expansive views over fields and forests, before you slice along the steep edge of the valley beneath a thick covering of trees. Pass quaint Kilmersdon, a village that prides itself on being the setting for the Jack and Jill nursery rhyme, before joining the short road into the centre of Radstock. The town's museum in the old Market Hall makes a great mid-ride break for discovering the history of the Somerset Coalfield, to which the route name 'Colliers Way' refers. In fact, on leaving Radstock you'll ride beside some of the spoil heaps or "batches" from the old coal mines as you join up with the former Somerset & Dorset Railway Line, with glimpses towards the stone arches of the old railway viaduct along the way.

At Shoscombe, steep country lanes lead to the little village of Wellow, with views of Stoney Littleton Long Barrow, a Neolithic burial chamber, on the limestone escarpment to the right of the trail. At Wellow, pass beneath the viaduct and rejoin the railway

---

Train station: Frome or Freshford

Grade: Moderate

Terrain, gradients and access: Steep gradients along an on-road route between Frome and Great Elm, and between Shoscombe and Wellow. In between, the route is a flat tarmac path with some road crossings. Dismount at the short, very steep section by Monkton School in Monkton Combe.

Loops, links and longer rides: NCN 4 Kennet & Avon Canal (**Ride 17**). NCN 4, 24 and 244 Two Tunnels Greenway (**Ride 14**).

Stay: The George Hotel, Frome (01373) 462584 georgehotelfrome.co.uk

Eat and drink: In Frome, The Griffin pub, The Garden Café and The Café at the Cheese and Grain are all popular. Along the way try Mells Café and The Talbot Inn at Mells. In Radstock, Victoria Hall Coffee Bar or the tea room at Radstock Museum are both good. Fox and Badger Inn and Wellow Trekking Centre café are both at Wellow, Hope and Anchor pub is at Midford and Wheelwright's Arms is in Monkton Combe. At the route's end, try Angelfish Restaurant at Brassknocker Basin.

Cycle hire: Bath & Dundas Canal Co, Monkton Combe (01225) 722192 **bathcanal.com**

Wider area cycle map: Somerset Levels

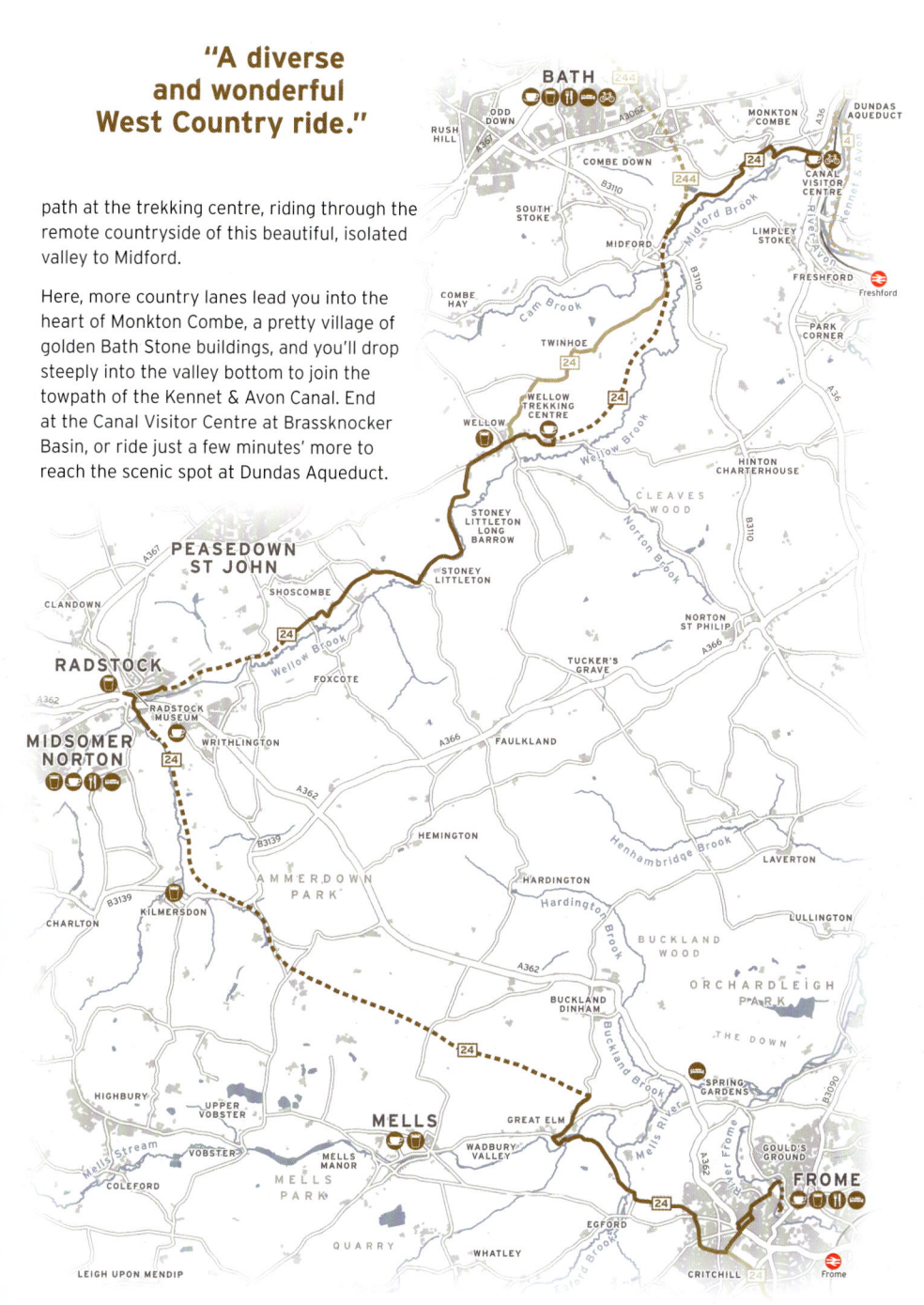

Finish: Canal Visitor Centre, Brassknocker Basin, Monkton Combe

RIDE 13

"A diverse and wonderful West Country ride."

path at the trekking centre, riding through the remote countryside of this beautiful, isolated valley to Midford.

Here, more country lanes lead you into the heart of Monkton Combe, a pretty village of golden Bath Stone buildings, and you'll drop steeply into the valley bottom to join the towpath of the Kennet & Avon Canal. End at the Canal Visitor Centre at Brassknocker Basin, or ride just a few minutes' more to reach the scenic spot at Dundas Aqueduct.

TWO TUNNELS GREENWAY

RIDE 14 — 5 miles

Start: Hope and Anchor pub, Midford

The two reopened railway tunnels that give the greenway its name are the stars of this route, but the views over the Cotswolds countryside and the World Heritage Site of Bath are equally stunning.

Start from the Hope and Anchor pub in Midford, which sits right beside the old railway path. Within moments, look to the left to see the intricate, Gothic-style Midford Castle on the hillside, before crossing over Tucking Mill Viaduct where views stretch down to the aquamarine waters of the fishing lake and across Tucking Mill Wood.

The highlight of the ride, Combe Down Tunnel, appears after less than a mile and carves a gently curved path through the steep limestone hillside. At over a mile long, it's the longest walking and cycling tunnel in the UK, and passing through it is a unique, deeply atmospheric experience. The chill from its inner depths can be felt long before you enter, and once inside it's a lovely long glide through the fridge cold air under subdued spotlights. You may hear the melodic strains of string music from time to time, too, part of a motion-activated art installation in the deepest parts of the tunnel.

Emerge blinking into the daylight for a section of leafy, open-air riding, before dipping back into the murky depths of the much shorter Devonshire Tunnel. Once both the tunnels have been left behind, it's a tranquil, tree-lined ride beside Linear Park in the south of the city. It's worth pausing on top of the bridge here to take in the knockout views over the Georgian buildings of Bath, where the long, golden arc of the city's famous Royal Crescent is particularly prominent.

Near the route's end, cross the River Avon and join the riverside path that leads into Bath. A short and signed on-road route then takes you from the river into the city centre to end at Upper Borough Walls just a short walk from the beautiful Bath Abbey.

Tucking Mill Viaduct fishing lake

RIDE 14

Finish: Upper Borough Walls, Bath

Train stations: Oldfield Park and Bath Spa

Grade: Easy

Terrain, gradients and access: Flat tarmac path with some road crossings and quiet, on-road sections at Bath. Take care riding through the Combe Down and Devonshire tunnels.

Loops, links and longer rides: Turn the Two Tunnels Greenway into a mostly traffic-free, 13-mile loop by joining the Kennet & Avon Canal at Bath and riding to Dundas Aqueduct, before following quiet country lanes through Monkton Combe back to the start at Midford. NCN 24 Colliers Way (**Ride 13**). NCN 4 Kennet & Avon Canal (**Ride 17**). NCN 4 Bristol & Bath Railway Path (**Ride 16**).

Stay: YHA Bath, 0345 3719673 yha.org.uk or Brooks Guesthouse, Bath (01225) 425543 brooksguesthouse.com

Eat and drink: The Hope and Anchor is at the start in Midford, whilst Wheelwrights Arms is nearby at Monkton Combe. Bath is full of wonderful places to eat and drink. Seek out Marshfield organic ice cream, made on a local farm and sold at several spots in the city, or try the exceptional coffee at Colonna and Small's. The Star Inn is one of Bath's finest and most traditional pubs.

Cycle hire: Nextbike, Bath (020) 8166 9851 nextbike.co.uk or Bath Bike Hire (01225) 447276 bathbikehire.com

Wider area cycle map: Somerset Levels

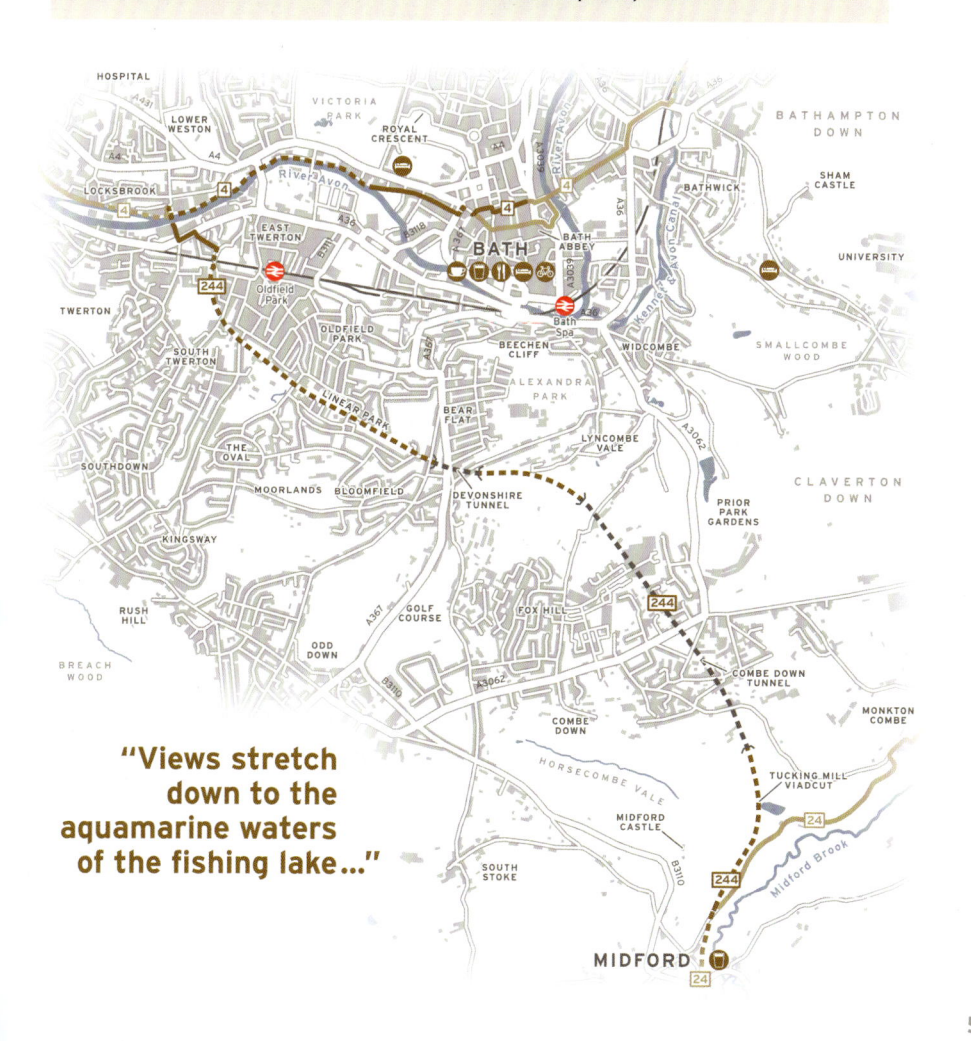

"Views stretch down to the aquamarine waters of the fishing lake…"

RIDE 15 — 11 miles — **Start:** Yatton train station

THE STRAWBERRY LINE

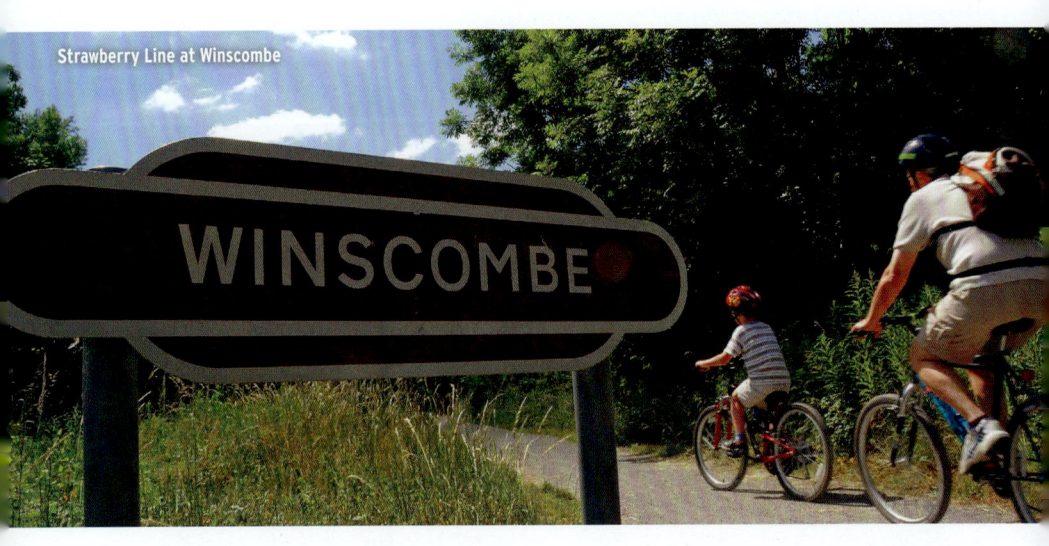

Strawberry Line at Winscombe

The landscape transforms spectacularly on this ride into the Mendip Hills, starting in the low lying land of the North Somerset Levels and ending beneath the dramatic vertical cliffs of Britain's biggest limestone gorge.

Start at Yatton train station and immediately enter Cheddar Valley Railway Local Nature Reserve (LNR) to ride beside rustling reeds, ponds and the special wetland habitat at Biddle Street. It's a beautifully peaceful area, and you'll soon be among the flat, atmospheric grazing marshes of Congresbury Moor and will cross the River Yeo.

The route follows a former branch line of the Great Western Railway, and is named after the sweet Cheddar strawberries that were transported on it. However, apples are the most notable fruit along the trail these days as the path traverses the vast Thatchers cider orchards at Sandford. You'll pass between soldier-straight rows of ripening apples with the intoxicating tang of the fermenting fruit in the air.

Around five miles in, pause at Sandford Station, an elegantly restored old railway station with a lovely little heritage centre and shop. Or, ride on for another mile to reach Old Station Green in Winscombe, which has bike parking and picnic benches on the former platform for an excellent mid-way stop.

From here, the landscape takes a wild and dramatic turn, and the flat pastures give way to oak- and ash-covered hillsides as you cut through steep limestone and ancient woodland into the Mendips Area of

Finish: Cheddar Gorge

RIDE 15

Train station: Yatton

Grade: Moderate

Terrain, gradients and access: Fine gravel track and stony trail with short, quiet on-road sections at Sandford, Axbridge and Cheddar. Take extra care passing through Shute Shelve Tunnel around seven miles in.

Loops, links and longer rides: At Yatton, follow NCN 26 north to connect to the Avon Cycleway, an 85-mile circular route around Bristol, following quiet country lanes through Thornbury, Chew Stoke, Clevedon and other attractive towns and villages. NCN 33 Festival Way.

Stay: YHA Cheddar 0345 3719730 yha.org.uk

Eat and drink: Try Strawberry Line Café at Yatton Station, Thatchers Cider Shop in Sandford and The Pantry at Winscombe. The Almshouse Tea Shop at Axbridge is very popular. Good choices in Cheddar include The Bath Arms pub and Edelweiss Café.

Cycle hire: Strawberry Cycles, Yatton 07983 816426 strawberrycycles.com or Cheddar Bikes 07864 329840 cheddarbikes.co.uk

Wider area cycle map: Somerset Levels

Outstanding Natural Beauty. Pass through the dark recesses of Shute Shelve Tunnel in the second half of the ride, before quiet roads lead you through the historic town of Axbridge. This is a real highlight of the ride, with quaint and characterful buildings such as the timber-framed King John's Hunting Lodge in the town square, and The Roxy, one of England's smallest cinemas.

Climb steadily out of the town to Cheddar Reservoir, where views over the twinkling, still water to the right of the path make a stark contrast to the craggy, weathered rocks of the gorge looming to the left. Pass through pretty Cheddar village to reach the mouth of the gorge, ending beneath the incredible vertical limestone cliffs and entrances to the deep caves.

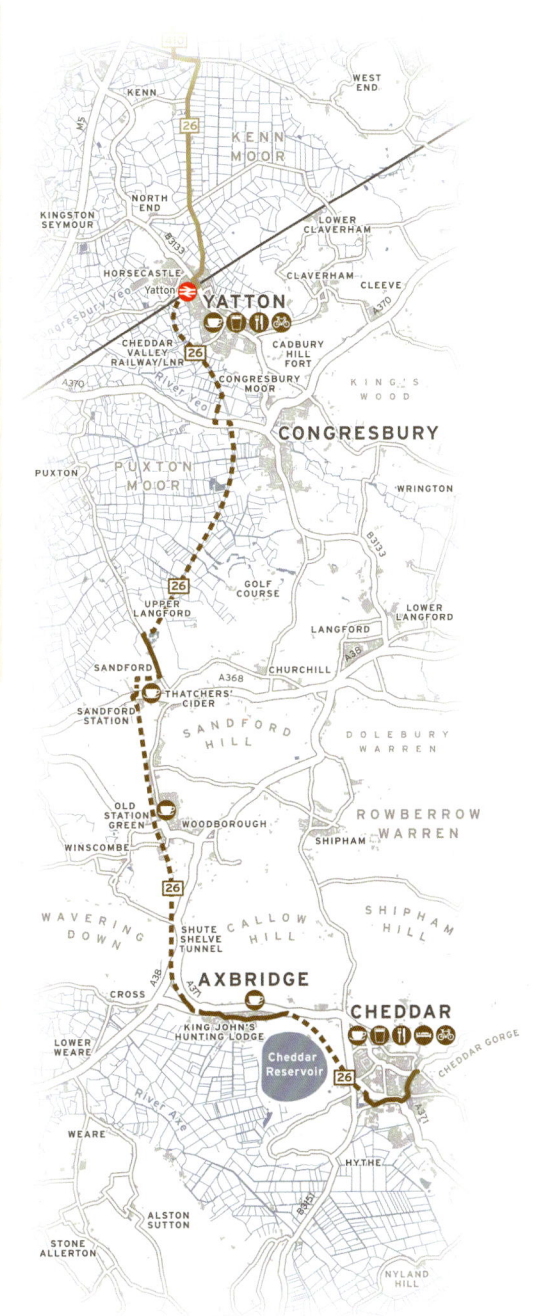

BRISTOL
&
BATH RAILWAY PATH

As one of the original paths to be built on the National Cycle Network, this route has lost none of its charm. It curves through the Avon Valley and into the south Cotswolds, linking up the wonderful West Country cities of Bristol and Bath.

Start among the café bars and pleasure boats of Bristol Harbourside, one of the nicest parts of the city, and see Bristol Cathedral rising up majestically behind. Cross leafy Queen Square and head for the east side of the city to join the railway path, the former route of the Midland Railway. It's a very gentle climb in the opening miles through the suburbs of Bristol, and you'll enter the dark depths of Staple Hill Tunnel on the way to the triangle of old train tracks at Mangotsfield Junction. This is where Carson's Chocolate Factory once stood, just one of the many chocolate factories in Bristol during the city's confectionery heyday. The only sweet treats here now, however, are the fruit trees in the community orchard on the station platform, which makes a great place for a secluded picnic.

The climb steadily continues, before a lovely sweeping descent leads you into Warmley Station and the ever-popular Waiting Room tearoom, another great place to stop for snacks. The hoppy scent that often wafts over this section of route comes from Bath Ales, a brewery just a short distance further down the track, where visitors can take a tour and sample the beer.

Artworks can be spotted throughout the ride, but Gaius Sentius, a giant sculpture of a Roman at the ride's halfway point, is one of the most well-known and marks the spot where a Roman Road crosses the path.

In the second half, join up with the tracks of the steam-powered Avon Valley Railway to ride from its busy Bitton Station to the Avon Riverside Station, where benches on the raised platform are great for soaking up the rolling South Gloucestershire scenery. Between the two stations you'll cross the River Avon, and it's worth looking out for the snaking path that leads down to a picnic area and locally-popular wild swimming spot on the river.

More river crossings follow as the Avon wriggles its way to Bath, and there are some lovely open views to be had from the bridges before entering the thick woodland of Kelston Park. The railway path ends just short of the city centre, so it's the river that leads you in to the fabulous World Heritage Site of Bath. Leave the river at the balconied Georgian terraces of Nelson Place and ride through attractive, narrow streets to end at the doors of the Theatre Royal in the heart of the city.

Cycling into the sunset near Fishponds

RIDE 16

Finish: Theatre Royal, Bath

Train stations: Bristol Temple Meads and Bath Spa

Grade: Moderate

Terrain, gradients and access: A steady ascent in the first half and steady descent in the second half along tarmac path. Some road crossings and short, quiet on-road sections at Bristol and Bath. Take care passing through Staple Hill Tunnel.

Loops, links and longer rides: From Saltford, follow the on-road Avon Cycleway to Chew Valley Lake. NCN 244 Two Tunnels Greenway (**Ride 14**). NCN 4 Kennet & Avon Canal (**Ride 17**).

Stay: Premier Inn Lewins Mead, Bristol 0333 0037734 premierinn.com

Eat and drink: Bristol Harbourside is lined with great cafés, restaurants and bars; Watershed, Arnolfini Harbourside Bar and The Bristol Stable are among the best. Along the route, try Warmley Waiting Room tearoom, The Buffet at Bitton Station and the Bird in Hand pub at Saltford. Society Café, The Star Inn and Boston Tea Party are favourites in Bath.

Cycle hire: Bristol Cycle Shack, Bristol (0117) 955 1017 bristol-cycle-shack.co.uk, Webbs Cycle Shop, Willbridge (0117) 932 5763 webbscycleshop.co.uk or Bath Bike Hire (01225) 447276 bathbikehire.com

Wider area cycle map: Somerset Levels

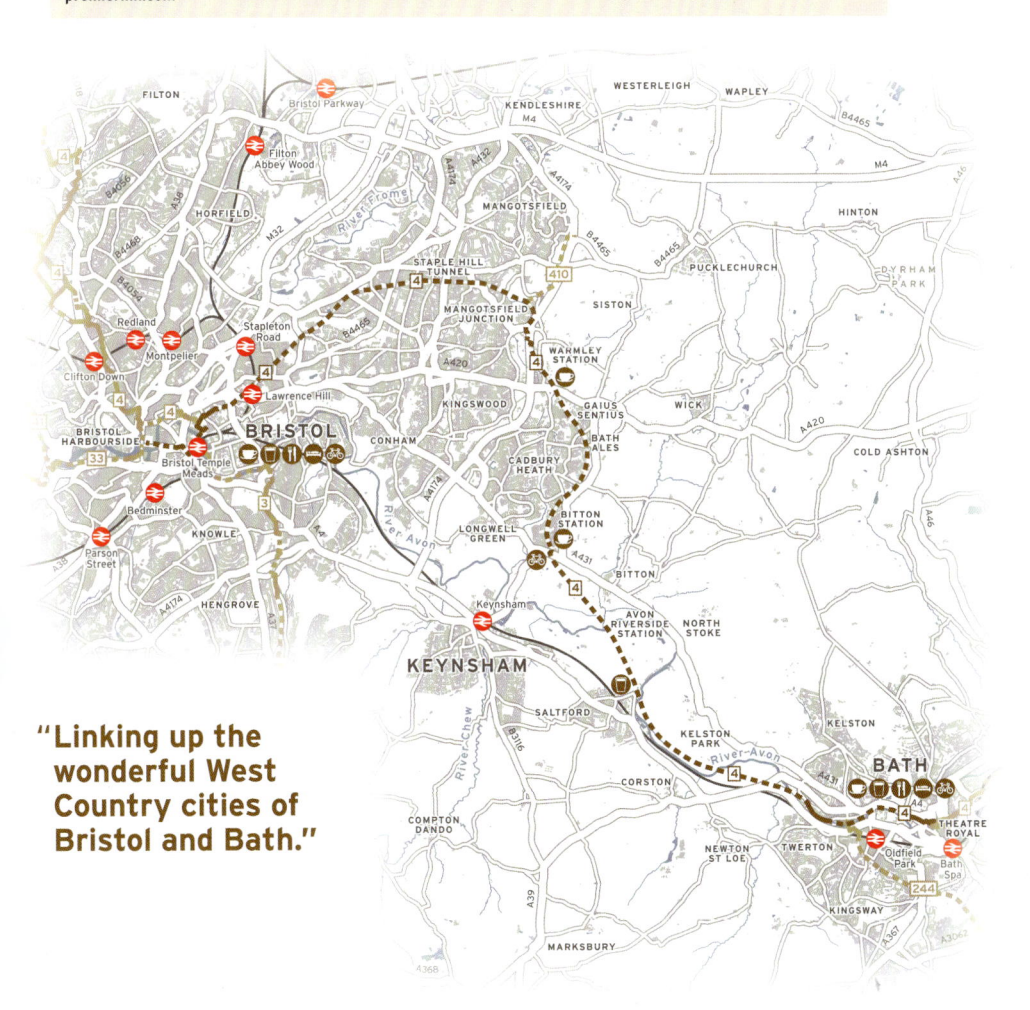

"Linking up the wonderful West Country cities of Bristol and Bath."

RIDE 17

Start: The Wharf Centre, Devizes

12 miles Devizes to Bradford-on-Avon Wharf or
22 miles Devizes to Bath

KENNET & AVON CANAL

This ride into the Cotswolds along the towpath of the Kennet & Avon Canal is entirely effortless, with views over the honey-gold buildings of Bath providing an exquisite ending.

Start at the Wharf Centre in Devizes and follow the towpath west to the Caen Hill Locks, regarded as the most impressive lock flight in the UK. The steep descent beside them and their pretty reed-fringed side ponds is joyful. The locks attract a lot of visitors, particularly in summer, so extra care is needed around here. However, you'll soon leave this busy spot behind and enter a more tranquil environment, with mile upon mile of gentle trail threading through the wide open Wiltshire countryside and alongside calm canal waters.

At Hilperton Marina, a one-mile link route from the towpath leads into Trowbridge, Wiltshire's county town, or stay on the path for a couple more miles to reach the Kennet & Avon Canal Trust tearooms at Bradford-on-Avon Wharf. This is an incredibly popular spot among cyclists, and an excellent endpoint for a shorter ride.

If energy allows then following the route all the way to Bath is thoroughly recommended, as the views that start to emerge over the southern tip of the Cotswolds are just stunning. Leave the charming town of Bradford-on-Avon behind and ride between the River Avon and canal through the lovely woodland of Barton Farm Country Park. The two aqueducts, Avoncliff and Dundas, are real highlights in this second half of the ride, and there are great views from the tops of both.

In the final miles, look across the thick trees of Conkwell Wood and Warleigh Wood covering the hillside to the east, and spot the square tower of Brown's Folly, known locally as 'The Pepperpot', peeping up above the village of Bathford. Eventually, the sweeping curve of the canal reveals the elegant buildings of Bath creeping up the hillside, a skyline so perfect and precious that the city is a World Heritage Site.

Leave the water before the Beckford Road tunnel and descend into the city, riding between the tall Georgian town houses on Great Pulteney Street and across the River Avon to end in front of the magnificent Bath Abbey.

Finish: Bradford-on-Avon Wharf or Bath Abbey

RIDE 17

Train stations: Bath Spa and Bradford-on-Avon

Grade: Devizes to Bradford Wharf – Easy
Devizes to Bath – Moderate

Terrain, gradients and access: Mostly flat, stony towpath with a steep descent past Caen Locks near the start. Several gates, some road crossings and short, on-road sections at Bradford-on-Avon and Bath.

Loops, links and longer rides: At Semington, join NCN 403 to Melksham and Chippenham on the quiet roads or along the Wilts & Berks Canal towpath as far as Melksham. At Dundas Aqueduct, join NCN 24 and follow quiet country lanes to Monkton Combe and Midford. At Midford, join NCN 244 Two Tunnels Greenway (**Ride 14**) or continue along NCN 24 Colliers Way (**Ride 13**). NCN 4 Bristol & Bath Railway Path (**Ride 16**).

Stay: Brooks Guesthouse, Bath (01225) 425543 **brooksguesthouse.com** or YHA Bath, 0345 3719103 **yha.org.uk**

Eat and drink: Waterside cafés and pubs abound on this route: The Wharf tearooms at Devizes, Caen Hill Café at Caen Locks, Kennet & Avon Canal Trust tearooms at Bradford-on-Avon Wharf, The Lock Inn Café and The Barge Inn at Bradford-on-Avon and The Cross Guns at Avoncliff. The Café on the Barge and The George are both at Bathampton and The Bathwick Boatman Riverside Restaurant is at Bathwick. Bath favourites include The Raven, The Star Inn and Boston Tea Party.

Cycle hire: Bath Bike Hire (01225) 447276 **bathbikehire.com** or TT Cycles, Bradford-on-Avon (01225) 867815 **ttcycles.co.uk**

Wider area cycle map: Severn & Thames

"Mile upon mile of gentle trail threading through the wide open Wiltshire countryside and alongside calm canal waters."

Evening ride along the Kennet & Avon Canal towpath

SWINDON TO MARLBOROUGH

RIDE 18 — 11.5 miles
45 403 482
Start: Coate Water Country Park, Swindon

This lovely rural ride between the rolling chalk hills of the Marlborough Downs leads into the beautiful town of Marlborough, with the chance to ride beside one of the famous Wiltshire white horses at the end.

Start at Coate Water Country Park and ride along the banks of its vast reservoir, before crossing over the water and entering the small copses of the park's nature reserve. Lovely views across the chalk downlands make the opening miles to Chiseldon particularly pleasant, with birds of prey soaring over the valley, and a tangle of gangly, noisy herons in the reserve's heronry visible from the viewing hides.

The spiralling climb over the M4 is a momentary reminder of a more hectic world, but it is quickly left behind as you undulate through mature woodland filled with birdsong, where there's a very good chance of spotting muntjac deer between the trees. Pass pretty thatched cottages and neat gardens along the country lanes through Chiseldon village, before joining a long, arrow-straight trail, with panoramic views across the farmland and steep downland ridges.

The pub at Ogbourne St George is a good halfway rest stop, before continuing through superb scenery. Views stretch across the steep, tractor-combed crop fields, before you enter pleasant, shady woodland for the final miles of the ride, looking out for red kites along the way.

A severe and stony descent leads out of the woodland and into residential streets on the edges of Marlborough, with a short, on-road ride into the heart of the town. End on the High Street by The Merchant's House, the elegant 17th Century home of a prosperous silk merchant, and take a stroll around this picturesque market town.

Alternatively, instead of dropping down into Marlborough town, continue along NCN 403 beside the River Kennet. You'll soon reach the grounds of the College, where the Marlborough White Horse can be found. Designed and cut into the earth by local schoolboys in 1804, it is the smallest of Wiltshire's famed chalk white horses and is on such a shallow slope that the cycle route is one of the few places from which it can be viewed. From here, it's just a few minutes' ride along the road into the pretty thatched village of Manton to end at The Outside Chance pub.

Grade II listed diving board at Coate Water

RIDE 18

Finish: High Street, Marlborough

Train station: Swindon

Grade: Moderate

Terrain, gradients and access: Undulating along tarmac path, fine gravel track and stony trail with a short grassy section near Ogbourne St George. Some road crossings and on-road sections at Chiseldon, Ogbourne St George and Marlborough.

Loops, links and longer rides: From Marlborough, follow NCN 403 on a mix of traffic-free and on-road route across Fyfield Down National Nature Reserve to Avebury, Chippenham and the Kennet & Avon Canal (**Ride 17**). From Swindon, follow NCN 45 on a mostly traffic-free route to Cotswold Water Park.

Stay: Premier Inn Swindon Central 0333 3219063 premierinn.com or The Sanctuary, Ogbourne St George (01672) 841473 the-sanctuary.biz

Eat and drink: There is a café at Coate Water Country Park at the route's start, or try Chiseldon House Hotel and Three Trees Farm Shop and Café, both at Chiseldon. The Inn with the Well is at Ogbourne St George, and The Oddfellows pub is at Manton. Marlborough is full of choice, including the popular The Lamb Inn, St Peters Coffee Shop & Restaurant and Rick Stein's Marlborough Restaurant.

Wider area cycle map: Severn & Thames

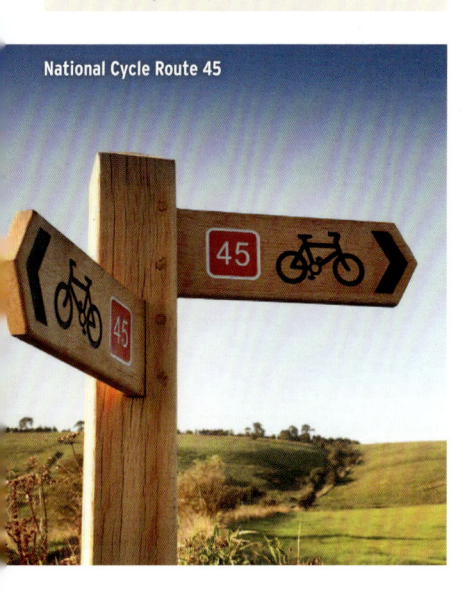

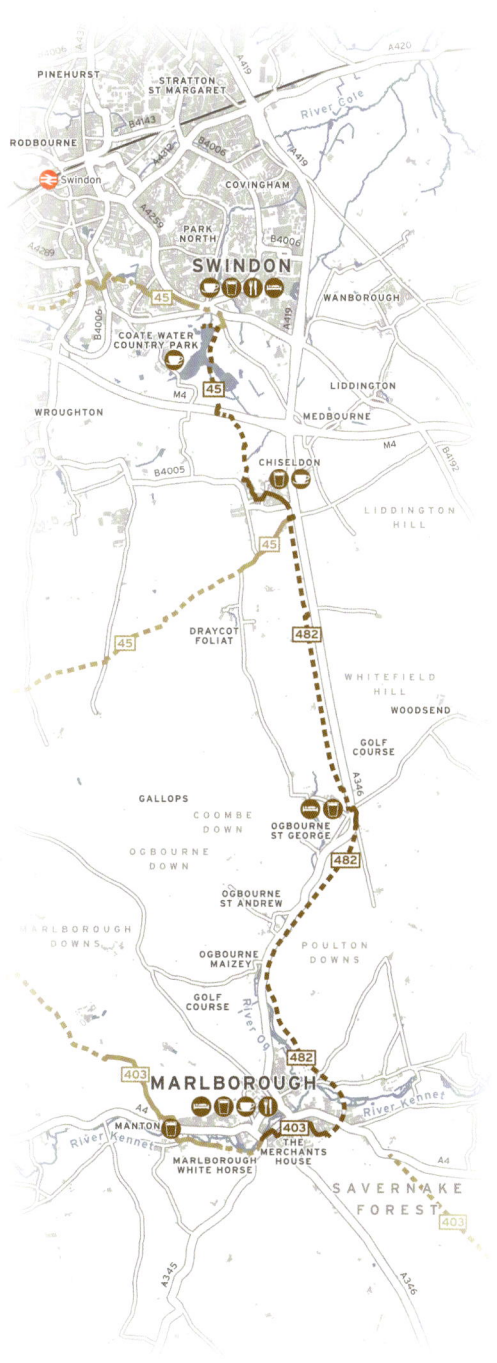

National Cycle Route 45

RIDE 19
5 miles

Start and finish: Lockkeepers' Café, Stroud

STROUD VALLEYS TRAIL
&
STROUDWATER CANAL

Your route out to the busy little Cotswold village of Stonehouse is along a leafy railpath; you need to briefly negotiate some busy town centre roads to get to the start of the trail and then a set of ramped steps and some winding paths through housing estates. Once you are on it though, it's a lovely level, leafy corridor all the way to the large roundabout on the outskirts of Stonehouse.

If you need any town centre services you can check out Stonehouse, though there is even more provision in Stroud. The attractive centre is worth a visit in its own right - it was recently voted the UK's Best Place to Live in a national newspaper. Plenty of green spaces, a Saturday farmers' market and old market hall and an outdoor swimming pool are a few of the reasons it won the accolade. All this surrounded by the Cotswolds Area of Outstanding Natural Beauty.

At the Stonehouse end of the route drop down onto the towpath (just under the road bridge here but but not easy to spot) and find a world of sound and light canal underpasses, restored sections of a once derelict canal teeming with flora and fauna and lovingly restored textile mill areas typified by Ebley Mill.

The canal leads back to your start point at the pretty and popular Lockkeeper's Café at Stroud and lets you really appreciate the hard work of the Cotswolds Canal Trust who continue to work to make the whole length of the canal navigable and open to all types of user.

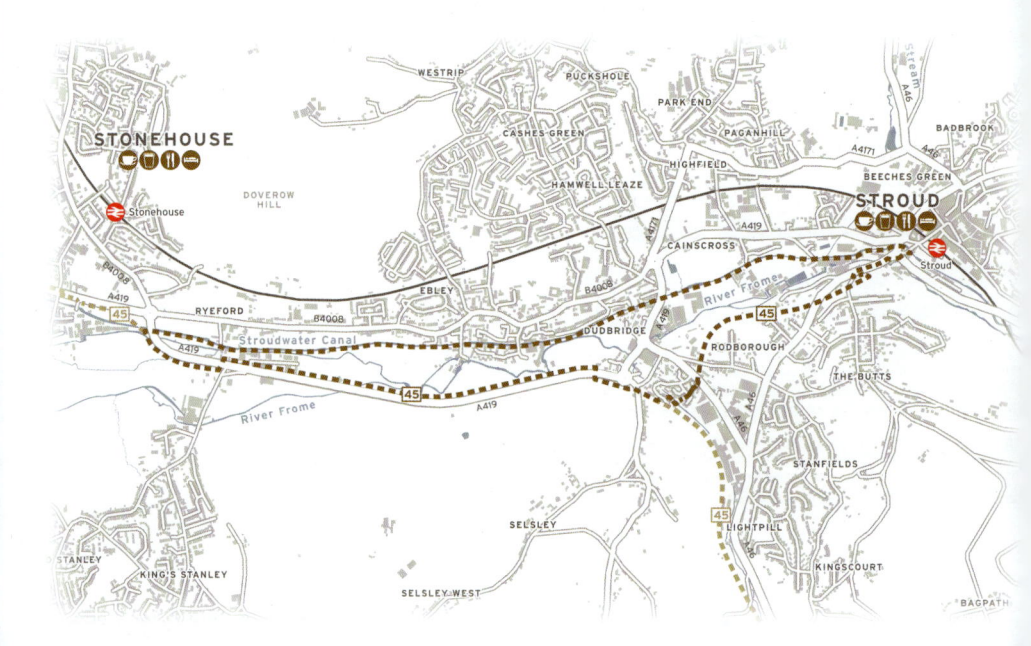

RIDE 19

Train Station: Stonehouse to Stroud is a four minute rail trip

Grade: Easy

Terrain, gradients and access: Very easy gradients along the valley floor of the River Frome on railpath then canal towpath. A couple of sets of steps, one small on the canal, one longer but with a cycle ramp on the Stroud to railpath link. The Stroudwater canal towpath is narrow in a few places and care is needed under some bridges but the quality of the path itself is good, level crushed stone.

Loops, links and longer rides: The railpath section of this route is part of NCN 45 which will link Cheshire and Wiltshire. You can follow NCN 45 east once you join the main section on leaving the Stroud spur behind and continue traffic-free all the way to Nailsworth (and the attractive Egypt Mill café and restaurant). From here it uses a mixture of minor roads and traffic-free sections to head to Swindon. Keeping on NCN 45 west of Stonehouse leads to NCN 41 which parallels the southern side of the Severn estuary here. The Stroudwater canal towpath becomes the Severn and Thames towpath at Wallend Lock and you can continue east on it, past the attractive Ship Inn at Brimscombe, all the way to Sapperton.

Stay: Five Valleys Aparthotel, Stroud has bike storage (01453) 764544 5va.co.uk

Eat and drink: Popular Lockkeepers Café at the route start by the canal in Stroud and canalside Kitsch café bar at Ebley Mill. Lots of places in Stonehouse and Stroud.

Wider area cycle map: Severn & Thames

Stroudwater Canal near Ebley Mill

"Restored sections of a once derelict canal teeming with flora and fauna and lovingly restored textile mill areas typified by Ebley Mill."

SOUTH EAST

Exceptional seaside routes and a reputation as one of the driest and sunniest parts of the UK make the South East a top choice for carefree, family-friendly cycling.

Offshore adventure awaits on the Isle of Wight across the sparkling waters of the Solent. The summer climate on its southern shores is a match for the Mediterranean, making the coast to coast Red Squirrel Trail a desirable blend of exotic island riding and traditional Hampshire home comforts. Coastal rides on the mainland are outstanding, too. Flat and effortless promenade routes take in the wild, shingly Thanet beaches and sheer chalk cliffs along the English Channel, as well as the classic seaside charm of Margate, Worthing and Whitstable, and the laidback cool of Brighton, where a growing cycling culture is being enthusiastically embraced.

Inland, the countryside rides are every bit as enticing, passing through the green hills of the Chilterns, the ancient woodland of The Bleanand skirting the edges of the South Downs, England's newest National Park. To say that many of the rides possess a storybook perfection is no exaggeration; the Forest Way will take you across the heart of 'Pooh Country' into the real-life woodland that inspired Hundred Acre Wood in the Winnie-the-Pooh tales, whilst the magnificent Windsor Castle at the start of the Jubilee River Path, and the stately buildings of Penshurst at the end of the Tudor Trail, could have been plucked straight from the pages of a fairytale.

But to indulge in some serious sightseeing from the saddle, head to London where gentle rides around the city's Royal Parks reveal a roll call of prestigious buildings, from the famous domes of St Paul's Cathedral and the Royal Albert Hall, to the sumptuous Buckingham and Kensington Palaces. Short and easy cycle rides simply don't get more impressive.

Brighton Pier

Routes overview

- **01** Red Squirrel Trail (15 miles)
- **02** Centurion Way (5.5 miles)
- **03** Shoreham Promenade (6 miles)
- **04** Downs Link North (18 miles)
- **05** Downs Link South (20 miles)
- **06** Brighton Seafront (7 miles)
- **07** Forest Way (10 miles)
- **08** Tudor Trail (5.5 miles)
- **09** Crab & Winkle Way (8 miles)
- **10** Oyster Bay Trail (8 miles)
- **11** Viking Coastal Trail (9 miles)
- **12** Tamsin Trail (7.5 miles)
- **13** Thames Path (14.5 miles)
- **14** Jubilee River Path (14.5 miles)
- **15** Two Palaces (4 miles)
- **16** Lee Navigation (South) (12.5 miles)
- **17** Phoenix Trail (8.5 miles)
- ⎯⎯ Featured ride
- ⎯⎯ National Cycle Network (traffic-free and on-road)

RIDE 01 — 15 miles | 23 🚲 | **Start:** Sandown Pier

RED SQUIRREL TRAIL

Sandown Pier

Nicknamed 'Britain in miniature', the Isle of Wight has the most superb coast to coast route in miniature too. Rolling hillsides, wisteria-covered tearooms, thatched cottages and traditional pubs are all quintessentially British, but the golden beaches, sapphire seas and balmy summer climate are more akin to the Mediterranean, making for a ride like no other.

Start beside the beach at Sandown, overlooking the sea and chalk cliffs at Culver Down. Quickly leave the sea behind, however, and head into the wet meadows, woodland and wildflower grassland of Alverstone Mead nature reserve. There are gorgeous views over the lush green hills here, and the viewing hide beside Skinners Meadow offers the best chance of seeing some of the island's well-loved red squirrels.

At Newchurch, a few miles further along the trail, the tangy scent of garlic wafts across the route from The Garlic Farm, which is open to visitors and worth the very short country lane detour. Try the garlic in the popular café, or stroll around the farm to see brown hares boxing in the wildflower meadows in spring. Continue following the course of the River Yar through the beautiful Arreton Valley to Merstone Station, where picnic benches beside the crop fields make a peaceful spot to rest at around the halfway point.

Gently crumpled hills are a beautiful backdrop in the ride's second half, and you'll pass beneath a canopy of ash trees at Blackwater, before joining up with the River Medina into Newport. This is the Isle of Wight's principal town and is well worth exploring. There's also the option here to follow a short, on-road section of NCN 22 to near Carisbrooke Castle, one of the most fascinating historic sites on the island.

Leaving Newport reach Medina Riverside Park where the river begins to widen and the extraordinary spires of St Mildred's church at Whippingham can eventually be seen on the horizon across the water.

End in the centre of Cowes, a lovely town for a stroll, and a particularly lively place in August when Cowes Week, its famous annual regatta, takes place. Cowes is divided in two by the mouth of the River Medina, so after exploring the western side of the water take a five-minute trip on the chain ferry to East Cowes (the ferry is free and bikes are permitted) to visit Osborne House, Queen Victoria's holiday home.

64

Finish: High Street, Cowes

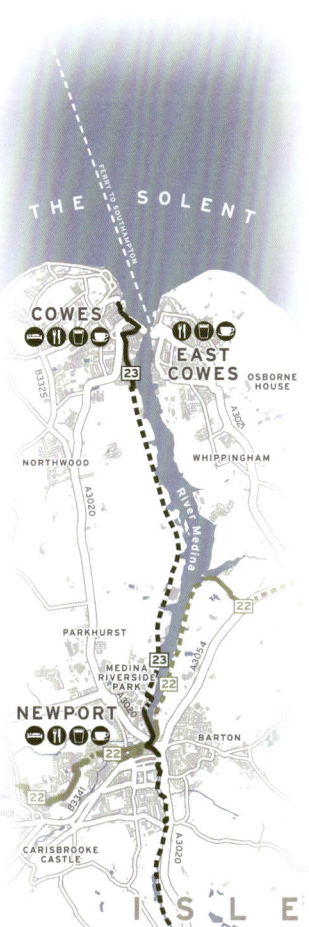

RIDE 01

Train stations: Sandown and Ryde. Reach the Isle of Wight by ferry from Portsmouth Harbour to Ryde, Southampton to East Cowes, or Lymington to Yarmouth or by hovercraft from Southsea to Ryde.

Grade: Moderate

Terrain, gradients and access: Mostly flat but with some gentle gradients. Tarmac path and stony trail, with a wooden boardwalk section at Horringford. Some small road crossings and short, on-road sections at Sandown, Newport, and Cowes.

Loops, links and longer rides: The Red Squirrel Trail (redsquirreltrail.org.uk) covers 23.5 miles in its entirety, which includes a signed loop via the pretty village of Godshill. Start in Cowes and follow the coast to coast route to Merstone where the route splits. Turn right to reach Godshill, Wroxall and Shanklin. Follow the shoreline north to Sandown before re-joining the coast to coast route and ending back at Merstone. The loop includes some steeper gradients and on-road riding. More experienced riders might also try the Round the Island Route, a challenging 64-mile, on-road loop of the Isle of Wight.

Stay: Rosemary Cottage, Newchurch (01983) 867735 rosemarycottagebreaks.co.uk or The Caledon Guesthouse, Cowes (01983) 293599 the-caledon.co.uk

Eat and drink: The Beach Café is at Sandown at the start. At Newchurch, try Pedallers' Cycle Café, The Pointer Inn and The Garlic Farm. Blue Door Café and Quay Arts Café Bar are all excellent in Newport. Sails Café in Cowes and Mrs Jones Tea Depot in East Cowes are both nice. Seek out Minghella ice cream, made on the island, and the Isle of Wight's speciality 'crab on chips'.

Cycle hire: Isle Cycle is in Sandown (01983) 400055 islecycle.co.uk, Routefifty7 in Shanklin 07491 000057 routefifty7.com or Wight Cycle Hire, Yarmouth (01983) 761800 wightcyclehire.co.uk

Wider area cycle map: Hampshire & Isle of Wight

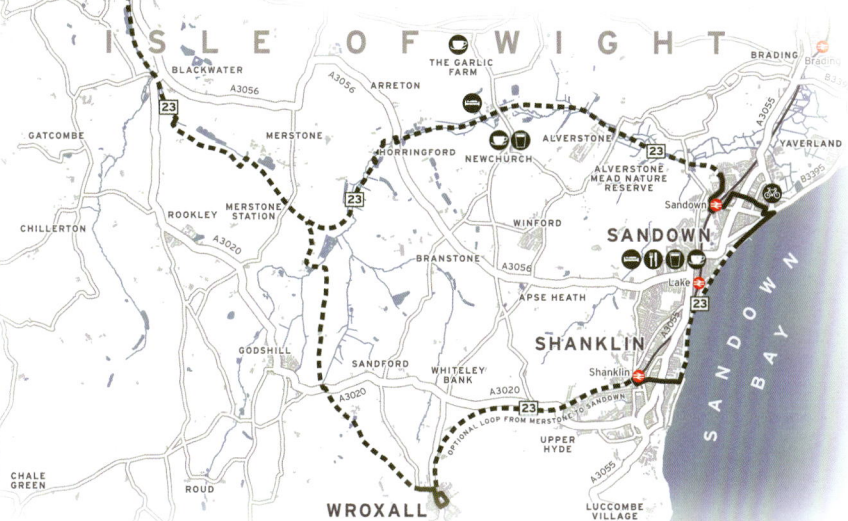

RIDE 02

88 🚲 **Start:** Westgate, Chichester

5.5 miles

CENTURION WAY

This rural ride through West Sussex starts from the edges of the beautiful cathedral city of Chichester and heads into the South Downs, Britain's newest National Park. Before setting off, it's worth taking the short ride along NCN 2 into Fishbourne to marvel at the spectacular remains of the Roman palace, or into the centre of the lovely walled city of Chichester to see the ornate Tudor Market Cross and the Norman cathedral, which has a pair of peregrine falcons nesting in its spire.

The route itself begins from Westgate, where you'll follow the old Chichester to Midhurst railway line, quickly entering peaceful countryside beneath the giant oak, sweet chestnut and sycamore trees of Brandy Hole Copse Local Nature Reserve (LNR).

Picnic mid-route surrounded by open meadows and an army of spade-wielding Roman workers called the Chichester Road Gang. This is a wonderful sculpture that marks the spot where a Roman road crosses the route.

A stony climb follows, leading through the sprawling farmland and rolling hills of the South Downs, before you join the tarmac, traffic-free path beside the road to the delightful little village of West Dean. The thatched cottages, village store and whitewashed pub make a picturesque ending.

Visit the attractive arboretum and Victorian glasshouses of West Dean Gardens near the route's end, or venture a little further east to Weald and Downland Open Air Museum.

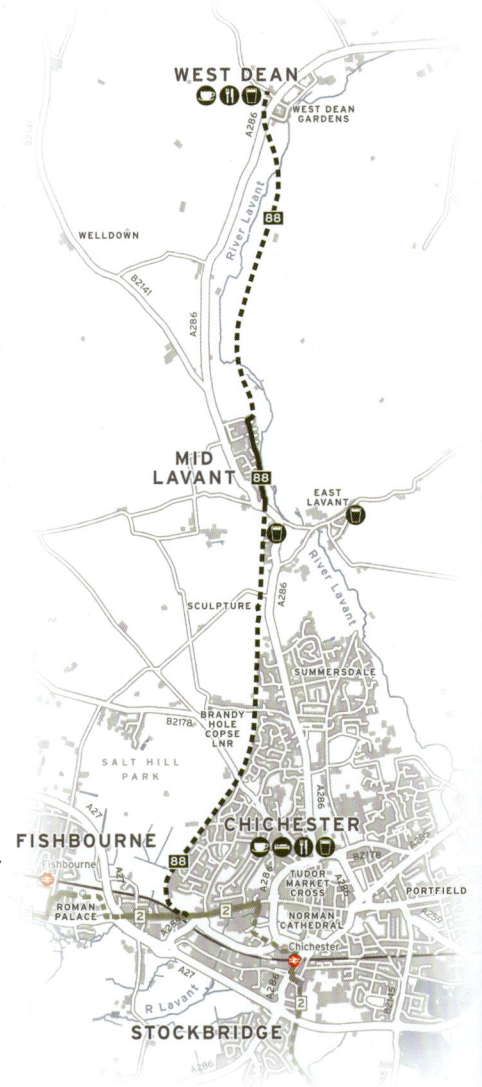

Finish: West Dean

RIDE 02

Mosaic floor at Fishbourne Roman Palace

Train station: Chichester

Grade: Easy

Terrain, gradients and access: A gentle climb along tarmac path and stony trail with short, quiet on-road sections at Lavant and West Dean.

Loops, links and longer rides: The South Downs Way is a 100-mile, mostly off-road mountain bike route along the ridges of the South Downs, through Sussex and Hampshire.

Stay: Cherry End B&B, Chichester (01243) 779495 chichesterbedandbreakfast.net

Eat and drink: The Earl of March pub at Lavant and The Royal Oak pub at East Lavant are both popular. At the route's end, try Gardens Restaurant at West Dean Gardens. Also The Tearoom at West Dean Stores and The Selsey Arms.

Cycle hire: Nearest is Summit Bikes, Selsey (01243) 697547 summitbikes.co.uk

Wider area cycle map: Central Sussex & South Surrey

"Marvel at the spectacular remains of a Roman palace..."

RIDE 03
6 miles

Start: Shoreham-by-Sea train station

SHOREHAM PROMENADE

This flat seaside ride along the sunny Sussex coast mixes wild, nature-filled shoreline with elegant seaside resorts.

Start from Shoreham-by-Sea train station and take the short, on-road route to the walking and cycling bridge over the wide water of the Adur Estuary. Boats bob around on the water here, and there are beautiful views in both directions from the bridge.

The saltmarsh and mudflats of the RSPB's Adur Estuary nature reserve are at the southern side of the bridge, and are a great spot to watch flocks of wading birds and wildfowl feeding and roosting. Indeed, the whole of Shoreham's shingly beach is designated as a Local Nature Reserve because of its unique habitat, and it certainly feels far wilder and more remote than Brighton, whose beach and chalk cliffs can be seen just a few miles to the east.

Sea views are concealed by the shingle ridge at the very start, so look inland across the rolling hills on the southern edges of the South Downs National Park. The most noticeable feature on the hillside is the impressive Lancing College chapel, a vast Victorian Gothic building that dominates the landscape above the Adur Valley.

The English Channel soon becomes visible as you pass between the shoreline and Widewater Lagoon, another Local Nature Reserve, before reaching Lancing. This is England's largest village and is a good spot for locking up to take a mid-ride paddle, picnic on Lancing Beach Green, or watch kite surfers from the shore (Lancing has one of the world's best beaches for the sport).

Leave Lancing and pass Brooklands boating lake to ride the final, gentle miles into the genteel seaside resort of Worthing. The Regency terraces and villas, handsome pier and ornate promenade shelters all feel very English, yet the sparkling blue sea and exotic palm trees lining the promenade are totally tropical on a sunny day.

End among the driftwood sculptures at the town's Waterwise Garden, a natural water saving garden on the shingly beach, where there are wonderful views out to sea.

Train stations: Shoreham-by-Sea and Worthing

Grade: Easy

Terrain, gradients and access: Flat tarmac path with a short, on-road section at Shoreham-by-Sea. Cyclists are advised to get off and push for very short sections around Lancing Beach Green.

Loops, links and longer rides: Downs and Weald is a 164-mile, on-road and traffic-free route from London to Hastings, via Brighton. Or try NCN 89 South Downs Way, a mainly traffic-free mountain bike route following the escarpments and ridges of the South Downs through Sussex and Hampshire or the Downs Link (**Ride 04** and **Ride 05**). NCN 2 Brighton Seafront (**Ride 06**).

Stay: The Burlington Hotel, Worthing (01903) 211222 theburlington.net

Eat and drink: Into the Blue restaurant or Ginger and Dobbs café in Shoreham-by-Sea are both popular. There's a snack kiosk at Widewater Lagoon and several cafés in Lancing. At Worthing, eat on the beachside decking of Coast Café or at Beach House bar and café.

Cycle hire: Adur Outdoor Activities Centre, Shoreham-by-Sea 0333 3407100 adurcentre.org.uk

Wider area cycle map: Central Sussex & South Surrey

Finish: Waterwise Garden, Worthing

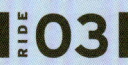

RIDE **03**

Cyclists on Worthing promenade

69

RIDE 04
18 miles

Start: Guildford High Street

DOWNS LINK NORTH

(GUILDFORD TO HORSHAM)

From Guildford's impressive High Street (with the equally impressive castle nearby) NCN 22 signs guide you through attractive back streets. Cross a main road to wend your way traffic-free style through meadows and parks, joining the Downs Link (which actually starts east of Guildford at Marthas Hill). You are soon cycling alongside the Wey and Arun canal, a hugely atmospheric section. The canal was built in 1816 to link the Wey Navigation near Guildford to the south coast and is known as 'London's lost route to the sea'. Today a local canal society is working to reopen the Wey & Arun Canal for leisure - several miles of the Canal are in regular use by small boats and canoes.

The Downs Link, as the name suggests, joins the North and South Downs, meaning you are passing over the Weald area in this ride, a lower lying area that is sandwiched between the two ridges of chalk hills. The wooded and watery Low Weald is a quintessentially medieval landscape; small-scale, intimate and tranquil with a pattern of small irregular pasture fields, formed by piecemeal woodland clearance which began in the 12th and 13th centuries featuring an abundance of ponds.

There's plenty of interest in nearby villages too, from the attractive buildings on Cranleigh high street just opposite the large modern square and supermarket that sits on the site of the old railway station. Rudgwick and Slinfold are also worth the short detours from the trail. Both feature characterful pubs and plenty of fine buildings with distinctive 'Surrey Style' architecture inspired by the Arts and Crafts Movement featuring lovely decorative red clay tiles.

Cyclist near Christ's Hospital

"Quintessentially medieval landscape; small-scale, intimate and tranquil..."

Finish: Christ's Hospital train station near Horsham

RIDE 04

Train Station: About an hour's return journey from Horsham to Guildford with a change at Dorking (very short ride from Dorking main to Dorking Deepdene but a carry up long, steep steps at Dorking Deepdene)

Grade: Moderate

Terrain, gradients and access: Compared to the southern half of the Downs Link, also covered here, the northern half has a few sections that are a little more challenging. Most noticeably just after the hamlet of Baynards, south of Cranleigh, there are forest tracks that require careful navigation and involve a couple of steep climbs. There are also more potentially muddy sections compared to the southern section, especially after rain. Access is generally good though, with few very restrictive access points.

Loops, links and longer rides: NCN 223 extends north of Guildford some 10 miles to Chertsey. A little less than 5 miles after starting at Guildford NCN 22 branches off to the east. Once complete route 22 will link London with Portsmouth, then Brockenhurst via the Isle of Wight. Currently, route 22 is open between Batt's Corner, south of Farnham and Banstead.

Stay: Puttenham Camping Barn (01483) 811001 puttenhamcampingbarn.co.uk Around 4 miles west of Guildford centre but a lovely ride in along NCN 22.

Eat and drink: Tons of choice at Guildford and Horsham, the latter just east of your finishing point of Christ's Hospital and a short train trip or bike ride away. Cranleigh is just off the trail and has a large pleasant area for sitting out with several pavement cafés near the attractive old town. The pretty village of Rudgwick has the Milk Churn café and the Kings Head pub. Attractive Red Lyon pub at Slinfold village which also has a village store.

Cycle hire: Surrey Hills Cycle Hire, Hambledon 07506 173480 surreyhillscyclehire.co.uk or Electric Bikes Guildford (01483) 808765 electricbikesguildford.com

Wider area cycle map: Central Sussex & South Surrey

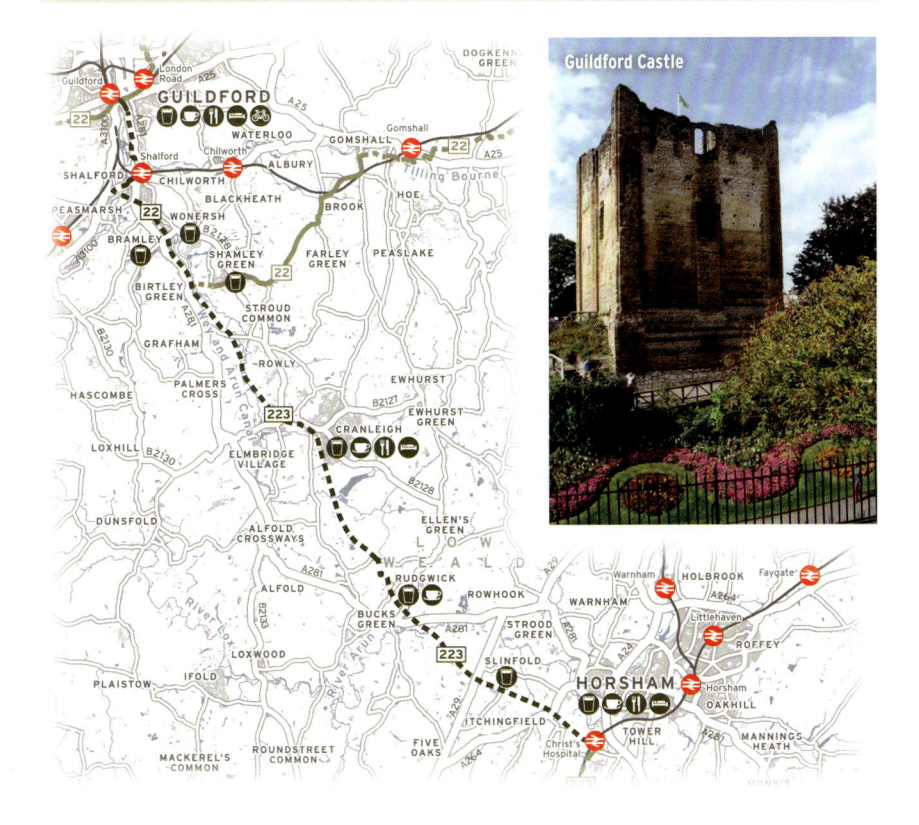

Guildford Castle

RIDE 05
20 miles — 223 — **Start:** Christ's Hospital train station

DOWNS LINK SOUTH

(HORSHAM TO SHOREHAM-BY-SEA)

At Christ's Hospital the Downs Link is soon heading away from the commanding brick tower of the private school that dominates the small settlement here. You can't miss the old West Grinstead station with a train carriage for company if you opt to make use of the lovely rest area here. After Partridge Green there are more open vistas as the trail crosses the River Adur at a lovely spot. It's worth taking time away from the trail to explore Henfield with some fine old buildings and bijou back lanes that pass by a pond and seating area at The Tanyard on the beautiful Blackgate Lane leading to a fine church.

There's more of a mixture of tracks and scenery after recrossing the river Adur, with tracks and roads leading right by the pretty main street of Bramber, with classy looking hotels and pubs overlooked by the crumbling remains of a Norman castle.

The final run in to Shoreham-by-Sea parallels the A283 here, the Downs Link heading through a gap in the South Downs and giving you a good look at the gentle outline of the hills of the country's newest National Park. The trail heads over a bridge as you roll alongside the river Adur for the last few miles, passing the amazing 18th Century wooden tollbridge – now a popular traffic-free link following a maintenance overhaul of it in 2008.

Although the Downs Link ends by one end of the busy main road through Shoreham it's worth making your way down to pick up NCN 2 on the elegant traffic-free bridge across the estuary and heading straight on to the beach here, a popular relaxing and bathing spot.

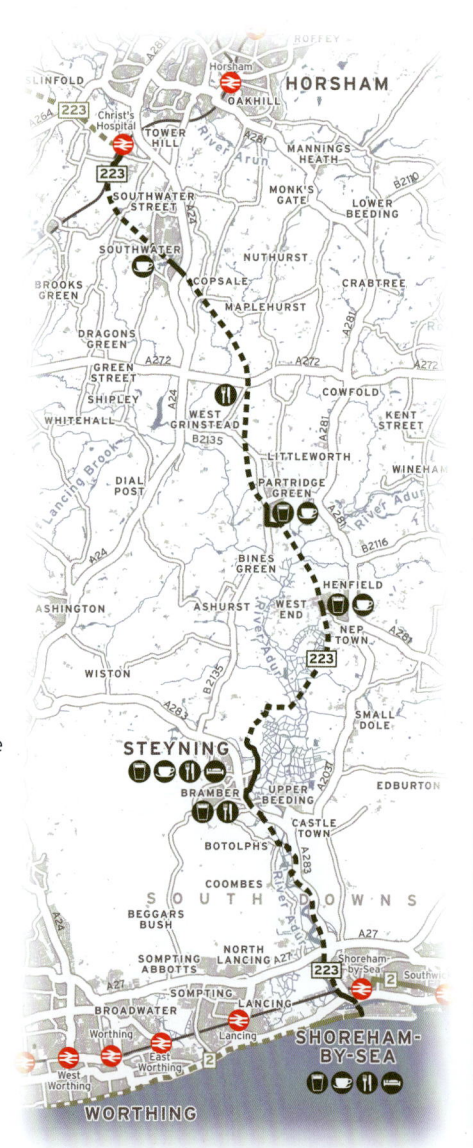

Finish: Shoreham-by-Sea seafront

RIDE 05

Train Station: Stations at Christ's Hospital, Horsham and Shoreham-by-Sea (return takes a little over an hour with a change at Barnham)

Grade: Easy

Terrain, gradients and access: It's pretty much all downhill from Christ's Hospital near Horsham, although very gradually. Mainly unsealed but smooth surfaces (occasionally a little stony) on a usually very broad track. Easy access with few if any restrictions at most access points. Signage for the Downs Link is generally excellent.

Loops, links and longer rides: There are local bridleway links from Christ's Hospital to lovely Horsham centre though mountain or trekking bikes with front suspension are recommended if not vital. At its southern end the Downs Link ends very near NCN 2 - a long-distance cycle route which, when complete, will link Dover in Kent with St. Austell in Cornwall via the south coast of England. NCN 2 is currently 361 miles long, with the only major gaps currently between Dawlish and Totnes, and Plymouth and St Austell. Suggested YHA accommodation here is on the South Downs Way, one of the few National Trails fully traversable by bike - though some sections are definitely mountain biker territory. The Downs Link itself joins the North Downs and South Downs Ways.

Stay: Truleigh Hill Youth Hostel 0345 371 9047 yha.org.uk

Eat and drink: There are some wonderfully varied opportunities en route. In Horsham, East Street is a real highlight (known locally as Eat Street) as is Kaya in the Park, whilst Southwater Country Park has a nice little café by the lake. West Grinstead station has The Orchard restaurant with a garden. Bike Side bike shop at Partridge Green offers coffee and snacks as well as spares and repairs. Right by the trail at Henfield is the lovely Old Railway pub with the Sidings Garden Kiosk café and a garden to enjoy and also by the trail at Henfield is the expansive Cabin at Berretts Farm with great views of the South Downs. There are a sprinkling of restaurants and pubs in lovely Bramber village and also plenty of choice in Shoreham-by-Sea.

Cycle hire: Southwater Cycles (01403) 701002 southwatercycles.com

Wider area cycle map: Central Sussex & South Surrey

Estuary Shoreham-by-Sea

RIDE 06
7 miles

Start: White Cliffs Café, Saltdean

BRIGHTON SEAFRONT

Man with bike, Brighton beach

This cliff top and promenade ride offers some wonderful views across the English Channel on its way to Brighton and Hove, one of the south coast's liveliest cities with a growing cycling culture.

Start at White Cliffs Café opposite Saltdean Park and Lido, where there are two options for heading west towards Brighton. NCN 2 follows the cliff top path, where the elevated position offers wonderful views of the chalk cliffs and sea. On this route you'll ride past the distinctive black Rottingdean Windmill and the colossal buildings of the world-renowned Roedean school overlooking the water.

Alternatively, take a more sheltered ride along Undercliff Walk and closely follow the shoreline beneath the white chalk cliffs, with views stretching across the Channel all the way.

It's a refreshing and easy cycle whichever route you choose, and the paths join together again at Madeira Drive near Brighton Marina. This is the biggest marina in Europe, so have a wander between the sleek boats and apartments, and around the parasol-covered terraces of the popular bars and restaurants here.

Leaving the marina behind, reach Black Rock and ride alongside the tracks of Volks Electric Railway, passing Brighton's naturist beach along the way, discreetly concealed behind a shingle ridge, and the elegant Victorian arches of Madeira Terrace. There's a real energy around Brighton, and the mix of cyclists, skaters, walkers and joggers that you'll meet along the path here gives it an almost Californian feel in high summer.

Ride past the 450ft i360 viewing tower and the famous Brighton Pier, and consider taking a short (five-minute) walk inland to find the 'extravagant pleasure palace' of the Royal Pavilion, the Prince Regent's over-the-top bachelor pad. Back on the promenade you can't miss the sad skeleton of West Pier out in the water but, derelict as it is, it still comes alive at dusk on winter evenings when one of the UK's most spectacular starling roosts takes place there.

In the final mile, ride past the magnificently restored Victorian bandstand and end at the grassy seafront spot of Hove Lawns. There's a signed, on-road route through Hove's wide streets to the train station, or continue a further mile from the Lawns to Hove Lagoon, where the route joins the road to Shoreham-by-Sea.

RIDE 06

Finish: Hove train station

Train stations: Brighton and Hove
Grade: Easy
Terrain, gradients and access: Tarmac path with short, on-road sections at Rottingdean, Black Rock and Hove.
Loops, links and longer rides: The Downs and Weald route is a 164-mile, on-road and traffic-free route from London to Hastings, via Brighton. NCN 2 Shoreham Promenade (**Ride 03**).
Stay: The White House, Brighton 0345 3719176 whitehousebrighton.com or YHA Brighton, 0800 019 1700 yha.org.uk
Eat and drink: Try White Cliffs Café at Saltdean or Molly's café and The White Horse pub at Rottingdean. There are lots of waterside restaurants at Brighton Marina Village, or near the route's end try Pavilion Gardens Café and Bandstand Café. The Upper Crust Bakery at Hove is also very popular.
Cycle hire: BTN (app bike share) **btnbikeshare.com** or Brighton Beach Bikes (01273) 601863 brightonbeachbikes.co.uk
Wider area cycle map: Central Sussex & South Surrey

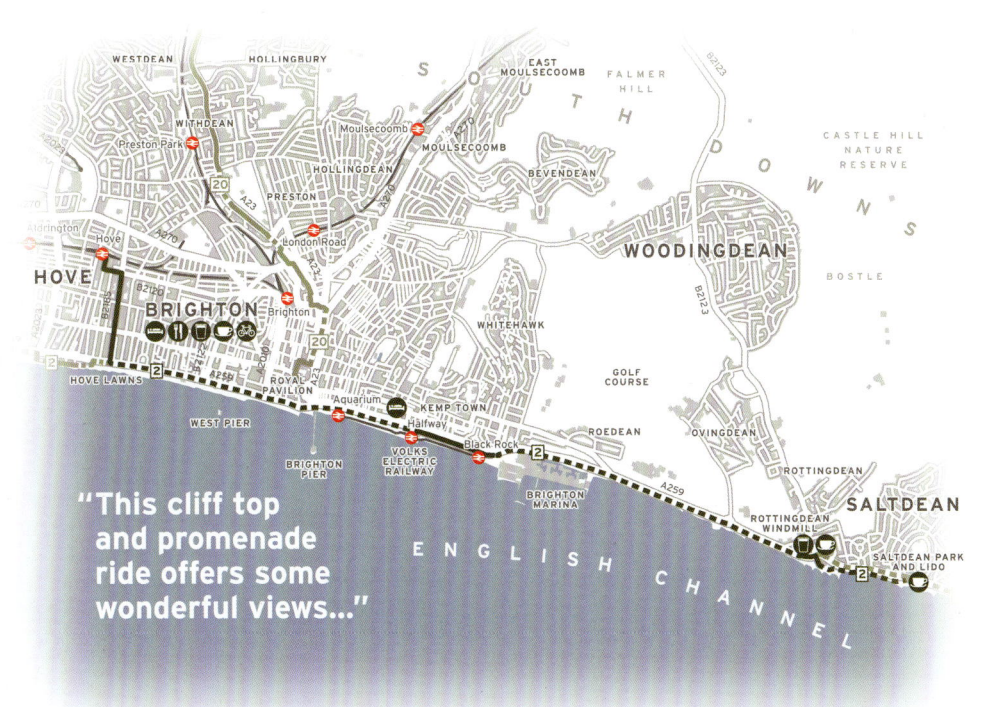

Hut on Brighton beach

"This cliff top and promenade ride offers some wonderful views..."

75

RIDE 07
10 miles | 21 🚲 | **Start:** Forest Way Country Park entrance, Corseley Road, Groombridge

FOREST WAY

This ride along a former railway path crosses beautiful woodland and meadows in the High Weald Area of Outstanding Natural Beauty. It's on the floodplain of the River Medway, meaning many of the trees beside the route are alder, willow or other species that flourish in wet ground. Despite the name, however, there is far more to this route than forest, and the views from the start at Groombridge stretch across open hillsides, crop fields and farmsteads.

Take a seat at the picnic spot in the opening mile to soak up the wide arable landscape and look at the round brick tower and conical roof of the nearby oast house. This is a hop kiln, used to dry locally grown hops in the days when beer was as vital in the daily diet as bread, and is a common sight around the region so keep a lookout for others nearby.

Wooded trail soon takes over, with fields and rolling hills visible beyond the trees and a series of path-side benches with cycle parking, making it easy to lock up and explore on foot. Cross little streams that lead off from the River Medway as you ride through the northern edges of Ashdown Forest, once a royal hunting ground.

It's worth venturing into Hartfield, around three miles in, as this little village is at the heart of Pooh Country; AA Milne lived here with his son, Christopher Robin Milne, and famous Pooh landmarks are known to be nearby.

At Forest Row, just a few miles further along the trail, pass Tablehurst community farm where you can see the animals and gardens or taste the organic produce. It's a gentle climb in the final miles, with glimpses of the pretty East Sussex countryside between the trees, before you join the short road into the ancient market town of East Grinstead.

End among the handsome buildings of the High Street and be certain to seek out Sackville College, a Jacobean Almshouse, that is one of the most attractive buildings in the town.

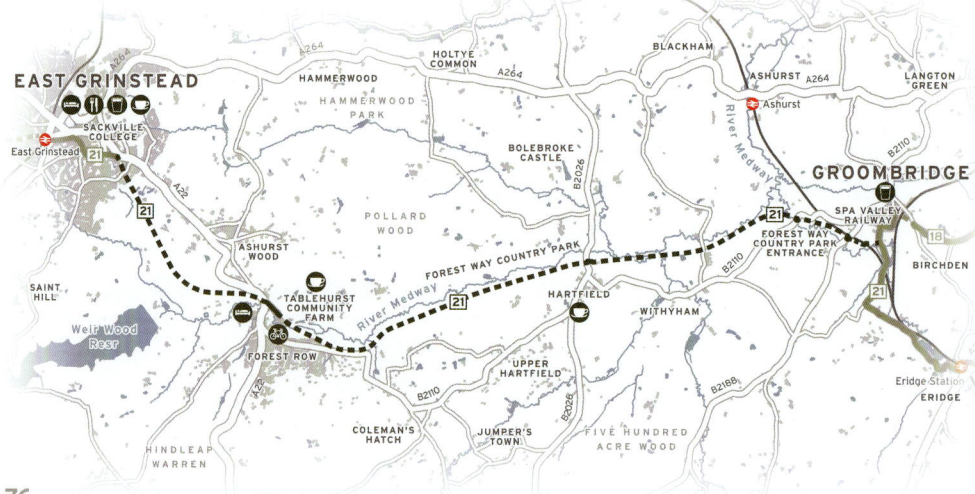

Finish: High Street, East Grinstead

RIDE 07

Train station: East Grinstead

Grade: Moderate

Terrain, gradients and access: Largely flat with a steady climb in the final miles. Tarmac path, stony trail and fine gravel track with some road crossings and short, on-road sections at Forest Row and East Grinstead.

Loops, links and longer rides: Forest Way is part of NCN 21 Avenue Verte, a 250-mile route that starts at the London Eye and crosses the channel to end at Notre Dame. It is also part of the Downs and Weald route, a 164-mile, on-road and traffic-free route from London to Hastings via Brighton. NCN 2 Brighton Seafront (**Ride 06**). NCN 2 Shoreham Promenade (**Ride 03**).

Stay: Cranston House, East Grinstead (01342) 323609 cranstonhouse.co.uk

Eat and drink: Try The Crown Inn at Groombridge, Piglet's Tearoom at Pooh Corner in Hartfield and Tablehurst organic farm shop and café at Forest Row. There are many places to eat in East Grinstead, including Market Square Food and Wine Co, Nest coffee shop and CJ's Café Bar.

Cycle hire: CountryBike 07858 595354 countrybike.co.uk

Wider area cycle map: Central Sussex & South Surrey

Signs along the way

Forest Way near Groombridge

RIDE 08

5.5 miles

Start: Tonbridge Swimming Pool car park

TUDOR TRAIL

This ride through charming countryside into the Weald of Kent is wonderful throughout, but it's the majestic view of Penshurst Place and Gardens in the final mile that makes it distinctly memorable.

The remains of Tonbridge Castle are near the route's start, and it's worth taking the small detour to visit them as the gatehouse is regarded as one of the finest in England.

Start at the Tonbridge Swimming Pool car park and follow the course of the River Medway as it weaves west, passing through scented woodland and crop fields to reach Haysden Country Park in the opening mile. The mosaic of woodland, meadows, marshland and lakes in this award-winning park is beautiful, and riding in the shade of the park's spinneys, and beside the white willow trees on the edges of Barden Lake, is just joyful. There are some great picnic spots near the water here, too.

From here, it's a gentle ride along quiet country lanes, before you re-join the traffic-free path to roll past brambly hedgerows and rich, green countryside. A long and steady climb along the concrete track of the Penshurst Estate in the route's second half is the only challenge of the ride, but even this is a pleasure, climbing between vast crop fields, with impressive over-the-shoulder views across the Kent hillsides.

The gradient gently eases, before a sharp turn at Well Place Farm and a final heart-lifting descent as the first wonderful views of Penshurst Place swell into sight ahead. The red roofs, towers and battlements of the magnificent 14th Century manor house, historic home of Viscount De L'Isle, are revealed in all their splendour here, completely stealing the scenery.

End at the Penshurst Place Visitor Centre for entry to the house and gardens, or ride for half a mile along the quiet road into the idyllic village of Penshurst. Its ivy-covered cottages and Tudoresque architecture are enchanting, and the little Forge Stores occupies one of the most unusual and alluring buildings of all.

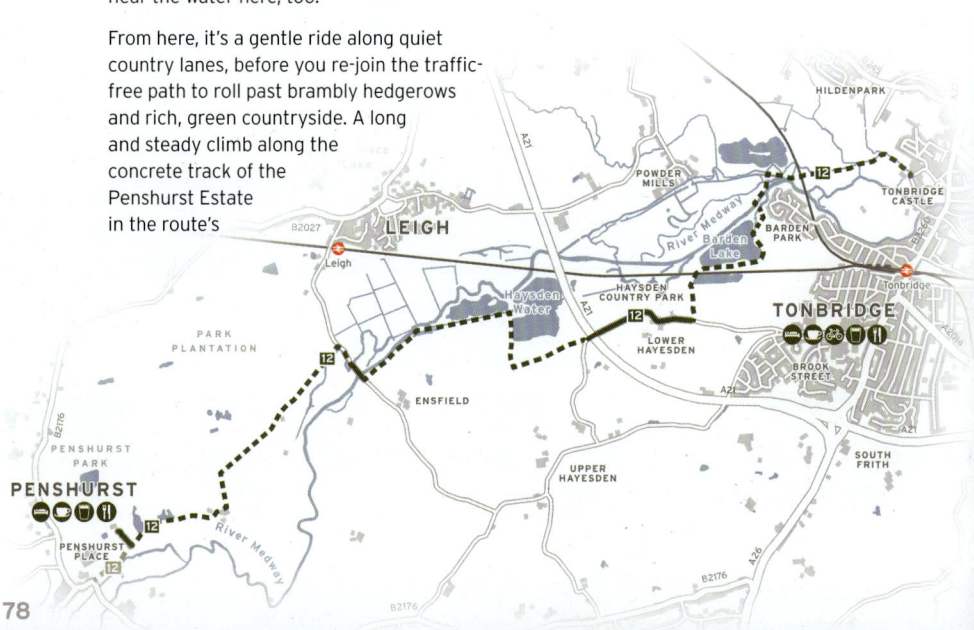

Finish: Penshurst Place and Gardens

RIDE 08

"The majestic view of Penshurst Place and gardens...makes it distinctly memorable."

Train stations: Tonbridge, Leigh and Penshurst
Grade: Easy
Terrain, gradients and access: Largely flat with one long climb near the end. Tarmac and concrete path, fine gravel track and stony trail. A short and quiet on-road section at Lower Haysden.
Loops, links and longer rides: The Downs and Weald is a 164-mile, on-road and traffic-free route between London and Hastings via Brighton. NCN 18 High Weald is a challenging and hilly route, mostly on-road, between Ashford and Royal Tunbridge Wells. NCN 21 Forest Way (**Ride 07**).

Stay: Charcott Farmhouse B&B, Leigh (01892) 870024 **charcottfarmhouse.com**
Eat and drink: Tonbridge has many places to eat, including popular Finch House café. Haysden Country Park has a snack bar. Porcupine Pantry is at Penshurst Place. The Leicester Arms Hotel, Forge Stores and Fir Tree House Tea Rooms are all in Penshurst village.
Cycle hire: Cycle-Ops, Tonbridge (01732) 500533 **cycle-ops.co.uk**, CountryBike 07858 595354 **countrybike.co.uk** or Brompton Dock, Tonbridge Station **bromptonbikehire.com**
Wider area cycle map: Kent

Penshurst Place and Gardens 79

RIDE 09
8 miles

Start: Westgate Gardens, Canterbury

CRAB
&
WINKLE WAY

Canterbury Cathedral

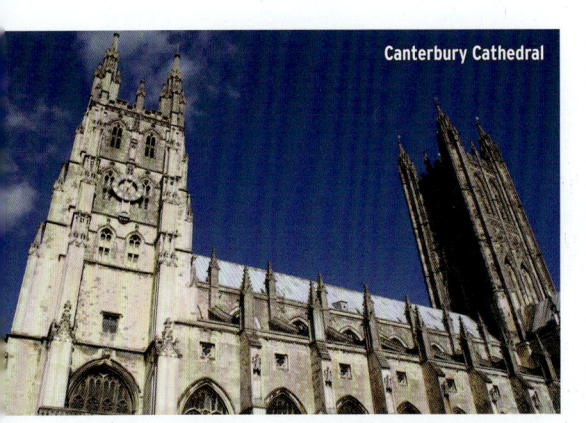

Other rides take in a beautiful city, coast or countryside setting, but few offer such magnificent examples of all three on an easy, family-friendly route. Eight miles of undulating trail take you through the 'Garden of England', from the historic city of Canterbury to the jaunty seaside town of Whitstable, with the ancient woodland of The Blean between.

Canterbury's pretty Westgate Gardens are a great start, particularly in summer when punts glide idly along the River Great Stour here. Before setting off, venture through the impressive medieval gateway at Westgate Towers to explore the cobbled streets and fine buildings of this grand city.

On the trail, be prepared for steady climbs and long descents as you head towards the Kent coast. The first climb occurs in the very first mile and leads up to the University of Kent, but stop at the top to rest and look back at the wonderful views across the city; the vast and majestic Canterbury Cathedral, the oldest cathedral in England, towers above the buildings around it.

Soon, arable Kent farmland dominates and crops stretch out beside the route, gloriously golden and dotted with wild poppies in summer. Another steady climb takes you to the picture perfect country church of St Cosmus and St Damian in the Blean, and past the edges of one of Kent's many orchards. Look and listen for skylarks hovering above the open meadows here, before riding deep into The Blean, one of the largest areas of ancient woodland in England.

Just beyond the halfway point, stop at a lovely quiet picnic spot in a glade of Clowes Wood where nightingales and heath fritillary butterflies might be spotted, or the churring call of secretive nightjars may be heard at dusk during May and June. The Winding Pond at the picnic spot used to supply water to the engine that helped haul train carriages up the long, steep hill from the coast when the Crab and Winkle path was a railway. However, no such boost is necessary for cycling in this direction, as it's just a long, gentle descent from here all the way to Whitstable, weaving in and out of the cool shade of woodland along the way.

In the final mile, enjoy snatched glimpses all the way down to the sea at Whitstable Bay, before riding through the quiet streets on the outskirts of the town to reach the route's end at the harbour. The buzzy cafés and market stalls at South Quay are great for browsing and sampling Whitstable's best-known delicacy, oysters.

Finish: Whitstable Harbour

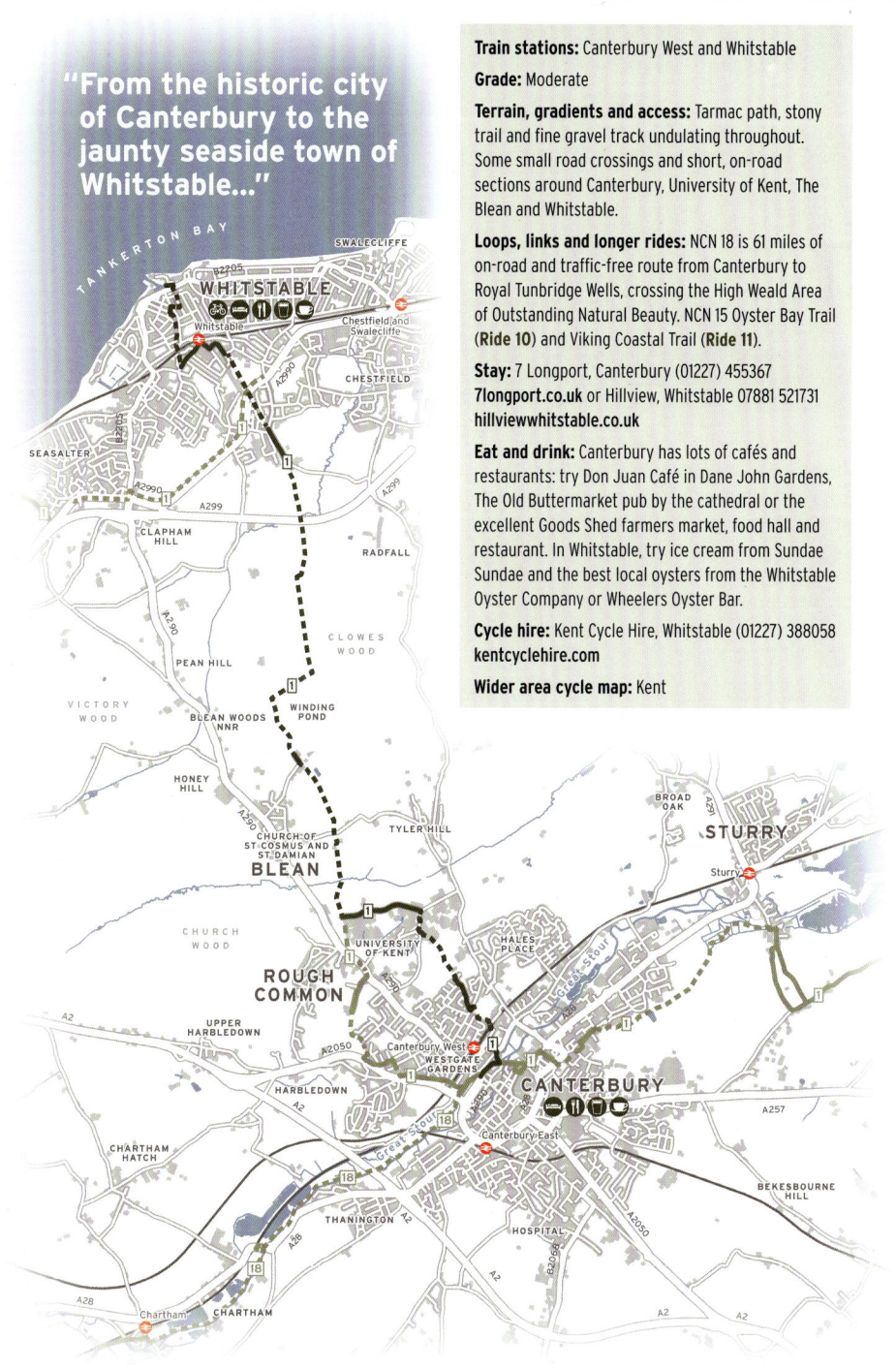

RIDE 09

"From the historic city of Canterbury to the jaunty seaside town of Whitstable..."

Train stations: Canterbury West and Whitstable

Grade: Moderate

Terrain, gradients and access: Tarmac path, stony trail and fine gravel track undulating throughout. Some small road crossings and short, on-road sections around Canterbury, University of Kent, The Blean and Whitstable.

Loops, links and longer rides: NCN 18 is 61 miles of on-road and traffic-free route from Canterbury to Royal Tunbridge Wells, crossing the High Weald Area of Outstanding Natural Beauty. NCN 15 Oyster Bay Trail (**Ride 10**) and Viking Coastal Trail (**Ride 11**).

Stay: 7 Longport, Canterbury (01227) 455367 7longport.co.uk or Hillview, Whitstable 07881 521731 hillviewwhitstable.co.uk

Eat and drink: Canterbury has lots of cafés and restaurants: try Don Juan Café in Dane John Gardens, The Old Buttermarket pub by the cathedral or the excellent Goods Shed farmers market, food hall and restaurant. In Whitstable, try ice cream from Sundae Sundae and the best local oysters from the Whitstable Oyster Company or Wheelers Oyster Bar.

Cycle hire: Kent Cycle Hire, Whitstable (01227) 388058 kentcyclehire.com

Wider area cycle map: Kent

OYSTER BAY TRAIL

The lively seaside town of Whitstable at this ride's start is a perfect contrast to the austere cliffs and untamed shoreline of Reculver Country Park at its end. Sweeping views across the north Kent coast are the real star, however, and remain spectacular from start to finish.

Start at the traditional yet independent little town of Whitstable and ride from its busy harbour alongside the shingly shore and charming, brightly coloured beach huts. Tankerton, in the opening miles, is a good place to pause and look back towards the Isle of Sheppey and Whitstable. Time it right and you may get the best view of all from half a mile out to sea at The Street, a shingle ridge that is exposed and accessible at low tide.

The path weaves delicately around the sensitive habitat of Long Rock so as not to disturb this vital feeding and breeding area for coastal birds, before the curve of land at Hampton comes into sight up ahead. The terracotta-coloured roofs and whitewashed houses here look every bit as enticing as a little Mediterranean village when the sun shines. However, a short climb up Western Esplanade quickly restores the classic English scenery, as the traditional seaside resort of Herne Bay appears.

Herne Bay's shingly beach, pier and ice cream kiosks are a timeless seaside treat, and make a great place to stop at around the ride's midway point.

Cycle past the seafront gardens, huge bandstand and beautifully ornate King's Hall, and begin to see a shift in the landscape as a quieter and wilder part of the north Kent coast emerges. At the steep-sided gully in the sandstone cliffs at Bishopstone Glen you'll need to leave the coastline momentarily and climb on the quiet road to enter Reculver Country Park, which occupies a beautifully undeveloped stretch of shore.

A vast green in the final mile offers the best sea views of the entire ride and makes a great late picnic spot, before a heavenly, gentle descent across the park's clifftop grassland. The sea and the imposing twin towers of the medieval St Mary's church perched on the edge of the land are a dramatic backdrop for the end of the ride.

Finish at the country park's visitor centre and lock up to explore the remains of the church, or walk along the shingle beach to take in the impressive views over the Thames Estuary and Kentish Flats wind farm.

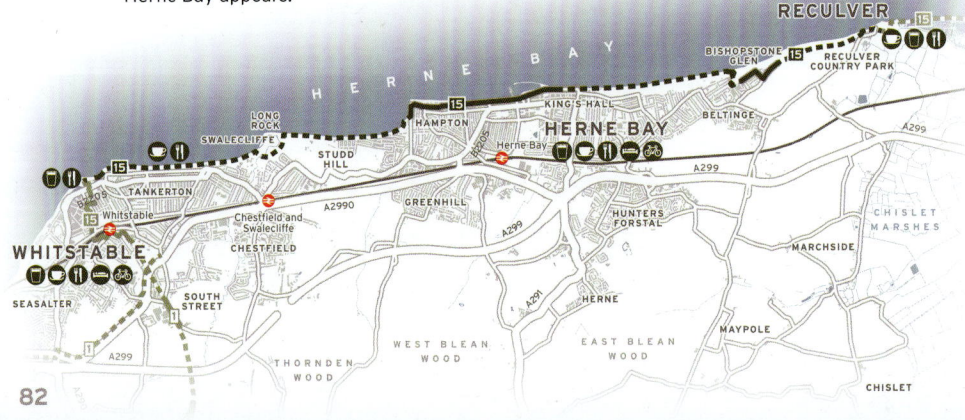

Finish: Reculver Country Park

RIDE 10

Train stations: Whitstable, Herne Bay and Birchington-on-Sea

Grade: Easy

Terrain, gradients and access: Largely flat along concrete, shared-use promenade with some climbs and on-road sections at Herne Bay and Bishopstone Glen. A short grassy section leads through Reculver Country Park.

Loops, links and longer rides: NCN 1 Crab and Winkle Way (**Ride 09**). NCN 15 Viking Coastal Trail (**Ride 11**).

Stay: Hillview, Whitstable 07881 521731 hillviewwhitstable.co.uk

Eat and drink: There are great places to eat among the community of local traders at Whitstable Harbour Market, South Quay, or The Old Neptune is a uniquely positioned pub on the beach at Whitstable. Along the way, try Sea View café, Tankerton Bay and the excellent JoJo's restaurant in Tankerton. At Herne Bay, the Hampton Inn has uninterrupted sea views, or try The King's Hall café. At the route's end, try The HatHats coffee company café in Reculver Country Park or the The King Ethelbert Inn with its own onsite seafood stall.

Cycle hire: Kent Cycle Hire, Whitstable and Herne Bay (01227) 388058 kentcyclehire.com

Wider area cycle map: Kent

Local oysters

Whitstable Harbour

83

RIDE 11 — 9 miles

Start: Reculver Country Park

VIKING COASTAL TRAIL

View over Broadstairs

On a sunny day, an endless expanse of turquoise sea stretches beside this glorious route along the wild and chalky Thanet Coast, where Vikings first landed in Britain.

Reculver Country Park at the route's start is a beautiful mix of clifftop grassland and shingly beach, with commanding views across the Thames Estuary.

Start beside the striking twin towers of St Mary's church and ride past the site of the Regulbium Roman fort, before heading over the blustery, concrete top of the Northern Sea Wall. The opening miles follow a particularly remote and invigorating stretch of coast, with oystercatchers speckling the pebbly foreshore and cormorants perching on the lifebuoys stretching out their wings.

Around three miles in, shingle gives way to golden sand at Minnis Bay, the first in a sequence of popular and sandy little beaches along this route. With its coloured beach huts, rickshaws, ice cream kiosks and a village-life feel, this is a quaint spot for an early stop, and there are lovely views all the way back to the sandstone cliffs of Reculver.

Finish: Turner Contemporary, Margate

RIDE 11

Train station: Margate
Grade: Easy
Terrain, gradients and access: Shared-use, concrete promenade and a short, on-road section from Epple Bay to Westgate-on-Sea. On short sections of the promenade at Westgate-on-Sea, St Mildred's Bay and Westbrook Bay, cyclists are required to dismount and push in the peak summer season.
Loops, links and longer rides: Follow the entire Viking Coastal Trail, a 21-mile ride around the Isle of Thanet peninsula following NCN 15 on a mix of traffic-free and on-road routes. From Margate, the trail continues along the coast to Broadstairs, Ramsgate and Cliffsend. NCN 15 Oyster Bay Trail (**Ride 10**).

Stay: Sands Hotel, Margate (01843) 228228
sandshotelmargate.co.uk
Eat and drink: At the start, try The HatHats coffee company café in Reculver Country Park or the King Ethelbert Inn with its own onsite seafood stall. Seaside eateries on the way include The Minnis Bay Bar and Brasserie at Birchington, West Bay Café at Westgate-on-Sea or The Margate Coffee Shed. The Ambrette restaurant and The Greedy Cow café in Margate's Old Town are both popular.
Cycle hire: Viking Coastal Trail Cycle Hire, Minnis Bay 07772 037609 or The Bike Shed, Margate (01843) 228866
thebikeshedkent.co.uk
Wider area cycle map: Kent

Leave Minnis Bay to swoop in and out of the deep, sea-carved grooves in the chalk cliffs to reach Birchington-on-Sea and Epple Bay, where a cobbled climb leads you away from the promenade and along the cliff top to a grassy picnic spot with fine panoramas. It's a descent from here to re-join the promenade at Westgate-on-Sea, before riding around sandy Westgate Bay and St Mildred's Bay, where the endpoint of Margate can be seen in the distance.

In the final miles you'll cross Westbrook Undercliffe Nature Park, a nice promenade area of wildflowers and coastal wildlife with chalk cliffs to one side and the sandy Westbrook Bay to the other, before reaching the spirited seaside resort of Margate. The wide sandy bay and tidal pool here are incredibly popular, as are the little vintage shops and cafés in the Old Town.

End at Turner Contemporary, a seafront art gallery inspired by romantic painter J M W Turner. And at sunset watch the dramatic changes in light and colour across the wide sky; Turner himself described the skies over Thanet as "the loveliest in all Europe".

RIDE 12
7.5 miles

Start and finish: Parkcycle at Roehampton Gate, Richmond Park

TAMSIN TRAIL

In the midst of this genteel and desirable London district lies the untamed retreat of Richmond Park, one of the 'Lungs of London'. This is the largest and wildest of the city's eight Royal parks, and the Tamsin Trail is a lovely loop around its edges, with incredible views from the highest points.

The ride is wonderful at any time of year, but come in autumn to see the leaves of the ancient oaks turn golden and witness the spectacular rut among the herds of red and fallow deer that roam the park.

Roehampton Gate is the best place to start the ride and to pick up a trail map from Parkcycle, Richmond Park's cycling centre. The gentle undulations on the route offer some fun ascents and descents throughout the ride, the most testing of which is the long and steady climb that follows Robin Hood Gate in the opening few miles. Look out for the flamboyant green of ring-necked parakeets flashing between the trees overhead, and take a small detour at Ham Cross to explore Isabella Plantation, an exotic, ornamental woodland garden.

In the ride's second half you'll pass the doors of Pembroke Lodge, an attractive Georgian mansion with elegant landscaped grounds. This is the highest point in Richmond Park and is a great spot for locking up to explore the Lodge, or simply taking in the great views over the Thames Valley. The most memorable spot near here is King Henry's Mound, with its protected 10-mile view down to the domed St Paul's Cathedral, one of the most iconic features of London's skyline.

Further along the trail reach Richmond Gate, where it's worth leaving the park momentarily to ride along the short road to Terrace Gardens on Richmond Hill, one of the finest gardens in London with a classic vista over the winding River Thames.

Back in the park, the final two miles of trail are a tumbling treat of open grassland and mature trees, taking in Bishops Pond and Adam's Pond on the way, just two of the thirty or so ponds within the park. End back at Parkcycle at Roehampton Gate.

Train stations: Barnes, North Sheen, Richmond (London) and Norbiton are all near the park.

Grade: Moderate

Terrain, gradients and access: Fine gravel track, undulating throughout with one reasonably long climb and some short, steep descents. Small crossings over the quiet roads within the park.

Loops, links and longer rides: There are other cycle trails around Richmond Park. Two Palaces (**Ride 15**). NCN 4 Thames Path (**Ride 13**). NCN 20 Wandle Trail.

Stay: Richmond Hill Hotel (020) 8940 2247 richmondhill-hotel.co.uk

Eat and drink: Roehampton Café at Roehampton Gate and The Tea Rooms in Pembroke Lodge are both within the park. Near Richmond Gate are the Roebuck, a traditional pub with fabulous views, Hollyhock Café in Terrace Gardens and Richmond Hill Bakery. Near Sheen Gate is Pearson Cycles, a popular London bike shop and café, and The Victoria, a very recommendable pub.

Cycle hire: Parkcycle, Richmond Park (020) 8878 2519 parkcycle.co.uk, Santander Cycles santandercycles.co.uk, Richmond Cycle Centre (020) 83320123 richmondcyclecentre.co.uk or Blazing Saddles Bike Hire (020) 8948 8240 blazingsaddlesbikehire.uk

Wider area cycle map: London

RIDE 12

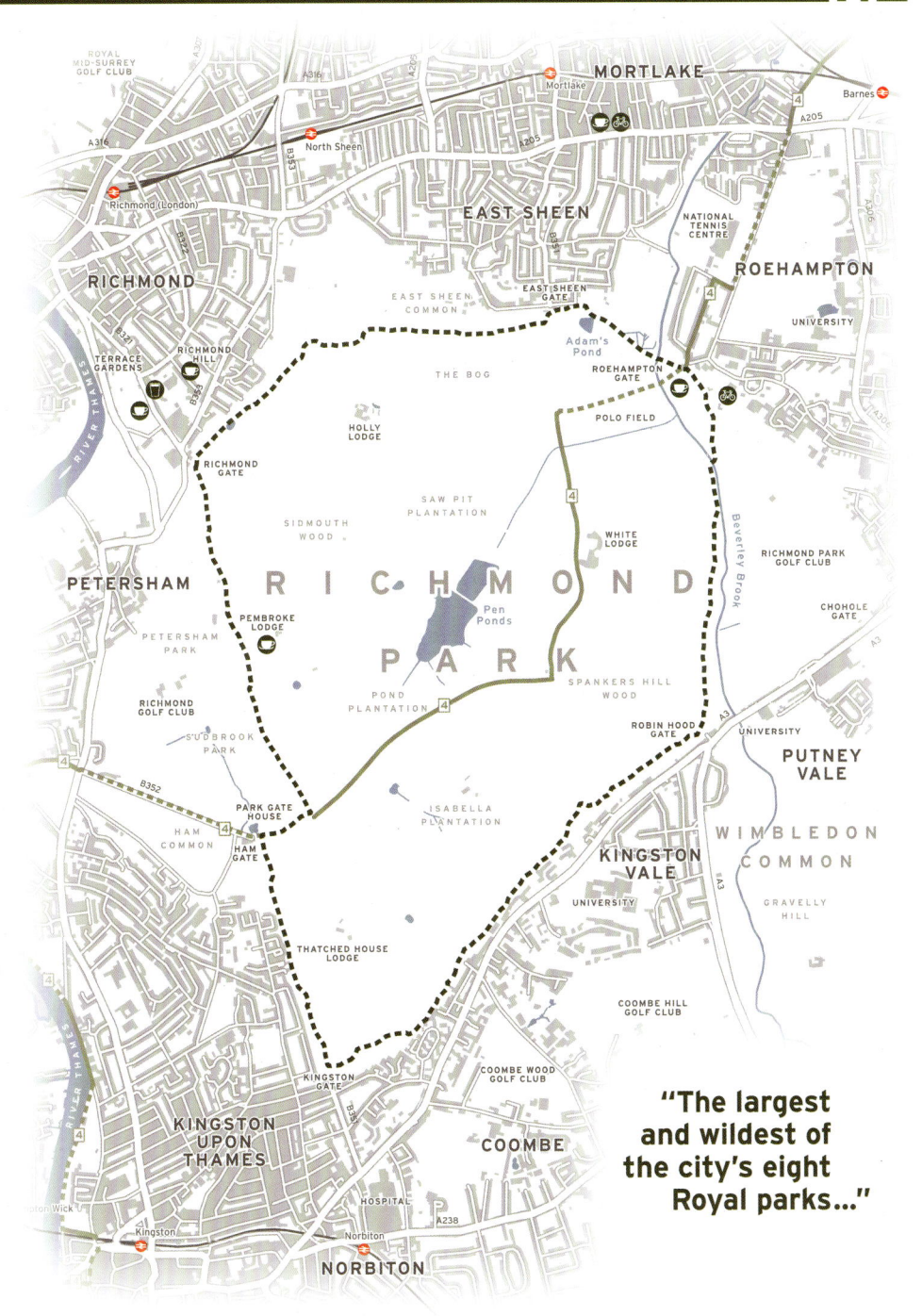

"The largest and wildest of the city's eight Royal parks..."

RIDE 13
14.5 miles

Start: Kingston Bridge, Kingston upon Thames

THAMES PATH

Thames riverside at Staines

One of the finest and most elegant riverside rides in the country, this route follows part of the Thames, England's longest river. Classic views up and down the waterway stretch to both sides of Kingston Bridge at the start, and the waterside scenery remains sensational all the way to Staines.

Start at the Home Park end of Kingston Bridge and ride through the park, where pleasure boats cruise leisurely along the water beside the path. Just three miles in, you'll ride past the gilded gates of the elaborate red-brick Hampton Court Palace, sumptuous home of Henry VIII and one of the ride's highlights, with the world-famous maze within its grounds.

There are some wonderful places to make an early stop on this ride. East Molesey, beside Hampton Court Bridge, is a particular delight in summer when the cafés and restaurants spill out onto the pavement, whilst Molesey Lock Café, a short while later, has become a real favourite among cyclists.

Beyond Molesey Lock, ride beside the wildflower meadows of pretty Hurst Park, which stretches for almost a mile along the riverbank and is the perfect place for picnicking whilst watching rowers glide past the beautiful St Mary's church in Hampton on the opposite bank. Reach the edges of Molesey Reservoirs nature reserve, former gravel pits that are now rich in bird and insect life, followed by the pretty Sunbury Lock at around the halfway point.

Near Weybridge, ten miles in, the route splits and you'll need to choose one of two options for passing around Chertsey Meads. Follow the northern option to stay most faithful to the riverside, and to take the brief but fun trip across the Thames on the Weybridge - Shepperton ferry.

A short, on-road section away from the waterside follows, but you'll soon re-join the riverside path and enter leafy Laleham Park, before reaching the attractive Penton Hook Lock and Marina. Here you can venture onto Penton Hook Island to be completely surrounded by the Thames.

Then it's just over a mile to the finish. The Thames continues all the way to its source in the Cotswolds, but end your ride at the handsome Victorian building of the Old Town Hall. It is just a short walk from here to the shops in the town centre.

RIDE 13

Finish: The Old Town Hall, Staines-upon-Thames

Train stations: Kingston and Staines

Grade: Moderate

Terrain, gradients and access: Flat, tarmac path, fine gravel track, stony trail and a short grassy section. Some short, on-road sections and road crossings at East Molesey, Shepperton, Laleham and Staines. Following the Shepperton side of the route means taking the Weybridge-Shepperton Ferry (adult single fare + bike: £4).

Loops, links and longer rides: There are a number of excellent cycling trails around the nearby Windsor Great Park. Tamsin Trail around Richmond Park (**Ride 12**). Jubilee River Path (**Ride 14**).

Stay: The White Hart Hotel, Hampton Wick (020) 8977 1786 **whitehartotel.co.uk**

Eat and drink: Pubs include The Mute Swan at Hampton Court Bridge, The Weir Hotel at Sunbury-on-Thames, and The Anglers, Walton-on-Thames. East Molesey has lots of open-air eateries, and Eight By the River or Molesey Lock Café are both nice tea stops near here. The Three Horseshoes in Laleham is very popular, as is Momo Café in Staines.

Cycle hire: Brompton Dock, Surbiton **bromptonbikehire.com**

Wider area cycle map: London

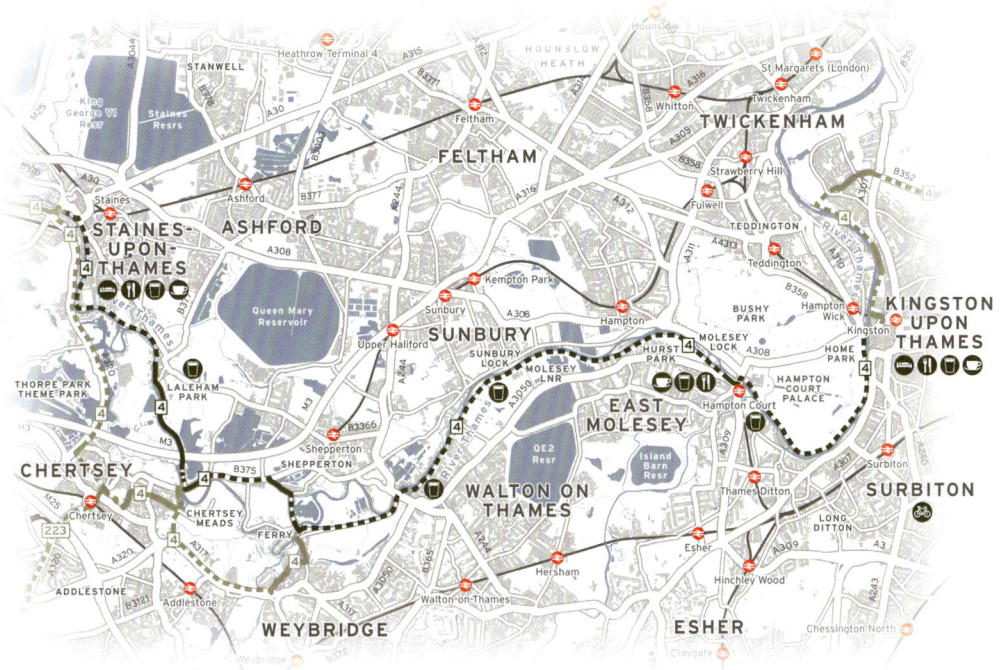

Cyclist on riverside path

JUBILEE RIVER PATH

This Royal Borough ride is ever so English, taking in the historic Windsor Castle, famous Eton College and two majestic rivers: the Thames and the Jubilee.

Start at Windsor Castle, the Queen's favourite weekend retreat, and take the swooping descent along its walls to join the River Thames. They may not be as grand as the castle, but the buildings that follow are beautiful, nonetheless, from the spire of Eton Wick church that can be seen across the meadows, to the charming little St Mary Magdalene chapel at Boveney. Boveney Lock is one of the most attractive locks on the Thames.

Reach the northern edges of Dorney Lake for snatched glimpses of the long and linear Olympic rowing venue as you ride beside the cedar grove and conifer collection in Eton College's impressive arboretum.

The riverside village of Bray, with its half-timbered cottages and cosy pubs, is a real mid-ride highlight, and within this humble and charming little Berkshire village are some serious gourmet destinations: the Michelin-starred restaurants of the Roux brothers and Heston Blumenthal, making for a great high-end lunch stop.

Ride through the thick woodland of Braywick Local Nature Reserve (LNR) and emerge on-road around the edges of Maidenhead (take extra care on the A4 here), before reaching the open water of Amerden ponds and finally joining the banks of the route's namesake, the Jubilee River. This stretch of the Jubilee is remote, wild and surrounded by the scrubland, grazing marsh and thick reedbeds of Dorney Wetlands. It's a perfect contrast to the lively Thames at Windsor, and is the best place for a tranquil picnic whilst watching for lapwings, bitterns and warblers.

In the final miles, follow the many arches of the vast railway viaduct back to Windsor on the traffic-free path. Better still, take the quiet road that leads into Eton to ride past the beautiful buildings of the renowned college and the antique shops on the High Street.

Both routes join up again at Eton Bridge, where you'll cross the Thames with views of Windsor Castle's iconic Round Tower ahead, before the short, on-road climb back to the castle gates.

Dorney landscape

RIDE 14

Train station: Windsor & Eton Riverside

Grade: Moderate

Terrain, gradients and access: Tarmac path, fine gravel track and a short grassy section around Dorney Lake. Some road crossings and on-road sections at Windsor, Bray, Maidenhead and Eton. The A4 around Maidenhead Bridge is the busiest on-road section, so opt to push along the pavement here if desired.

Loops, links and longer rides: NCN 4 passes through Windsor Great Park, a magnificent Royal Park with its own network of walking and cycling trails. NCN 4 Thames Path (**Ride 13**).

Stay: Manor Cottage B&B, Old Windsor (01753) 856075 manorcottagewindsor.co.uk

Eat and drink: Monty Café, Sebastian's Italian and The Alma pub at Windsor are all popular. Bray village is a foodie haven, home to the Roux Brothers' Waterside Inn and three of Heston Blumenthal's eateries: The Fat Duck, The Crown at Bray and The Hinds Head. Alternatively, try the award-winning sandwiches at The Pineapple in Dorney.

Cycle hire: Extreme Motion, Windsor (01753) 830220 extrememotion.com

Wider area cycle map: Thames Valley

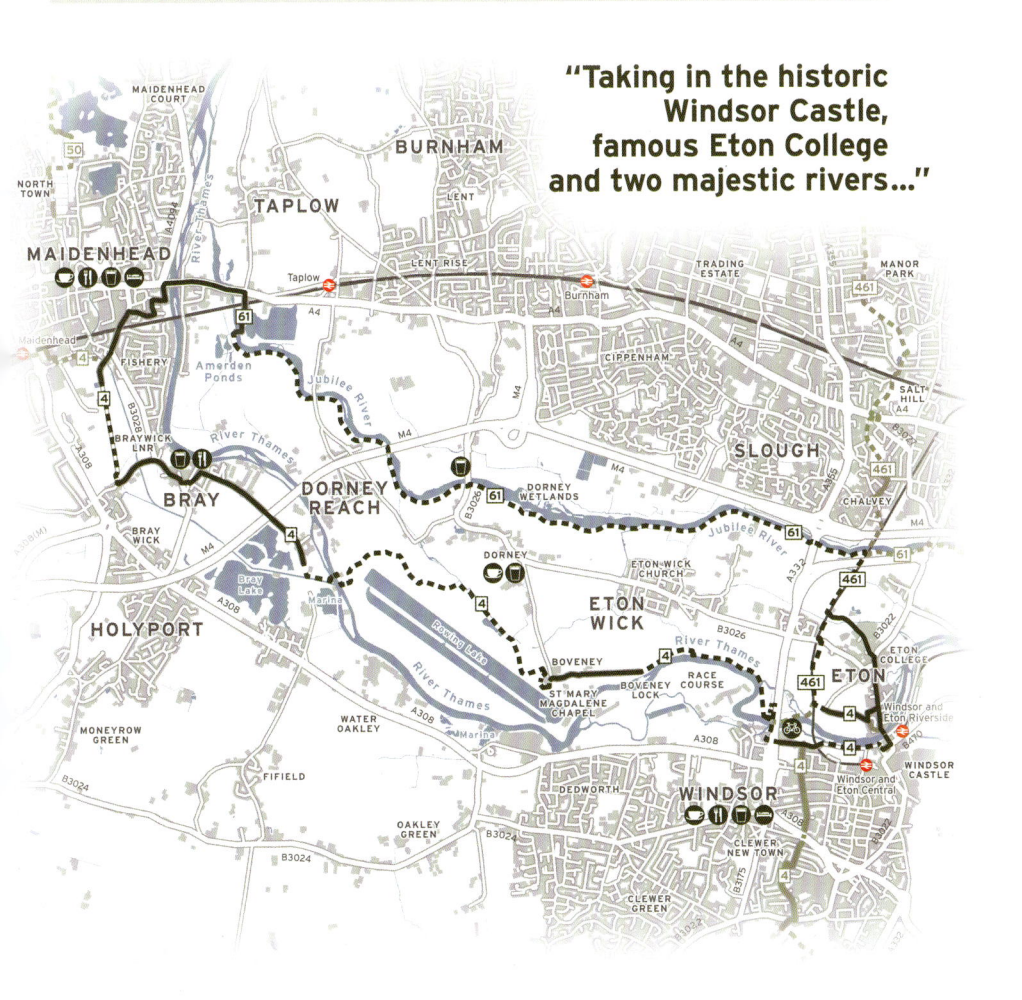

"Taking in the historic Windsor Castle, famous Eton College and two majestic rivers..."

RIDE 15
4 miles

Start: Buckingham Palace

TWO PALACES

Two Royal residences and three leafy Royal parks in just four gentle miles make this an unforgettable trip through the green heart of London, following part of the Jubilee Greenway.

It's a tick list of famous London sights all the way, starting at Buckingham Palace, the Queen's official London home. Take care here as it's a very busy spot that teems with tourists, especially mid-morning during the Changing of the Guard ceremony.

From the palace, ride along the southern edge of Green Park, the smallest of London's eight Royal parks, and beneath Wellington Arch at Hyde Park Corner. The arch is topped by the largest bronze sculpture in Europe, the angel of peace landing on the chariot of war.

Ride through Hyde Park along Rotten Row, a name derived from the French 'Route de Roi' meaning 'King's Road', passing the fountains and formal rose gardens at the bottom of the park, and the stripy deckchairs casually scattered on the banks of the Serpentine in summer.

You'll leave Hyde Park behind at the Diana Memorial Fountain and enter Kensington Gardens, following Mount Walk for lovely views down its boulevards of sentry-straight trees to the gilded Gothic Albert Memorial and the unmistakeable red dome of The Royal Albert Hall.

At the ride's midway point, the impressive facade of Kensington Palace appears, the birthplace and childhood home of Queen Victoria. Ride up to the middle of Broad Walk to get the best view of the palace and its grounds, and to reach Round Pond, or continue to the top for the Diana Memorial Playground.

There are some restrictions on cycling around Kensington Gardens, so from here you'll need to retrace the route back along Mount Walk, before riding up West Carriage Drive, crossing Serpentine Bridge and heading back into Hyde Park at the Serpentine North Gallery.

The return ride along the north bank of the Serpentine is particularly lovely, with great views over the water and boats. End at Hyde Park Corner, or ride up to the top of the park to reach the renowned Speakers' Corner.

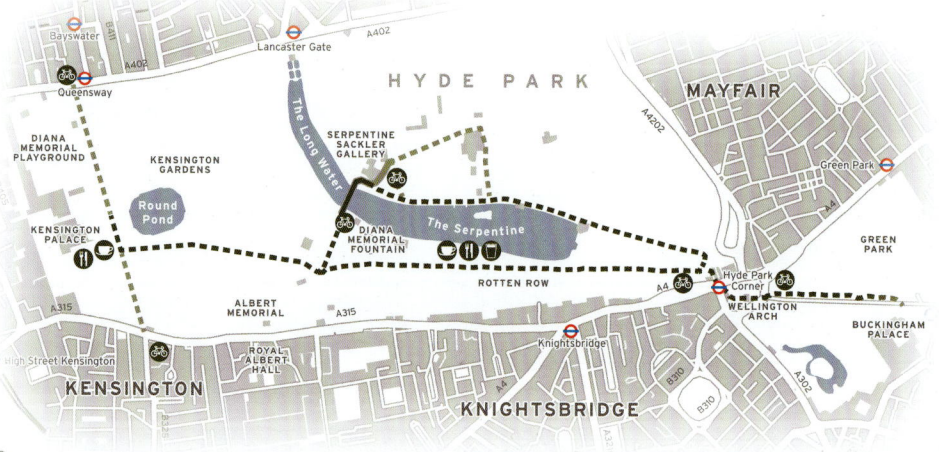

Finish: Hyde Park Corner

RIDE 15

Train station: London Paddington

Grade: Easy

Terrain, gradients and access: Flat tarmac path. Some road crossings.

Loops, links and longer rides: Tamsin Trail through Richmond Park (**Ride 12**). NCN 4 Thames Path (**Ride 13**). NCN 20 Wandle Trail.

Stay: YHA Earls's Court 0345 371 9114 **yha.org.uk**

Eat and drink: The Palace Café and The Orangery are both at Kensington Palace, whilst The Broad Walk Café is within Kensington Gardens. The Magazine Restaurant at the Serpentine North Gallery, The Lido Café Bar and The Serpentine Bar and Kitchen are all in Hyde Park. Coffee and snack kiosks along the route include Tri angle, Boathouse and Hyde Park Corner. Venture a little further to Covent Garden for the cycle-themed café Brompton Junction.

Cycle hire: Santander Cycle Hire docking stations are at Wellington Arch and Hyde Park Corner, as well as Palace Gate and Queen's Gate in Kensington Gardens and both sides of the Serpentine bridge. **santandercycles.co.uk**

"An unforgettable trip through the green heart of London..."

Buckingham Palace

LEE NAVIGATION

(SOUTH)

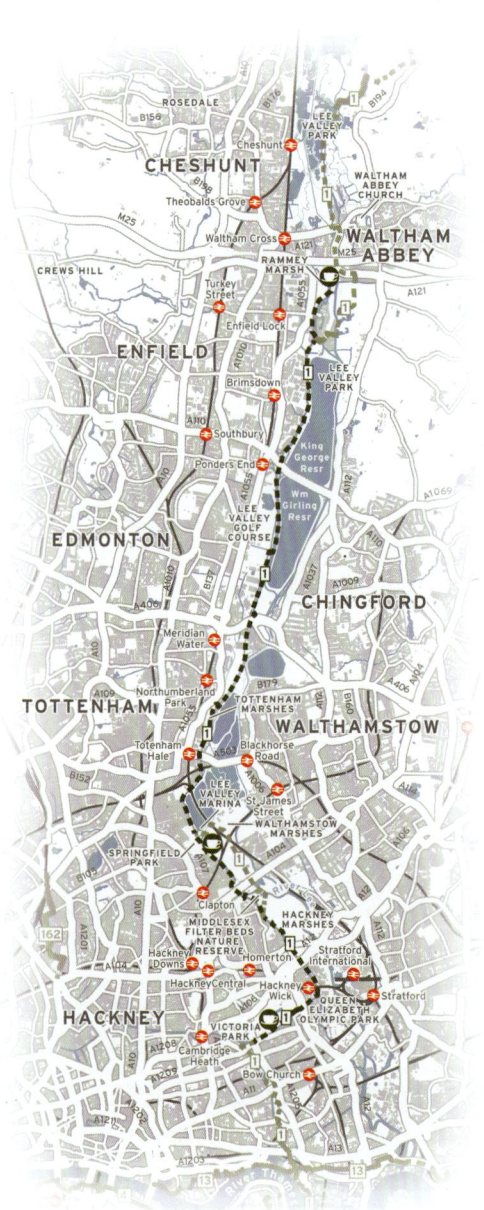

RIDE 16 — 12.5 miles
Start: West Boating Lake, Victoria Park

This ride along the River Lee Navigation starts in London's characterful East End and finishes among pretty Essex countryside at Waltham Abbey.

Start from the West Boating Lake at Victoria Park, riding along the edges of its vast grassy space before immediately joining the banks of the River Lee Navigation and sticking to them closely for the remainder of the ride. The most remarkable feature of the landscape here is Queen Elizabeth Olympic Park, a legacy of the London 2012 Games that has transformed Stratford.

The natural world holds hands with urban London throughout these opening miles, and you'll ride through some of the many riverside parks and nature reserves that make London one of the greenest cities in the world. Discover the neat, trimmed grass of more than 80 sports pitches on Hackney Marshes, and then move swiftly into the wild reedbeds, wet woodland and lagoons of Middlesex Filter Beds nature reserve. It's a particularly busy and popular towpath in these early stages, so you'll find yourself among many other cyclists, walkers and joggers on the route, as well as friends gathering outside the traditional London pubs that nudge at the water's edge, and families using the local parks. Springfield Park, just four miles in, makes a particularly pleasant detour as the views from its grassy banks overlook Walthamstow Marshes and the moored boats of Lee Valley Marina.

Reach Tottenham Marshes at around the halfway point, a vast wild wetland where nature starts to dominate the ride and the city begins to lose its hold. Look out for

Finish: The Narrowboat Café, Waltham Abbey

RIDE 16

Train stations: Cambridge Heath and Waltham Cross
Grade: Moderate
Terrain, gradients and access: Flat, tarmac path, fine gravel track and stony trail with raised cobbles on some sections of the towpath and some road crossings.
Loops, links and longer rides: NCN 21 Waterlink Way is a seven-mile, mostly traffic-free route from the Cutty Sark in Greenwich to Cator Park in the London Borough of Bromley. Or visit Epping Forest, near Waltham Abbey; cyclists are permitted to ride across most of the forest, and there are several way-marked trails within its 6,000 acres. NCN 1 Lee Navigation (North) (**Ride 02**).
Stay: YHA Lee Valley, 0345 3719057 yha.org.uk
Eat and drink: Crate craft brewery and pizzeria or The Hackney Pearl are all popular in Hackney Wick, or try the Pavilion Café at Victoria Park or Springfield Café in Springfield Park. The Narrowboat Café is at the route's end at Rammy Marsh, Waltham Abbey.
Cycle hire: Santander Cycle Hire santandercycles.co.uk

kingfishers and kestrels here, and large flocks of linnets feeding on the seed heads of the plants in winter.

The landscape grows increasingly rural in the second half of the ride, following the river's very straight course with extensive views over the fields. Ride past the neatly groomed greens of Lee Valley golf course to reach Enfield Lock. This is the best part of the river for fishing, so you're likely to see anglers sitting patiently along the banks here.

Cross the water to ride along the edges of Rammey Marsh, where the transformation from urban to rural starts to feel complete.

Keep a lookout in this beautiful area for water voles, pipistrelle bats and orchids. In the final mile, the peace of these natural surroundings is disturbed by the London Orbital Motorway passing over the towpath, but the traffic zipping overhead just makes the quiet stillness of the river all the more appealing.

Ride into the fringes of Essex and end at The Narrowboat Café on the waterside. The towpath can be ridden all the way to Hertford if you desire (a further 13 miles), or climb up to join the road here for the short ride to the attractive Waltham Abbey church, said to be the last resting place of King Harold II.

Cyclist in Lee Valley nature reserve

"Starts in London's characterful East End and finishes among pretty Essex countryside…"

RIDE 17
8.5 miles | 57 | **Start:** Thame Leisure Centre

PHOENIX TRAIL

Wide open views across the Chilterns Area of Outstanding Natural Beauty accompany this lovely route from Oxfordshire into Buckinghamshire.

Start at Thame Leisure Centre, where the sweeping scenery across the hillsides sets the tone for a lovely rural ride. In the opening mile it's worth following the signed, quarter of a-mile link path into the centre of Thame, where the thatched buildings on the High Street, the red brick Town Hall, and little Thame Museum are all beautiful.

The trail follows a former railway line and is arrow-straight for most of the way, largely passing through open farmland with panoramic Chilterns views. However, you'll occasionally duck into the cover of trees, or ride between fat green hedgerows dotted with pink hollyhocks in summer.

Towersey, around three miles in, is the only trailside village along the way, so The Three Horseshoes pub here has become a popular spot among Phoenix Trail walkers and cyclists.

There are some lovely artworks to watch out for on the route, too; 'Winged Seat' in the early miles is one of the most striking, and its gently raised position makes it one of the best spots to sit and look across the countryside.

Another favourite is the collection of copper creatures perilously balanced on top of telegraph poles at around the halfway point. Whilst looking up at these curious characters, there's a chance you'll see a kestrel hunting over the farmland, or even a red kite, a bird of prey that has thrived in this area and can easily be recognised by its distinctive forked tail. Climb up the short and stony trail to cross over the tracks of the Chinnor & Princes Risborough Railway, where there are marvellous views across the thick, dark forests on the edges of the Chiltern Hills.

Leave the path in the final miles and join a quiet country lane through the idyllic hamlet of Horsenden, passing its pretty little church and manor house, before taking the gentle, on-road descent into Princes Risborough. Take a walk around this market town and you'll see the Whiteleaf Cross carved into the steep chalk hillside above; it has dominated the landscape here for centuries.

Sculpture by Lucy Casson

Finish: Market Square, Princes Risborough

RIDE 17

Train stations: Haddenham & Thame Parkway and Princes Risborough

Grade: Easy

Terrain, gradients and access: Mostly flat tarmac path, fine gravel track and stony trail. Some small road crossings, and a short, on-road section at Princes Risborough.

Loops, links and longer rides: Princes Risborough is one of the gateway towns for The Chilterns Cycleway, a 170-mile, on-road route around the Chilterns Area of Outstanding Natural Beauty. From Thame, follow NCN 57 along an on-road route to Oxford, one of the UK's most cycle-friendly cities.

Stay: The Peacock Country Inn, Henton (01844) 353519 peacockcountryinn.co.uk

Eat and drink: In Thame there is lots of choice including Rumsey's Chocolaterie, The Thatch or The Six Bells. The Three Horseshoes is in Towersey, or in Princes Risborough try the George & Dragon pub or La Crepe Escape café.

Cycle hire: Chilterns Cycle Hire (01296) 696343 otec.bike

Wider area cycle map: Thames Valley

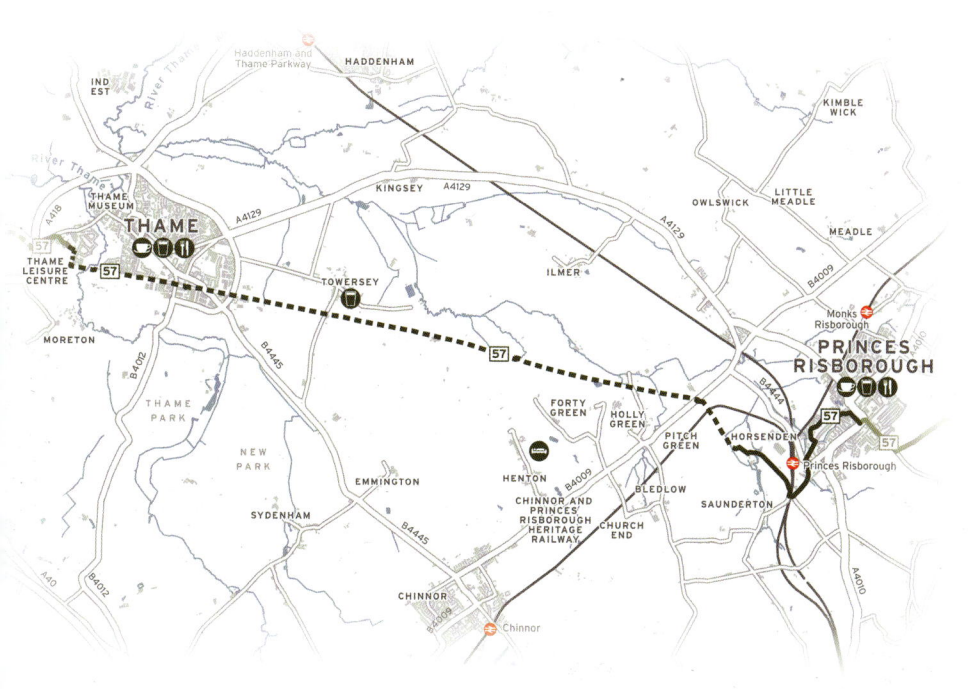

Red kite

97

WALES

If ever a country was made for exploring by bike, it was Wales. Top quality cycle routes criss-cross its dramatic and diverse landscape, from remote and romantic island rides on Anglesey at the very northern tip of the country, to stylish city cycling through Cardiff, the contemporary capital in the south.

In between, you'll experience the magnificent Snowdonia, Cambrian and Brecon Beacon mountain ranges, and the alpine-like slopes of the Afan and Sirhowy Valleys. If that conjures up expectations of long and gruelling out-of-the-saddle hill climbs then be reassured, there's nothing more demanding than a few steady inclines in this collection of rides.

Wales' colourful history and industrial past are revealed at every turn. You'll ride through the unique and striking landscape of the slate quarries in the north, former coal mining communities in the lush green South Wales Valleys, and beside peaceful waterways that were once the energetic lifeblood of the Industrial Revolution. Indeed, the most memorable canal ride in the UK is right here in Wales; a dizzying glide across the incredible Pontcysyllte Aqueduct, the highest navigable aqueduct in the world.

The Peregrine Path through the ancient woodland in the Forest of Dean offers exceptional opportunities for wildlife watching, as do the rides along the nature-rich Mawddach Estuary and vast golden beaches of the Gower. But to spot the most iconic species in Wales, the red kite, head for the Elan Valley Trail or Ystwyth Trail, where a glimpse of these graceful birds of prey is almost guaranteed.

The rides featured here are all under 30 miles but will undoubtedly give you an appetite for more, in which case you might tackle one of Wales' popular multi-day rides like the Celtic Trail or Lôn Las Cymru, available to buy at **shop.sustrans.org.uk**. Whichever routes you choose, you can always be sure of spectacular scenery and a sincere welcome in cycle-friendly, warm-hearted Wales.

Looking down on Talybont Reservoir

Routes overview

- **01** The Brunel Trail (9.5 miles)
- **02** Millennium Coastal Path (6.5 miles)
- **03** Swiss Valley Trail (12 miles)
- **04** Clyne Valley Country Park (5 miles)
- **05** Swansea Bike Path (6 miles)
- **06** Afan Valley Trail (6 miles)
- **07** Three Parks Trail (12 miles)
- **08** Cardiff Bay Trail (6 miles)
- **09** Taff Trail (South) (28.5 miles)
- **10** Taff Trail (North) (25 miles)
- **11** Abergavenny to Pontypool (20.5 miles)
- **12** Monmouthshire & Brecon Canal (Newport to Pontypool) (10 miles)
- **13** Monmouthshire & Brecon Canal (Pontypool to Abergavenny) (13 miles)
- **14** Peregrine Path (5.5 miles)
- **15** Elan Valley Trail (8.5 miles)
- **16** Ystwyth Trail (8.5 or 17.5 miles)
- **17** Montgomery Canal (14 miles)
- **18** Dolgellau to Tywyn (21 miles)
- **19** Mawddach Trail (9.5 miles)
- **20** Llangollen Canal (9.5 miles)
- **21** Lôn Eifion (12 miles)
- **22** Lôn Las Menai (4 miles)
- **23** Lôn Las Ogwen (11 miles)
- **24** Lôn Las Cefni (8 miles)
- **25** North Wales Coast Cycle Route (16 miles)

— Featured ride
— National Cycle Network (traffic-free and on-road)

RIDE 01
9.5 miles

Start: Haverfordwest train station

THE BRUNEL TRAIL

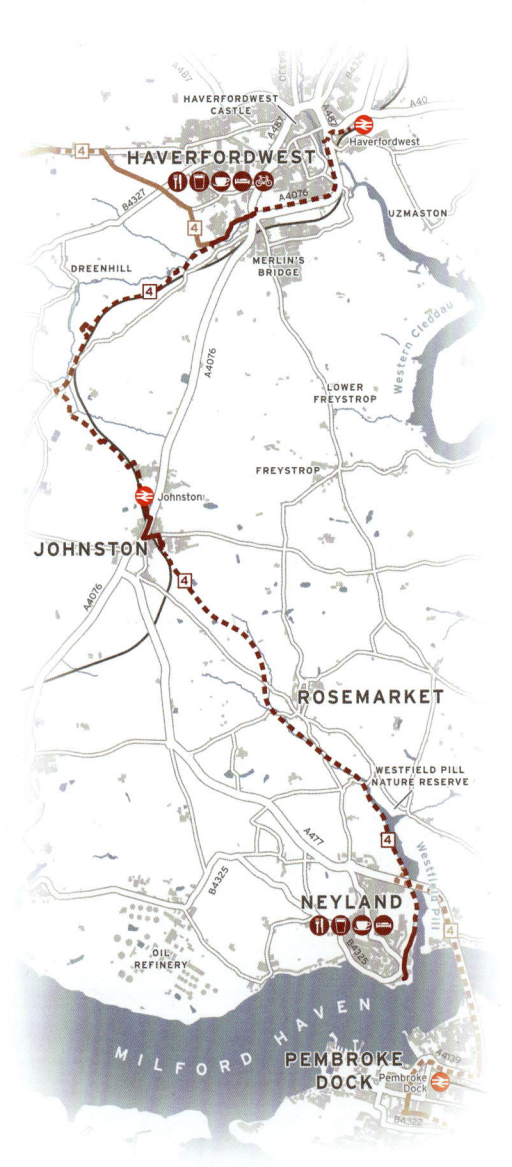

This tumbling ride passes through peaceful Pembrokeshire countryside to the pretty quayside at Neyland. It is named after Victorian engineer Isambard Kingdom Brunel and partly follows the route of his Great Western Railway.

From the train station, take a short detour into the centre of Pembrokeshire's county town to explore Haverfordwest Castle and Town Museum before following the local link along Freemens Way to reach Merlin's Bridge. Here you'll enter Pembrokeshire's rich green landscape, crossing the little stone bridge over Merlin's Brook and climbing gently alongside lush meadows, trickling streams and grazing ponies. The views become more extensive as you climb and descend along the winding route, before ducking into Bolton Hill Wood to ride between the fat, twisted tree trunks.

At Johnston, around the midway point, it becomes a gentle descent along former railway path, making for easy pedalling all the way to the beautifully undisturbed woodland and wetland of Westfield Pill, one of the highlights of the ride. This Wildlife Trust nature reserve is an important spot for little grebes and runs along a sheltered inlet from the main Daugleddau Estuary. Water views open up throughout the reserve and benches alongside the inlet are perfect for picnicking or watching for the electric blue flash of a kingfisher flitting over the water's surface.

Leave Westfield Pill to see the tall masts of the moored yachts at Neyland Marina come into view and ride along the waterside. End at Brunel Quay next to a bronze statue of the great engineer himself, resplendent in his trademark stovepipe hat.

RIDE 01

Finish: Brunel Quay, Neyland

Train stations: Haverfordwest, Johnston and Pembroke Dock

Grade: Moderate

Terrain, gradients and access: Undulating tarmac path with several gates, road crossings and quiet on-road sections around Merlin's Bridge and Brunel Quay.

Loops, links and longer rides: The Brunel Trail is part of NCN 4 Celtic Trail, a long-distance route across Wales from Fishguard to Chepstow. At Westfield Pill follow NCN 4 along traffic-free path over Cleddau Bridge to Pembroke Castle, or take the traffic-free link to Milford Haven.

Stay: St Davids Guest House, Haverfordwest (01437) 766778 stdavidsguesthouse.com

Eat and drink: In Haverfordwest try The George's, a mix of pub, café, restaurant and shop. The Bar at Neyland Yacht Haven has a nice outdoor terrace overlooking the water.

Cycle hire: Mike's Bikes, Haverfordwest (01437) 760068 mikes-bikes.co.uk

Wider area cycle map: South West Wales

"Take a short detour into the centre of Pembrokeshire's county town to explore Haverfordwest Castle…"

Haverfordwest Castle

RIDE 02
6.5 miles

Start: Pembrey Country Park

MILLENNIUM COASTAL PATH

Miles of golden shoreline and the breezy open landscape of the magnificent Millennium Coastal Park, a scenic linear park that attracts more than a million visitors each year, make for one of the finest bike routes imaginable. Pembrey Country Park at the start is worth exploring as it has sprawling sands edged by dunes at Cefn Sidan, pine forests, nature trails, horse riding, a dry ski slope and the longest toboggan run in Wales.

From the country park you'll join the Wales Coast Path with the vast expanses of sea, sky and sand inducing a joyous sense of freedom. In the opening miles skirt around the pretty little harbour at Burry Port with its red-capped lighthouse, backdrop of vivid green hills and the gorgeous Gower Peninsula visible over the Loughor Estuary. The sandy beach at Burry Port is very popular too.

The path leaves the waterside only momentarily to weave between placid lagoons and flower-rich grasslands being cultivated for wildlife, before re-joining the magnificent seafront for the remaining miles. End at St Elli's Bay café overlooking Llanelli Beach. There's cycle parking for locking up and exploring the adjacent North Dock Dunes Local Nature Reserve (LNR).

Millennium Coastal Path

Finish: St Elli's Bay Café, Llanelli

RIDE 02

Train stations: Pembrey & Burry Port and Llanelli

Grade: Easy

Terrain, gradients and access: Flat, wide tarmac path and fine gravel track.

Loops, links and longer rides: An alternative end point is the WWT National Wetland Centre Wales; continue along NCN 4 from the Discovery Centre in Llanelli for a further four miles on traffic-free path to reach the Wetland Centre's entrance. Millennium Coastal Path is part of NCN 4 Celtic Trail, a long-distance route across Wales from Fishguard to Chepstow. NCN 47 Swiss Valley Trail (**Ride 03**).

Stay: Pembrey Country Park Caravan Club site (01554) 834369 **caravanclub.co.uk**

Eat and drink: Pembrey Country Park has an ice cream parlour, café, bar and restaurant. Harbour Light Tearoom mid-route at Burry Port Harbour is popular, or visit St Elli's café in the former Discovery Centre with wonderful views of Llanelli Beach, Loughor Estuary and the Gower Peninsula.

Cycle hire: Ski Pembrey at Pembrey Country Park (01554) 834443 or Brompton Dock at Burry Port Interchange **bromptonbikehire.com**

Wider area cycle map: South West Wales

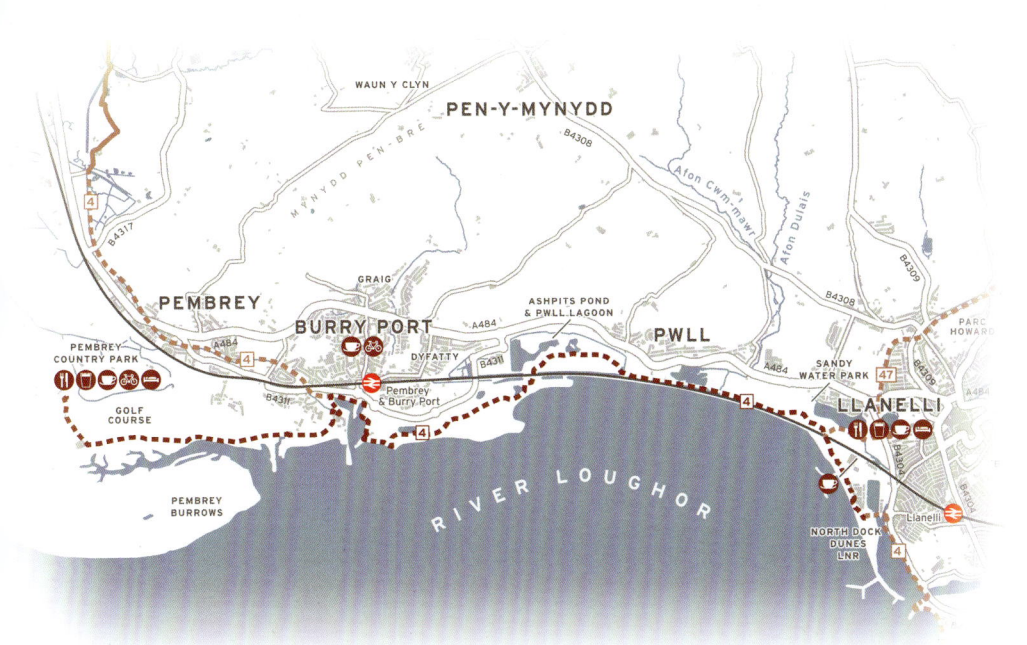

Millennium Coastal Path

103

RIDE 03 — 12 miles
Start: Sandy Water Park, Llanelli

SWISS VALLEY TRAIL

Swiss Valley Trail

At one time this was a horse-drawn railway route, now it's a pretty walking and cycling trail. It winds gently upwards from the Millennium Coastal Park through Carmarthenshire's Swiss Valley and among glorious Welsh woodland into the hills above Llanelli.

Start at Sandy Water Park, a lake created on the site of a former steelworks, before crossing Pont d'Agen walking and cycling bridge to Llanelli's Old Castle Pond, where Carnwyllion Castle once stood.

Rows of Welsh terraces in the opening mile and views up to the splendid mansion and grounds of Parc Howard on the right are quickly left behind as you climb through rural landscape into deeper woodland, with glimpses of the placid waters of the Lliedi reservoirs through the trees. A clearing in the woods at Horeb and a cluster of picnic benches make a good resting place in the ride's first half before the landscape opens up and views of the rolling Carmarthenshire hills make the steady uphill riding worthwhile.

Close to the village of Tumble, ride along the edge of the steep hillside and enjoy sweeping views across the Gwendraeth Valley. It's the best scenery of the entire ride and there are benches thoughtfully placed along the route for absorbing it at leisure. Ride close to the edges of Mynydd Mawr Woodland Park at Tumble before entering the little village of Cross Hands and ending beside the beautiful Art Deco public hall and cinema.

Finish: Cross Hands

RIDE 03

"Ride along the edge of the steep hillside and enjoy sweeping views across the Gwendraeth Valley."

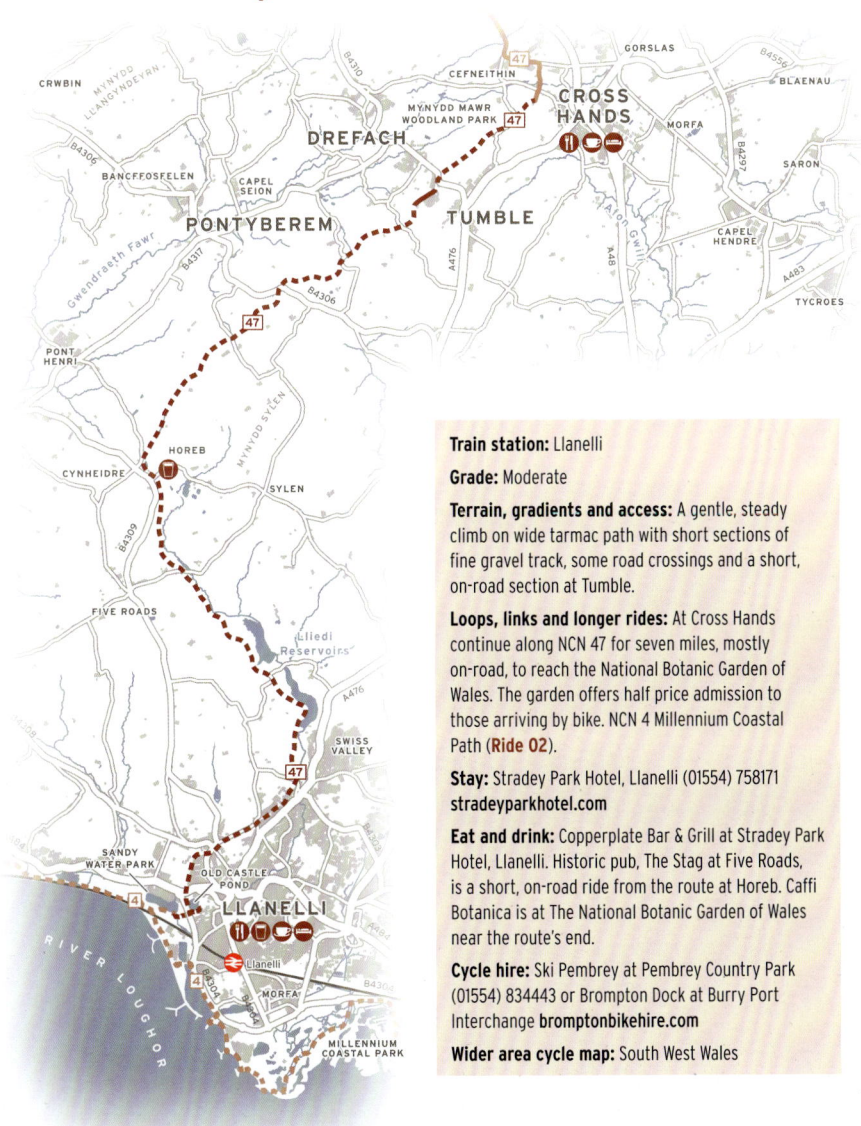

Train station: Llanelli

Grade: Moderate

Terrain, gradients and access: A gentle, steady climb on wide tarmac path with short sections of fine gravel track, some road crossings and a short, on-road section at Tumble.

Loops, links and longer rides: At Cross Hands continue along NCN 47 for seven miles, mostly on-road, to reach the National Botanic Garden of Wales. The garden offers half price admission to those arriving by bike. NCN 4 Millennium Coastal Path (Ride 02).

Stay: Stradey Park Hotel, Llanelli (01554) 758171 stradeyparkhotel.com

Eat and drink: Copperplate Bar & Grill at Stradey Park Hotel, Llanelli. Historic pub, The Stag at Five Roads, is a short, on-road ride from the route at Horeb. Caffi Botanica is at The National Botanic Garden of Wales near the route's end.

Cycle hire: Ski Pembrey at Pembrey Country Park (01554) 834443 or Brompton Dock at Burry Port Interchange bromptonbikehire.com

Wider area cycle map: South West Wales

105

RIDE 04
5 miles

Start: Gowerton train station

CLYNE VALLEY COUNTRY PARK

This short ride passes through Swansea's only country park, swooping between the wooded hillsides of the Clyne Valley along a section of the popular long-distance Celtic Trail cycle route.

Start at Gowerton train station and quickly join the wooded trail, crossing the Clyne River several times before settling alongside it and following its course between the oak, birch and beech trees of Clyne Wood.

At the halfway point the outdoor benches of The Railway Inn at Upper Killay are a good resting point and a chance for you to sample ale brewed locally on Gower. Alternatively, picnic in the thick woodland of the country park near the route's end.

At the park's entrance on Mumbles Road the adjacent Clyne Gardens are worth exploring and are internationally famed for the collection of rhododendrons, at their best in May when the vivid pink flowers are in full bloom. Or cross the road to Swansea Bay at Black Pill. This area comes alive with migratory birds in winter and is extremely popular with families using the lido, play area and picnic spot in summer.

Clyne Gardens

"The adjacent Clyne Gardens are worth exploring and are internationally famed…"

106

Finish: Black Pill, Swansea Bay   RIDE 04

Train stations: Gowerton or Swansea
Grade: Easy
Terrain, gradients and access: A gentle descent along tarmac path with a short, on-road section at Gowerton and a road crossing at Black Pill.
Loops, links and longer rides: This ride is part of NCN 4 Celtic Trail, a long-distance route across Wales from Fishguard to Chepstow. At Black Pill join Swansea Bike Path (**Ride 05**).

Stay: Somerfield Lodge, Mumbles (01792) 401989 somerfieldlodge.co.uk
Eat and drink: The Railway Inn, Upper Killay, at the route's halfway point, The Junction Café at the route's end near Black Pill or the many cafés of nearby Mumbles.
Cycle hire: Santander Cycles santandercycles.co.uk
Wider area cycle map: South West Wales

107

RIDE 05
6 miles

Start: National Waterfront Museum, Swansea

SWANSEA BIKE PATH

Swansea Bay

This gloriously scenic ride hugs the sweeping golden arc of Swansea Bay where you'll be blissfully assisted by the wind in parts and battling against a sea breeze in others.

Start at the National Waterfront Museum in Swansea's Maritime Quarter and quickly reach the seafront to roll alongside the vast sandy beach where the sea stretches away to the left and the tall square clock tower of Swansea Guildhall dominates the skyline to the right. The beautiful Singleton Park and Botanical Gardens (at their best in August) are right beside the route and worth a visit, before Black Pill appears up ahead, a vital overwintering spot for wading birds. This is around the halfway point and has a lido, play area and picnic benches that make a great family-friendly rest stop. Take in the sea views here or venture over the road to explore the wooded hillsides of Clyne Valley Country Park.

Pretty coloured houses at Mumbles come into view on the second part of the ride and it's only a short detour inland if you want to explore the village and the hill-top Oystermouth Castle. Scoop around the outdoor terrace of popular waterfront ice cream parlour Verdi's before ending at the Victorian Mumbles Pier. Mumbles marks the start of the Gower Peninsula's stunning coastline and the pier is the perfect spot for locking up and taking a stroll to neighbouring Bracelet Bay to delve among the rock pools.

Finish: Mumbles Pier

RIDE 05

Train station: Swansea

Grade: Easy

Terrain, gradients and access: Flat tarmac path.

Loops, links and longer rides: NCN 43 Swansea Valley Trail leads north on a mostly traffic-free path from Swansea waterfront to Ystradgynlais, following the River Tawe in parts. NCN 4 Clyne Valley Country Park (Ride 04).

Stay: Chapel House, Mumbles (01792) 362129 thechapel.house

Eat and drink: Cafés, bars and restaurants abound in Swansea's Maritime Quarter at the route's start and Mumbles near the end. It's worth making a small detour to the Joe's Parlours on either Mumbles Road or St Helens Road for some of the best ice cream in Wales. Verdi's ice cream is wonderful, too, and is right on the route.

Cycle hire: Santander Cycles santandercycles.co.uk

Wider area cycle map: South West Wales

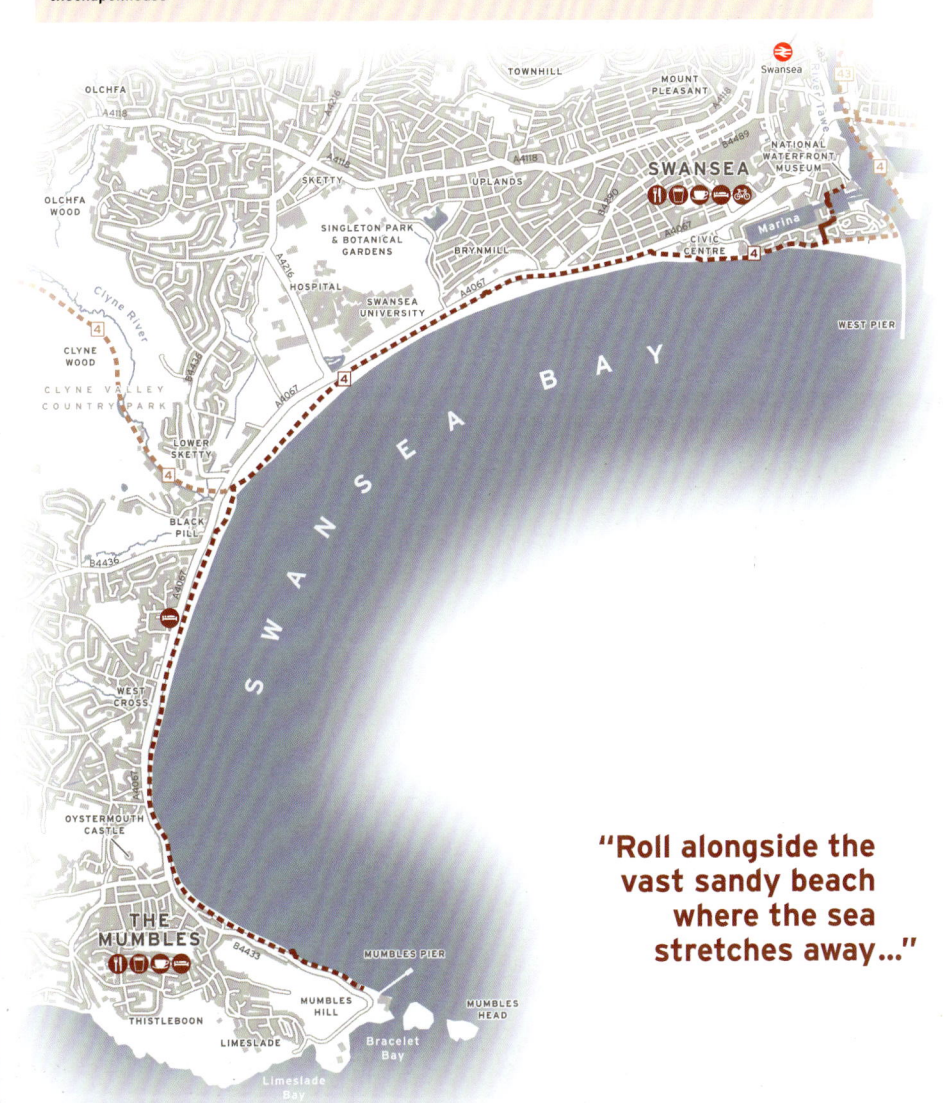

"Roll alongside the vast sandy beach where the sea stretches away..."

109

RIDE 06 — 6 miles — 887 — Start: Port Talbot Parkway train station

AFAN VALLEY TRAIL

This enchanting route climbs mountain slopes and through Alpine-like forests known locally as 'Little Switzerland' to Afan Forest Park at the top of the former coal mining Afan Valley.

Start from Port Talbot Parkway train station, quickly leaving the town behind to follow the River Afan between rounded green hillsides thick with woodland. The 'portrait bench' at around the halfway point is a wonderful place to rest and take in the scenery in the company of three of the area's most significant sons: actor Richard Burton, comedian and actor Rob Brydon and local forest ranger Dick Wagstaff, all depicted here in steel.

Roll across the fine railway viaduct at Pontrhydyfen and enjoy panoramic views across the valley before entering Afan Forest Park at the Rhyslyn car park.

This is a popular forest for mountain biking, so sightings of adventure-seekers tackling the rugged trails are guaranteed. However, the Afan Valley Trail sticks to smooth and gently climbing path (marked as a green 'rookie' trail), only turning to loose, stony track at the very end where you'll zig-zag steeply upwards to the visitor centre, perched at the top like a welcoming Swiss mountain lodge. Alternatively, the old Cynonville Station is nearby and has a cluster of picnic benches and a BBQ shelter.

Afan Valley

Finish: Afan Forest Park Visitor Centre

RIDE 06

Train station: Port Talbot Parkway

Grade: Moderate

Terrain, gradients and access: A steady climb on tarmac path and stony trail. Some gates, road crossings and short, quiet, on-road sections at the start and at Pontrhydyfen, where there are also some short, steep climbs.

Loops, links and longer rides: NCN 887 continues along traffic-free path up the Afan Valley to Cymer, where it connects with the scenic NCN 885 Llynfi Valley Trail to Maesteg. The Afan Forest is a world-class centre for mountain biking and the Glyncorrwg Mountain Bike Centre is accessible via a link route from NCN 887 at Cymer.

Stay: Afan Lodge, Duffryn Rhondda (01639) 852500 afanlodge.wales

Eat and drink: Cedars Tearoom at Afan Forest Park Visitor Centre and the Corrwg Cwtch Café at Afan Lodge in Duffryn Rhondda both offer hearty food and great views.

Cycle hire: Afan Valley Bike Shed (01639) 851406 afanvalleybikeshed.co.uk

Wider area cycle map: South East Wales

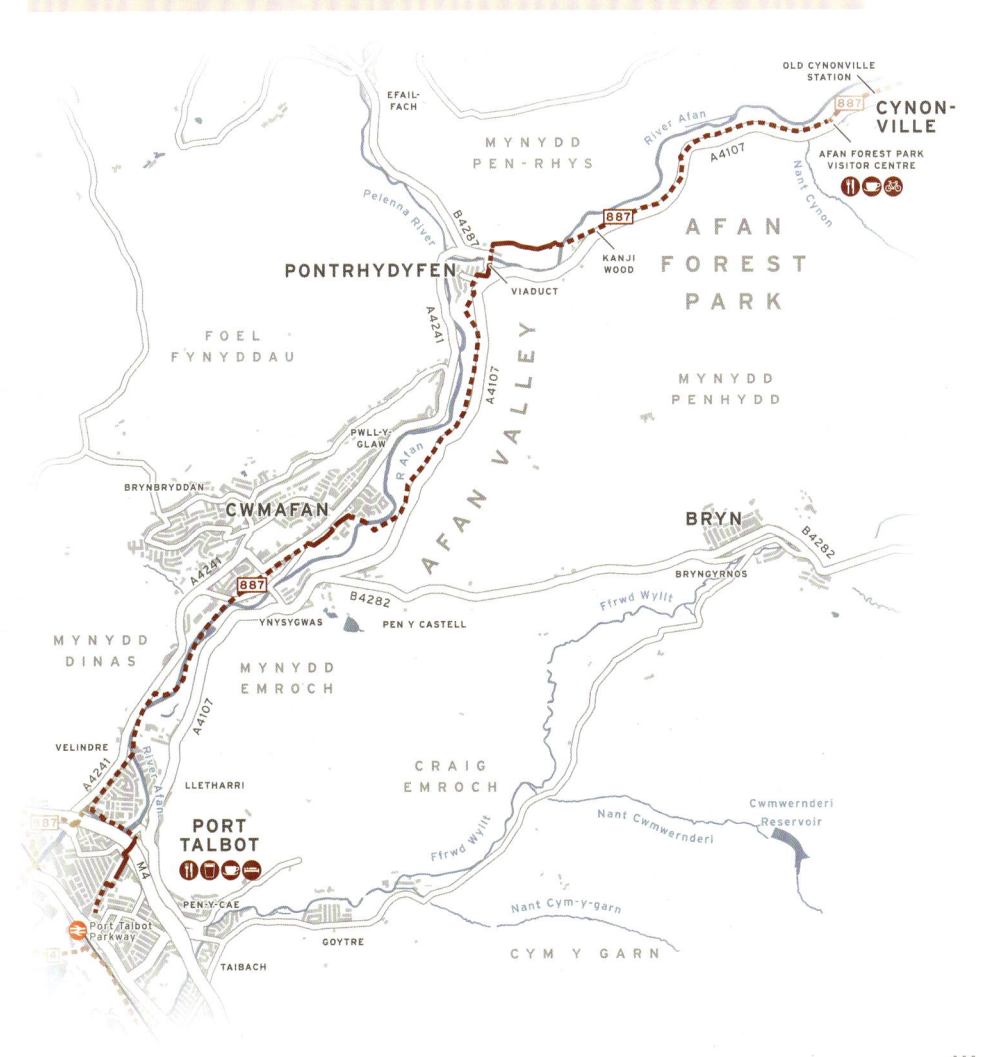

THREE PARKS TRAIL

Start: Summit Centre, Taff Bargoed
RIDE 07 — 12 miles

This route links up three beautiful parks across three lush South Wales Valleys, with traces of the region's once dynamic mining industry still evident along the way.

Start beneath vast, rounded hillsides among the reedbeds and lakes of Parc Taf Bargoed and follow the fast-flowing river that once ran black with coal but is now teeming with nature.

On leaving the park you'll cross into the Rhymney Valley and will be close to the beautiful Tudor manor house of Llancaiach Fawr at Nelson before entering Parc Penallta, a wildlife haven of marshes, lagoons and reedbeds carved from a former coal tip. An uphill climb through the park along stony trail is only a slight detour from here, and leads to 'Sultan' the pit pony, a massive equine earth sculpture galloping across the ground.

The 16-arch Hengoed Viaduct, just before the midway point, is the real highlight of the ride and the raised viewing points along its top give wonderful views to either side over the tumbling tree-covered hills of the Rhymney Valley. Stop at the Maesycwmmer end of the viaduct to look at 'The Wheel of Drams' sculpture, a modest tribute to the area's mining past.

From here, enter the steep and Alpine-like Sirhowy Valley and gently descend under a thick canopy of trees with snatched views across the sheer valley sides. The Sirhowy River gushes vigorously beneath whilst the ancient oak and beech woodland of Graig Goch climbs sharply up the hillside to the right.

In the final miles there's a lovely picnic spot at Nine Mile Point beside Flatwoods Meadows nature reserve, before dropping steeply down to join the riverside. Leave the trail for a very short, on-road ride to Crosskeys train station or turn right into Parc Waunfawr to add a bonus fourth park to the end of the ride.

'The Wheel of Drams' sculpture

Finish: Crosskeys train station   RIDE **07**

Train stations: Quakers Yard, Hengoed and Crosskeys
Grade: Moderate
Terrain, gradients and access: Tarmac path and stony trail, gently descending all the way with one short, steep descent at Full Moon. Some road crossings throughout and a short, on-road section at Crosskeys.
Loops, links and longer rides: The route is part of the long-distance Celtic Trail that runs across Wales from Fishguard to Chepstow. NCN 8 Taff Trail (**Ride 09**).

Stay: Cwmcarn Forest Caravan, Camping and Glamping site, Crosskeys (01495) 272001 **cwmcarnforest.co.uk**
Eat and drink: Refreshments are available at Summit Centre at the route's start, or along the way, try Blas restaurant at Bryn Meadows in Maesycwmmer, The Halfway House at Wyllie and Crosskeys Fish Bar.
Cycle hire: BikePark Wales, Merthyr Tydfil 07730 382501 **bikeparkwales.com**
Wider area cycle map: South East Wales

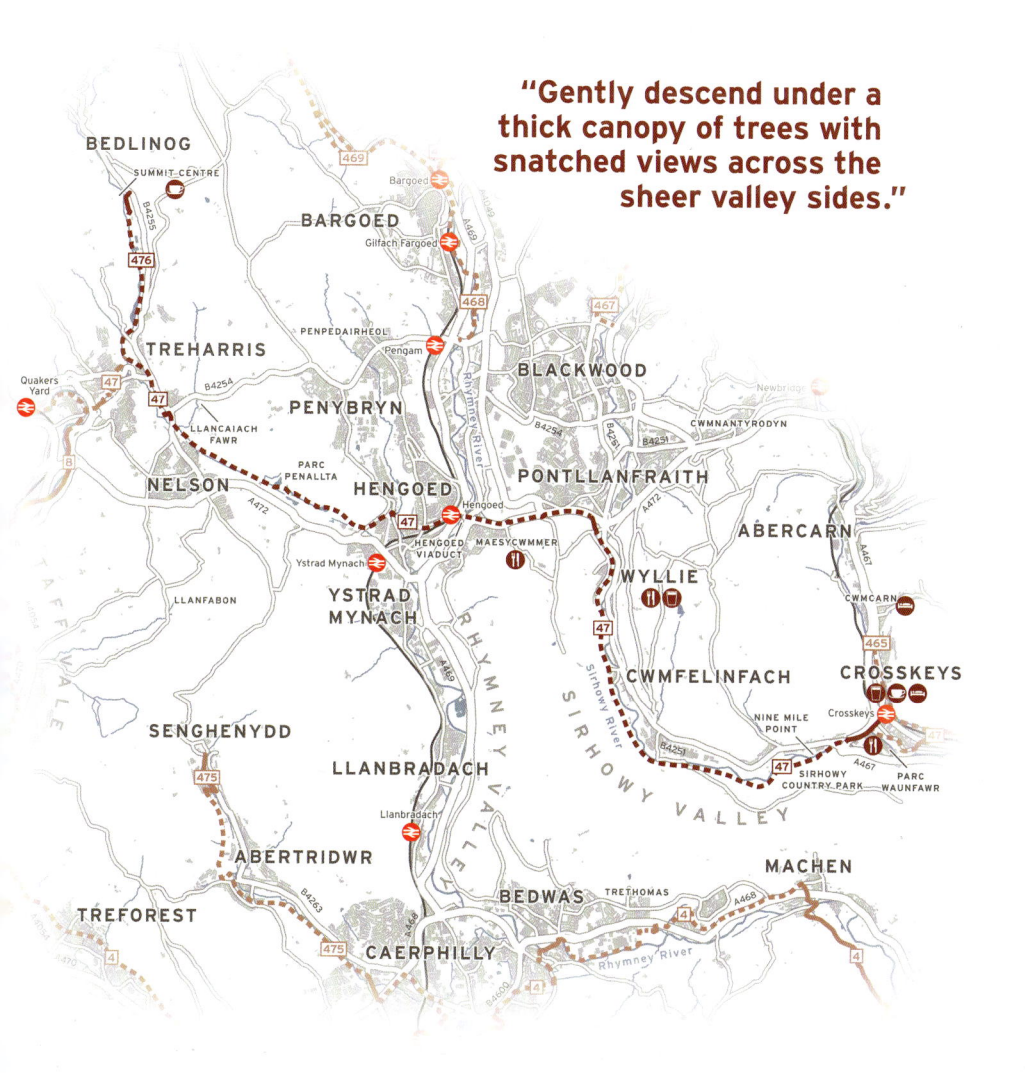

> "Gently descend under a thick canopy of trees with snatched views across the sheer valley sides."

113

RIDE 08
6 miles

Start and finish: Roald Dahl Plass, Cardiff Bay

CARDIFF BAY TRAIL

This circular ride takes in Cardiff Bay's masterful fusion of contemporary and classic features, as well as the desirable seaside town of Penarth.

Start at Roald Dahl Plass, named after the Cardiff-born author, and immediately ride past the historic red Pierhead building and the sleek modern Senedd building. Both belong to the National Assembly for Wales but are wildly different in design, which sets the tone for an exceptionally eclectic ride. The pretty white Norwegian church follows and is beside the Antarctic 100 Memorial, overlooking the very point where Captain Scott's expedition ship SS Terra Nova left Cardiff in 1910.

From here, it's a wonderfully windswept, effortless glide over Cardiff Bay Barrage, flanked by giant boulders and with views across the Bristol Channel to Flat Holm and Steep Holm islands and the Somerset coast. Across the barrage, take a short detour to explore Penarth town and pier, or simply continue along the route to pass the luxurious yachts of Penarth Quays Marina and cross Pont y Werin (People's Bridge), looking out for the famous sportspeople depicted in steel at either end.

The thundering rapids of Cardiff International White Water make for exciting spectating before entering the more restful green spaces of Hamadryad Park and Cardiff Bay Wetlands with its freshwater marshland and vast reed-fringed lake. This is the most peaceful spot for enjoying the views over to Penarth and there are warblers and water rails hidden among the reeds. In winter, you may even see the swirling dark cloud of a starling murmuration as dusk falls.

From the deep peace of this nature haven head into Mermaid Quay, a popular and lively spot full of cafés, bars, shops and restaurants, before ending back at Roald Dahl Plass.

Schedule extra time on this ride to visit the many family-friendly attractions along the route including the BBC's Doctor Who Experience, Techniquest Science Centre and the magnificent armadillo-like Wales Millennium Centre where there are often free daytime performances in the foyer.

Train stations: Cardiff Bay and Penarth

Grade: Easy

Terrain, gradients and access: Flat paved path with small on-road sections mid-route, and some road crossings and gates.

Loops, links and longer rides: Cardiff Bay Trail intersects with Ely Trail, a mostly traffic-free walking and cycling route along the River Ely from Cardiff Bay to St Fagans National History Museum. NCN 8 Taff Trail (South) (**Ride 09**).

Stay: Holm House Hotel, Penarth (02920) 706029 holmhousehotel.com

Eat and drink: Mermaid Quay in Cardiff Bay is bursting with cafés and restaurants; favourites are Cadwaladers Ice Cream, 'Fabulous' welsh cakes, ffresh Bar and Restaurant in Wales Millennium Centre, the Galley at Penarth Marina and the RSPB Hafren Café by the Barrage. In Penarth centre visit The Busy Teapot Café.

Cycle hire: Pedal Power, Cardiff Bay (029) 2039 0713/07775 616411 cardiffpedalpower.org

Wider area cycle map: South East Wales

RIDE 08

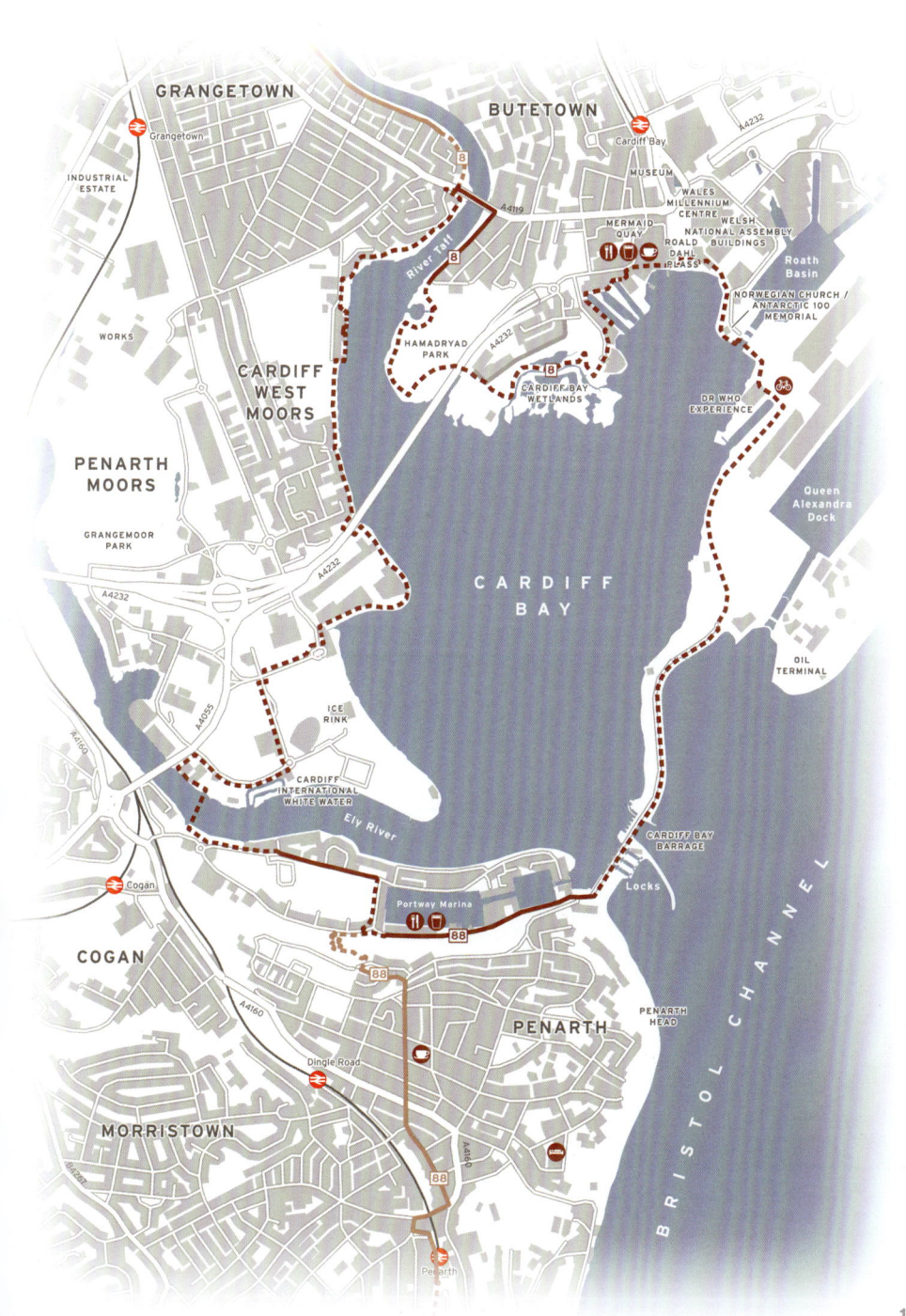

Map Labels

GRANGETOWN
- Grangetown (station)
- INDUSTRIAL ESTATE
- WORKS

BUTETOWN
- Cardiff Bay (station)
- MUSEUM
- WALES MILLENNIUM CENTRE
- MERMAID QUAY
- WELSH NATIONAL ASSEMBLY BUILDINGS
- ROALD DAHL PLASS
- Roath Basin
- NORWEGIAN CHURCH / ANTARCTIC 100 MEMORIAL
- A4232
- A4119

CARDIFF WEST MOORS
- River Taff
- HAMADRYAD PARK
- CARDIFF BAY WETLANDS
- DR WHO EXPERIENCE

PENARTH MOORS
- GRANGEMOOR PARK
- A4232

CARDIFF BAY
- Queen Alexandra Dock
- OIL TERMINAL
- ICE RINK
- CARDIFF INTERNATIONAL WHITE WATER
- Ely River
- CARDIFF BAY BARRAGE
- Locks

COGAN
- Cogan (station)
- A4160

PENARTH
- Portway Marina
- PENARTH HEAD
- Dingle Road (station)
- A4160

MORRISTOWN
- Penarth (station)

BRISTOL CHANNEL

115

TAFF TRAIL

(SOUTH)

This descent through the Taff Valley sees the landscape evolve from rugged, rounded hillsides around former mining villages in the Heads of the Valleys to the sleek buildings of Wales' capital city Cardiff and its vibrant Bay.

Start from Merthyr Tydfil train station, leaving the vast Brecon Beacons behind. The scenery remains hilly and untamed, however, as the tufty moorland ridge of Merthyr Common tumbles away in the east while Gethin Woods spread across the hillside to the west. The densely packed trees here conceal the feverish activity of mountain bikers at the popular BikePark Wales within the forest.

Some of the best views of the ride appear between the steep slopes of the valley near Aberfan, and the wide open scenery here is a perfect contrast to the shady woodland that follows through thick oak, birch and ash forest at Pontygwaith Nature Reserve. Wild strawberries and harebells carpet the forest floor here in summer as you join the Trevithick Tramroad, famous for carrying the first steam engine in history.

At Pontypridd, the lovely open green space of Ynysangharad War Memorial Park nestled in a bend of the River Taff is a highlight, with pretty gardens, bandstand, toilets and a refreshment kiosk that make it a great rest stop around the midway point.

It's worth taking a couple of minor detours in the ride's second half to visit two impressive Welsh castles; Caerphilly Castle, the largest in Wales, is just a two-mile, traffic-free ride along part of the Celtic Trail, whilst a short link from Tongwynlais leads to the fairytale towers of Castle Coch or 'Red Castle' hidden in the wooded hillside.

Back on the Taff Trail the gentle giant of Garth Mountain becomes visible against the sky at Taffs Well before you descend into the flatter suburbs of the city. The path clings to the shores of the River Taff from now on with great views over the fast-flowing water and weirs.

Cardiff's parks are easily some of the finest in any UK city and Bute Park, in the ride's final miles, is a particular gem. The trees of the arboretum are heavy with cherry blossom in spring and ablaze with red and orange leaves in autumn, creating a beautiful backdrop for Cardiff Castle which sits on the edge of the park.

Cardiff's giant Principality Stadium and the former Brains Brewery buildings dominate the cityscape on the way into the buzzy and popular Bay. End at one of the open air cafés on Cardiff Bay waterfront for views over the seaside town of Penarth and the North Somerset coast.

Cardiff Bay

Finish: Millennium Centre, Cardiff Bay

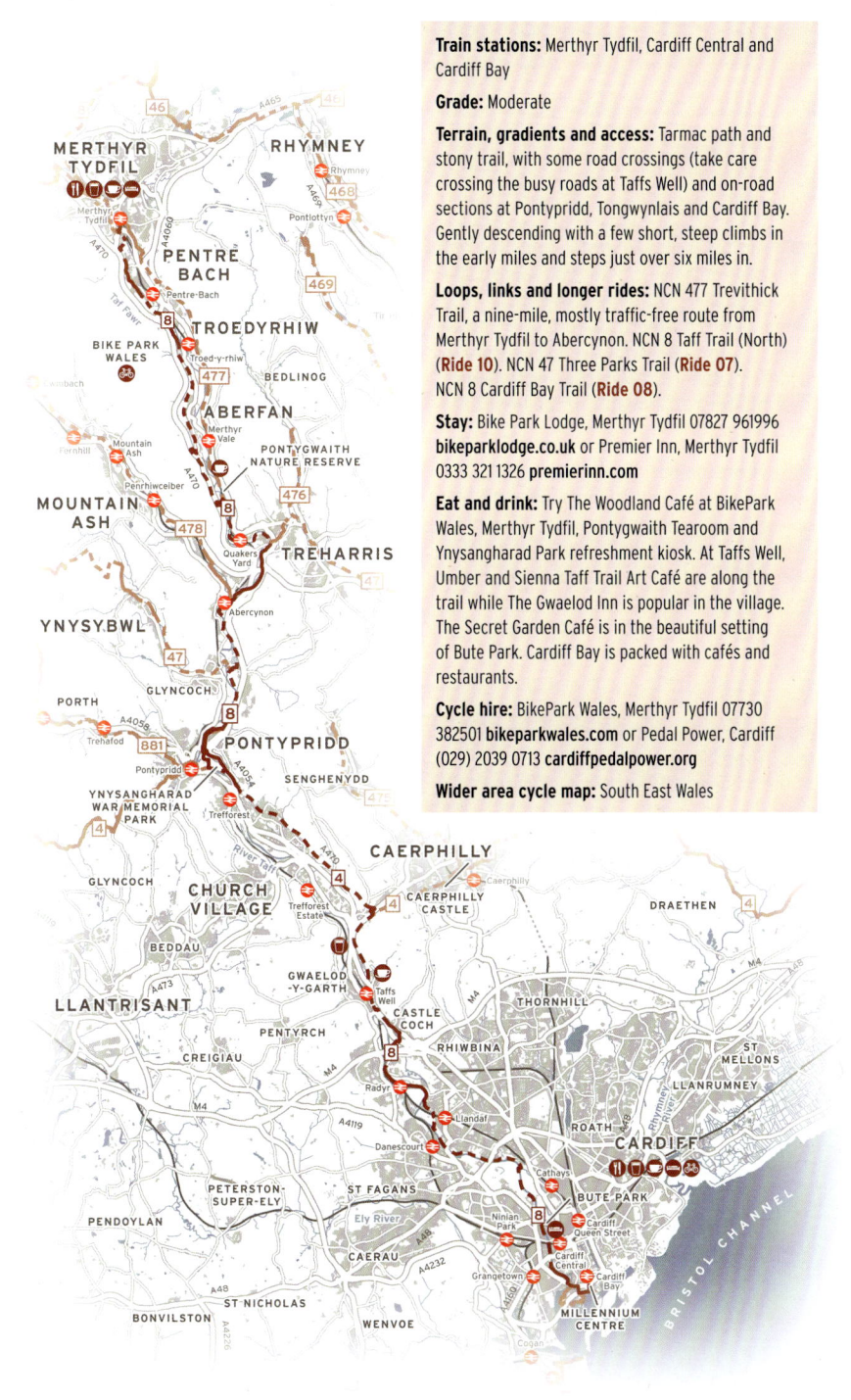

RIDE 09

Train stations: Merthyr Tydfil, Cardiff Central and Cardiff Bay

Grade: Moderate

Terrain, gradients and access: Tarmac path and stony trail, with some road crossings (take care crossing the busy roads at Taffs Well) and on-road sections at Pontypridd, Tongwynlais and Cardiff Bay. Gently descending with a few short, steep climbs in the early miles and steps just over six miles in.

Loops, links and longer rides: NCN 477 Trevithick Trail, a nine-mile, mostly traffic-free route from Merthyr Tydfil to Abercynon. NCN 8 Taff Trail (North) (**Ride 10**). NCN 47 Three Parks Trail (**Ride 07**). NCN 8 Cardiff Bay Trail (**Ride 08**).

Stay: Bike Park Lodge, Merthyr Tydfil 07827 961996 bikeparklodge.co.uk or Premier Inn, Merthyr Tydfil 0333 321 1326 premierinn.com

Eat and drink: Try The Woodland Café at BikePark Wales, Merthyr Tydfil, Pontygwaith Tearoom and Ynysangharad Park refreshment kiosk. At Taffs Well, Umber and Sienna Taff Trail Art Café are along the trail while The Gwaelod Inn is popular in the village. The Secret Garden Café is in the beautiful setting of Bute Park. Cardiff Bay is packed with cafés and restaurants.

Cycle hire: BikePark Wales, Merthyr Tydfil 07730 382501 bikeparkwales.com or Pedal Power, Cardiff (029) 2039 0713 cardiffpedalpower.org

Wider area cycle map: South East Wales

117

TAFF TRAIL

(NORTH)

Start: Theatr Brycheiniog, Brecon
Ride 10 — 25 miles

The Taff Trail is a flagship route for Wales and splits neatly into two manageable segments. The more challenging terrain of this northern half offers incredible scenery from start to finish, leading from the mountains of the Brecon Beacons National Park into the rustic beauty of the Heads of the Valleys.

Start at Brecon Basin and enjoy a gentle two-mile ride along the Monmouthshire & Brecon Canal towpath to Brynich Lock before a country lane takes over, leading through the Vale of Usk into the foothills of the Beacons. Views across the bulging, shadowy hill of Bryn come first, then the stunning mountains of Pen y Fan, the highest in southern Britain, Cribyn and Fan y Big. An undulating ride along country lanes follows, with the mountainous scenery still visible over the tops of the high-sided hedgerows.

At the glittering expanse of Talybont Reservoir, climb steadily beside the water along the traffic-free trail before seeking out the picnic spot at Blaen-y-Glyn at the tip of Talybont Forest. This is around the ride's midway point and close to pretty woodland waterfalls. It also provides a nice opportunity to rest before more climbing over Torpantau Pass where you'll reach the highest point of the Taff Trail in the upland forest of Taf Fechan. The views across the valley are astonishing and a tumbling trail follows with swooping descents along the banks of the Pentwyn Reservoir and a long stony climb past Pontsticill Reservoir.

Crossing the Pontsticill dam gives picture postcard views back across the water as well as final glimpses of Pen y Fan and its rugged neighbours. Here you'll be close to the vintage Brecon Mountain Railway before crossing two viaducts in quick succession; Pontsarn comes first, followed by the superior sweeping curve

Pontsticill Reservoir

Finish: Merthyr Tydfil train station

Train station: Merthyr Tydfil.

Grade: Challenging

Terrain, gradients and access: Undulating throughout with some steep climbs and descents. Gravel towpath, loose stony trail, tarmac path, several road crossings and quiet, on-road sections.

Loops, links and longer rides: At Pontsticill Reservoir the Taff Trail intersects with NCN 46, a mix of traffic-free and on-road route leading to Brynmawr and Abergavenny. NCN 477 Trevithick Trail, a nine-mile, mostly traffic-free route from Merthyr Tydfil to Abercynon. NCN 8 Taff Trail (South) **(Ride 09)**.

Stay: The Lodge, Llanfrynach (01874) 665714 thelodgebreconbandb.co.uk or YHA Danywenallt, Talybont-on-Usk 0345 371 9548 yha.org.uk

Eat and drink: There are lovely cafés in Brecon including The Hours Café and Bookshop and the café at Theatr Brycheiniog. The Three Horseshoes at Brynich Aqueduct and The Royal Oak at Pencelliare are both popular. Try The Butchers Arms at Pontsticill or Julie's Castle Tea Rooms at Cyfarthfa Castle near the route's end.

Cycle hire: Bikes and Hikes, Talybont-on-Usk 0790 996 8135 bikesandhikes.co.uk

Wider area cycle map: South East Wales

---

of Cefn Coed, which was built to carry the Brecon and Merthyr Railway over the River Taff and is simply wonderful to ride across.

Descend past wildflower meadows and see the towers of Cyfarthfa Castle emerge from the trees ahead before passing Cyfarthfa Iron and Steelworks. This was once the largest ironworks in the world and it signals your entry into the former industrial heartland of Merthyr Tydfil. End at Merthyr train station or, if energy allows, follow the rest of the Taff Trail all the way to Cardiff Bay; it's a further 28.5 miles but descends gently all the way.

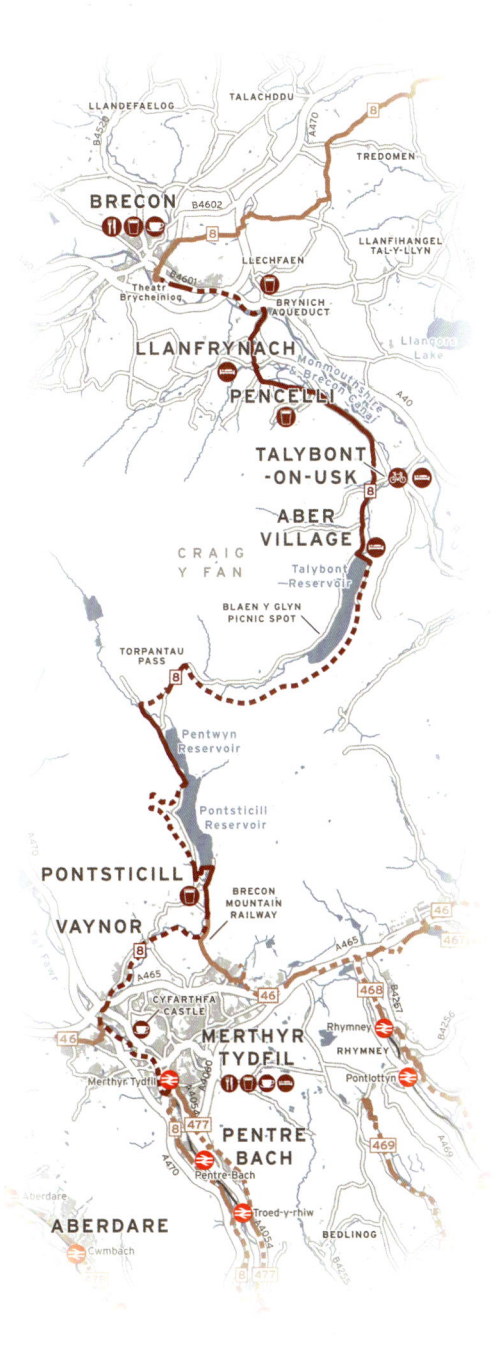

ABERGAVENNY
TO
PONTYPOOL

If you arrive in Abergavenny via train there is a well signed and very handy link into Abergavenny centre. This wonderfully scenic ride starts out gently enough, following NCN 46 signs out of Abergavenny's picturesque centre and dropping down past its crumbling castle remains to a lovely path alongside the River Usk, through quiet meadowland.

A new traffic-free cycle bridge is planned here in future that will avoid the current need to hop over the busy road bridge. Once across the Usk, climb to Llanfoist to pick up a lengthy stretch of high quality railpath that parallels the pretty Brecon and Monmouthshire canal, passing by attractive Govilon village en-route to Clydach village. If you take a brief detour off NCN 46 in Clydach village you will find the spectacularly located Cambrian Inn.

Turn left at a path junction onto NCN 492 as it zig-zags over the hills that form the Heads of the Valleys on wonderfully quiet paths and roads with great views down the Clydach valley. It's now pretty much all downhill but don't speed on without stopping to admire the 3.5-mile long volunteer-run Pontypool and Blaenavon heritage railway with a wonderful little platform halt opposite the Whistle Inn public house. The tranquil setting of the Garn Lakes doesn't give a hint of the industrial heritage to come, as you parallel the cheerful little railway line and pass close by the Big Pit National Coal Museum that lets visitors trip underground like real coal miners once did. This whole area is a World Heritage Site known as Blaenavon Industrial Landscape.

You are soon on a wonderful downhill stretch of fast railpath, high above the valley with an alpine feel to it. At Pontypool take care not to miss the underpass under the A4043 to take you into Pontypool's attractive old centre. The lovely Italian Gardens here are a green oasis and a fine place for some R&R at the end of your ride.

Above Blaenavon

Finish: Pontypool centre

Train Station: From Pontypool to Abergavenny there are regular services for the 10 minute train return

Grade: Challenging

Terrain, gradients and access: Although the majority of this route is on railpaths, that doesn't tell the whole story. There are plenty of brief yet very steep road sections around Clydach village but the final downhill run to Pontypool is all wonderfully fast coasting on a moderately steep downhill tarmac path. It makes the initial, usually gradual climb out of Abergavenny to above the Heads of the Valleys all worth it.

Access controls are a mixture of easy-to-navigate U-chicanes, L-chicanes, small cattle grids and some gates (many are left open) and A-frames. Mainly tarmac but with brief sections of grassy path and various off-road surfaces after Clydach.

Loops, links and longer rides: NCN 46 is followed as far you turn away from the Heads of the Valleys route where you pick up NCN 492 which is a local route linking Cwmbran to Brynmawr via Blaenavon.

NCN 46 will link Neath to Bromsgrove when complete but currently there are long stretches open across the Heads of the Valleys (with a gap west of Merthyr Tidfill) and a fully complete route east of Abergavenny to Hereford.

Stay: Angel Hotel, Abergavenny (01873) 857121 angelabergavenny.com is a pricey 4 star, cycle friendly option. More basic but with a spectacular location is the Whistle Halt Inn campsite above Blaenavon (01495) 790403

Eat and drink: Not a great deal of provision on the way but there are pretty pubs with great scenic locations at Govilon, just off the route (Tafarn y Bont), at Clydach (Cambrian Inn) and above Blaenavon railway (Whistle Halt Inn) - the latter with campsite.

Cycle hire: Hopyard Cycles, Abergavenny (01837) 830219 hopyardcycles.co.uk

Wider area cycle map: South East Wales

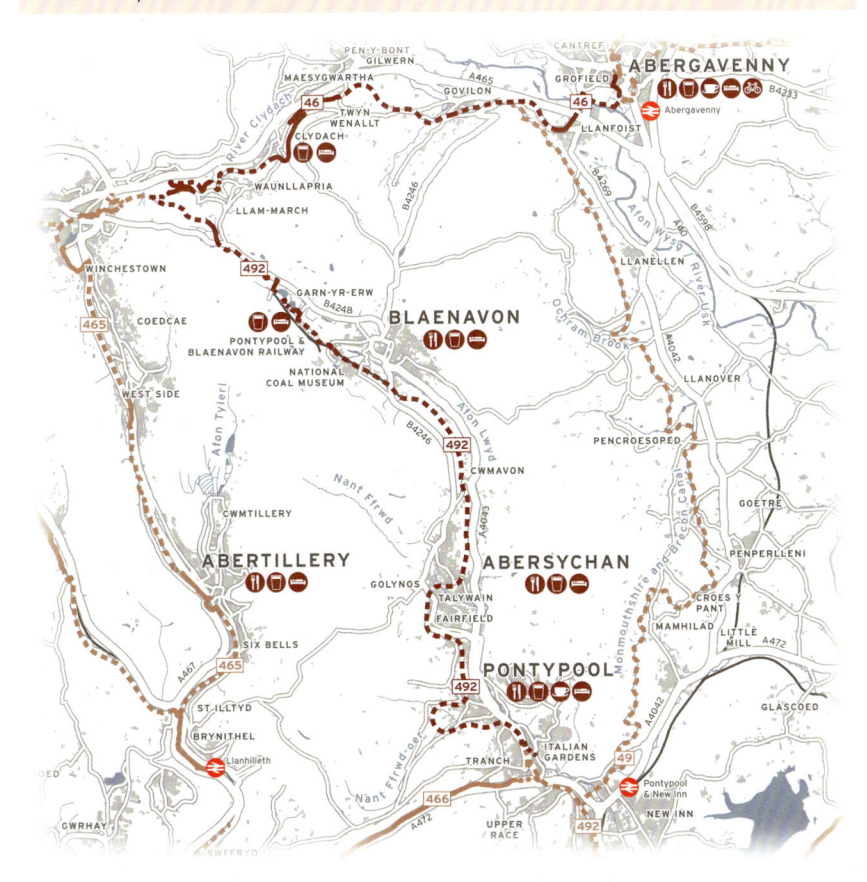

MONMOUTHSHIRE & BRECON CANAL

(NEWPORT TO PONTYPOOL)

This pleasant ride climbs gently up to the southern tip of the Brecon Beacons along the towpath of the Monmouthshire & Brecon Canal, once a busy and active waterway that transported coal, iron and limestone from the Welsh valley towns to Newport.

From the train station, pass the remains of Newport Castle on the banks of the River Usk and leave the city behind to join the green and bushy fringes of the canal where total tranquillity awaits. Swans, moorhens and dragonflies are easy to spot from the very start but look out for the canal's less conspicuous kingfishers, otters and bats as well as bee orchids, named after the shape of their flowers that resemble fat bumblebees.

Vast green meadows can be seen over the hedgerows, and the hills build gradually as the canal progresses north towards the Beacons. There are several locks along this stretch of canal meaning short bursts of pronounced climbing, however, valley towns and villages feature along the way so there are plenty of places for you to stop and rest. Cwmbran, just after the halfway point, is a good place to seek refreshments or The Open Hearth pub at Sebastopol in the ride's second half is in a wonderfully scenic spot with picnic benches along the water's edge.

In the final mile there are opportunities to leave the canal early and head into Pontypool town centre, or follow a signed route along quiet roads to end in the lovely Pontypool Park. Alternatively, carry on along the towpath to cross Pontymoile Aqueduct and watch the Afon Lywd or 'Grey River' gushing ferociously underneath; it's known locally as 'rock breaker' because of the extreme force with which it flows. Leave the towpath after the aqueduct to join the short road to Pontypool & New Inn train station, whilst the canal continues on its long journey into the Brecon Beacons National Park.

Canalside riding

"Leave the city behind to join the green and bushy fringes of the canal..."

Finish: Pontypool & New Inn train station

RIDE 12

Train stations: Newport and Pontypool & New Inn
Grade: Moderate

Terrain, gradients and access: Climbing throughout on tarmac path and narrow stony trail with some road crossings and a short and quiet on-road section approaching Cwmbran. Take care passing under low bridges close to the water's edge.

Loops, links and longer rides: The Monmouthshire & Brecon Canal can be cycled all the way from Newport to Brecon, a distance of 45 miles (**Ride 13**). NCN 492 Afon Lwyd Trail is a nine-mile, traffic-free route from Pontypool to the Blaenavon World Heritage Site and The Big Pit: National Coal Museum. NCN 46 Clydach Gorge is an eight-mile, traffic-free trail from Llanfoist to Brynmawr (**Ride 11**). Combine the canal towpath, Afon Lwyd Trail and Clydach Gorge route to create a 31-mile, traffic-free loop.

Stay: Great House B&B, Caerleon (01633) 420216
greathousebb.co.uk

Eat and drink: The Riverfront café and The Secret Garden Café in Newport are both popular. At Cwmbran try Llantarnam Grange Arts Centre café, or The Open Hearth pub and Page's Fish and Chips both at Sebastopol. The Boatyard tearoom is at Pontymoile Marina.

Cycle hire: Newport Cycle Hire, Fourteen Locks 07538 721922/07972 285771

Wider area cycle map: South East Wales

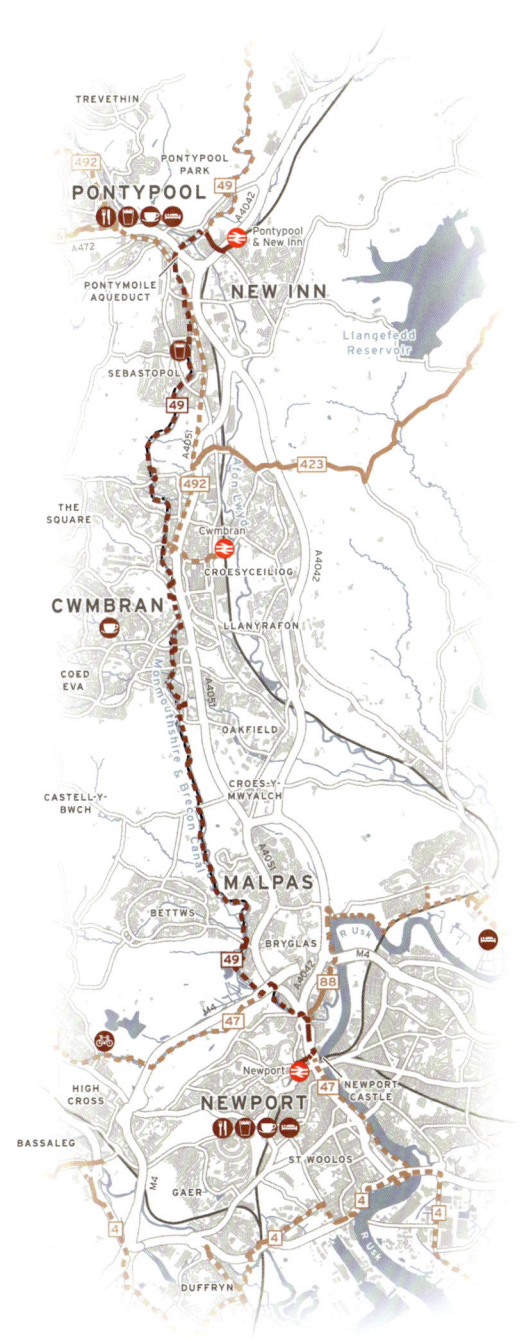

Canal bridge near Pontymoile Basin

RIDE 13
13 miles

Start: Pontypool & New Inn train station

MONMOUTHSHIRE & BRECON CANAL

(PONTYPOOL TO ABERGAVENNY)

Cycle through part of the remarkable landscape of the Blaenavon World Heritage Site on this section of the Monmouthshire & Brecon Canal, once a vital artery when the region was one of the world's most important producers of iron. Local life moves at a more restful pace now with barges drifting slowly by, shaggy-hooved ponies grazing the banks and the timeless beauty of the grassy and heather-clad Black Mountains in the distance.

The scenery is incredible from the very start with views over the tumbling meadows and patchwork of fields. This part of the towpath is less populated than the southern section of the canal between Newport and Pontypool, creating a more remote and peaceful ride. The only interlude in the tranquillity is around the halfway point at Goytre Wharf, a busy mooring spot for boats with a canal visitor centre over the water, toilets, shop, café and picnic areas, plus the option to hire a boat or follow one of the woodland walks and sculpture trails.

The scenery on the second half of the ride is the best by far as you pass around the base of the huge Blorenge hill and beside the broad-leaved woodland of Goytre Hall Wood. Gentle hills and crop fields stretch away into the distance and The Black Mountains in the Brecon Beacons National Park appear on the horizon. The iconic point of Sugar Loaf comes first, then the smaller mound of Skirrid or 'Holy Mountain' with its distinctive landslip that seems to open the mountainside into a gaping yawn.

Come away from the canal near Llanfoist and zig-zag downwards along the wooded trail to end at Church Lane car park, Llanfoist. From here, a mix of traffic-free trail and on-road route leads through Castle Meadows and beside the River Usk into the heart of Abergavenny, a lovely market town with handsome castle ruins.

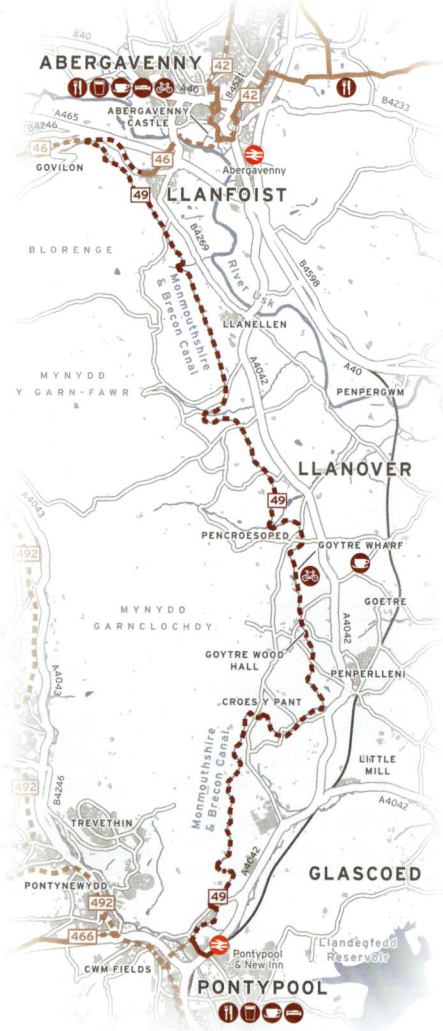

Finish: Car park at Church Lane, Llanfoist, near Abergavenny

RIDE 13

Train stations: Pontypool & New Inn and Abergavenny

Grade: Moderate

Terrain, gradients and access: Mostly flat, fine gravel track and stony trail. The path narrows following Goytre Wharf. Take extra care passing under low bridges where the trail narrows and runs close to the water's edge.

Loops, links and longer rides: The towpath of the Monmouthshire & Brecon Canal can be cycled all the way from Newport to Brecon (**Ride 12**). NCN 492 Afon Lwyd Trail is a nine-mile, traffic-free route from Pontypool to the Blaenavon World Heritage Site and The Big Pit: National Coal Museum. NCN 46 Clydach Gorge is an eight-mile, traffic-free trail from Llanfoist to Brynmawr (**Ride 11**). Combine the canal towpath, Afon Lwyd Trail and Clydach Gorge route to create a 31-mile, traffic-free loop.

Stay: The Guesthouse, Abergavenny (01873) 854823 theguesthouseabergavenny.co.uk

Eat and drink: Try Goytre Wharf Café and Coffee Bar on the banks of the canal mid-route. Abergavenny is known for its foodie credentials and annual food festival, with a huge amount of choice from fine dining at The Walnut Tree just outside the town to more modest options like Emmeline's Homebaking or the cosy Cwtch Café.

Cycle hire: Hopyard Cycles, Abergavenny (01873) 830219 **hopyardcycles.co.uk** or Goytre Wharf, Llanover (01873) 880516 **goytrewharf.com**

Wider area cycle map: South East Wales

"Local life moves at a more restful pace now..."

Canal route view

RIDE 14 — 5.5 miles
Start: New Weir car park, Symonds Yat East

PEREGRINE PATH

The Forest of Dean is a fairytale setting for a gentle ride into Wales through the steeply wooded Wye Valley, bookended by the famous viewpoints of Symonds Yat Rock and the Kymin. Symonds Yat Rock is a raised point near the route's start that offers sweeping Wye Valley scenery and a chance to spot the Peregrine Falcons that nest on the limestone cliffs in summer and lend the route its name.

The route itself starts at New Weir car park in the valley bottom and immediately joins the wide trail through the thick and scented trees of Highmeadow Woods. Follow the path around the curve of the River Wye, one of the best places in Britain for canoeing and kayaking, and after a mile or so cross the border into Wales to reach a wonderful picnic spot near Biblins youth campsite. The river's shores are wide and stony here, rope swings dangle tantalisingly over the water and Biblins Bridge spans the Wye, a wobbly Indiana Jones-style suspension bridge with marvellous views down the valley from its swaying centre.

Ride along the edges of Lady Park Wood National Nature Reserve, a beautiful untouched ancient woodland climbing the slopes of Upper Wye Gorge, before leaving the river and shade of the trees temporarily to emerge onto open farmland.

The old platform of Hadnock Halt, a stop on the former Ross and Monmouth Railway, makes a good resting spot around the halfway point before joining the quiet road along the edges of the Woodland Trust's pretty Priory Grove.

In the final mile, the white castellations of the National Trust's Round House can be seen on the renowned local viewpoint of the Kymin, high on the hillside to the left. If you want to end at the Kymin, and enjoy incredible panoramas over the Wye Valley and Brecon Beacons, then be prepared for a tough climb on steep and narrow roads. Alternatively, opt for a gentler ending by crossing Wye Bridge to ride into the market town of Monmouth and finish outside the beautiful Shire Hall in Agincourt Square, close to the remains of Monmouth Castle.

The Peregrine Path

"A fairytale setting for a gentle ride into Wales through the steeply wooded Wye Valley..."

RIDE 14

Finish: Shire Hall, Monmouth

Train stations: Nearest is Abergavenny

Grade: Easy

Terrain, gradients and access: Flat stony trail with an on-road section from Hadnock to Monmouth and through Monmouth town centre.

Loops, links and longer rides: From Symonds Yat East take the ancient hand ferry across the water to Symonds Yat West. From Monmouth follow NCN 423 on-road to Cwmbran. Family Cycle Trail is a popular 11-mile circular ride around the Forest of Dean from the Pedalabikeaway centre at Cannop Valley. NCN 49 Monmouthshire & Brecon Canal (**Rides 12** and **13**).

Stay: The Saracens Head, Symonds Yat East (01600) 890435 **saracensheadinn.co.uk** or YHA Wye Valley 0345 371 9666 **yha.org.uk**

Eat and drink: The Royal Lodge, Rose Cottage Tearoom and Terrace and The Saracens Head Inn are all at Symonds Yat East. Favourites in Monmouth include Farringtons and Scrumptious Monmouth at the Beaufort Arms Hotel.

Cycle hire: Nearest is Pedalabikeaway, Cannop Valley (01594) 729000 **pedalabikeaway.co.uk**

Wider area cycle map: South East Wales

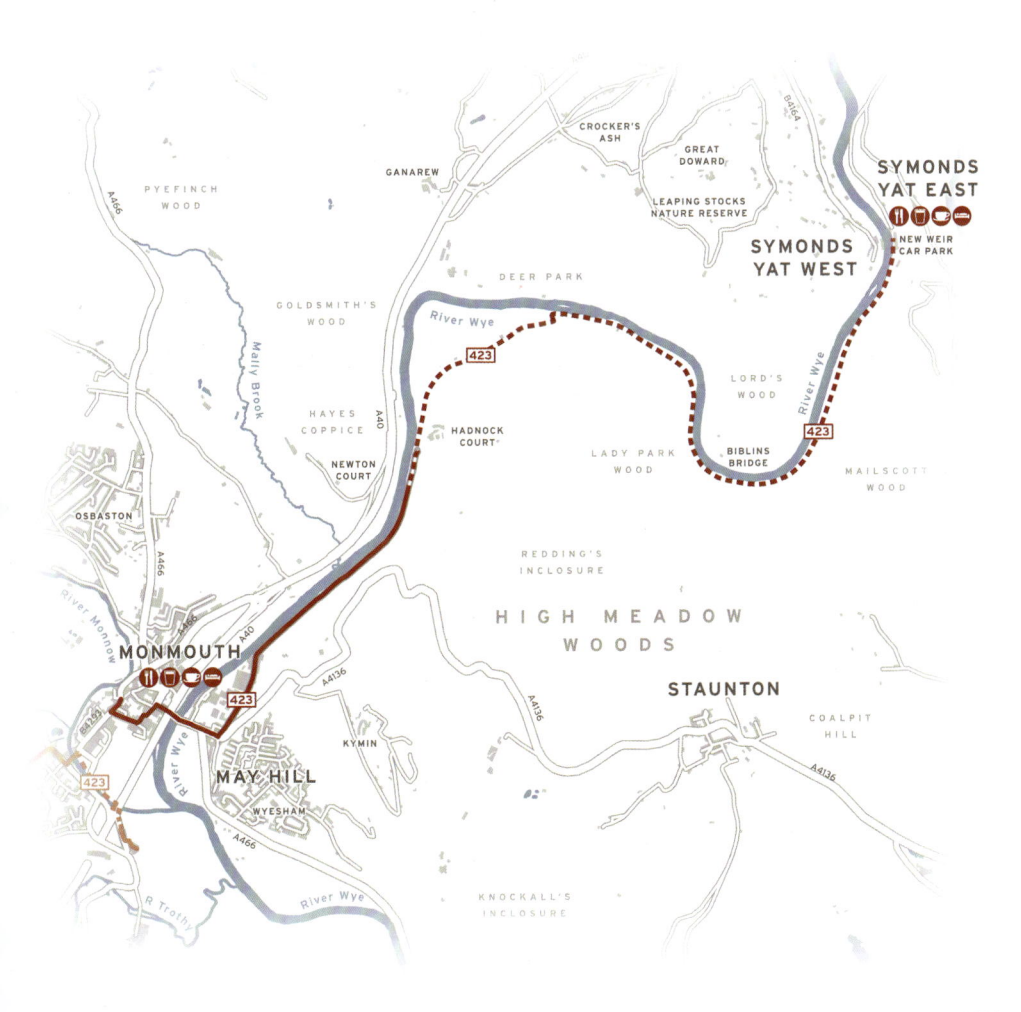

RIDE 15
8.5 miles

Start: Cwmdauddwr, near Rhayader town centre

ELAN VALLEY TRAIL

Garreg-ddu Reservoir

This ride through the heart of Wales takes in the rugged beauty of the Cambrian Mountains and the placid waters of four Elan Valley reservoirs. Keep a look out overhead for the distinctive forked tail and gliding flight of red kites; Gigrin Farm, a red kite feeding centre, is nearby so these iconic Welsh birds are a familiar sight in the sky around here.

It's an undulating ride from the very start as you climb through the rolling Radnorshire hills and across the rich grassland of the Radnorshire Wildlife Trust's Rhayader Tunnel Nature Reserve, an important haven for bats and other species. The Elan Valley Visitor Centre, almost three miles in, is a good stop for finding out more about this beautiful valley, or visit the RSPB Carngafallt nature reserve near here too, with its ancient oaks and summertime carpet of heather moorland.

Caban-coch is the first dam and reservoir to be reached on the trail and it sits beneath the craggy mound of Craig Cnwch and the Caban quarries. At Garreg-ddu Reservoir there's a lovely climb between giant conifers, where the musky, resinous scent of the trees fills the air. In the final miles the views become ever more spectacular and a secluded bench tucked discretely beneath the main trail makes the best picnic spot on the ride, overlooking the beautiful Pen-y-garreg Reservoir. End at the big and elegant arches of Craig-goch dam.

RIDE 15

Finish: Pen-y-garreg Reservoir

Train stations: Nearest is Llandrindod Wells or Caersws

Grade: Easy

Terrain, gradients and access: Gently climbing along tarmac path and stony trail, becoming more rugged in the second half. Several gates and small roads to cross.

Loops, links and longer rides: NCN 81 continues on-road to the opposite end of Craig-goch Reservoir, with a country lane back to Rhayader. Alternatively, loop Pen-y-garreg Reservoir by turning left over Craig-goch dam and taking the quiet road back to the Elan Valley Trail, re-joining it at Garreg-ddu Reservoir. This is around the same distance as doubling back on the trail but offers a sweeping descent and fabulous water views. From Rhayader NCN 8 links with the Radnor Ring, National Route 825, to Llandrindod Wells, home of The National Cycle Museum.

Stay: Beili Neuadd B&B and Bunkhouse, St Harmon (01597) 810211 **beilineuadd.co.uk**

Eat and drink: The Triangle Inn is a 16th Century drovers' inn just moments from the start of the trail or visit the café at Elan Valley Visitor Centre or Penbont House traditional Welsh tearoom on the road close to Pen-y-garreg dam. There are many eateries in Rhayader, including popular pub The Lamb and Flag.

Cycle hire: Clive Powell Bikes, Rhayader (01597) 811343 **clivepowellbikes.com** or Elan Valley Visitor Centre (01597) 810880 **elanvalley.org.uk**

Wider area cycle map: Mid South Wales

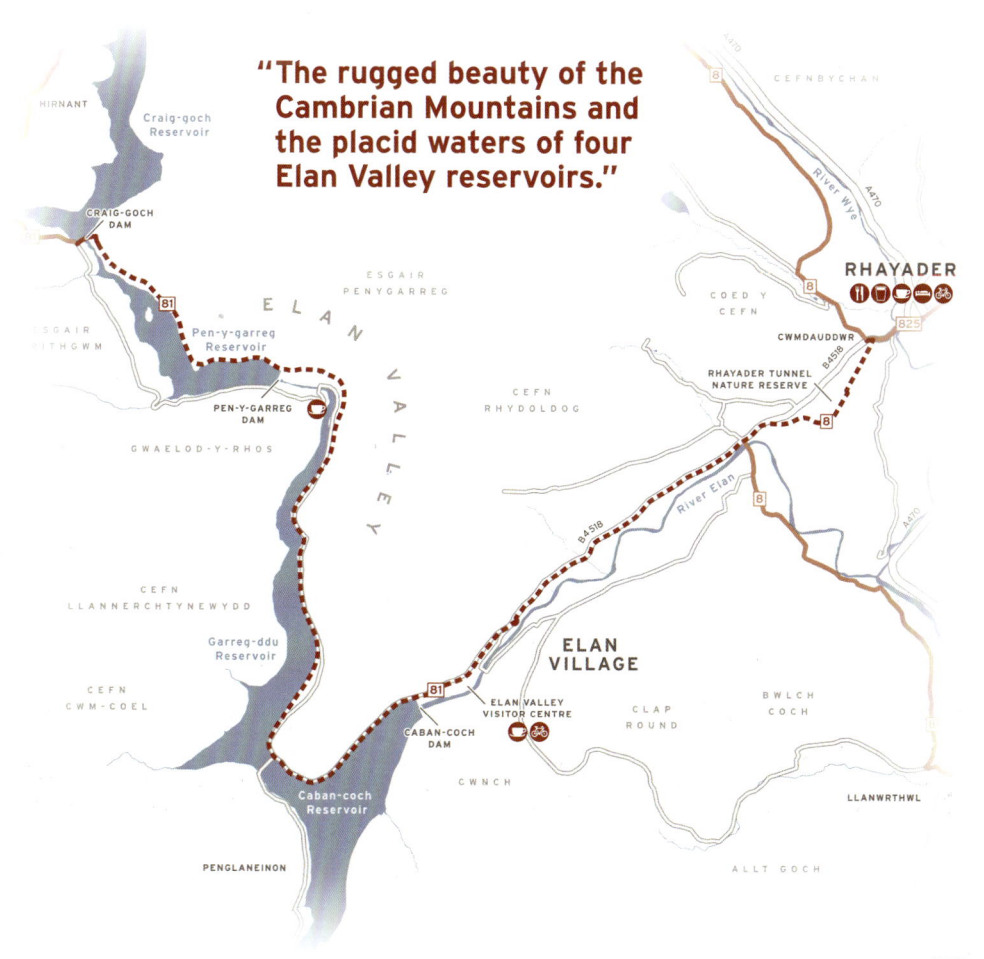

> "The rugged beauty of the Cambrian Mountains and the placid waters of four Elan Valley reservoirs."

RIDE 16 | 81 | 82 | **Start:** Pen Dinas LNR, Aberystwyth

8.5 miles to Trawsgoed or
17.5 miles to Cors Caron

YSTWYTH TRAIL

The Ystwyth trail follows the line of the former Manchester and Milford Railway and links the beautiful Ystwyth and Teifi valleys. It leads from the stunning Ceredigion coast at Aberystwyth to Cors Caron National Nature Reserve (NNR), against an impressive backdrop of the Cambrian Mountains.

Start at the charming little Pen Dinas Local Nature Reserve (LNR) at Aberystwyth where oystercatchers can be seen picking their way along the foreshore. Look out for choughs and Welsh cobs too, and the vast coastal peak of Pen Dinas looming above. It's a steep, stony climb in the opening mile but remember to take a look behind for magnificent views of Wellington Monument, the towering chimney-style structure on top of Pen Dinas.

The trail quickly leaves the sea and shingle ridge behind in favour of the deep woodland and hillsides of Ceredigion. The path aligns with the pale grey pebbly shores of the attractive River Ystwyth in the first half of the ride, with a long and straight section to the Black Covert picnic spot at Trawsgoed. This is a lovely riverside picnic spot beneath the shade of the ash, birch and sweet chestnut trees within Ystwyth Forest and is the ideal endpoint for a family ride.

Only follow the Ystwyth Trail all the way to Cors Caron if you're seeking a challenge. Steep road climbs between high-sided hedgerows make this second half much more testing, but the views are undeniably sensational, particularly looking back near the Tynybedw picnic site. A steep, twisting descent follows between tall conifers on a narrow stony trail, which is best tackled on a mountain bike.

However, the route mellows again at Cors Caron National Nature Reserve where there are unspoilt views across three raised bogs. These areas of deep peat have built up over 12,000 years and are internationally important for wildlife; look out for red kites, hen harriers, curlews and skylarks overhead, and dragonflies, lizards and otters that live in the bogs.

Cross land that was once part of Strata Florida Abbey and consider taking the bridleway and short on-road section from the reserve to the beautiful abbey ruins. Or, simply follow the long straight path through Cors Caron to the car park and toilets where the traffic-free route ends. From here a one and a half-mile, on-road ride leads to the market town of Tregaron, home to the Red Kite and Welsh Gold centres.

Aberystwyth Promenade

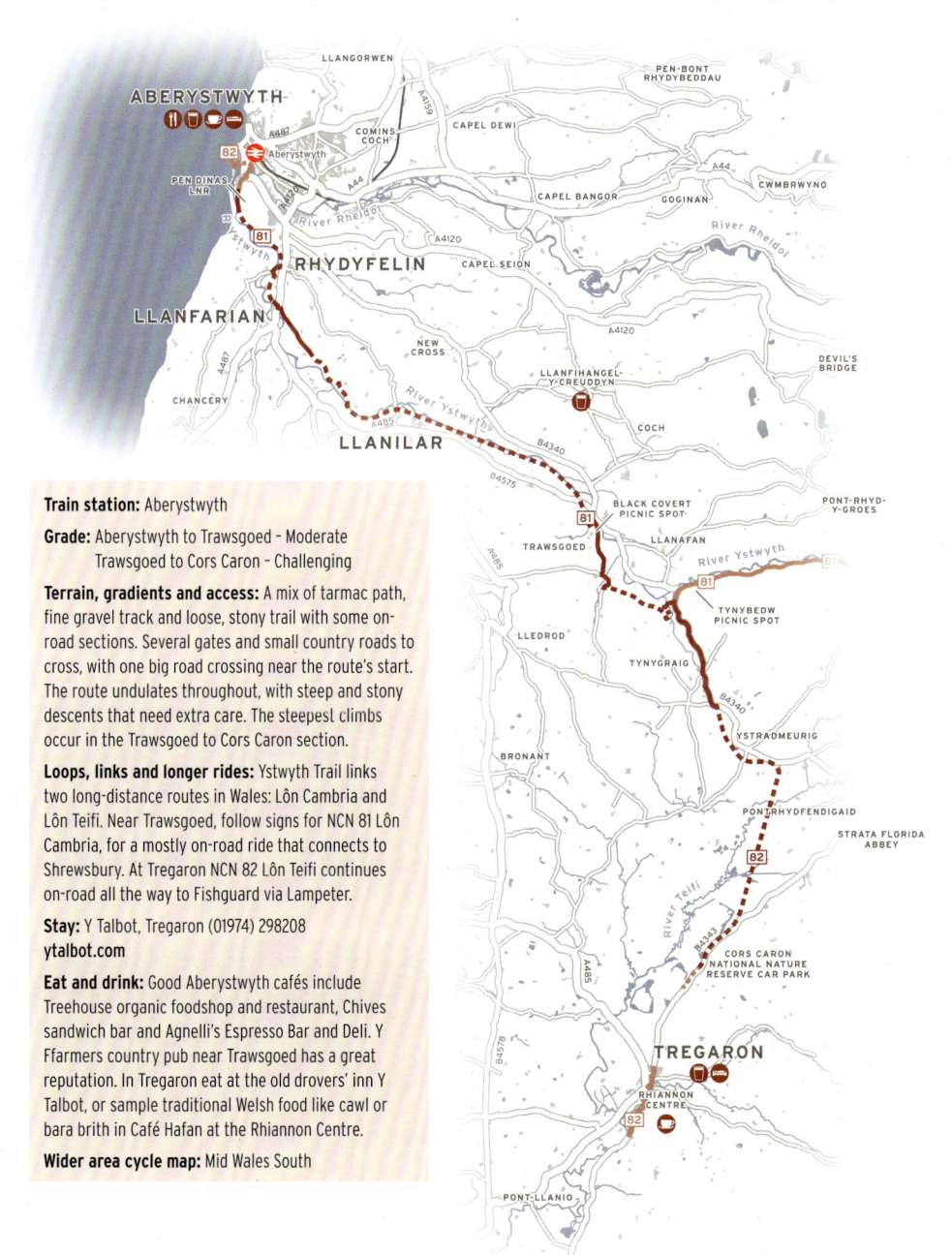

Finish: Black Covert car park and picnic site at Trawsgoed or Cors Caron NNR car park **RIDE 16**

Train station: Aberystwyth

Grade: Aberystwyth to Trawsgoed - Moderate
Trawsgoed to Cors Caron - Challenging

Terrain, gradients and access: A mix of tarmac path, fine gravel track and loose, stony trail with some on-road sections. Several gates and small country roads to cross, with one big road crossing near the route's start. The route undulates throughout, with steep and stony descents that need extra care. The steepest climbs occur in the Trawsgoed to Cors Caron section.

Loops, links and longer rides: Ystwyth Trail links two long-distance routes in Wales: Lôn Cambria and Lôn Teifi. Near Trawsgoed, follow signs for NCN 81 Lôn Cambria, for a mostly on-road ride that connects to Shrewsbury. At Tregaron NCN 82 Lôn Teifi continues on-road all the way to Fishguard via Lampeter.

Stay: Y Talbot, Tregaron (01974) 298208
ytalbot.com

Eat and drink: Good Aberystwyth cafés include Treehouse organic foodshop and restaurant, Chives sandwich bar and Agnelli's Espresso Bar and Deli. Y Ffarmers country pub near Trawsgoed has a great reputation. In Tregaron eat at the old drovers' inn Y Talbot, or sample traditional Welsh food like cawl or bara brith in Café Hafan at the Rhiannon Centre.

Wider area cycle map: Mid Wales South

RIDE 17
14 miles

Start: Halfpenny Bridge, Newtown

MONTGOMERY CANAL

This towpath trail beside 'The Monty' canal passes through the lush green Severn Valley with views over the rolling Shropshire Hills Area of Outstanding Natural Beauty along the way.

It is river rather than canal that features in the opening miles, as you follow the magnificent Severn out of Newtown to the pools and lagoons of Montgomeryshire Wildlife Trust's Pwll Penarth Nature Reserve where the towpath takes over. The tumbling countryside of the Welsh Marches, the borderlands between England and Wales, is an enchanting setting as you thread between the wriggling river and linear canal, lifted over Bechan Brook by the Aberbechan Aqueduct.

Cross the canal twice near Abermule and pass beneath the attractive old Glanhafren Bridge into the shade of the wet woodland at Montgomeryshire Wildlife Trust's Red House Nature Reserve. Intersections with the fast road at Fron and Garthmyl interrupt the tranquillity mid-route but the meadows, dingles and fishing lakes in between help to restore a sense of peace.

Some wonderful picnic spots feature in the ride's second half, particularly at Berriew Aqueduct amid colourful yellow iris and pink flowering rush, and later at the pretty Belan Locks next to the curious black and white houses of the area's former limekiln workers.

Near the end, the Shropshire Hills rise up to the right and the dramatic peaks of the Breidden Hills and Rodney's Pillar can be seen up ahead. End at Powysland Museum on the edge of the bunting-strewn streets of Welshpool town centre. From the High Street a walking route leads up to the National Trust's Powis Castle where the views from the famous terraced gardens are unrivalled.

Powis Castle gardens

Finish: Powysland Museum, Welshpool

RIDE 17

"An enchanting setting as you thread between the wriggling river and linear canal..."

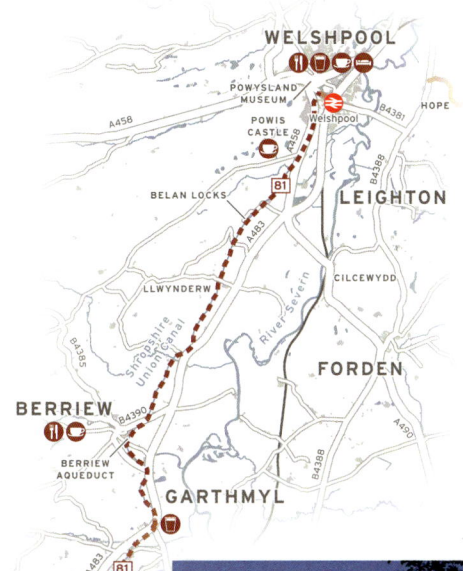

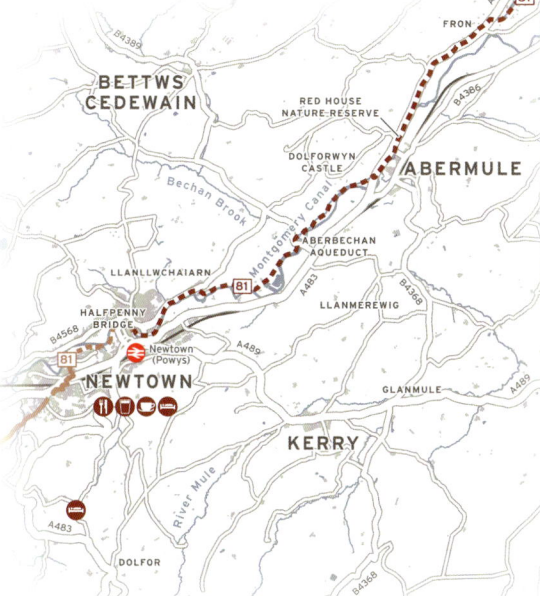

Train stations: Newtown and Welshpool

Grade: Moderate

Terrain, gradients and access: Flat tarmac path and fine gravel track, with several gates and fast road crossings around Fron and Garthmyl. Take particular care passing beneath low bridges and on a sharp, steep bend joining the towpath near Abermule.

Loops, links and longer rides: Turn the ride into a more challenging loop by returning to Aberbechan along the more undulating, parallel on-road section of local cycle route. NCN 81 Lôn Cambria crosses the heart of mid Wales between Aberystwyth and Shrewsbury on mostly on-road route.

Stay: The Old Vicarage Dolfor, Newtown (01686) 629051 theoldvicaragedolfor.co.uk

Eat and drink: The Waggon and Horses is near the route's start in Newtown or try The Nag's Head Inn at Garthmyl and Upper Rectory restaurant or Lychgate Cottage Tea Room and Deli both at Berriew. In Welshpool, Bay Tree Vintage Tea Room is popular, whilst the Courtyard Restaurant and Garden Coffee Shop is at Powis Castle.

Wider area cycle map: Mid North Wales

Powis Castle

133

RIDE 18
21 miles

Start: Eldon Square, Dolgellau

DOLGELLAU
TO
TYWYN

As stressed in the Terrain section, probably the most challenging route in the book and one of the most challenging sections on the whole of the NCN. That's because you are heading off-road and along the northern lower slopes of Cadair Idris which contains the highest peak in southern Snowdonia, Penygadair. The rewards on this undeniably strenuous route include amazing views over sandy Barmouth Bay and jaw-dropping mountain landscapes; more often than not the upper slopes of Cadair Idris are swathed in wild-looking cloud, but this only adds to the drama.

NCN 82 signs are hard to find in the maze of streets around Dolgellau's neat and characterful main square but you soon pick them up on the outskirts along with the signs for Cadair Idris itself. It's a steady climb on a minor road before the gradient levels out somewhat along the shoulder of the massif after passing pretty Gwernan Lake.

Just keep bearing left across the increasingly spectacular upland plateau to pick up the rough track that climbs to a staggering viewpoint north along the coast, with views over Barmouth Bay and north along the coast.

Track quality improves and the climb levels out through an area of forestry before a long sweeping descent as views over the Dysenni valley come into sight. Now on tarmac, this is still virtually traffic-free and remains so as you hit the valley bottom and circle the broad valley floor in front of the spectacularly isolated Birds' Rock (so named after the large number of birds that nest on its rocky peak, including the rare Chough).

The final run in to Tywyn sees a little more motor traffic in places before a traffic-free path leads to the jolly seaside resort where you can café sit on the seafront or pay a visit to the Talyllyn steam railway, with trains running daily into the southern Snowdonia hills.

Snowdonia views from the route

Finish: Tywyn seafront

RIDE 18

Train Station: From Tywyn you can get a train back to Mawddach and use part of the current ride 19 to return along the Mawddach Trail to Dolgellau.

Grade: Challenging

Terrain, gradients and access: Perhaps the most challenging route in the book and a mountain bike for the very fit or an electric mountain bike for the reasonably fit would be ideal for tackling it. There are plenty of steep climbs and a very loose, rubbly one that climbs to the viewpoint above Barmouth Bay. There's plenty of tarmac at either end too, and although this is not technically traffic-free, much of it sees so little traffic as to be virtually traffic-free (a little care mixing with traffic required on small sections at Bryncrug and Tywyn). Access controls are mainly in the form of farm gates on the off-road section, though there aren't a huge number of these.

Loops, links and longer rides: This ride uses part of NCN 82, planned to run from Bangor to Fishguard, with many sections already open. For much of the middle and northern sections it roughly parallels with another north-south route, NCN 8 – Lôn Las Cymru – which means there are good opportunities for some longer circular rides too.

Stay: Trem Hyfryd Guest House, Dolgellau B&B aimed specifically at hikers and bikers (01341) 470030 tremhyfrydwales.co.uk

Eat and drink: Dolgellau has plenty of eateries around the main square and there is a seafront café at journey's end at Tywyn, though very little in between.

Cycle hire: Dolgellau Cycles (town centre location) (01341) 423332 dolgellaucycles.co.uk

Wider area cycle map: Mid-Wales North

Views across Barmouth Bay

RIDE 19
9.5 miles — Start: Barmouth seafront

MAWDDACH TRAIL

Possibly the finest and most memorable traffic-free trail of all, this is nine miles of perfection along the heavenly Mawddach Estuary in North Wales.

Start at the sandy beach and dunes in charming Barmouth, once a fashionable Victorian seaside resort, and quickly reach the highlight of the ride: a joyful clatter over the wooden planks of the long Barmouth Bridge that spans the estuary. There are tremendous views in every direction from the bridge, but the jagged Cadair Idris and neighbouring peaks are particularly impressive and reveal the mythical Old Man of Barmouth, the profile of an upturned face where the mountains meet the sky.

Pass through Morfa Mawddach, once the site of a busy junction of the Great Western Railway that ran to Ruabon but now a more peaceful RSPB nature reserve. The estuary banks follow a sweeping curve, which is wonderful to ride along, with swallows flitting overhead in summer and a series of perfectly placed picnic benches at the water's edge. Ride through the conifer, oak and birch woodland of Abergwynant woods and stop to look across the water at Bontddu village; the hills above it were at the centre of a gold rush in the last century.

Penmaenpool, in the final miles of the ride, was once one of the Mawddach's main shipbuilding sites, and here you'll pass the scenic staggered terraces of the George III Hotel, an ideal spot for a drink. From here, cross the river twice to end at Marian Mawr car park in Dolgellau, or take the very short ride along the road into the attractive town centre.

Mawddach Trail

"Nine miles of perfection along the heavenly Mawddach Estuary..."

136

RIDE 19

Finish: Marian Mawr car park, Dolgellau

Train stations: Barmouth and Morfa Mawddach

Grade: Easy

Terrain, gradients and access: Flat, wide promenade, tarmac path, and fine gravel track with some road crossings and short, on-road sections at Barmouth and Penmaenpool. Some gates to pass through.

Loops, links and longer rides: Half a mile from the end of the trail at Dolgellau, the route intersects with NCN 82 where a seven-mile ride north, mostly on-road, leads to the mountain bike hotspot of Coed y Brenin. Or, return to Barmouth via Cregennen Lakes for a more challenging alternative to the trail; follow NCN 82 south west from Dolgellau and be prepared for a long, scenic on-road climb. Turn right to pass the lakes and take the steep descent to the valley bottom before joining the A493 for a short way and re-joining the Mawddach Trail near Arthog. If you keep following NCN 82 here it uses a rocky track to climb to amazing views over the coast before descending to Bryncrug and Tywyn (**Ride 18**).

Stay: Bryn Melyn Guesthouse in Barmouth has exceptional estuary views (01341) 280556 **brynmelyn.co.uk**

Eat and drink: Barmouth favourites include Bath House Café on the seafront, The Last Inn overlooking the water or The Harbour Fish Bar. At Penmaenpool the route passes the door of the George III Hotel and its lovely beer garden. Dolgellau has many eateries, including the highly-regarded T H Roberts café.

Cycle hire: Dolgellau Cycles (01341) 423332 **dolgellaucycles.co.uk** or Birmingham Garage, Barmouth (01341) 280644

Wider area cycle map: Mid Wales North

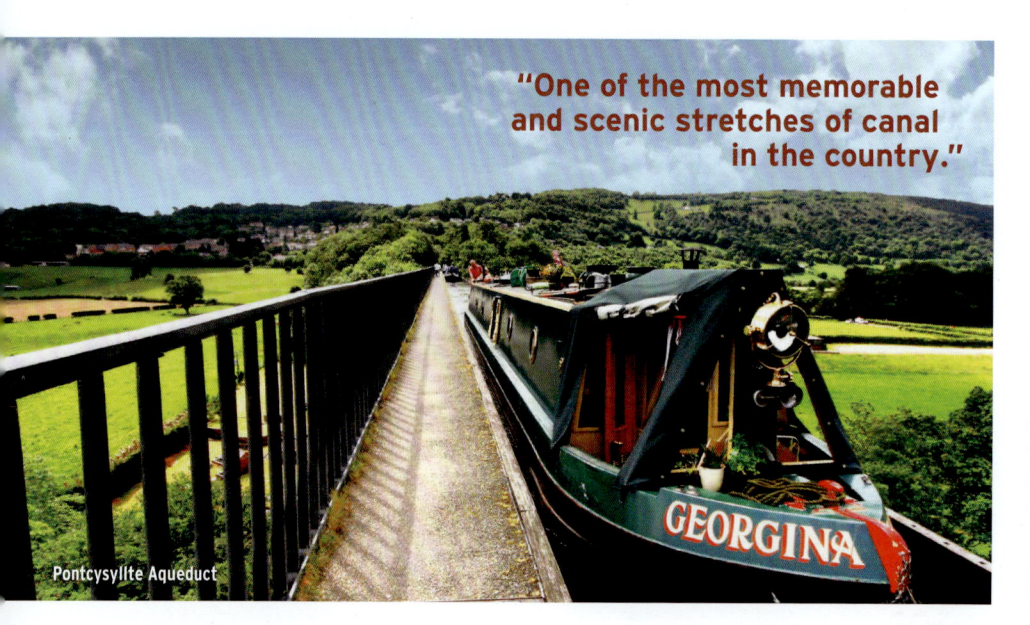

LLANGOLLEN CANAL

Ride 20 — 9.5 miles — **Start:** Horseshoe Falls, Llantysilio

"One of the most memorable and scenic stretches of canal in the country."

Pontcysyllte Aqueduct

This route follows one of the most memorable and scenic stretches of canal in the country. It passes through the picturesque Dee Valley in North Wales and over the sensational Pontcysyllte Aqueduct, one of the finest in the world.

The gushing water of Horseshoe Falls is a pretty start before setting off along the towpath between the River Dee and Llangollen Canal beneath the Llantysilio Mountains. Reach the little town of Llangollen after just two miles; it sits below the tumbling remains of the medieval Castell Dinas Bran and is a great place for an early stop, particularly in July during its famous International Eisteddfod. The raised aspect of the canal here gives great views over the town and pretty Dee Bridge, while just half a mile later the dramatic limestone ridge of The Panorama stretches out ahead. Benches near Trevor Uchaf in the ride's first half are the most scenic spot to picnic whilst looking across the wide river and the lush green Vale of Llangollen.

There are glimpses of Pontcysyllte Aqueduct's nineteen elegant arches as you approach Trevor Basin, and the basin itself buzzes with visitors all eager to cross 'the stream in the sky'. Dismount here to push across the highest navigable aqueduct in the world, designed by great Victorian engineer Thomas Telford more than 200 years ago. Its status

RIDE 20

Finish: Chirk town centre

Train stations: Chirk, Llangollen and Berwyn (no connection to main rail network)

Grade: Easy

Terrain, gradients and access: Flat tarmac and gravel path. There are some small steps at Trevor Basin and cyclists must dismount and push over Pontcysyllte Aqueduct. Take care passing under low bridges along the canal close to the water's edge and through the unlit Whitehouse Tunnel near the route's end.

Loops, links and longer rides: From Horseshoe Falls cycle west along the quiet lanes of the Dee Valley towards Glyndyfrdwy, Carrog and the little town of Corwen. From Chirk follow Ceiriog Cycle Route, a circular on-road ride around the Ceiriog Valley. NCN 5 Chester to Connah's Quay (Ride 02).

Stay: Llangollen Hostel, Llangollen (01978) 861773 llangollenhostel.co.uk or The Hand Hotel, Chirk (01691) 773472

Eat and drink: Try The Chainbridge Hotel near the route's start, Wharf Tea Room at the canalside in Llangollen or Vintage Rose Tea Rooms and Dee Side Café Bistro in Llangollen town centre. Refreshments can be found at Trevor Basin and there is a visitor centre here. In Chirk try the community-managed Caffi Wylfa or Teddybears Tea Rooms.

Cycle hire: Drosi Bikes, Llangollen 07396 658 501 drosibikes.org or SAS Outdoors (01978) 860471 sasoutdoors.co.uk

Wider area cycle map: Shropshire, Staffordshire & The Black Country

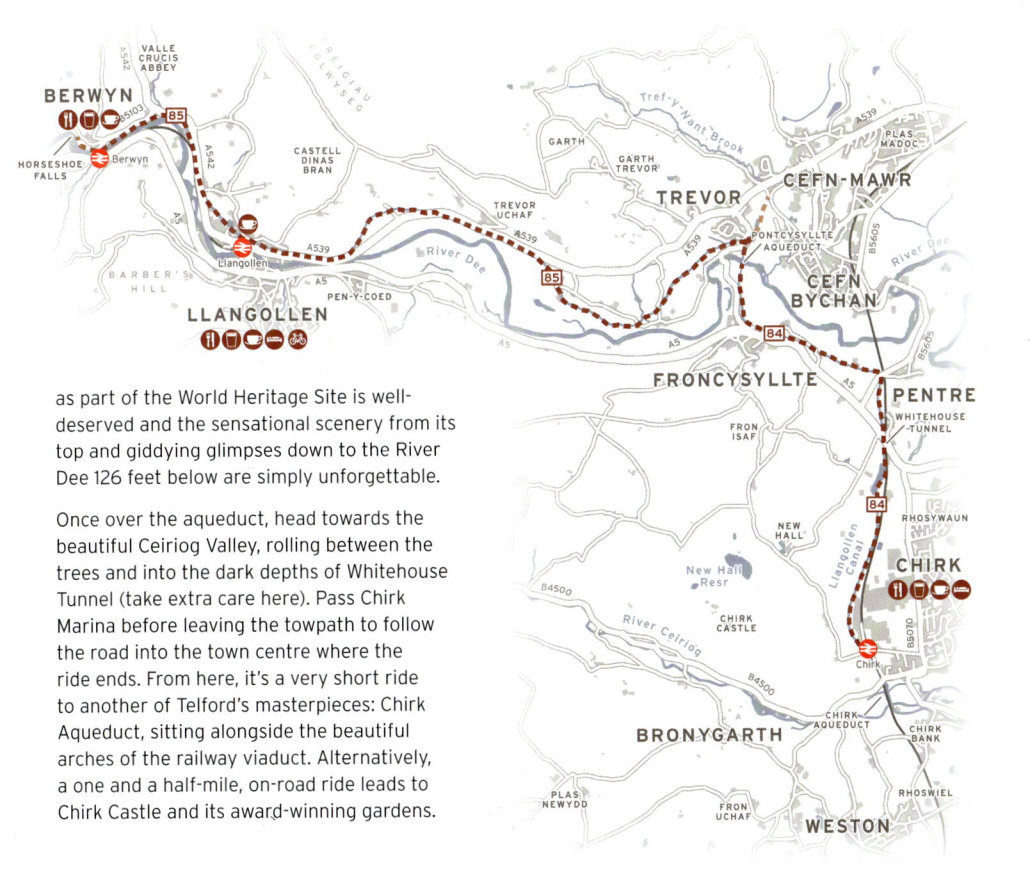

as part of the World Heritage Site is well-deserved and the sensational scenery from its top and giddying glimpses down to the River Dee 126 feet below are simply unforgettable.

Once over the aqueduct, head towards the beautiful Ceiriog Valley, rolling between the trees and into the dark depths of Whitehouse Tunnel (take extra care here). Pass Chirk Marina before leaving the towpath to follow the road into the town centre where the ride ends. From here, it's a very short ride to another of Telford's masterpieces: Chirk Aqueduct, sitting alongside the beautiful arches of the railway viaduct. Alternatively, a one and a half-mile, on-road ride leads to Chirk Castle and its award-winning gardens.

RIDE 21
12 miles

Start: Caernarfon Castle

LÔN EIFION

This route is sandwiched between the sea and Snowdonia Mountains, meaning the views as it climbs into the slate valleys of Gwynedd are out of this world.

The Maes at the start is one of Caernarfon's highlights. Historically the town's gathering place, the cobbled square buzzes with people chatting amiably and sitting at pavement cafés. From here, descend past the grand towers of Caernarfon Castle, a World Heritage Site, and join a leafy traffic-free trail on the dormant bed of a railway that ran between Caernarfon and Afon Wen for almost a hundred years. The tracks of the Welsh Highland Railway mirror the cycle route in the opening miles so you may be raced by a steam train chugging its way to the foot of Snowdon.

The scenery opens up, mountains loom ahead, and the views over Caernarfon Bay are staggering before you enter the thick cover of Welsh woodland. Inigo Jones Slate Works near the halfway point is a good rest stop to see the local slate being expertly crafted, and the café here has become a popular spot with cyclists.

The views increase in magnitude in the second half of the ride, with sheep-grazed meadows and wildflower-fringed farmland in the foreground, the flinty grey peaks of Snowdonia's Nantlle Ridge to one side and the vast Bwlch Mawr on the Llŷn Peninsula to the other.

Join up with the pretty Afon Dwyfach or 'little holy river' in the final miles with views towards the dark and moody peak of Mynydd Graig Goch in the distance. The traffic-free path ends abruptly at Bryncir but the garden centre and its café are nearby and make a good endpoint.

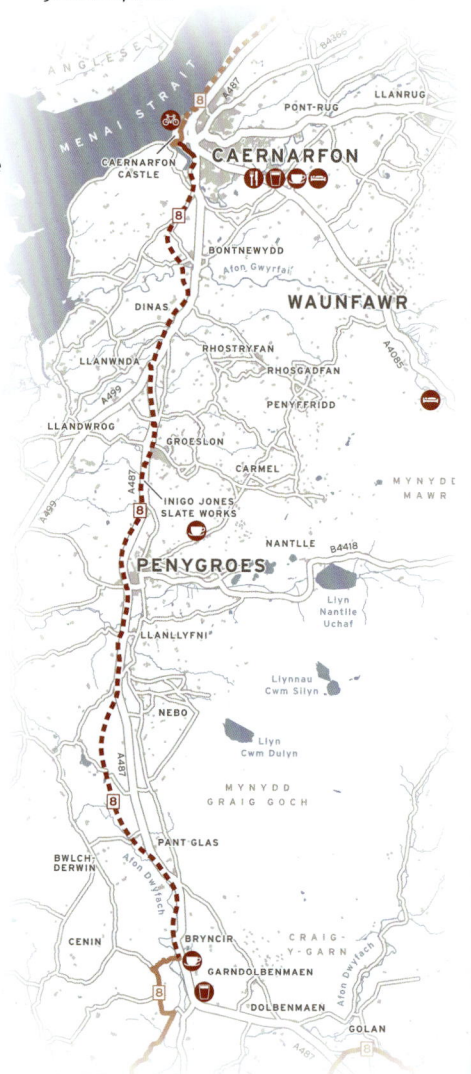

140

Finish: Bryncir

RIDE 21

Train station: Nearest is Bangor or Criccieth

Grade: Moderate

Terrain, gradients and access: Gradually climbing with a gentle descent in the final miles. Tarmac path with a short and quiet on-road section leaving Caernarfon. Several gates and road crossings.

Loops, links and longer rides: The route intersects with regional route 61, Lôn Gwyrfai, a mostly on-road route to Waunfawr. From the route's end at Bryncir, follow NCN 8 along country roads for a further eight miles to Criccieth, the gateway to the Llŷn Peninsula, with sandy and pebbly beaches and a medieval castle perched on the headland. NCN 8 Lôn Las Menai (**Ride 22**).

Stay: Pentre Bach bunkhouse and campsite at Waunfawr 07798 733 939 pentrebachbunkhouse.co.uk

Eat and drink: Caernarfon has some great cafés, including Caffi Maes at Castle Square. The Welsh Rock Café at the Inigo Jones Slate Works is a good mid-route stop. At the route's end, Bryncir Garden Centre has a café or Tafarn yr Afr "The Goat Inn" is at Glandwyfach.

Cycle hire: Beics Antur Bikes, Caernarfon (01286) 672622 anturwaunfawr.org

Wider area cycle map: North Wales

Lôn Eifion

RIDE 22
4 miles | **8** | **Start:** Caernarfon

LÔN LAS MENAI

This short and gentle ride through Gwynedd takes in the glittering water of the Menai Strait and offers marvellous views of the Isle of Anglesey.

Caernarfon's cobbled streets and the arched entrance in the medieval town walls are a wonderful start before you roll into Victoria Dock, home to the award-winning Galeri Caernarfon arts venue on the waterfront.

Further along the trail there are benches surrounded by vertical slabs of jagged local slate, which make an ideal raised spot for looking over the tidal strait. The water here may be speckled with dinghies, powerboats and kayaks from the nearby Plas Menai National Outdoor Centre, which can be reached by following a short stretch of road just after the ride's halfway point.

Water views in the ride's first half are replaced by shady Gwynedd woodland in the second half, before you join the road for a short descent into the little village of Y Felinheli, a former shipping harbour for slate. The waterfront benches on Beach Road are a peaceful place to end whilst watching the boats bob across the Menai Strait.

Caernarfon Castle

RIDE 22

Finish: Y Felinheli

Train station: Nearest is Bangor

Grade: Easy

Terrain, gradients and access: Mostly flat tarmac path with some road crossings and short, quiet on-road sections at Caernarfon and Y Felinheli.

Loops, links and longer rides: From Y Felinheli, follow NCN 8 Lôn Las Cymru north for four miles along a mix of on-road and traffic-free route to the attractive Menai Suspension Bridge leading over to Anglesey. Or, close to Y Felinheli pick up signs for Lôn Adda that leads into the centre of Bangor and Bangor train station. NCN 8 Lôn Eifion (**Ride 21**).

Stay: Totters Independent Hostel, Caernarfon (01286) 672963 **totters.co.uk**

Eat and drink: Cafés on The Maes next to Caernarfon Castle spill out into the square in summer and nearby Palas Caffi is renowned for ice cream. Café Bar in Galeri Caernarfon uses local produce, and has excellent views of Victoria Dock. At Y Felinheli, Garddfon Inn has a little waterfront beer garden but Swellies Café is favoured for food.

Cycle hire: Beics Antur Bikes, Caernarfon (01286) 672622 **anturwaunfawr.org**

Wider area cycle map: North Wales

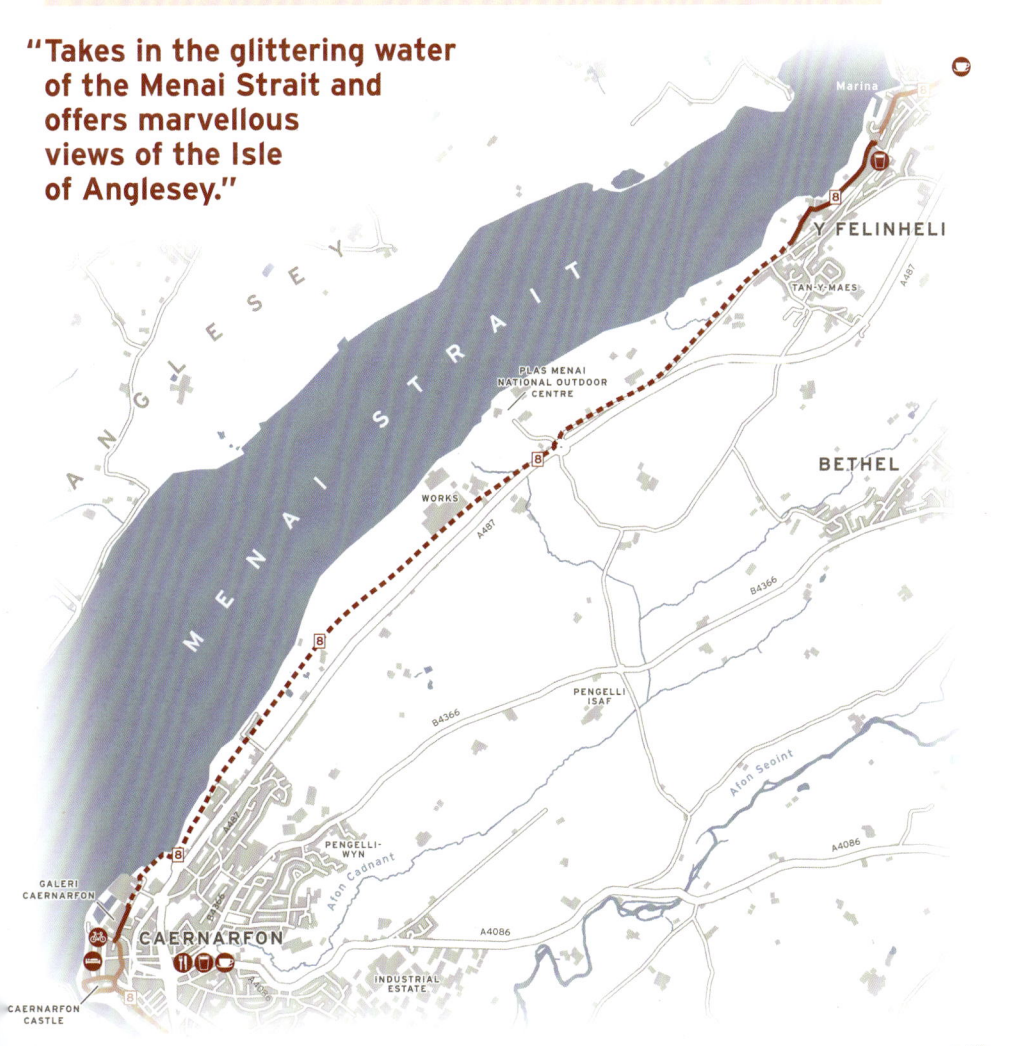

"Takes in the glittering water of the Menai Strait and offers marvellous views of the Isle of Anglesey."

RIDE 23
11 miles | 82 5 | **Start:** Porth Penrhyn, Bangor

LÔN LAS OGWEN

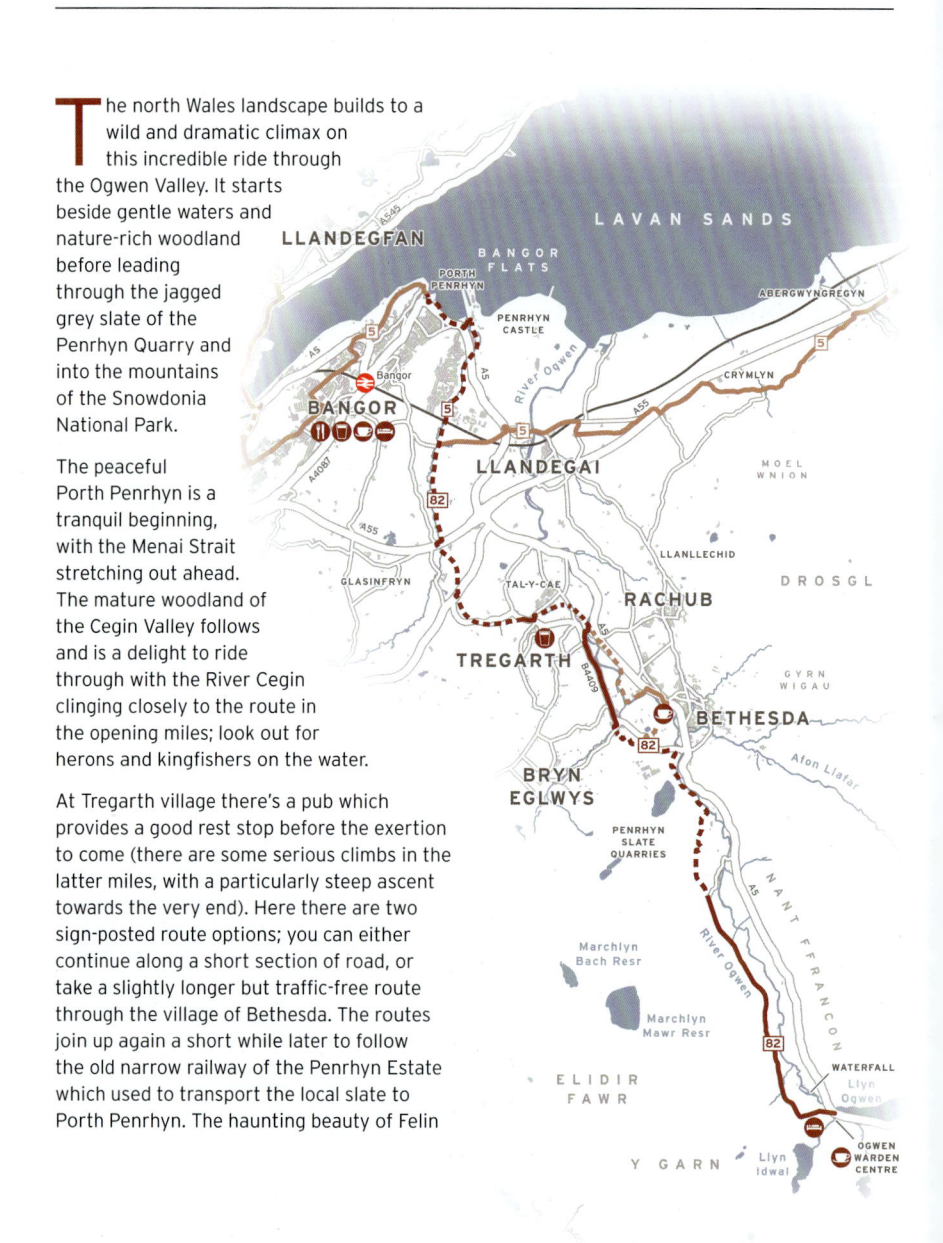

The north Wales landscape builds to a wild and dramatic climax on this incredible ride through the Ogwen Valley. It starts beside gentle waters and nature-rich woodland before leading through the jagged grey slate of the Penrhyn Quarry and into the mountains of the Snowdonia National Park.

The peaceful Porth Penrhyn is a tranquil beginning, with the Menai Strait stretching out ahead. The mature woodland of the Cegin Valley follows and is a delight to ride through with the River Cegin clinging closely to the route in the opening miles; look out for herons and kingfishers on the water.

At Tregarth village there's a pub which provides a good rest stop before the exertion to come (there are some serious climbs in the latter miles, with a particularly steep ascent towards the very end). Here there are two sign-posted route options; you can either continue along a short section of road, or take a slightly longer but traffic-free route through the village of Bethesda. The routes join up again a short while later to follow the old narrow railway of the Penrhyn Estate which used to transport the local slate to Porth Penrhyn. The haunting beauty of Felin

Finish: Ogwen Warden Centre, Llyn Ogwen

RIDE 23

Train stations: Bangor or Betws-y-Coed
Grade: Challenging
Terrain, gradients and access: Stony and uneven track, steep in parts. On-road sections at Tregarth and between Bethesda and Llyn Ogwen.
Loops, links and longer rides: NCN 5 North Wales Coast Route (**Ride 25**) NCN 8 Lôn Las Menai (**Ride 22**). NCN 8 Lôn Las Cymru is a long-distance route across Wales from Holyhead to Chepstow or Cardiff.

Stay: YHA Idwal, an eco-friendly hostel and campsite 0345 371 9744 yha.org.uk
Eat and drink: Try the Pant Yr Ardd pub in Tregarth in the route's first half, Caffi Seren at Bethesda or the café at Ogwen Warden Centre at the end.
Cycle hire: Nearest is Llanberis Bike Hire, Llanberis (01286) 872787 llanberisbikehire.co.uk
Wider area cycle map: North Wales

"Beside gentle waters and nature-rich woodland..."

Llyn Ogwen

Fawr, a complex of slate buildings that served the Penrhyn Quarry for 150 years, is lovely to ride through before climbing around the foothills of the austere grey quarry itself.

Ride along the banks of the River Ogwen, thunderous after heavy rain and a popular whitewater river among canoeists and kayakers, before joining a quiet road to cycle the final two and a half miles amid breathtaking views of the Carneddau and Glyderau mountain ranges. End at the edges of Llyn Ogwen beneath the craggy slopes of Tryfan, one of Snowdonia's most challenging peaks, where Sir Edmund Hilary and team trained for their Everest ascent. Keep an eye out for wild mountain goats nearby and seek out Rhaeadr Ogwen, beautiful gushing waterfalls close to Ogwen Warden Centre.

RIDE 24 | 566 | **Start:** Malltraeth

8 miles a further mile in either direction at the finish leads along the reservoir

LÔN LAS CEFNI

The Isle of Anglesey, or Ynys Môn in Welsh, is at the tip of north Wales and is a beautifully unspoilt and uncrowded environment in which to cycle. This ride follows the River Cefni to Llyn Cefni, a secluded reservoir at the heart of the island, with the forbidding grey shapes of the Snowdonia Mountains on the mainland visible along the way. It's worth exploring the miles of unbroken sand that form Llanddwyn Beach near the route's start, which is backed by dunes and the coastal pine plantation of Newborough Forest. This is a perfectly romantic setting as Llanddwyn Island here is linked to the legend of St Dwynwen, the Welsh patron saint of lovers.

From the village of Malltraeth follow almost two miles of very quiet road before joining the traffic-free trail at Pont Marquis. It's a wonderfully remote experience riding beside the long, straight line of the river past the RSPB's Malltraeth Marsh nature reserve. Look out for herons sitting in the small pools or even rare bitterns concealed among the reeds.

At the town of Llangefni you'll reach the pretty St Cyngar church and The Dingle Local Nature Reserve (LNR), one of the highlights of the ride. This ancient woodland could be straight from a storybook and is thick with oak, ash, wild cherry and sycamore trees with artful timber sculptures marking the entrance. The trail undulates through the wooded valley on its way to the Llyn and you might want to stop and explore Coed Plas just behind the church. This is the oldest part of the woodland and is planted with sweet chestnut, beech and scots pine trees, with a carpet of buttery yellow wild daffodils across the forest floor in spring. Cross the river on wooden boardwalks, looking out for kingfishers along the way, before reaching the shores of Llyn Cefni. Here there are paths along the water to the left or right; there are great views of the reservoir along the path to the left or a nice picnic spot at the end of the trail to the right.

Cefni Reservoir

Finish: Llyn Cefni

RIDE 24

Train station: Bodorgan

Grade: Easy

Terrain, gradients and access: Tarmac path and stony trail. Flat from Malltraeth village but undulating throughout The Dingle. A quiet, on-road section leads from Malltraeth to Pont Marquis with some road crossings at Llangefni.

Loops, links and longer rides: From Llyn Cefni join the on-road NCN 566 to Llanerchymedd and follow the Copper Trail around the northern part of the island. NCN 8 Lôn Las Cymru, a long-distance route across Wales, starts from Holyhead on Anglesey and leads all the way to Chepstow or Cardiff on a mix of on-road and traffic-free route.

Stay: Pen-y-Bont Farm campsite and holiday cottage, Bodorgan (01407) 840209 pen-y-bontfarm.co.uk

Eat and drink: Riverside Café in Malltraeth is close to the route's start. Llangefni, in the route's second half, has many eateries including Mona House Coffee Shop and the café at Oriel Ynys Môn, Anglesey's Centre for Art and History.

Cycle hire: Cybi Bikes, Anglesey 07717 453806 cybibikes.co.uk or Cycle Wales in Llangefni cyclewales.net

Wider area cycle map: North Wales

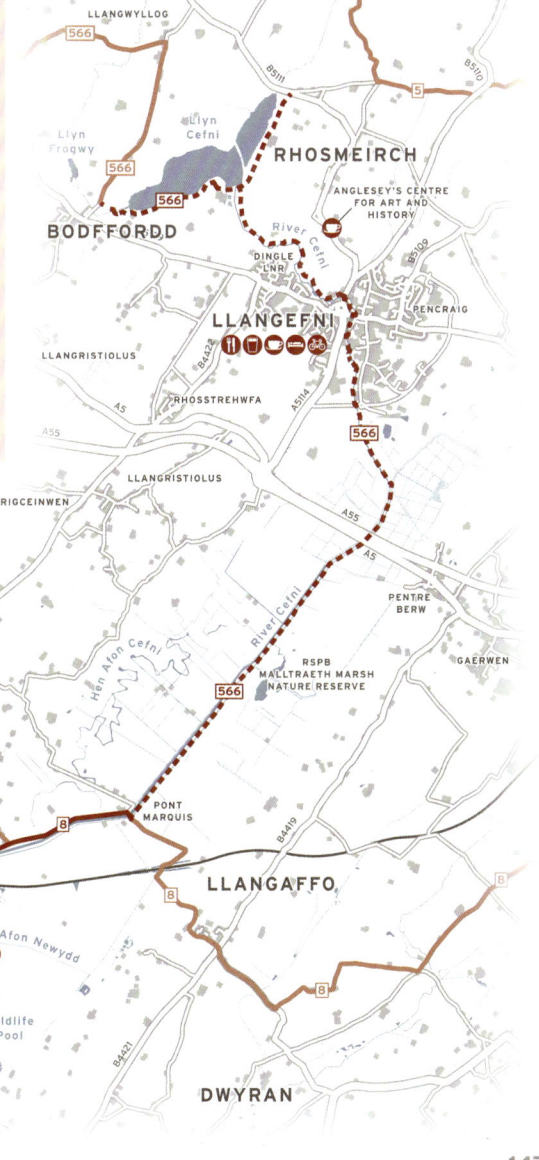

147

RIDE 25 — 16 miles — Start: Prestatyn train station

NORTH WALES COAST CYCLE ROUTE

This ride through Denbighshire and Conwy along the Wales Coast Path is entirely faithful to the coastline, resulting in exceptional sea views from start to finish against a mountainous backdrop of the Snowdonia National park.

It's a short on-road ride from Prestatyn train station to reach the seafront and join the traffic-free route along the gentle curve of the land. Dunes tumble away to the left, whilst waves lap at the sand and shingle to the right. Wonderful north Wales beaches feature throughout the ride, including miles of family-friendly golden sands between Prestatyn and Rhyl, the rare habitat of the shingly Pensarn beach and Honeycomb Reef at Llanddulas.

Rhyl is a classic bucket-and-spade seaside resort where you'll cross the harbour on the sleek Pont y Ddraig or Dragon's Bridge, a walking and cycling link to Kinmel Bay that has transformed the area. Look inland at around the halfway point to see the fairytale turrets of Gwrych Castle near Abergele peeping out from the surrounding woodland.

At Colwyn Bay there are great views across the water from the rooftop viewing area of the contemporary Porth Eirias Watersports Centre and a very short traffic-free link leads into Colwyn Bay town centre. Continue along the promenade to reach the pretty seaside resort of Rhos-on-Sea and end at the tourist information point. The tiny St Trillo's chapel is near here, worth a visit as it is believed to be the UK's smallest chapel.

Colwyn Bay

Finish: Rhos-on-Sea Tourist Information Point

RIDE 25

Train stations: Prestatyn, Rhyl, Abergele & Pensarn and Colwyn Bay

Grade: Moderate

Terrain, gradients and access: Flat, wide concrete promenade with a couple of very short ascents and descents around Llanddulas. Short, quiet on-road section from Prestatyn train station. Be prepared for a headwind when riding westwards.

Loops, links and longer rides: NCN 5 runs from Chester to Holyhead. From Rhos-on-Sea a mostly traffic-free ride west leads to Llandudno, Conwy and Penmaenmawr. From Prestatyn follow a local route to Talacre and the wild Gronant Dunes, or head on-road along NCN 5 to Flint, followed by a mostly traffic-free path to Connah's Quay and over the England/Wales border to Chester.

Stay: Beaches Hotel, Prestatyn (01745) 853072 thebeacheshotel.com or Whitehall Guest House, Rhos-on-Sea (01492) 547296 whitehall-hotel.co.uk

Eat and drink: Beach Hut café and bar at the Nova Complex with Harbour Hub Café and other seafront kiosks at Rhyl, as well as Pantri Bach shop and café at Abergele. Rhos-on-Sea has many cafés and kiosks including the Coast café and gift shop near the route's end.

Cycle hire: The Bike Hub, Rhyl (01745) 339758 bikehubrhyl.uk

Wider area cycle map: North Wales

"The Wales Coast Path is entirely faithful to the coastline, resulting in exceptional sea views from start to finish..."

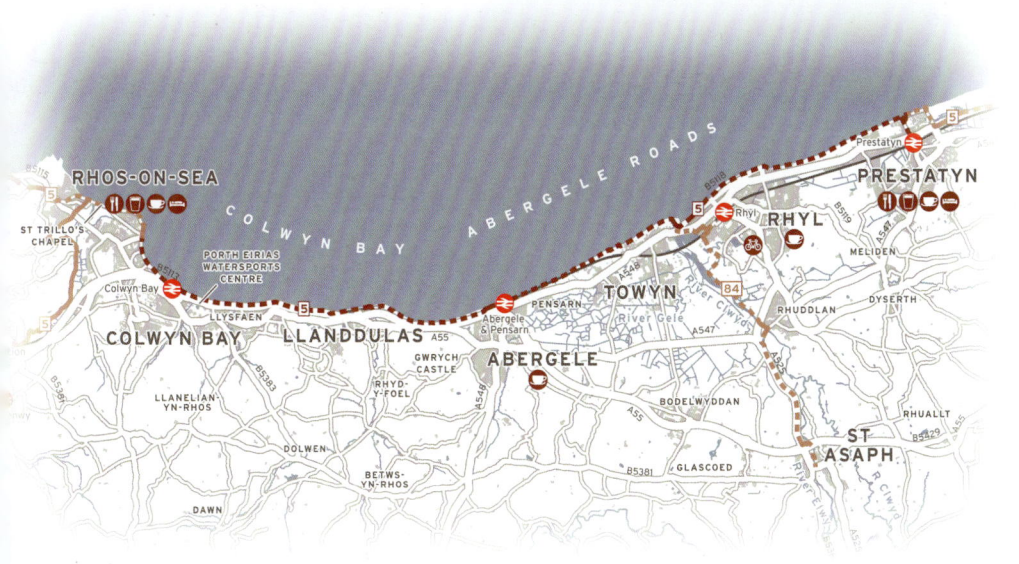

Rhyl Promenade

149

MIDLANDS

This collection of rides across the heart of the country encapsulates some of England's most diverse and distinguished architecture, history and landscapes.

The Stratford Greenway is one of the most quintessentially English experiences of this entire guide, taking in rural Warwickshire and the historic, half-timbered cottages of Shakespeare Country. By contrast, there's a distinctly cosmopolitan edge to the towpath rides across the buzzy urban core of Birmingham, the Venice of the Midlands with its mile upon mile of city centre canals.

A ride through Leicester spans thousands of years of evolution in just a few miles, leading from the bulbous rocket tower at the National Space Centre to the woolly mammoth sculpture in Watermead Park, an untamed wetland where ice age remains have been unearthed. The scenic trail around the shores of Rutland Water offers the chance to explore England's smallest county, but it's the Silkin Way in Shropshire that makes for a truly memorable ride. This glorious woodland descent through the Ironbridge Gorge ends with a triumphant crossing of the River Severn on the world's first ever iron bridge.

In the north of the region, the rugged limestone landscape of the Peak District dominates, and two former railway routes within the National Park are featured here; Tissington Trail takes you beside the mouth of the cavernous Dovedale ravine, but it's the Monsal Trail that families flock to. The dim, mysterious depths of six long railway tunnels on this gentle ride are guaranteed to ignite a cycling passion among younger riders, and are a perfect contrast to the area's dramatic limestone cliffs and deep green Derbyshire Dales. If just one route can sum up the masterful diversity of the Midlands, it's this one.

Ironbridge with poppies

Routes overview

- **01** Stratford Greenway (4.5 miles)
- **02** The Brampton Valley Way (14.5 miles)
- **03** Grand Union Canal (Market Harborough Arm) (6 miles)
- **04** Rea Valley Cycle Route (6 miles)
- **05** Birmingham to Sandwell Valley (7 miles)
- **06** Silkin Way (7 miles)
- **07** Rutland Water (15.5 miles)
- **08** Leicester to Watermead Park (5 miles)
- **09** Derby Canal & The Cloud Trail (13 miles)
- **10** Mickleover Trail (6 miles)
- **11** Nutbrook Trail (10.5 miles)
- **12** Biddulph Valley Way (12 miles)
- **13** Tissington Trail (13.5 miles)
- **14** Monsal Trail (9 miles)
- **15** Clumber Park & Sherwood Forest (26 miles)
- **16** Water Rail Way (15.5 miles)
- **17** Longdendale Trail (13 miles)

— Featured ride
— National Cycle Network (traffic-free and on-road)

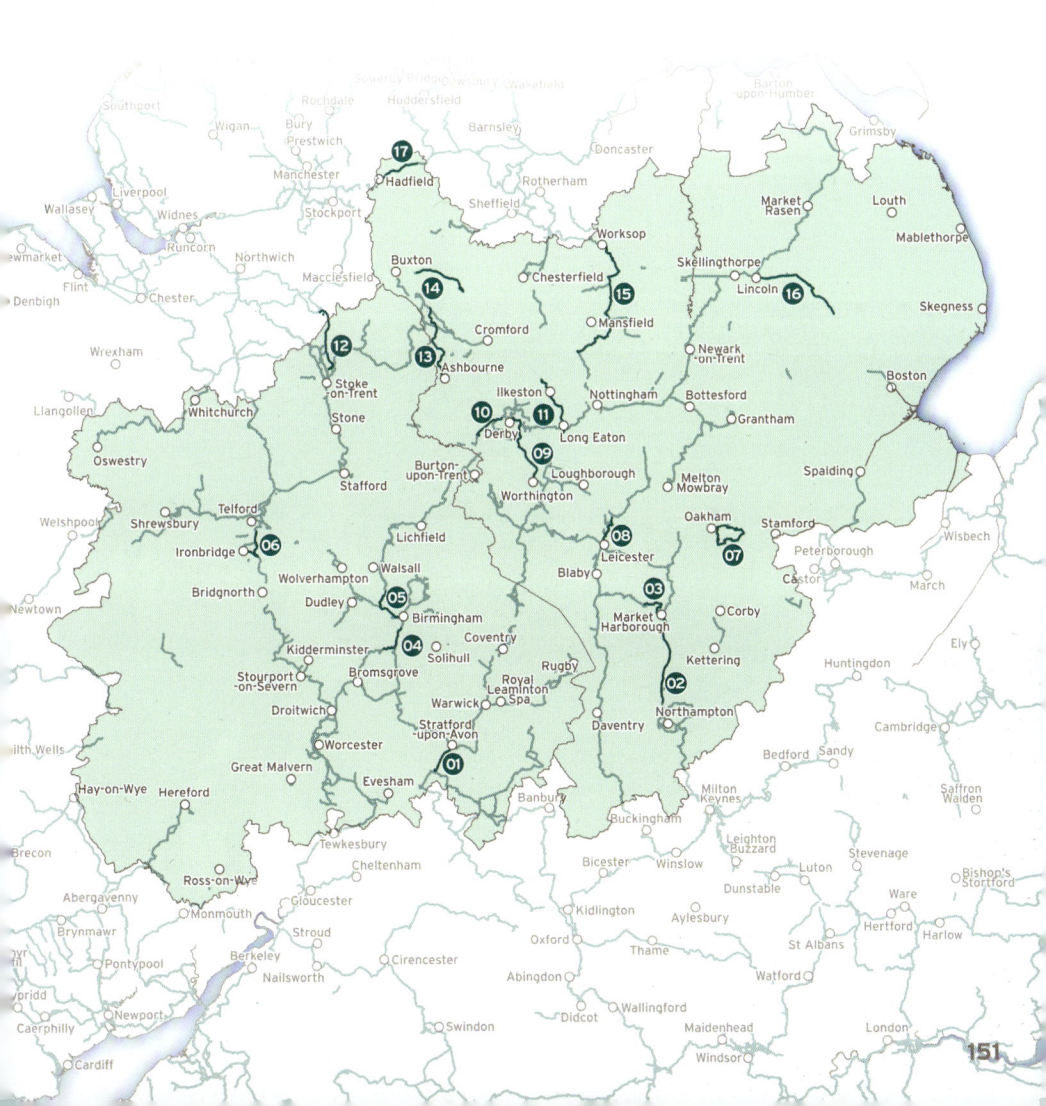

RIDE 01
4.5 miles

Start: Seven Meadows car park, Stratford-upon-Avon

STRATFORD GREENWAY

This short ride manages to capture the essence of Olde England, from the timber-fronted Tudor buildings at Stratford-upon-Avon, the birthplace of Shakespeare, to the chocolate box villages of romantically rural Warwickshire.

To visit the beautiful town centre, take a short, on-road ride along NCN 41 from Seven Meadows Road near the car park at the start of the greenway. Alternatively, simply join the trail and head towards Stratford Racecourse. You'll cross the Avon on the steel Stannals Bridge, before crossing the River Stour and following a long, straight route into deep and peaceful countryside.

Milcote picnic area is a great halfway stop, with a railway carriage café on the trackside and benches offering mellow views over the surrounding meadows and farmland. Or, take a short, on-road detour into Welford-on-Avon, a pretty village of thatched cottages tucked into a loop of the River Avon, where the lovely St Peter's church and 17th Century Bell Inn are worth a visit.

Leave the greenway at Long Marston and follow a rugged trail to join the short, quiet road into the little village centre. The country pub with its skittles alley is a cosy and traditional ending that entirely befits the route.

Thatched houses and St Peter's church in Welford-on-Avon

Finish: Long Marston

RIDE 01

Train station: Stratford-upon-Avon

Grade: Easy

Terrain, gradients and access: Flat, fine gravel trail with some narrow gates and road crossings. A short, on-road section at Long Marston.

Loops, links and longer rides: From Stratford-upon-Avon, follow NCN 5 for around three and a half miles on a traffic-free route along the canal towpath to Wilmcote and Mary Arden's Farm, one of the Shakespeare Birthplace Trust properties (closed in winter).

Stay: YHA Stratford, 0345 371 9661 **yha.org.uk**

Eat and drink: HR Coffee Bar, The Garrick Inn and The Dirty Duck are all popular in Stratford-upon-Avon. Carriages Café can be found on the route at Stratford Racecourse and at Milcote picnic area, or try The Bell Inn at Welford-on-Avon. The Mason's Arms country pub is at the route's end at Long Marston.

Cycle hire: Stratford Bike Hire, 07711 776340 **stratfordbikehire.com**

Wider area cycle map: Warwickshire & The South Midlands

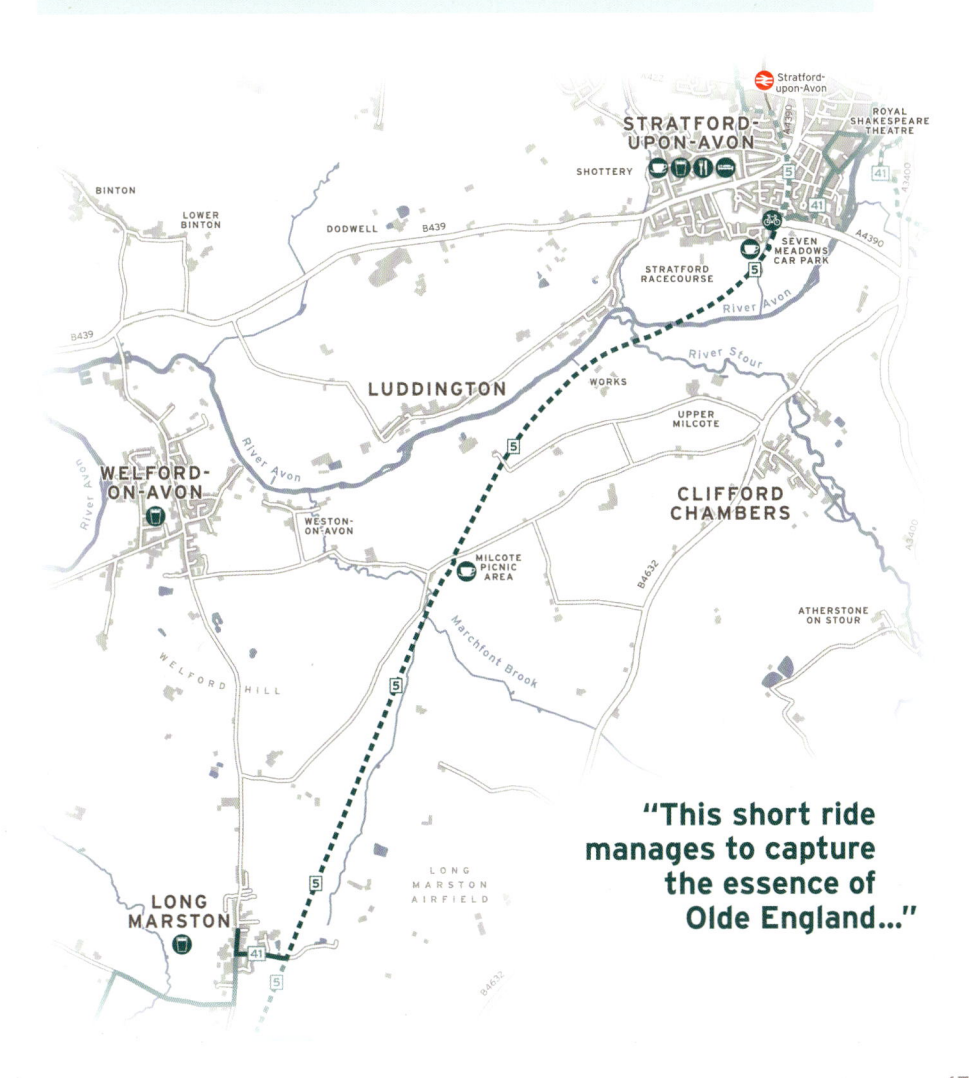

"This short ride manages to capture the essence of Olde England..."

153

RIDE 02
14.5 miles

Start: Windhover pub, Northampton

THE BRAMPTON VALLEY WAY

This long, former railway path leads through the attractive rural landscape of Northamptonshire and Leicestershire. There are two long, dark railway tunnels that add a touch of adventure along the way, and some excellent links to the area's fine country houses and parks.

Start at The Windhover pub near Northampton and immediately enter a rich pastoral landscape with wide open views across the fields. In the opening miles you'll link up with Northampton & Lamport heritage steam railway, and will pass its carriages on the track at Pitsford & Brampton Station where the volunteer-run shop and café make a nice early stop. Apple trees line the path around here, and little windfall fruits squelch under wheel during late summer as you ride onwards, alternating between wide open countryside and leafy, sheltered cuttings.

At Merry Tom Crossing there's a good opportunity to deviate from the railway path by following the link route to Brixworth village or Brixworth Country Park, where a seven-mile, traffic-free loop around the shores of Pitsford Reservoir is a fun distraction. Or, simply stay on the trail to reach the pleasant picnic spot at Spratton Crossing, followed by the bulrushes and meadows of Spring Marsh, where there are benches for looking back towards Brixworth and its handsome Romanesque church. In fact, there are benches dotted all along the route, often with intricate mosaic artworks alongside them, and also a series of excellent picnic spots at the former stations of the railway line; one of the best is at Draughton Crossing around the halfway point of the ride.

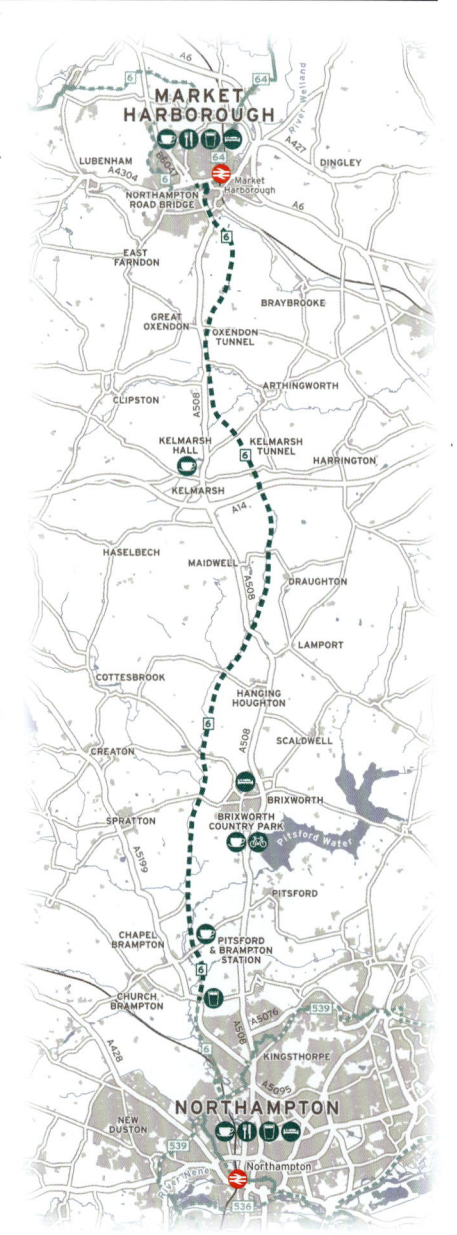

154

Finish: Britannia Walk, Market Harborough

RIDE 02

Train stations: Northampton and Market Harborough

Grade: Moderate

Terrain, gradients and access: Fine gravel track and stony trail, with some gates and road crossings. Steadily ascending in the first half and descending in the second. Take particular care through Kelmarsh Tunnel and Oxendon Tunnel; they are both unlit and more than 400 metres in length, so use very good lights and ride slowly or dismount and walk carefully through. There are longer on-road routes around both tunnels.

Loops, links and longer rides: A seven-mile, traffic-free circuit of Pitsford Water at Brixworth Country Park is close to the route. NCN 6 Grand Union Canal (**Ride 03**).

Stay: The Coach and Horses, Brixworth (01604) 880329 **coachandhorsesbrixworth.co.uk**

Eat and drink: The Windhover pub is at the start in Northampton, or try Platform 3 Buffet at Pitsford & Brampton Station, The Willow Tree café at Brixworth Country Park or Kelmarsh Hall Tea Room. In Market Harborough, Milo's Café, Ascough's and Veneto restaurant are all popular.

Cycle hire: Rutland Cycling, Brixworth Country Park (01604) 881777 **rutlandcycling.com**

Wider area cycle map: East Midlands

"Enter a rich pastoral landscape with wide open views across the fields."

Brampton Valley Way

With around five miles to go, reach the dark opening of Kelmarsh Tunnel. There is a longer, on-road route that leads around it, and this is a particularly rewarding detour as it passes the delightful 18th Century Kelmarsh Hall and Gardens. Alternatively, take a deep breath and ride into the dark. There are 480 metres of unlit tunnel so it's a bit of an adventure, and the darkness closes in from the moment you enter, which can be both exhilarating and unsettling. It's advisable to have excellent bike lights and ride very slowly through, before popping out at the other side for lovely open views across the fields.

It's only a few miles of open-air riding before Oxendon Tunnel appears. At 418 metres long it's a shade shorter than Kelmarsh, but still needs nerve, bright lights and some extra care. Once through, it's a steady descent all the way to the outskirts of Market Harborough, passing allotments and parks on the edges of the town, before riding into the centre and ending at Britannia Walk.

RIDE 03
6 miles

Start: Union Wharf, Market Harborough

GRAND UNION CANAL

(MARKET HARBOROUGH ARM)

Following the wriggling Market Harborough Arm of the Grand Union Canal, this route passes through lovely rural Leicestershire along the meandering course of the waterway. It reaches a superb climax at the famous Foxton lock flight, where the canal is raised dramatically up the hillside.

Start at Union Wharf in Market Harborough, where the route immediately becomes a classic towpath ride of toyshop-coloured barges, snoozing swans and droopy willow trees trailing along the water's surface. After just a mile and a half, at Kosi Korna, take the short and steep climb over the bridge to follow the opposite canal bank for the remainder of the ride.

Narrow boats occasionally chug cheerily past, but otherwise it's an undisturbed ride through the pastoral Leicestershire landscape along a wild and nature-rich trail. In late summer the elderberry and blackberry bushes beside the route are thick with fruit and the brown sausage-like tops of bulrushes tower almost head-high in places.

Pass under a series of attractive red brick humpback bridges on the way to Foxton, where you'll continue along the towpath rather than following NCN 6 which digresses onto the road here. In the final half-mile the towpath becomes alive with walkers, and the popular waterside gardens of the cafés and inns at Foxton Locks come into view.

Dismount and push over the steep and cobbled Rainbow Bridge to visit the 10 magnificent Foxton locks, now more than 200 years old. The grassy banks alongside the locks are perfect for a picnic whilst watching boats make the steady journey upwards – it can take each vessel around 45 minutes to traverse all the locks – or take a walk to the top lock for pretty views and to visit the little Foxton Canal Museum.

Bridge in Market Harborough

Finish: Foxton Locks

RIDE 03

Train station: Market Harborough
Grade: Easy
Terrain, gradients and access: Flat, stony towpath with several gates. Cyclists are asked to dismount around the Union Wharf area at the start. Take care passing under the low bridges that span the canal.
Loops, links and longer rides: Brixworth Country Park can be found a few miles south of Market Harborough and there's a seven-mile, traffic-free route around the shores of Pitsford Reservoir within the park. NCN 6 Brampton Valley Way (**Ride 02**).

Stay: The Three Swans Hotel, Market Harborough (01858) 466644 threeswans.co.uk
Eat and drink: Ascough's in Market Harborough is highly regarded, as is Milo's café. Welland Park near the route's start has a café or try The Waterfront Restaurant and Bar at Union Wharf. The Black Horse pub and restaurant is at Foxton, or Bridge 61, Foxton Locks Inn, The Old Boathouse and Top Lock Café are all at Foxton Locks.
Cycle hire: Rutland Cycling, Brixworth Country Park (01604) 881577 rutlandcycling.com
Wider area cycle map: East Midlands

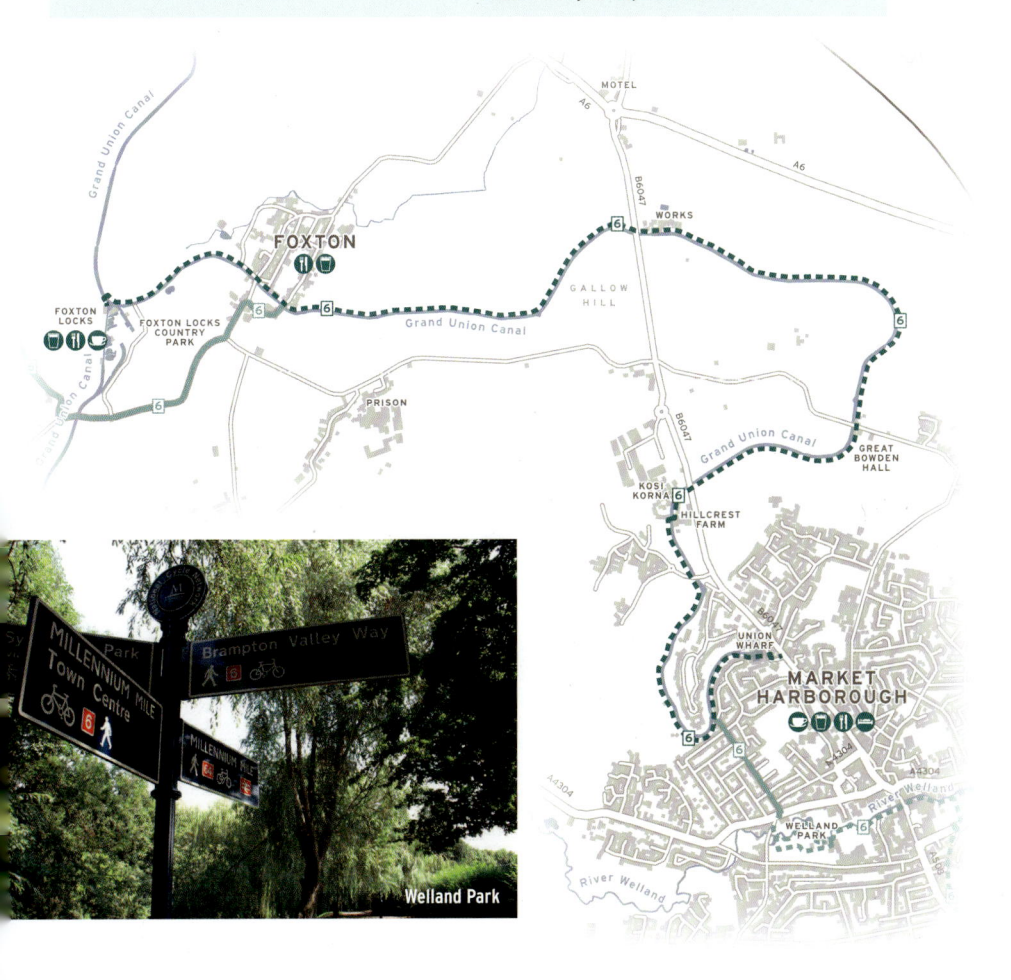

Welland Park

157

RIDE 04
6 miles

Start: Cannon Hill Park, Birmingham

REA VALLEY CYCLE ROUTE

This ride through the Rea Valley passes through some of Birmingham's finest parks, and has an irresistibly sweet surprise in the middle. Cannon Hill Park, to the south of the city, is a very attractive beginning. Start at its Edgbaston Road entrance and ride right across the centre, passing the colourful gardens, tearoom and bandstand, all completely charming. mac (formerly Midlands Arts Centre) is here, too, where you can see, hear and create your own art.

From here, join up with the little River Rea, where the surrounding thick greenery is entirely untamed compared with the neatly groomed park. Ride through the open space of Pebble Mill playing fields and the pleasant greenery of Hazelwell Park at Stirchley. Here, you'll pass the site of Hazelwell Mill, a 17th Century mill that ground corn for the manor and was just one of the many watermills that could once be found along the hard working River Rea.

At around the halfway point of the ride, join the towpath of the Worcester & Birmingham Canal at Lifford. This is where you have the option to take a one-mile detour that children will love. Simply turn right on the towpath and follow it to Bournville, home to Cadbury World, a real-life version of Willy Wonka's chocolate factory. Alternatively, stick to the Rea Valley route and turn left along the towpath, following it for just half a mile to Kings Norton Junction.

At the junction, the brief flirtation with the canal is over, and you'll leave it behind to descend into the vast green space of Kings Norton Park, where the giant spire of St Nicolas' church is beautifully framed by the trees. This is another of Birmingham's classic and popular parks, with the River Rea running peacefully along its edge and picnic benches beneath colossal conifer trees. It's a good place to end the ride before heading back into Birmingham. However, it would be a shame not to continue just a little further to reach the Wychall Meadows, part of Kings Norton Local Nature Reserve. This is a wonderfully wild retreat, and the big open water of the reservoir is a prime spot to look for herons, ducks and moorhens.

In the final mile, leave the nature reserve and follow the River Rea to Northfield, where it's just a short, on-road ride to the train station.

Cannon Hill Park, Birmingham

RIDE 04

Finish: Northfield train station

Train stations: Five Ways and Northfield

Grade: Easy

Terrain, gradients and access: Tarmac path and fine gravel track. Some road crossings and short, on-road sections at Pebble Mill, Lifford and Northfield.

Loops, links and longer rides: From Cannon Hill Park it's a two-mile, mostly on-road ride along NCN 5 into Birmingham city centre. From Northfield, the Rea Valley route can be followed for a further four miles, mostly on-road, to Waseley Country Park. NCN 5 Birmingham to Sandwell Valley (**Ride 05**).

Stay: Woodbrooke B&B, Birmingham (0121) 472 5171 woodbrooke.org.uk

Eat and drink: Try Garden Tea Rooms or Bridges Café at the mac in Cannon Hill Park, Cadbury World Café at Bournville, or Wild Bean café near Kings Norton Park.

Cycle hire: On Your Bike, Birmingham (0121) 666 6933 onyourbike.com or Brompton Dock outside Birmingham Moor Street train station bromptonbikehire.com

Wider area cycle map: Shropshire, Staffordshire & The Black Country

"An irresistibly sweet surprise in the middle."

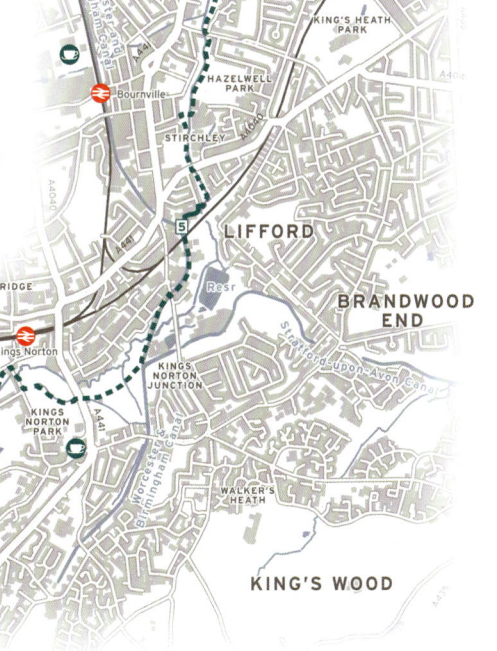

159

RIDE 05 — 7 miles

Start: Centenary Square, Birmingham

BIRMINGHAM
TO
SANDWELL VALLEY

'The Golden Boys' statue in Birmingham's Centenary Square

This ride starts in one of Britain's biggest and busiest cities, yet is surprisingly scenic and peaceful as it follows the canal through the Black Country into Sandwell Valley Country Park. Centenary Square is a vibrant start, with the vast Symphony Hall and unusual tiered Library of Birmingham at its edges and 'The Golden Boys' glinting in the sunlight across the road, a gilded statue of three Industrial Revolution pioneers.

Leave the square to join the canal towpath at Tindal Bridge, following the water to Old Turn Junction where two canals meet. It's often said that Birmingham has more miles of canal than Venice, and it certainly appears that way among the basins, wharves and junctions of the waterways that criss-cross the city centre. You'll follow the Birmingham Canal Main Line from here, with a backdrop of red brick buildings and towering black chimneys making a stark contrast to the flat and placid water.

Within just a mile, busy central Birmingham is left behind and the towpath becomes fringed with green rushes and blackberry bushes. Cross the water at Smethwick Junction. This is where the canal splits in two and both waterways run side by side through the Galton Valley, but you'll stick to the banks of the lower New Main Line and will pass the attractive brick Smethwick Pumping Station.

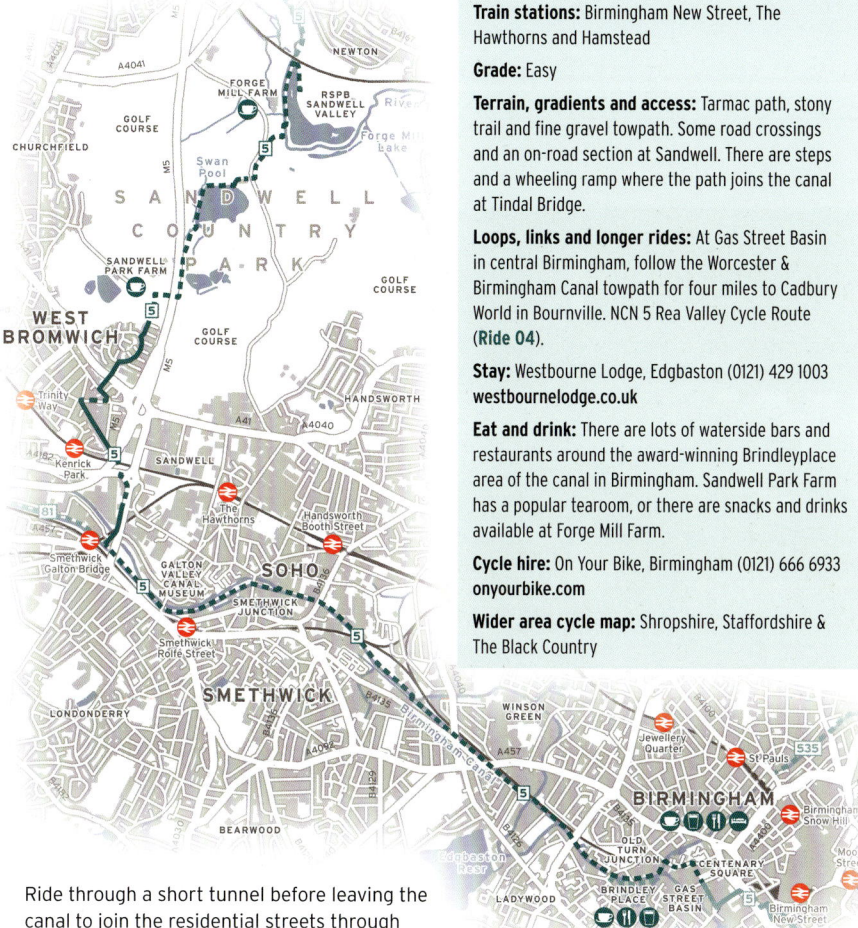

Finish: Sandwell Valley Country Park

RIDE 05

Train stations: Birmingham New Street, The Hawthorns and Hamstead

Grade: Easy

Terrain, gradients and access: Tarmac path, stony trail and fine gravel towpath. Some road crossings and an on-road section at Sandwell. There are steps and a wheeling ramp where the path joins the canal at Tindal Bridge.

Loops, links and longer rides: At Gas Street Basin in central Birmingham, follow the Worcester & Birmingham Canal towpath for four miles to Cadbury World in Bournville. NCN 5 Rea Valley Cycle Route (**Ride 04**).

Stay: Westbourne Lodge, Edgbaston (0121) 429 1003 westbournelodge.co.uk

Eat and drink: There are lots of waterside bars and restaurants around the award-winning Brindleyplace area of the canal in Birmingham. Sandwell Park Farm has a popular tearoom, or there are snacks and drinks available at Forge Mill Farm.

Cycle hire: On Your Bike, Birmingham (0121) 666 6933 onyourbike.com

Wider area cycle map: Shropshire, Staffordshire & The Black Country

Ride through a short tunnel before leaving the canal to join the residential streets through Sandwell and reach the country park.

Sandwell Park Farm is one of two working farms with visitor centres in the country park and is well-positioned near the entrance. It's worth pausing here to meet the animals or explore the Victorian kitchen garden. Shortly afterwards, the M5 slices through the park, but it is only a brief interruption and is quickly forgotten on the pleasant descent that leads into the tranquil heart of the park. Swan Pool is a good spot to picnic whilst watching the wildlife, and from here it's a lovely woodland descent to Forge Mill Lake and Forge Mill Farm.

The farm visitor centre is a nice place to end, or better still, ride along the banks of the River Tame and follow the signs for RSPB Sandwell Valley. The nature reserve is less than a mile away from the farm, with hides offering great views of the wading birds and wildfowl on the beautiful open water of the lake.

RIDE 06
7 miles

Start: Telford Bike Hub at Telford Town Park

SILKIN WAY

Ironbridge Village

Ironbridge's status as the birthplace of the Industrial Revolution doesn't do justice to the tremendous natural beauty that this World Heritage Site also offers. This gentle ride through Ironbridge Gorge takes in Shropshire's industrial past and scenic present, but the real highlight is the enchanting market town of Ironbridge climbing the wooded hillside at the route's end and giving a tantalising glimpse into times gone by.

Telford Town Park at the route's start is everything a town park should be, a hive of activity and play, with gardens, pools, historical ruins and wildlife. From here, it's a pleasant descent through thick and dreamy woodland for much of the way, with nature and industry neatly intertwined throughout.

Reach the edges of Hinkshay Meadow in the opening miles, the best place in the park for spotting butterflies, before passing the old platform of Dawley & Stirchley Station, a relic from the days when this route was a working railway line. After just three miles, you'll enter Ironbridge World Heritage Site and pass the gates of Blists Hill Victorian Town, one of ten Ironbridge Gorge museums. It's worth pausing here to get a taste of life as it was more than 100 years ago.

Finish: Ironbridge

Train station: Telford Central

Grade: Easy

Terrain, gradients and access: Tarmac path, fine gravel track and stony trail. A steady descent that levels off in the final miles, with just a couple of very short, steep climbs. Some road crossings and quiet, on-road sections at Coalport and Jackfield.

Loops, links and longer rides: From Telford continue on NCN 81 along a mostly on-road route to Shrewsbury.

Stay: Holiday Inn, Telford (01952) 527000 ihg.com

Eat and drink: Telford Town Park at the start has a snack bar, or there are refreshments at Blists Hill Victorian Town near the halfway point. The Woodbridge Inn at Coalport, in the ride's second half, occupies a lovely riverside spot, or try Tile Press Café in the Maws craft centre, The Boat Inn and The Black Swan all at Jackfield. Ironbridge has many eateries; popular places include Darby's 1779 café, Eley's of Ironbridge pork pies, The White Hart, The Swan or The Malthouse. For something sweet, visit Vanilla Ice or Queenies Cupcakery.

Cycle hire: Shropshire Raft Tours, Ironbridge (01952) 427150 shropshirerafttours.co.uk

Wider area cycle map: Shropshire, Staffordshire & The Black Country

At Coalport, the picnic benches beneath a canopy of trees overlooking the River Severn make a peaceful place to rest, before crossing the river on the pretty Coalport Bridge. Here, you'll join the Severn Valley Way and enter the thick woodland of the gorge. Enchanting valley views are visible through the trees in the final miles, and at Jackfield the distinctive spire of St Mary's church looms into sight, followed by the elegant plum-coloured building of Jackfield Tile Museum, another great spot for locking up and exploring.

Less than a mile later, finish the ride in momentous style by crossing over the world's first ever iron bridge. The pretty town here seems suspended in time, with St Luke's church taking centre spot on the hillside and the other handsome, historic buildings of the town clustered around it. It's just a short, on-road descent beside the river from here to The Museum of the Gorge, where the fascinating history of Ironbridge is revealed.

RIDE 07
15.5 miles

Start and finish: Giant bike shop, Normanton car park

RUTLAND WATER

Rutland's motto, 'Much in little', suits both the diminutive county itself and this superb cycle route around its heart. The best of the area's storybook villages, rolling countryside, rare wildlife and vast water views are condensed into one neat and satisfying ride that follows a scenic trail around the reservoir.

Start at the Giant bike shop on the southern shores of the water and within the first half mile reach Rutland's most famous landmark: the arrestingly beautiful Normanton church perched on the reservoir's edge. A mile later, take the refreshingly blustery ride over the top of the dam, where you're likely to see cormorants stretching their wings on the rocks beneath, before reaching Rutland Water Visitor Centre. This is the best spot on the ride for families; there's even a manmade sandy beach and swimming area here in summer, and the views from the grassy banks are beautiful, extending all the way back to Normanton church on the south shore.

From here, there are steep climbs and descents along the northern shores of the water, especially through Barnsdale Wood which is an enchanting area of woodland blanketed with bluebells in spring. At the halfway point, take a detour and follow the one-mile, traffic-free link into Oakham, the county town of Rutland, where there are good pubs, cafés and a 12th Century castle to explore.

Back on the trail you'll ride amid sheep-grazed pastures and rumpled hills to reach the pretty cottages and church of Egleton village. Be sure to look to the left around here to see the impressive square mansion house at Burley-on-the-Hill on the skyline; it's visible many times throughout the ride's second half.

The western side of the reservoir is taken up by the Rutland Water Nature Reserve which hosts the renowned annual Birdfair and is home to the Anglian Water Bird Watching Centre. It's worth locking bikes outside the centre and taking a look at the wildlife from one of the 31 viewing hides that are scattered around the reserve. However, it's the blissful descent to the Lyndon Visitor Centre that reveals the true wildlife highlight of the ride: a pair of nesting ospreys visible on the centre's nest-cam during the breeding season.

In the final miles, the attractive moored boats of Rutland Sailing Club can be seen bobbing around at the water's edge, and there are some final glimpses of Normanton church up ahead before you return to the Giant bike shop.

Rutland Water and Normanton church

Train station: Oakham

Grade: Moderate

Terrain, gradients and access: Gently undulating throughout with some short, steep gradients in parts. Fine gravel track and tarmac path with a short, on-road section at Egleton and several gates.

Loops, links and longer rides: Near Oakham, follow signs for the Hambleton Peninsula and ride an additional seven-mile, traffic-free loop around the land within the centre of the reservoir. NCN 6 and 48 Leicester to Watermead Park (**Ride 08**).

Stay: Wisteria Hotel, Oakham (01572) 722844 wisteriahotel.co.uk

Eat and drink: Oakham is home to the very good Hambleton Bakery, or try The Admiral Hornblower pub, and Otters Smokehouse and Deli. Along the route, try Crazy Fox Café, Funky Fox Café at Rutland Water Visitor Centre, Harbour Café Bar and Restaurant at Whitwell and The Horse and Jockey pub at Manton.

Cycle hire: Rutland Cycling at Whitwell (01780) 460705 and Normanton (01780) 720888 rutlandcycling.com

Wider area cycle map: East Midlands

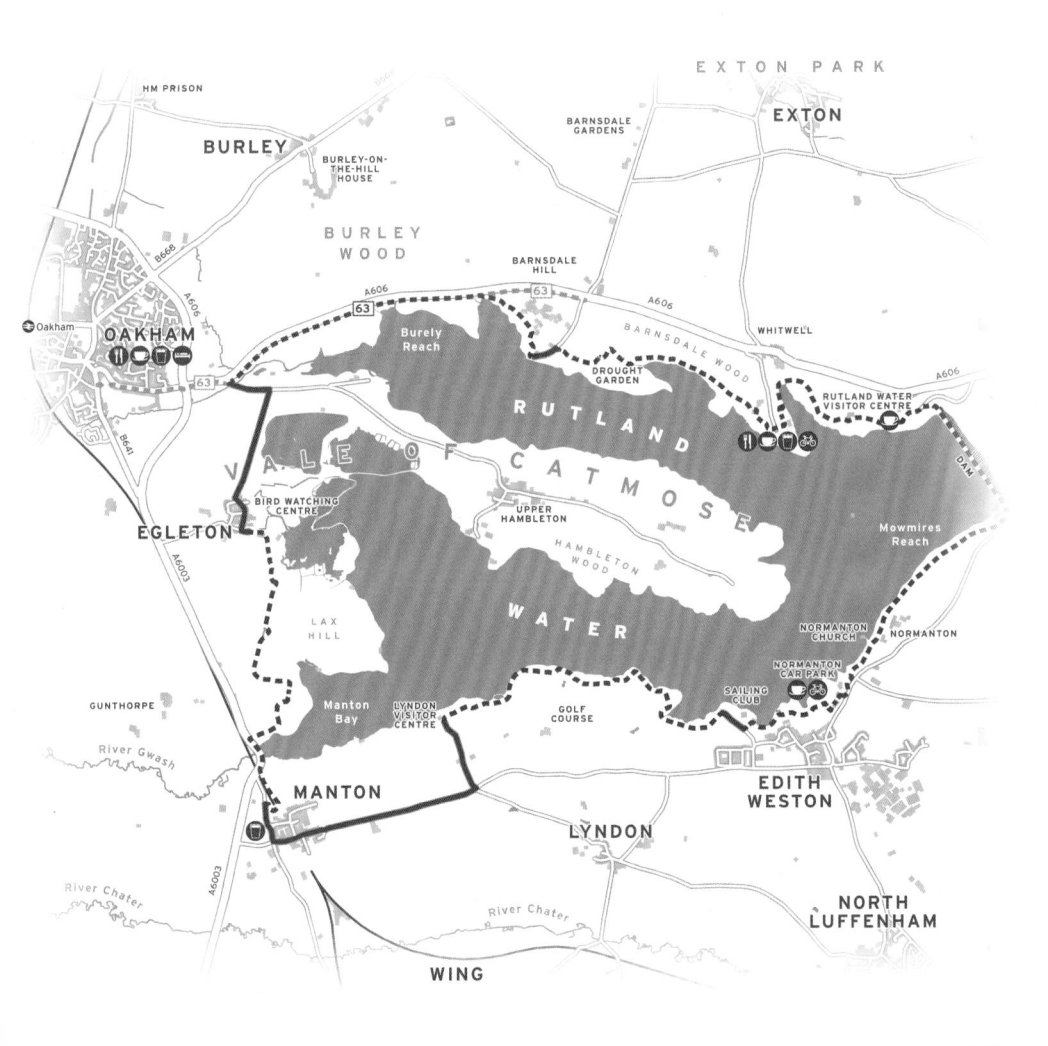

RIDE 08
5 miles · Start: Abbey Park, Leicester

LEICESTER
TO
WATERMEAD PARK

Bulrushes at Watermead Park

This ride follows the River Soar between two dramatically different Leicester parks; the groomed gardens of Abbey Park at the start perfectly contrast with the primal, wild wetland habitat of Watermead Park at the end.

Start at Abbey Park, Leicester's most beautiful city park, and ride past the delicately scented Lavender Maze and the Abbey Park Pavilion café. The River Soar divides the park neatly in two, and it's a good idea to cross the attractive arched bridge beside the tearooms to reach the Victorian gardens, bandstand and boating lake on the decorative east side. Return to the west bank to start the ride, following the river through the park and passing near to the remains of Leicester's 12th Century abbey and Cavendish House, a 17th Century mansion.

Less than a mile in, the bulging 42-metre high rocket tower of the National Space Centre comes into view beside the towering Victorian red brick chimney of the beautiful Abbey Pumping Station that houses Leicester's Museum of Science and Technology; both are equally fascinating and worth a visit. Join the quiet roads through Belgrave and keep a keen lookout for the old manor house, Belgrave Hall; it's tucked modestly into the residential streets and concealed behind the high brick walls of its gardens, so is easily missed.

Around the halfway point, enter the wildlife haven of Watermead Country Park on the Soar Valley floodplain. The remainder of the ride is spent coasting around the open water of the beautiful large lakes and little ponds, and among wildflower meadows and reedbeds between the River Soar and Grand Union Canal. BBQ spots, picnic areas and viewing hides are dotted all around, and there are a variety of cycle-friendly paths criss-crossing the park.

Finish: John Merrick's Lake, Watermead Park

RIDE 08

Train stations: Leicester and Syston

Grade: Easy

Terrain, gradients and access: Flat, tarmac path with some road crossings and a short, on-road section at Belgrave.

Loops, links and longer rides: From Leicester, follow a three-mile, traffic-free route south along NCN 6 Great Central Way, passing through Aylestone Meadows to reach Glen Parva and Glen Hills Local Nature Reserves.

Stay: Abbey Hotel, Leicester (01162) 256599 trivelleshotels.com/abbey

Eat and drink: In Leicester, try Hollys Coffee Shop and Sandwich Bar, Peppercorns café in the Abbey Park Pavilion or Boosters Café at the National Space Centre. The White Horse at Birstall and The Hope and Anchor pub at Syston are both beside Watermead Park.

Cycle hire: Rutland Cycling Leicester (0116) 344 0200 rutlandcycling.com

Wider area cycle map: East Midlands

Following NCN 6 through the southern end will lead to the Millennium Mammoth, a life size woolly mammoth created to commemorate the discovery of Ice Age remains at Watermead, and just one of many prehistoric-themed sculptures to be discovered here. The path between Trilakes and Keys Lake is particularly good, too, offering a refreshing breeze off the water and great views to both sides.

End beside the shores of John Merrick's Lake, or join the banks of the canal to exit the park and end at the Hope and Anchor pub across the road. Alternatively, follow the road for around one mile to reach Syston station and return to Leicester by train.

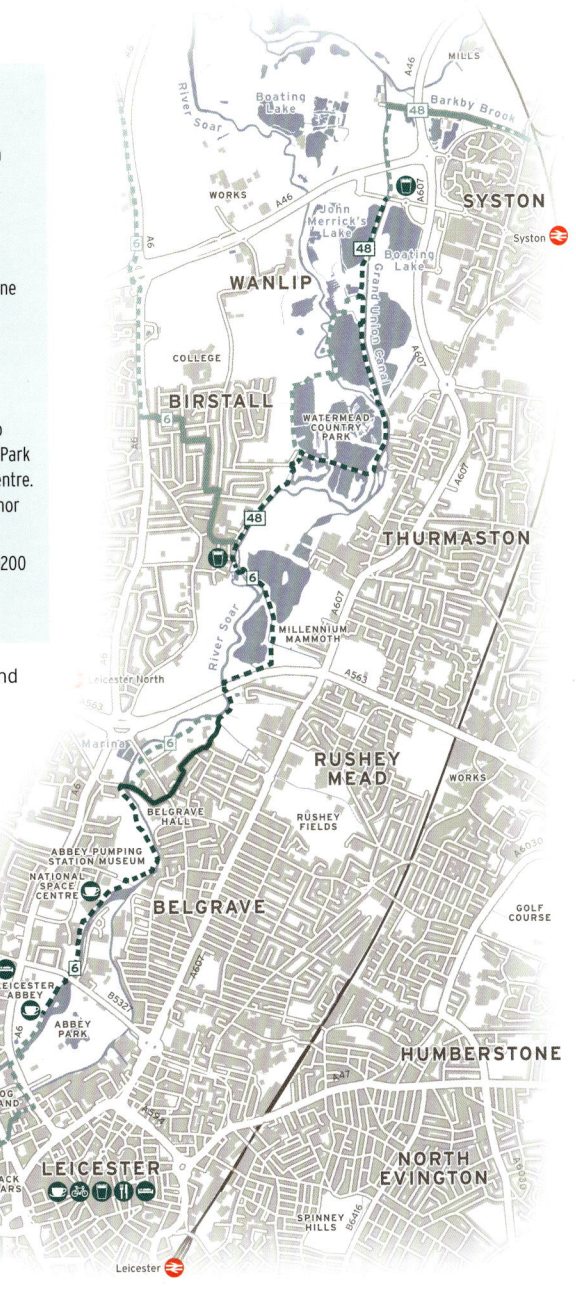

167

RIDE 09

13 miles

Start: Riverside Gardens, Derby

DERBY CANAL
&
THE CLOUD TRAIL

Riverside trails, canal towpaths and old railway paths are the holy trinity of traffic-free cycle routes, and this ride is a pleasant mix of all three, weaving through the beautiful Derbyshire and Leicestershire countryside.

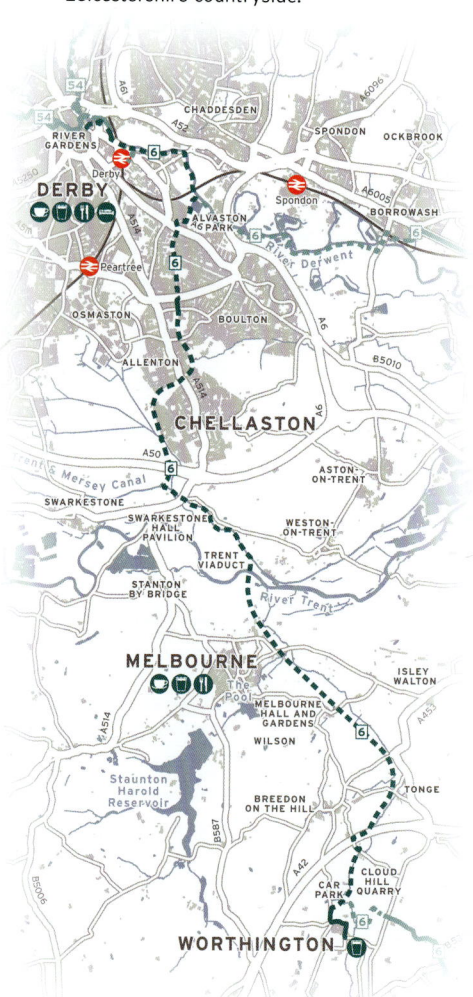

Start beside the gushing weir and attractive red-brick Council House at Riverside Gardens and follow the River Derwent out of the city through some of Derby's fine riverside green spaces; Bass's Recreation Ground and The Sanctuary Local Nature Reserve are both nice but best of all is Alvaston Park. Riding along the shores of the lake at Alvaston Park is particularly pleasant, and there is a café and benches around the water here for an early break.

On leaving the park, follow a long, green corridor along the Derby Canal path through the southern fringes of the city, before emerging into deeply rural Derbyshire where you'll join the towpath of the Trent & Mersey Canal at Swarkeston. There are glimpses of Swarkestone Hall Pavilion across the farmland to the right of the path with its twin turrets standing out proudly against the surrounding flat landscape.

After just a mile and a half of towpath riding, leave the canal and join the former railway line, crossing the River Trent on the elegant Trent Viaduct and pausing in the centre for great views up and down the river. In the final miles, the little Georgian market town of Melbourne on the edges of The National Forest is a thoroughly recommendable detour. It's less than a mile from the trail to reach the pubs and restaurants in Melbourne's town centre, or visit the picturesque old mill pool and the exquisite Melbourne Hall and Gardens.

Back on the trail, pass beside hedgerows, wheat fields and apple orchards as you cross the border into Leicestershire and begin the gentle climb to Worthington. The views over

Finish: Worthington

RIDE 09

Train station: Derby
Grade: Moderate
Terrain, gradients and access: Mostly flat with a steady ascent in the final miles. Tarmac path, fine gravel track and stony trail with some road crossings and very short, on-road sections at Boulton and Worthington. Take care passing under low bridges along the canal close to the water's edge.
Loops, links and longer rides: From Alvaston Park, continue along the riverside path for a further two miles to reach Elvaston Castle Country Park. NCN 67 Nutbrook Trail (**Ride 11**). NCN 54 Mickleover Trail (**Ride 10**).
Stay: Flowerpot Pub, Derby (01332) 204755 flowerpotderby.com
Eat and drink: Acropolis café in Market Place, Derby. Try Waterside café at Alvaston Park or Welcome Café and Melbourne Hall Tea Rooms, both in Melbourne. The Malt Shovel inn is at the route's end in Worthington village.
Wider area cycle map: East Midlands

Trent & Mersey Canal near Swarkestone

the steep limestone hills are splendid, and the priory church at Breedon on the Hill is a particularly striking sight, perched on the sheer limestone cliff. Pass around the edges of the dramatic limestone Cloud Hill Quarry, before the traffic-free trail comes to an end at a little car park on the northern edge of Worthington. It's a very short, on-road ride from here into the village centre to end at the pub.

RIDE 10 — 6 miles | 54 | **Start:** Mickleover Meadows, Derby

MICKLEOVER TRAIL

This short and rural ride follows part of the former Great Northern Railway route through the lush south Derbyshire countryside to the pretty village of Etwall. Start at Mickleover Meadows Local Nature Reserve on the west side of the city, and climb up through its open grassland and wildflower meadows.

Around two miles in, reach Hackwood Farm, an excellent place for an early break. Eat in the rustic little tearoom or walk around the orchards, farmland and woodland to glimpse the beautiful 18th Century country house of Radbourne Hall through the trees. Back on the route, woodland engulfs you as you pass beneath the thick trees of Black Wood, before emerging among crop fields and open farmland to begin a gentle descent towards Etwall.

It's a short climb from the traffic-free path to join the road into the attractive little village centre, where you can lock up and take a walk past the pretty St Helen's church and the Sir John Port Almshouses, or eat in Blenheim House, a former 18th Century farmhouse.

Gate to the trail in the sun

Finish: Etwall

RIDE 10

Train stations: Derby or Tutbury & Hatton

Grade: Easy

Terrain, gradients and access: Gently climbing in the opening miles followed by a steady descent. Tarmac path with some gates, road crossings and on-road sections at Mickleover and Etwall.

Loops, links and longer rides: From Mickleover, follow NCN 54 along a mix of traffic-free path and on-road route into the centre of Derby. At Etwall, you can follow a 14-mile, on-road ride to Ashbourne to join the Tissington Trail (**Ride 13**), which in turn links up with the High Peak Trail. NCN 6 Derby Canal & the Cloud Trail (**Ride 09**). NCN 67 Nutbrook Trail (**Ride 11**).

Stay: Derby Mickleover Hotel 03330 035442 bestwestern.co.uk

Eat and drink: Hackwood Farm Shop and Tea Rooms is near the start of the route. Highfields Happy Hens Tea is close to the route's end. The Hawk & Buckle pub is in in Etwall village.

Cycle hire: Nearest is Ashbourne cycle hire centre, Ashbourne (01335) 343156
peakdistrict.gov.uk/visiting/cycle

Wider area cycle map: East Midlands

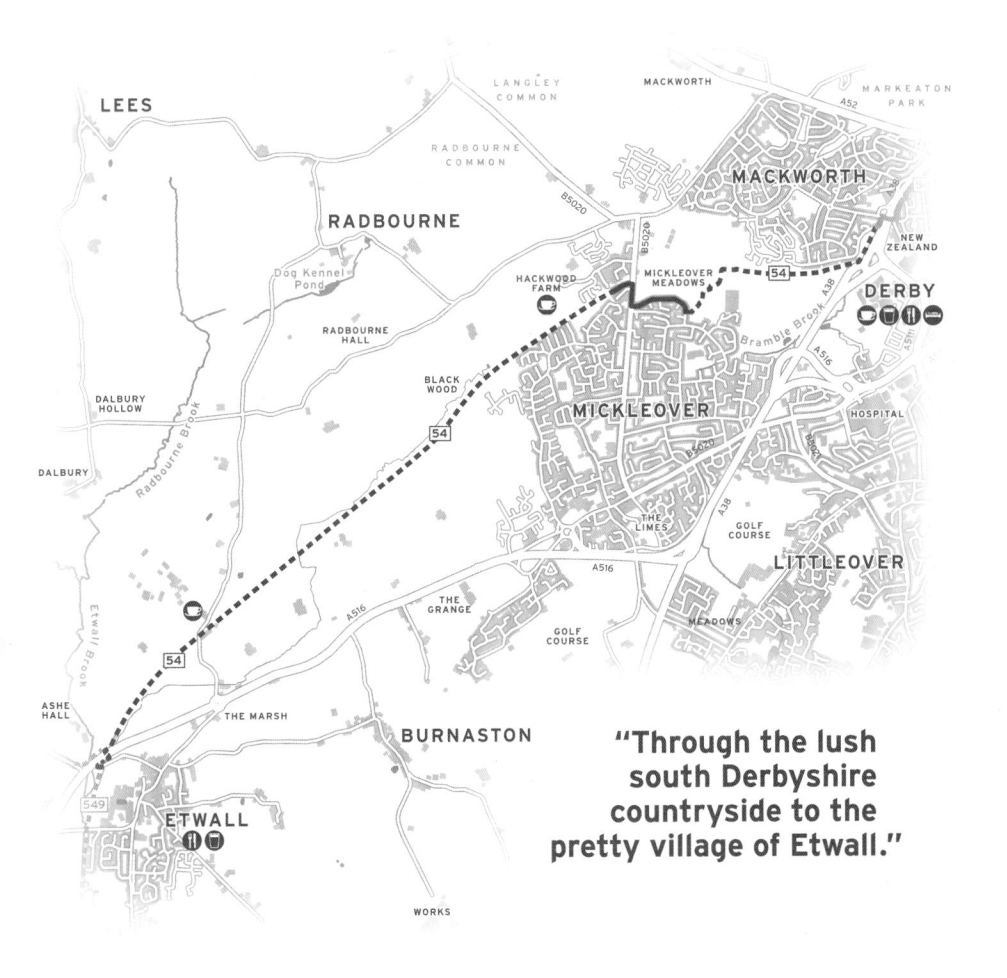

"Through the lush south Derbyshire countryside to the pretty village of Etwall."

171

RIDE 11 — 10.5 miles

Start: Erewash Canal towpath at Tamworth Road, Long Eaton

NUTBROOK TRAIL

Cycling along the Nutbrook Trail

The pleasant pastoral setting is incredibly relaxing, and the views from the flat towpath stretch up over the big sandstone escarpment of Stoney Clouds. At Stanton Lock, cross the water and leave the canal behind to join the old railway path, loosely following the course of the River Nutbrook which gives the route its name. It's a tranquil, tree-lined route here, with beautiful broadleaved woodland at Kirk Hallam and a series of lakes at Straws Bridge nature reserve.

Wild, open scrubland follows, before you enter the southern edges of Shipley Country Park through the Derbyshire Wildlife Trust's Woodside Nature Reserve on the site of the old Woodside Colliery. There's an impressive viewing tower just off the Nutbrook Trail here, giving great views across the wetlands, wildflower meadows and grassland of the nature reserve, and the surrounding Derbyshire countryside.

From here, a trail through thick woodland leads to the edges of the large Shipley Lake, followed by the smaller Osborne's Pond. The Nutbrook Trail cuts right through the park, but there are 20 miles of paths and bridleways that can be cycled within it, so it's a good idea to leave the trail and explore.

This route crosses Derbyshire's Amber Valley, following the attractive Erewash Canal in the first half and route of the old Stanton Branch Line railway in the second.

Wetlands dominate the ride from the moment you start beside Tamworth Road in Long Eaton, threading along the towpath between the Erewash Canal and River Erewash to the wet meadows of Toton Washlands. Pretty locks and red brick mill buildings feature in the opening miles, but the most beautiful are the lock keeper's cottage at Sandiacre Lock, and Springfield Mill, a vast Victorian lace mill with elegant arched windows and a huge chimney towering over the path.

Seek out the open water of Mapperley Reservoir and the site of the old Shipley Hall (the hall itself is gone but the woodlands and gardens around it remain). End at the park's visitor centre and café, or better still, at the volunteer-run Derby Lodge Tea Room in the heart of the park, a charming old building with lovely views across Derbyshire from its gardens.

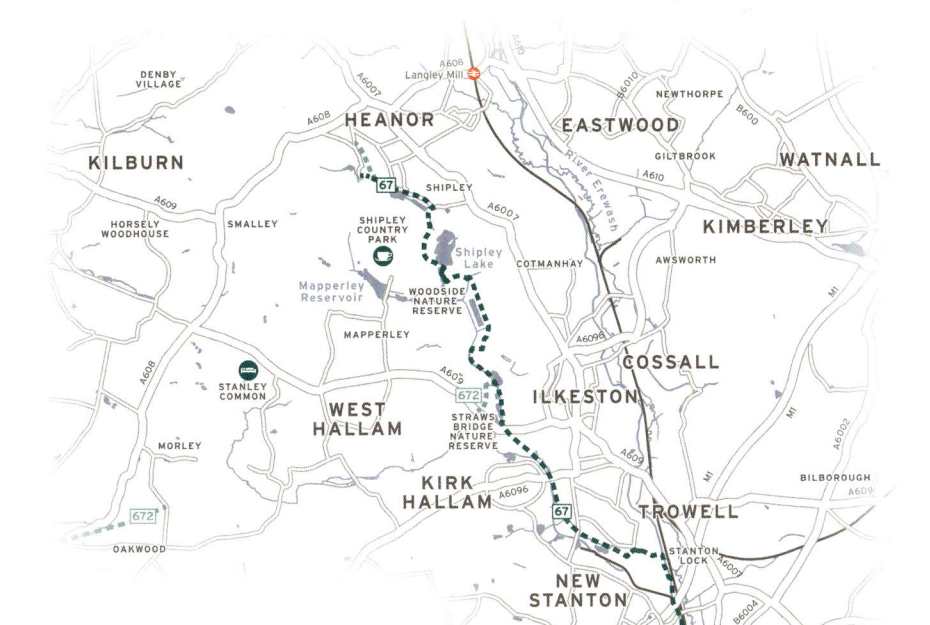

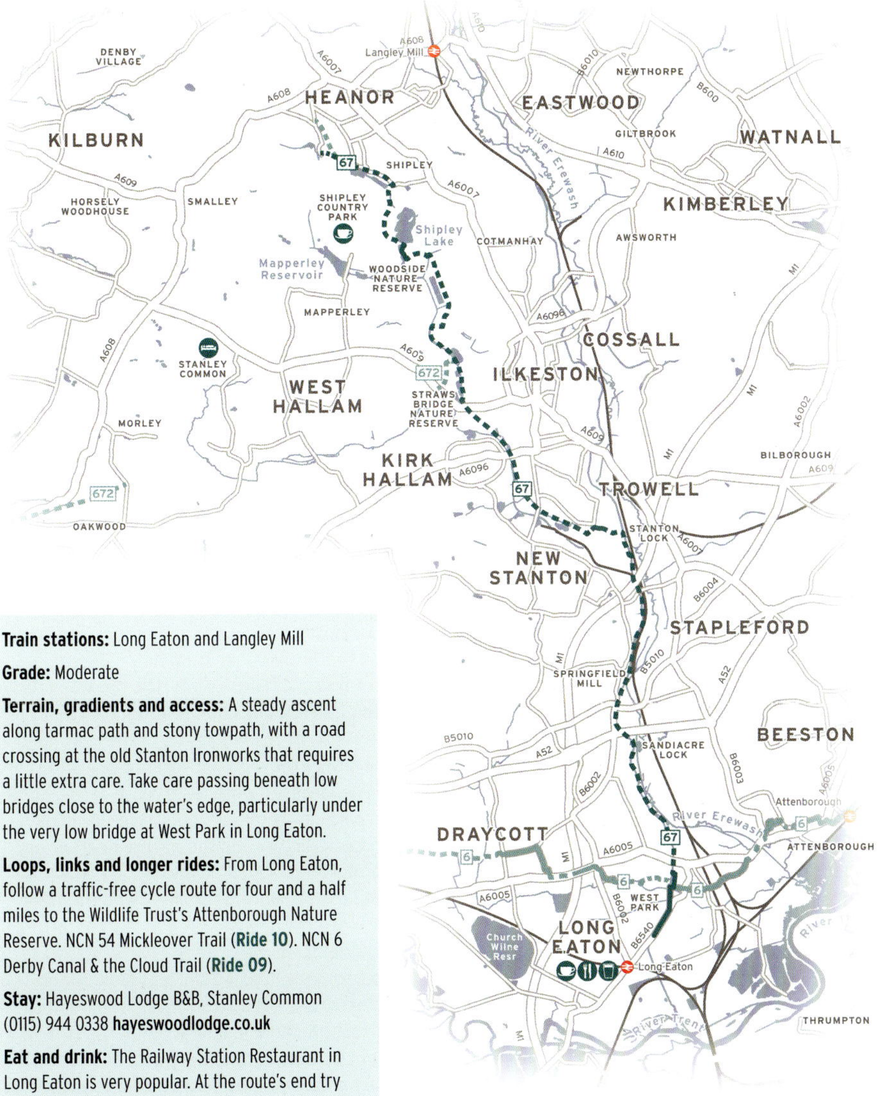

Finish: Shipley Country Park, Heanor

RIDE 11

Train stations: Long Eaton and Langley Mill

Grade: Moderate

Terrain, gradients and access: A steady ascent along tarmac path and stony towpath, with a road crossing at the old Stanton Ironworks that requires a little extra care. Take care passing beneath low bridges close to the water's edge, particularly under the very low bridge at West Park in Long Eaton.

Loops, links and longer rides: From Long Eaton, follow a traffic-free cycle route for four and a half miles to the Wildlife Trust's Attenborough Nature Reserve. NCN 54 Mickleover Trail (**Ride 10**). NCN 6 Derby Canal & the Cloud Trail (**Ride 09**).

Stay: Hayeswood Lodge B&B, Stanley Common (0115) 944 0338 **hayeswoodlodge.co.uk**

Eat and drink: The Railway Station Restaurant in Long Eaton is very popular. At the route's end try Derby Lodge Tea Room or Ramblers Coffee Shop in Shipley Country Park.

Cycle hire: Nottingham City Card Cycles (0115) 832 0264 **citycardcycles.com**

Wider area cycle map: East Midlands

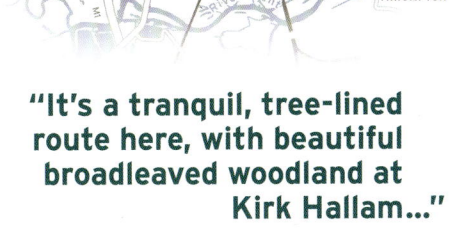

"It's a tranquil, tree-lined route here, with beautiful broadleaved woodland at Kirk Hallam..."

173

BIDDULPH VALLEY WAY

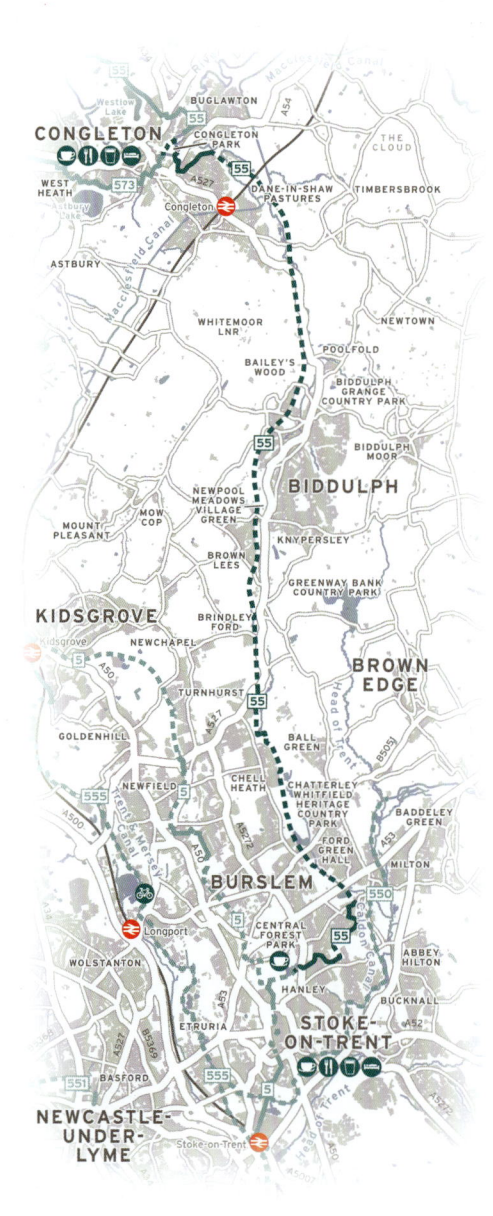

Peak District views and the magnificent Chatterley Whitfield Colliery buildings make this a scenic and memorable ride.

Start at the shores of the lake in Central Forest Park on the north side of Stoke-on-Trent, before climbing up the quiet road to Birches Head, where the views across the surrounding Staffordshire hills are wonderful. An enjoyable descent through the grassland, and a short stretch of residential riding, leads to the former route of the Biddulph Valley railway line. It was built to transport coal from the huge north Staffordshire coalfield, and you'll follow it all the way to Congleton.

Just two miles in, look to the right and see the beautiful timber-framed 17th Century farmhouse of Ford Green Hall, before entering the Chatterley Whitfield Heritage Country Park, one of the highlights of the ride. It's on the site of the old Whitfield Colliery and is one of the largest nature reserves in Stoke. Look for rare dingy skipper butterflies, orchids and kestrels around the patchy heather and shrubs on the spoil heaps, or kingfishers by the little ponds and brooks. Climb the trail between the spoil heaps and reed beds to get a magnificent view of the Chatterley Whitfield Colliery, a Scheduled Ancient Monument. The colossal brick chimney stack, winding houses, mineshafts and headgears make up Britain's biggest remaining colliery site, and are dramatically silhouetted against the sky.

From here, continue to climb gently into the woodland around Brindley Ford, before starting a lovely long and steady descent through the trees. Newpool Meadows Village Green, just after the halfway point of the

Finish: Congleton Park

RIDE 12

"The colossal brick chimney stack, winding houses, mineshafts and headgears..."

Chatterley Whitfield headgear

ride, is a wild and tranquil spot for a mid-ride picnic, before rolling through open farmland with glorious views over the Peak District in the east.

Ride through the beautiful ancient woodland of Bailey's Wood and into Whitemore Local Nature Reserve (LNR), where you'll cross the border into Cheshire. In the final miles of the ride, the raised aspect of the trail offers wonderful views across the Congleton Viaduct and Dane-in-Shaw Pastures, whilst the prominent hill of The Cloud is visible in the east, towering above the Cheshire Plains.

It's a short but very steep climb from the railway path to emerge on the quiet road that leads into Congleton. End at Congleton Park, a beautiful and relaxing green space around the banks of the River Dane.

Train stations: Stoke-on-Trent and Congleton

Grade: Moderate

Terrain, gradients and access: Some steady climbs and descents throughout, along tarmac path, fine gravel track and stony trail. Some gates, road crossings and a couple of steps at Brindley Ford. Short, on-road sections at Stoke-on-Trent and Congleton.

Loops, links and longer rides: NCN 549 Manifold Trail can be found east of Stoke-on-Trent, on the edges of the Peak District. It's a nine-mile, largely traffic-free route between Hulme End and Waterhouses.

Stay: Best Western Stoke-on-Trent City Centre Hotel (01782) 202361 **bestwesternstokecitycentre.co.uk**

Eat and drink: Central Forest Park snack bar is at the route's start and Six Towns Oatcakes is nearby. Stock at the Pavilion is a café bar within Congleton Park, or Crema deli in Congleton town centre is a popular choice.

Cycle hire: Green Door, Westport Lake, Stoke 07824 473432 **green-door.org.uk**

Wider area cycle map: Merseyside & Manchester

TISSINGTON TRAIL

Ride 13 — 13.5 miles
Start: Cycle hire centre, Parsley Hay

This is a beautiful descent through the gently rolling hills of the White Peak in the Peak District National Park, with astounding views over the rocky tors and limestone ravine of Dovedale midway.

Leave the cycle hire centre at Parsley Hay amid a scenic patchwork of fields rolling away into the distance and views over Pilsbury Castle Hills. Within two miles reach Hartington, once one of the busiest railway stations on the Ashbourne Line and now a tranquil picnic spot with the beautifully restored old signal box beside the track. Here, you'll find the flower-rich pastures and hay fields of Derbyshire Wildlife Trust's Hartington Meadows Nature Reserve, and it's worth taking a look around to see the twittering skylarks, colourful orchids and butterflies in summer.

Sweeping views are suspended momentarily whilst you ride along the deep railway cutting between steep banks of rock, before the scenery opens up once more over rumpled hills and rugged tors. Look to the west and see the uppermost edges of Dovedale appear, a dramatic limestone ravine with thick, dark woodland at its tip.

In the route's second half, green and fertile countryside takes over, and a stretch of lush woodland riding leads to the café at Tissington Station. This is a good place for a tea stop, or take a short, on-road detour from here to reach the Jacobean Tissington Hall at the heart of one of the prettiest villages in the country.

Back on the trail, enter the wildlife haven of Fenny Bentley Cutting before reaching the Tissington Trail car park and cycle hire centre at Mapleton Road in the final mile. From here, it's a cool, dark ride through the short Ashbourne Tunnel to Ashbourne Leisure Centre where the traffic-free path comes to an end. Take the very short, on-road ride into the centre of town where you'll find Church Street, regarded as one of the best Georgian streets in Derbyshire.

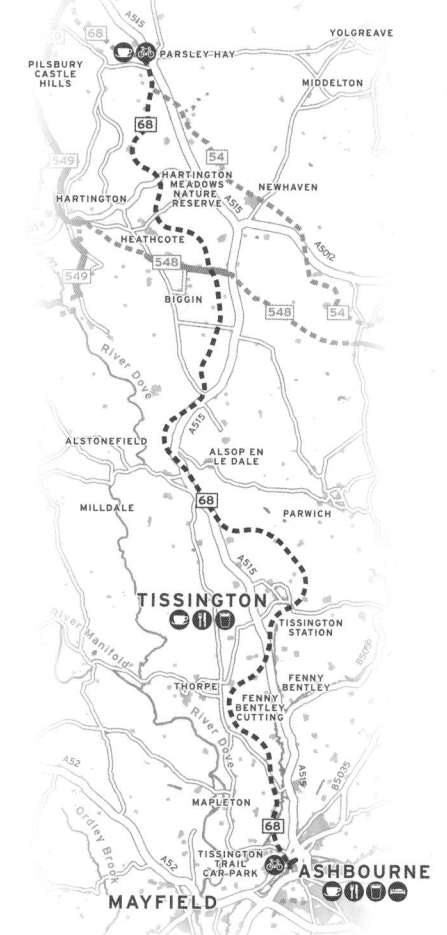

Finish: Ashbourne

RIDE 13

Train stations: Nearest are Belper and Buxton

Grade: Moderate

Terrain, gradients and access: A gentle descent along stony trail.

Loops, links and longer rides: From Ashbourne, follow an on-road route to Etwall, before joining the traffic-free NCN 54 Mickleover Trail into Derby (**Ride 10**). NCN 549 Manifold Trail is close to the Tissington Trail, and is a nine-mile, largely traffic-free route between Hulme End and Waterhouses. NCN 54 High Peak Trail.

Stay: YHA Ilam 0345 371 9023 **yha.org.uk** or Compton House, Ashbourne (01335) 343100 **comptonhouse.co.uk**

Eat and drink: Parsley Hay Refreshments are at the route's start or try the Snack Kiosk at Tissington Station. In Tissington, try Herbert's Fine English Tearooms at Tissington Hall. Café Impromptu and The Cheddar Gorge deli in Ashbourne are both popular.

Cycle hire: Parsley Hay cycle hire centre (01298) 84493 or Ashbourne cycle hire centre (01335) 343156 **peakdistrict.gov.uk/visiting/cycle**

Wider area cycle map: South Yorkshire & The Peak District

Railway cutting on the Tissington Trail at Heathcote

MONSAL TRAIL

Ride 14 — 9 miles
Start: Blackwell Mill Cycle Hire

This popular path through the Peak District National Park is a particular favourite among children, who take great pleasure in delving into the dim secrecy of the six old railway tunnels along the route. Dramatic views across the limestone cliffs and steep-sided river gorge offer a sensational open-air contrast.

Start at the cycle hire centre at Blackwell Mill and head east into the heart of the Derbyshire Dales. Two short tunnels feature in the opening mile, but both are just teasers before the longer and atmospheric Chee Tor Tunnel that immediately follows, a pleasure to breeze through with its moody lighting and smooth surface.

View of houses from Monsal Trail

You'll emerge back into the sunlight to reach Miller's Dale Bridge, where there's a good chance adventurers will be abseiling down to the banks of the River Wye below. Continue along the path beneath the old lime kilns that tower above the trail to reach Miller's Dale Station. This is a great early stopping point with its picnic area, toilets, coffee van and surrounding ash woodland that blooms with purple orchids and wood anemone in spring.

Through Miller's Dale Quarry there are wonderful spots for surveying the wriggling River Wye and the craggy limestone hills. The route's first half also provides views over two handsome cotton mills. Litton Mill comes first, a light and beautiful building with a dark and unsettling history, directly followed by the long Litton Tunnel. Cressbrook Tunnel follows with Cressbrook Mill beyond, once a producer of high-quality cotton for the lacemaking industry.

At the midway point, cross over the beautiful Monsal Viaduct, a real highlight of the ride. It's one of Britain's most impressive viaducts, with five vast arches and first-rate views over the rugged hills and river. Headstone Tunnel is the last tunnel on the route, and once you're through, the few remaining miles are a pleasant, open-air ride in expansive scenery to Hassop Station, a scenic picnic spot with a café and cycle hire.

Near the ride's end, catch glimpses of the pretty market town of Bakewell on the hillside, dominated by the mighty spire of its parish church, before ending at Coombs Road. From here, a steep and stony track leads down to the quiet road, where it's just a short ride into the centre of Bakewell, the ancient capital of the Peak on the banks of the River Wye. It's a popular and pretty town full of good cafés and tearooms, but forget about finding the traditional Bakewell Tart here, the area's real authentic treat is Bakewell Pudding.

Finish: Coombs Road, Bakewell

Train station: Buxton

Grade: Easy

Terrain, gradients and access: Gently descending all the way along a stony trail, with a tarmac surface through the six tunnels. Take extra care passing through the tunnels.

Loops, links and longer rides: From the Wye Dale car park at the route's start, it's less than four miles on-road to the spa town of Buxton. NCN 54 High Peak Trail is just a short distance to the south. NCN 68 Tissington Trail (**Ride 13**).

Stay: YHA Ravenstor, Miller's Dale 0345 371 9655 **yha.org.uk** (Restricted opening times) or Hassop Station B&B (01629) 815668 **hassopstation.co.uk**

Eat and drink: Lazy Days Tuck Shop at Blackwell Mill Cycle Hire, Miller's Dale Station coffee and snack van and Hassop Station café are all along the route. In Bakewell there are many eateries including the excellent Ricci's Italian café and The Lavender Tea Rooms. Visit The Old Original Bakewell Pudding Shop and seek out the award-winning Frederick's of Chesterfield ice cream.

Cycle hire: Blackwell Mill Cycle Hire (01298) 70838 **peakblackwellcyclehire.com** or Monsal Trail Cycle Hire, Hassop Station (01629) 815668 **hassopstation.co.uk**

Wider area cycle map: South Yorkshire & The Peak District

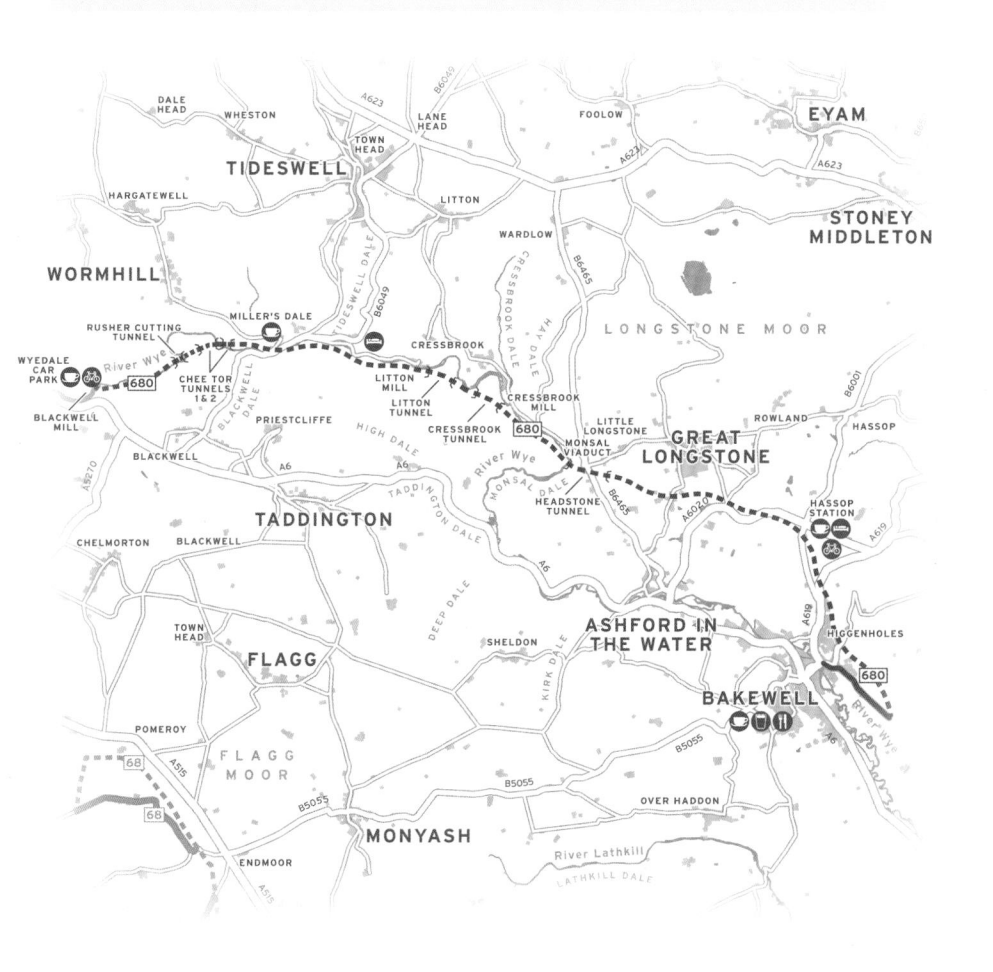

CLUMBER PARK
&
SHERWOOD FOREST

There's plenty of forest riding on this route, as you would expect from a route passing through Sherwood Forest (amongst many other forests). There is lots of variety within that description; there are the open spaces of Boundary Wood near Blidworth, a mix of older pines and larch and a much younger forest in Sherwood itself. Perhaps most special of all is the RSPB reserve of Budby South Forest which the route passes right by - a blend of historic heathland and ancient woodland with unusual bird species including nightjars and crossbills as seasonal visitors.

The route is bookended by scenic highlights in the form of romantic poet Lord Byron's ancestral home, Newstead Abbey, and the National Trust's Clumber Park. Although the magnificent house at Clumber burnt down in 1938 there remain countless acres of country estate and a wonderful cycle trail around the lake to the lovely estate village of Hardwick. In between there's some wonderful forest riding and some fantastic tracks and roads through the rolling, open countryside of north Nottinghamshire in this often overlooked but very attractive area known as The Dukeries.

You need to keep an eye on signage and Sustrans' detailed Peak District Cycle Map (26) would be helpful as there are few landmarks or navigation clues other than signage on the many wooded sections, so a missing sign means it's easy to go wrong. In particular in Sherwood Pines Forest Park look out for signs leaving the main track onto a smaller one to pick up NCN 645, rejoining NCN 6 at the lovely lakeside tranquil spot of Vicar Water Country Park.

The ride continues on NCN 6, north of Clumber Park, giving you the chance to head along the pretty Chesterfield Canal at Worksop. There you can visit the remains of a once important priory and the National Trust's Mr Straw's House, a 1930s period dwelling. It's also handy if you want to get a train back to Newstead or Nottingham.

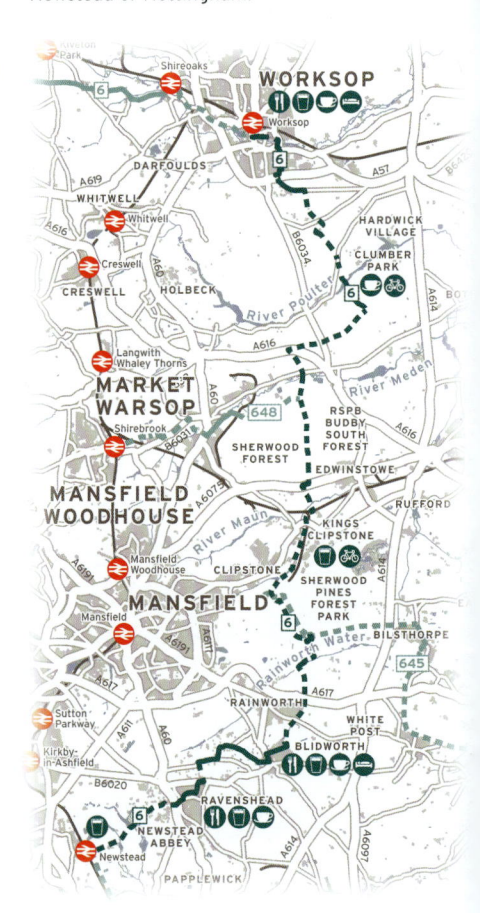

Finish: Worksop centre

RIDE 15

Newstead Abbey

"Romantic poet Lord Byron's ancestral home Newstead Abbey..."

Train Station: Direct 45 minute return from Worksop to Newstead

Grade: Moderate

Terrain, gradients and access: Some A-frames and horse controls to contend with plus a few gates – but not too many to spoil the route, with plenty of fast riding in between on flat or gently rolling tracks and minor roads. Tracks are generally good quality crushed stone with plenty of sealed surface interludes too.

Loops, links and longer rides: From Newstead NCN 6 heads south via pretty Linby village (pub and tearoom) and Hucknall and Bulwell to lovely Wollaton Park and the Trent Valley on the outskirts of Nottingham. At Clumber Park NCN 647 splits off NCN 6 eastwards to Lincoln. Lots of forest trails Sherwood Pines and Clumber Park too. After Worksop NCN 6 heads towards Sheffield via attractive Rother Valley Country Park (**Ride 01**).

Stay: MGM Muthu Clumber Park Hotel and Spa, Worksop (01623) 835333 **muthuhotelsmgm.com**

Eat and drink: Newstead Abbey has a café as does Voltz bike shop at Blidworth and there is the aptly named Route 6 café (weekends only) on the off-road section coming into Blidworth. There are also pubs en route at Ravenshead (Little John), Blidworth (Black Bull) and Kings Clipstone (Dog and Duck). Blidworth itself has a small collection of convenience stores and eateries including a fish and chip shop with stained glass window! At Clumber Park is the Walled Kitchen Garden in fine surroundings.

Cycle hire: Sherwood Pines Cycle Hire (01623) 822855 **sherwoodpinescycles.co.uk** or Clumber Park Cycle Hub (01909) 544911 **nationaltrust.org.uk**

Wider area cycle map: The Peak District

RIDE 16
15.5 miles

Start: Woodhall Junction, Woodhall Spa

WATER RAIL WAY

'The Lady of Shalott' by Anwick Forge

The flat and fertile farmland of the Lincolnshire Fens makes this a unique and atmospheric ride through the Witham Valley to Lincoln. The route's name is both a salute to the former Lincolnshire Loop Line railway on which the path is built, and the secretive water rail, a wading bird occasionally glimpsed amid the surrounding wetlands.

Start at the old station of Woodhall Junction and join the banks of the River Witham, sticking closely to them for most of the ride. The best spots for scenery are the neatly preserved riverside stations at Stixwould and Southrey in the route's first half, where the gently raised platforms offer long views across Lincolnshire's immense crop fields. Against this backdrop of agricultural flatlands, you'll certainly notice the tall trees of Southrey Wood rising up on the east of the trail. It's one of Lincolnshire's limewoods and includes some of the most ancient forest in England.

Near the woods, leave the waterside momentarily to follow a rugged farmland trail into Bardney village, where the Bardney Heritage Centre makes an excellent halfway stop for tea, fish and chips, or a fascinating look into the industrial history of the area. Take a little detour in Bardney to seek out the remains of the village's 12th Century abbey, just one of the nine monasteries that were founded in the Witham Valley.

In the second half of the ride, the unquestionable star of the skyline is Lincoln's majestic cathedral, one of Europe's greatest

Finish: Titanic Bridge, Lincoln

RIDE 16

Train station: Lincoln

Grade: Moderate

Terrain, gradients and access: Flat tarmac path, fine gravel track and stony trail with some gates and on-road sections around Bardney and Lincoln.

Loops, links and longer rides: NCN 1 Water Rail Way is 33 miles in its entirety. From Woodhall Spa you can continue on-road to Langrick before joining traffic-free path into Boston. From Lincoln, follow NCN 64 along a six-mile, traffic-free route to the Nottinghamshire village of Harby.

Stay: Brayford Guesthouse, Lincoln (01522) 885007 brayfordguesthouse.co.uk

Eat and drink: Archie's Independent Coffee House, and The Petwood Hotel are both at Woodhall Spa, while The Bardney Fryer is at Bardney Heritage Centre. Brayford Waterfront in Lincoln has many bars and restaurants, or try the independent cafés and tearooms on Steep Hill, a pretty cobbled street near the cathedral; Bunty's Tea Room is a favourite here.

Cycle hire: Woodhall Country Park, Woodhall Spa (01526) 353710 woodhallcountrypark.co.uk or Woodhall Spa Bike Hire 0776 1480 922 woodhallspabikehire.co.uk

Wider area cycle map: Lincolnshire & Wolds

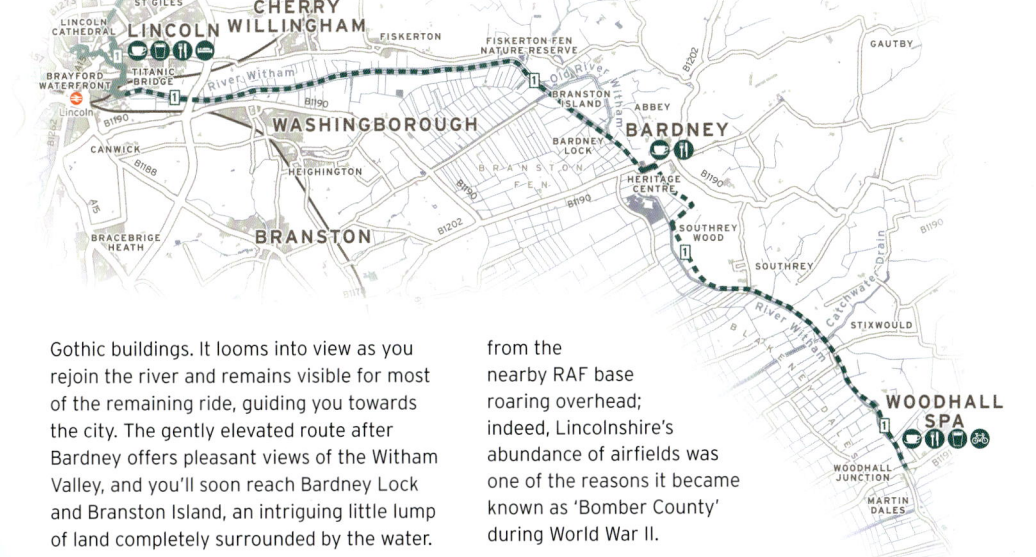

Gothic buildings. It looms into view as you rejoin the river and remains visible for most of the remaining ride, guiding you towards the city. The gently elevated route after Bardney offers pleasant views of the Witham Valley, and you'll soon reach Bardney Lock and Branston Island, an intriguing little lump of land completely surrounded by the water.

In the final miles, reach the wet wilderness of Lincolnshire Wildlife Trust's Fiskerton Fen Nature Reserve, one of the most beautiful spots on the ride, and one of the best places for attempting to spot the route's shy namesake, the water rail, hidden among the reed-planted islands. It's not all rural tranquillity, however, and there's a good chance of seeing (and hearing) aircraft from the nearby RAF base roaring overhead; indeed, Lincolnshire's abundance of airfields was one of the reasons it became known as 'Bomber County' during World War II.

Pass the old Washingborough Station before reaching the end of the traffic-free path at Titanic Bridge on the edges of Lincoln. The city centre and vibrant Brayford Waterfront are less than a mile from here, or continue to follow NCN 1 for more than a mile on uphill, on-road route to reach the gates of the wondrous Lincoln Cathedral.

RIDE 17 — 13 miles

Start: Hadfield train station or trail head car park on Platt Street

LONGDENDALE TRAIL

(HADFIELD TO WOODHEAD TUNNELS)

Your start point is Hadfield whose reputation as a characterful Peak District mill town was enhanced by its role in the BBC TV comedy League of Gentleman. It sits tucked away on the valley side at the bottom of a series of five magnificent Victorian reservoirs. They were built in the 19th Century to supply water for the rapidly expanding industrial centre of Manchester and its surroundings.

Located very near the train station, the trail heads on a gradual climb along the southern side of five historic dams: Bottoms, Valehouse, Rhodeswood, Torside and Woodhead. The views over them come and go as you progress along the trail, all backed by magnificent peat moorland scenery, in late summer and early autumn carpeted with purple heather.

Today's railpath is tranquilly idyllic but has a turbulent history. The railway was built in the mid nineteenth century by 1,500 navvies who suffered a terrible fatality and illness rate. The trail ends at the start of the three-mile-long Woodhead Tunnel - for a time, the longest tunnel in the country. It was only in 1970 that the passenger service along the line and under the Pennines stopped, followed by the goods service in 1981.

If you want more adventure when you reach the Woodhead tunnel then NCN 62 follows one of the toughest tracks on the whole of the NCN. It zig-zags on a rubbly track up the side of the Pennines to a stunning viewpoint down Longdendale. It's only a third of a mile extra but it will probably feel like a lot more!

For a different perspective try the Trans Pennine Trail alternative start from Hadfield that heads across the top of Bottoms reservoir dam, with its ornate architecture and views across to Tintwistle village. You can circle Valehouse and Rhodeswood reservoirs on a mixture of tracks. Small access roads are open to slow moving traffic and there is always some steeper off-road climbing on rougher tracks to get back up to the Longdendale trail itself.

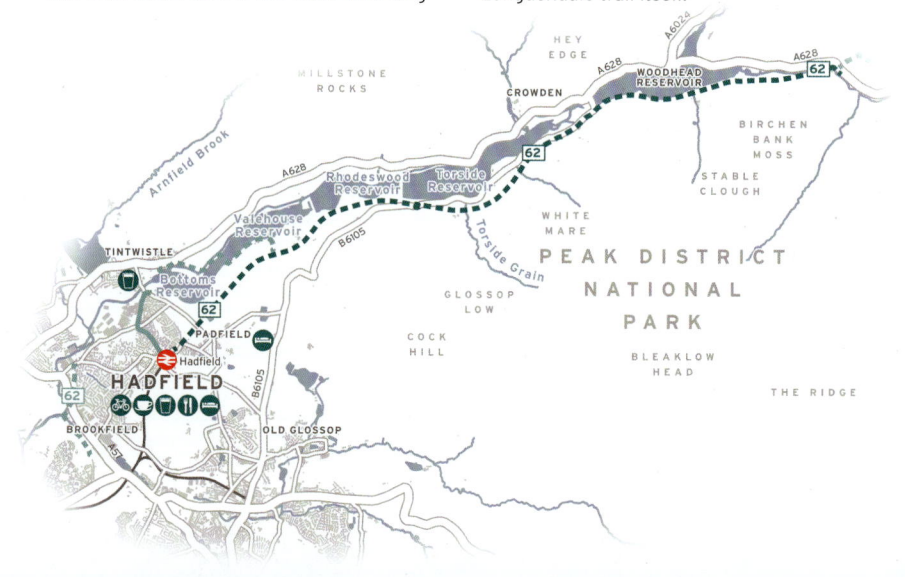

184

Finish: Woodhead Tunnel

RIDE 17

Train Station: There are regular trains from Manchester Piccadilly to Hadfield station which is the end of the line

Grade: Easy

Terrain, gradients and access: Whilst you are surrounded by the wild, occasionally craggy moorland of the Dark Peak area this former railway is largely flat or only slightly graded. There are some access controls, usually wide bridleway type gates and C-shaped stone wall chicanes. The trail itself is crushed stone and in places there is a parallel, rougher and often muddier track for horse riders. Occasional puddles and muddy sections after rain, usually where the trail passes through woods.

Loops, links and longer rides: It's easy to extend the length of your riding with loops around Valehouse or Rhodeswood reservoirs but note the latter loop involves some fairly bumpy mountain bike style track. The Longdendale Trail itself is part of NCN 62 which is part of the Trans Pennine Trail from Southport to Hornsea, yet another northern coast to coast option. Locally NCN 62 continues east from the Longdendale Trail on a very tough track over the Pennines whilst to the west it uses a mixture of smaller roads and tracks to weave its way towards Stockport eastwards. There is a small but tough spur through pasture along the Pennine Bridleway that crosses the NCN here. This takes you to the safety of a light controlled crossing of the busy and very dangerous A628 and into the pretty village of Tintwistle and the very characterful Black Bull pub.

Stay: Windy Harbour Farm Hotel and Campsite (01457) 853107 windyharbour.co.uk

Eat and drink: Plenty of choice in Hadfield but very little along the way. Tintwistle a short distance off the route has the excellent Bulls Head pub.

Cycle hire: Hadfield Bike Hire, bike drop off at trail head or train station. 07394 943 928 hadfieldbikehire.co.uk

Wider area cycle map: Peak District

"All backed by magnificent peat moorland scenery, in late summer and early autumn carpeted with purple heather..."

The Longdendale Trail in Upper Longdendale

EAST OF ENGLAND

Flat fenlands, big skies and faraway horizons play with your sense of size and space in the East of England, offering effortless cycling and an overwhelming sense of freedom.

Long and satisfying waterside routes are a highlight. A ride along the banks of the Grand Union Canal will lead you from Leighton Buzzard into Milton Keynes, passing 'Britain's best kept secret' along the way, the remarkable Bletchley Park, whilst the River Lee Navigation from Hertford takes you all the way to the lively East End of London and the remarkable Olympic Park. An abundance of railway paths make for simple and pleasant rides, too, including the well-loved Marriott's Way from the medieval city of Norwich, and five 'Lost Rails' across Hertfordshire, lost forever to the railways but rediscovered and given new life by walkers and cyclists.

Peterborough is particularly good for cycling thanks to its Green Wheel, a network of traffic-free paths and quiet roads that encircle the city, with linear routes or 'spokes' that lead into the centre. Indeed, this collection of rides features two Green Wheel routes that follow the banks of the River Nene.

However, it's the world-famous university city of Cambridge that is the star of the east. This is easily one of the most cycle-friendly cities in the UK, and you'll find you're just one of many cyclists riding contentedly through the streets. Keep pace with the impressive college rowing teams on a ride that follows the banks of the River Cam, or cross the ancient and atmospheric Cambridgeshire Fens on the Lodes Way where time seems to stand still.

By contrast, Letchworth and Stevenage are fine (and very differing) demonstrations of how cycling was key to New Town development in the 20th Century.

Cyclist in Cambridge

Routes overview

- **01** The Alban Way (7 miles)
- **02** Lee Navigation (North) (13 miles)
- **03** Cole Green Way (7.5 miles)
- **04** The Ayot Greenway (5 miles)
- **05** Flitch Way (8.5 miles)
- **06** Great North Way (28 miles)
- **07** Luton & South Beds Way (17 miles)
- **08** Grand Union Canal (15.5 miles)
- **09** The University Way (9 miles)
- **10** Grafham Water to St Neots (10 or 15.5 miles)
- **11** Cambridge to Waterbeach (8.5 miles)
- **12** Cambridge to Wicken Fen (16.5 miles)
- **13** Nene Park Loop (6.5 miles)
- **14** Celtic Causeway (7.5 miles)
- **15** Marriott's Way (14 miles)
- **16** King's Lynn to Sandringham (10 miles)
- — Featured ride
- — National Cycle Network (traffic-free and on-road)

RIDE 01
7 miles | 61 🚲 → **Start:** St Albans Abbey train station

THE ALBAN WAY

This pleasant ride through the Hertfordshire countryside is enhanced beyond measure by the magnificent St Albans Cathedral at the start and elegant Hatfield House at the end.

St Albans is a classic English cathedral city, and before setting off on the ride it's worth cycling through the picturesque Verulamium Park near the route's start. It stands on the ancient Roman city and is a gorgeous mix of riverside meadows, lakes and woodland.

Start the ride at St Albans Abbey train station, following a short, on-road route to Cottonmill Lane where you'll join the former Hatfield and St Albans branch line of the Great Northern Railway. Almost immediately, pause on the old railway bridge for an exceptional view of St Albans Cathedral poking up from among the trees on the skyline. Around two and a half miles in, there's the option to follow a short lane into Highfield Park, and you won't need to venture too far to find yourself in one of the park's orchards for a picnic beneath the blossom in spring, or under the ripening fruits in summer.

Back on the trail, it's a gentle and flat ride all the way to Hatfield, passing crop fields, fishing lakes and the old platforms of the village railway stations along the way. Ride underneath The Blackberry Arch, an attractive metal sculpture created by a local artist, before meeting the vast Galleria shopping centre. The path safely negotiates the busy road network here, but that is soon left behind as you enter the quieter outskirts of Hatfield.

The traffic-free path ends on Wrestlers Bridge over the railway tracks at Bull Stag Green. Turn around here and ride back to St Albans, or experienced cyclists can join Great North Road (or push along the pavement if less confident) for a short journey to the train station and the stunning Jacobean estate of Hatfield House. This is one of the 'Treasure Houses of England', a collection of ten of the most magnificent palaces, houses and castles in the country.

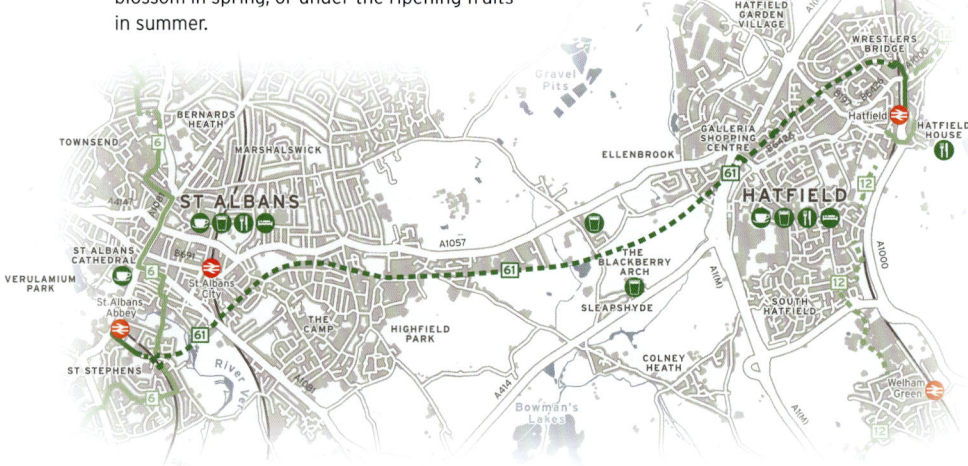

Finish: Wrestlers Bridge, Hatfield or Hatfield House

01

Train stations: St Albans Abbey, St Albans City and Hatfield

Grade: Easy

Terrain, gradients and access: Flat tarmac path with some small road crossings, an on-road section near St Albans Abbey train station and a bigger, busier road if ending at Hatfield House (extra care needed here).

Loops, links and longer rides: The Alban Way is one of Hertfordshire's five 'Lost Rails' traffic-free walking and cycling routes. The others are The Ayot Greenway (**Ride 04**), The Cole Green Way (**Ride 03**), The Ebury Way and The Nickey Line. NCN 6 Upper Lea Valley Way is a three and a half-mile, traffic-free route between Luton and Harpenden. NCN 12 Great North Way is a 32-mile cycle route along traffic-free paths and quiet lanes between Potters Bar and Letchworth Garden City. (**Route 06** covers part of the Great North Way)

Stay: The White Hart Hotel (01727) 853624 whitehearthotelstalbans.co.uk

Eat and drink: In St Albans, try Abbot's Kitchen at the cathedral, Lussmanns or The Pudding Stop. Along the route, visit The Three Horseshoes or The Plough, both in Smallford. The Coach House Restaurant is on the Hatfield House estate at the route's end.

Wider area cycle map: South Cambridgeshire, Beds & North Herts

"One of the 'Treasure Houses of England'..."

Hatfield House

RIDE 02
13 miles | 1 | 61 | **Start:** The Narrowboat Café, Waltham Abbey

LEE NAVIGATION

(NORTH)

The long River Lee Navigation runs all the way from London to Hertford, and this ride along its northern end is a more relaxed and rural experience than that at the lively London end.

Start beside the Narrowboat Café on the water's edge at Waltham Abbey and head north following NCN 1 into the marshes and lakes of the River Lee Country Park. The wide river, pretty locks and wildlife-rich wetlands are nicely peaceful, and there are some great opportunities to pause and enjoy them. Passing the wet meadows and grazing marshes of Silvermeade, just a few miles in, is particularly pleasant and you should keep a keen watch for endangered water voles in their riverbank habitat as you ride, especially in spring.

At Broxbourne Rowing Club the previously straight river starts to bend sharply, and you'll cross it a couple of times on the way to Dobb's Weir where the ride joins NCN 61. The weir is a pretty and popular place to lock up and explore, or continue a short way to the visitor centre of the RSPB's Rye Meads nature reserve, a short distance off the towpath around the halfway point of the ride.

Pass the yachts and boats of Stanstead Abbotts Marina and the pretty Stanstead Lock before discovering one of the most scenic stretches of the ride: a simple landscape of lush open meadows and lagoons. Take a small detour over the river at the Herts and Middlesex Wildlife Trust's Amwell Nature Reserve to look across the lake; it's a truly delightful spot and easily one of the nicest nature reserves on the route.

It's a return to civilisation at Hardmead Lock, and you'll ride beside the shops and cafés in the little town of Ware to one of the highlights of the route: rows of 18th Century gazebos, known as 'Dutch Summerhouses', overlooking the water. Cross the rich wetland habitat of The Meads before Hertford comes into view up ahead.

Just beyond Hertford Lock leave the waterside moments later to join the short road to Hertford East train station, or continue on-road from the station into the attractive town centre.

Train stations: Waltham Cross and Hertford East
Grade: Moderate
Terrain, gradients and access: Flat stony trail, fine gravel track and concrete path with some short cobbled sections. Some road crossings and short, on-road sections at Broxbourne and Hertford. Take extra care passing under low bridges and where the trail runs close to the water's edge.
Loops, links and longer rides: Lee Navigation (South) (**Ride 16**). NCN 12, 57 and 61 Cole Green Way (**Ride 03**).
Stay: YHA Lee Valley, 0345 371 9057 **yha.org.uk** or Number One Port Hill, Hertford (01992) 587350 **numberoneporthill.co.uk**
Eat and drink: The Narrowboat Café and the café bar at Lee Valley White Water Centre are both by the start at Waltham Abbey. Old Mill Retreat Café at Broxbourne is a favourite among cyclists. There are many places at Ware, including The Saracen's Head beside the route. Giambrone's Italian Deli, Lussmanns and Bebo café are all in Hertford town centre.
Cycle hire: Lee Valley Canoe Cycle, Broxbourne (01992) 676650 **lvcc.link**
Wider area cycle map: South Cambridgeshire, Beds & North Herts

Finish: Hertford East train station

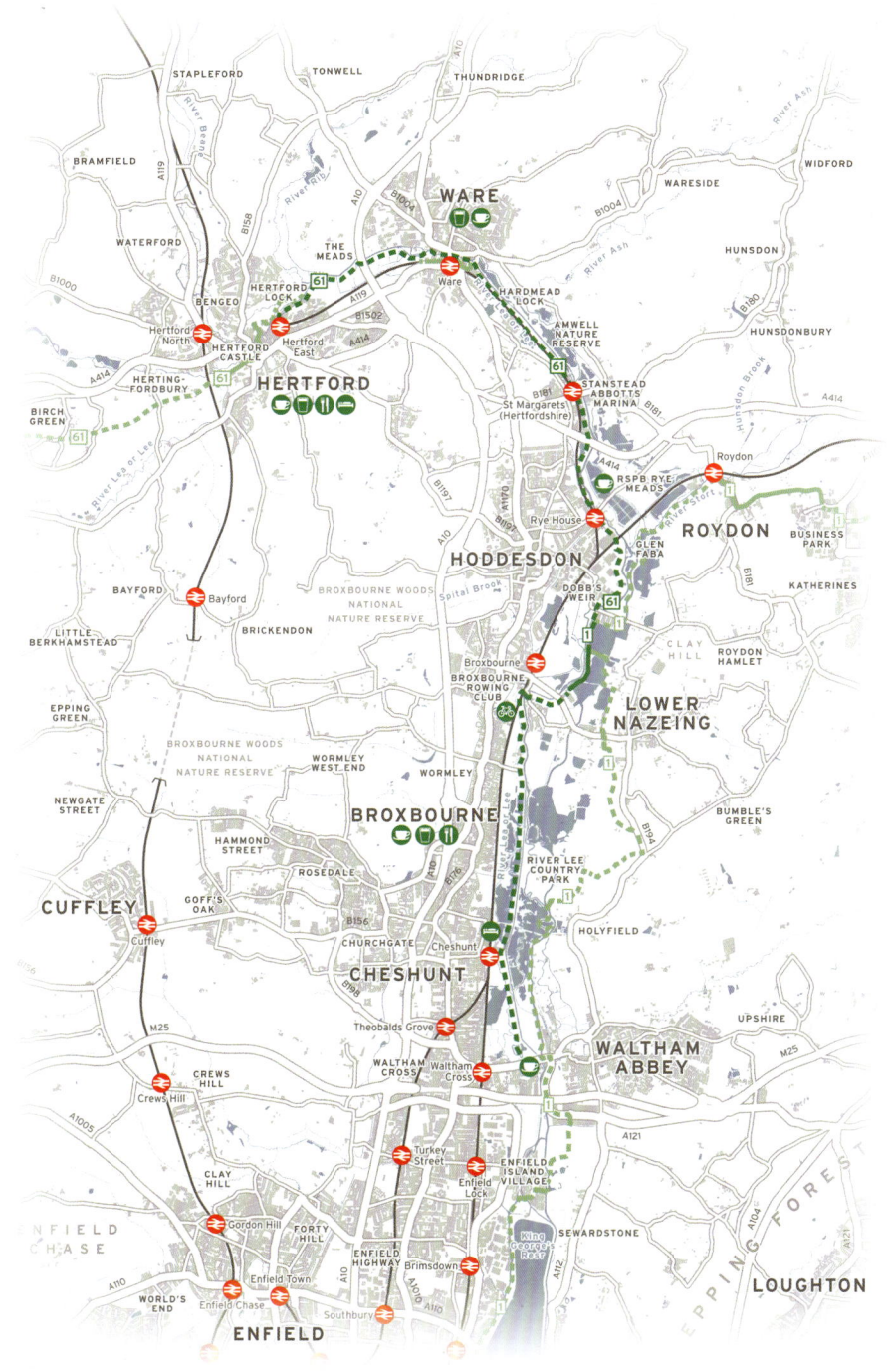

RIDE 02

RIDE 03
7.5 miles | 12 61 57 | **Start:** Hertford Tourist Information Centre

COLE GREEN WAY

This route between the Mimram Valley and Lea Valley is a pleasant countryside ride along a fine old railway path. Hertford is the county town of Hertfordshire and is a pretty spot to start from, with the long River Lea running right through its centre.

Before setting off, take a look around the little Hertford Museum and its Jacobean knot garden in Bull Plain near the start, and visit the 15th Century gatehouse in the town centre; it's all that remains of Hertford Castle. From here, ride through quiet streets on the edges of Hertford to join the traffic-free path beside the ground of Hertford Town FC and immediately pass beneath the arches of the huge railway viaduct. The trail becomes a mix of cool, shady woodland and open views across the farmland, passing beneath the former railway's Victorian brick bridges along the way.

At around the midway point of the ride, reach the old platform of Cole Green Station where there's a picnic area and pond among the trees. Or, try The Cowper Arms country pub beside the route for an indoor break.

The second half of the ride takes you alongside meadows and crop fields, and through the trees of Holwellpark Wood and Rolls Wood into the eastern fringes of Welwyn Garden City. At Stanborough Road it's just half a mile along traffic-free path to the lakes and parkland in Stanborough Park, which makes a scenic and relaxed ending. Alternatively, join the road into the centre of Welwyn Garden City to end at the pretty Howardsgate gardens and fountains beside The Howard Centre shopping plaza, all named in tribute to Welwyn Garden City's creator, Sir Ebenezer Howard.

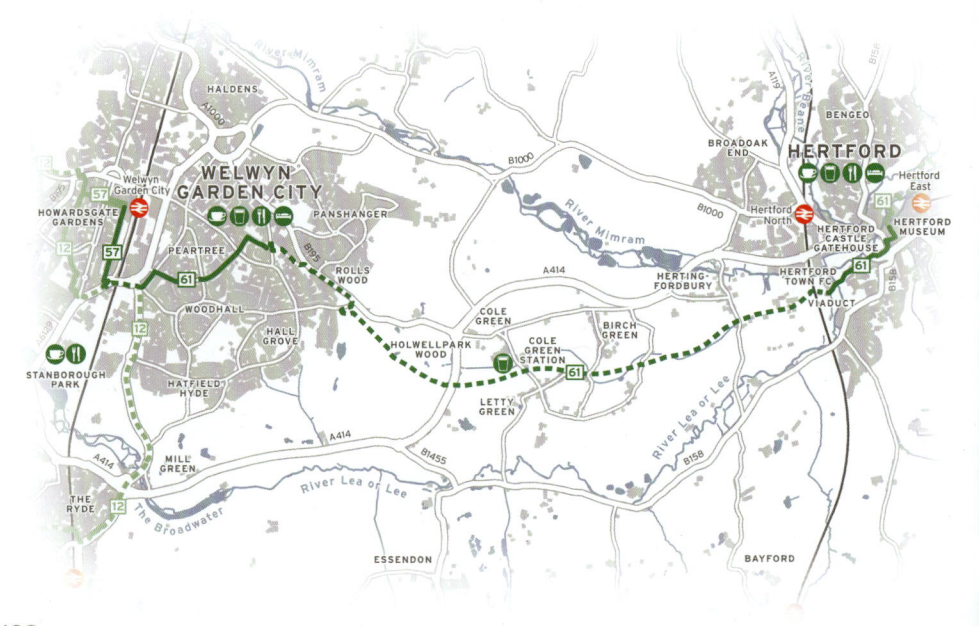

Finish: Howardsgate, Welwyn Garden City

RIDE 03

River Lea at Hertford

Train stations: Hertford East, Hertford North and Welwyn Garden City

Grade: Easy

Terrain, gradients and access: A very gentle ascent on tarmac path and fine gravel track, with some road crossings and on-road sections at Hertford and Welwyn Garden City.

Loops, links and longer rides: The Cole Green Way is one of Hertfordshire's five 'Lost Rails' traffic-free walking and cycling routes. The others are The Alban Way (**Ride 01**), The Ayot Greenway (**Ride 04**), The Ebury Way and The Nickey Line. From Hertford, follow NCN 1 and 61 Lee Navigation (North) (**Ride 02**). NCN 6 Upper Lea Valley Way is a three and a half-mile, traffic-free route between Luton and Harpenden. NCN 12 Great North Way is a 32-mile cycle route along traffic-free paths and quiet lanes between Potters Bar and Letchworth Garden City.

Stay: The A1 Bed & Breakfast, Welwyn Garden City (01707) 323868 a1bedandbreakfast.co.uk

Eat and drink: Giambrone's Italian Deli, Lussmanns and Bebo café are in Hertford town centre and are all very good. The Cowper Arms is mid-route at Cole Green, or at Welwyn Garden City try Stanborough Coffee Shop and Terranova Italian Restaurant in Stanborough Park.

Wider area cycle map: South Cambridgeshire, Beds & North Herts

Mid-summer on the River Lea

193

THE AYOT GREENWAY

Fountain in Welwyn Garden City

This short trail along a former railway path is a real gem, leading through beautiful Hertfordshire woodland and ending in the historic village of Wheathampstead.

Start at the pretty gardens and fountains of Howardsgate in Welwyn Garden City, before riding through quiet streets on the north western edge of the town to join a lovely wide trail through Sherrardspark Wood. Keep a look out for muntjac deer, foxes and woodland birds as you climb gently through the stands of ancient oak and hornbeam.

On leaving the woodland, it's just a short ride to Ayot Green for a tree-lined ride past the vast open greens and beautiful houses, followed by a heavenly country lane descent. The traffic-free trail continues again at the bottom of the hill, but before joining this it's worth continuing along the quiet road for just a quarter of a mile to get a close look at the beautiful and ornate red brick church in Ayot St Peter. It's an example of an Arts and Crafts church built in 1875, and is easily one of the loveliest churches in the country.

Back on the greenway, crop fields unfold all around and more gentle freewheeling leads to Robinson's Wood picnic area, a peaceful spot in a forest glade that makes the perfect place to take a break. The rural landscape of the Upper Lea Valley is a lovely setting for the final miles, before joining the banks of the River Lea into Wheathampstead.

End by the pretty little Diamond Jubilee Garden on the riverside and take a stroll through the centre of the attractive village. Alternatively, it's just a short, on-road ride to the south east edge of the village to visit Devil's Dyke and The Slad, massive earthworks that date back as far as 40BC.

Finish: Diamond Jubilee Garden, Wheathampstead

RIDE 04

Train station: Welwyn Garden City

Grade: Easy

Terrain, gradients and access: A gentle ascent in the opening miles and steady descent for the remainder along fine gravel track and stony trail. One gate, several road crossings and on-road sections in Welwyn Garden City, Ayot Green and Wheathampstead.

Loops, links and longer rides: The Ayot Greenway is one of Hertfordshire's five 'Lost Rails' traffic-free walking and cycling routes. The others are The Alban Way (**Ride 01**), The Cole Green Way (**Ride 03**), The Ebury Way and The Nickey Line. NCN 6 Upper Lea Valley Way is a three and a half-mile, traffic-free route between Luton and Harpenden. NCN 12 Great North Way is a 32-mile cycle route along traffic-free paths and quiet lanes between Potters Bar and Letchworth Garden City.

Stay: The A1 Bed & Breakfast, Welwyn Garden City (01707) 323868 a1bedandbreakfast.co.uk

Eat and drink: In Welwyn Garden City, Simmons Bakery on Howardsgate or Café Trio are both good choices. Miller and Carter steakhouse, artisan bakery Loafing and L'Olivo restaurant are all popular in Wheathampstead.

Wider area cycle map: South Cambridgeshire, Beds & North Herts

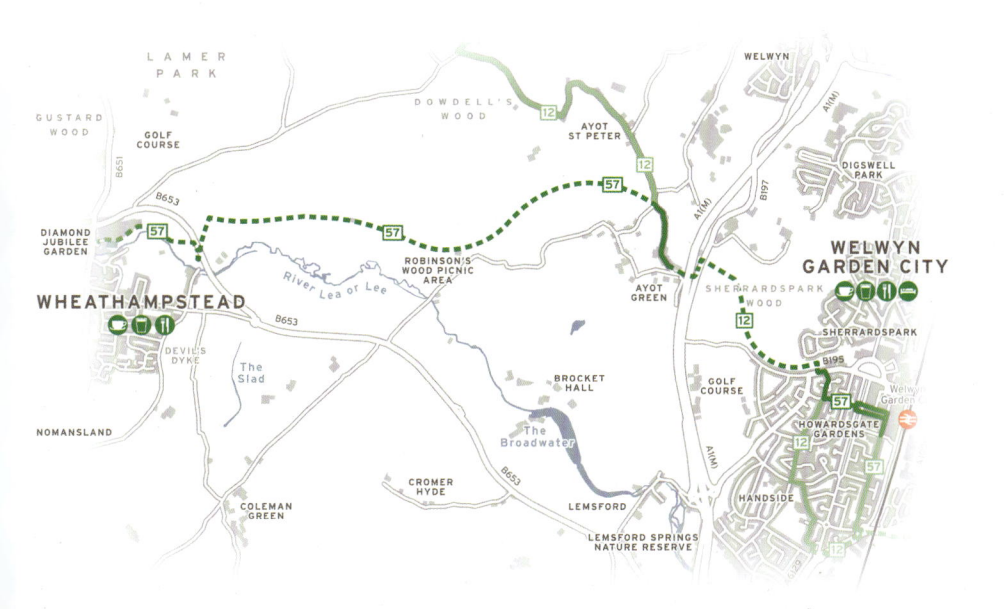

Ayot Greenway in the sunshine

195

RIDE 05
8.5 miles | 16 🚲 | **Start:** Braintree train station

FLITCH WAY

This rural Essex ride passes through the wonderful Flitch Way Country Park along the track of the former railway line between Braintree and Bishops Stortford.

Start at Braintree train station and immediately join the long and leafy traffic-free trail. There are elegant Victorian bridges and old stations all along the route, relics from the route's railway days that have been beautifully restored by volunteers. The nicest of all is Rayne Station in the opening miles, once one of the busiest stations on the line and now the site of a popular café, visitor centre and picnic spot, so it's a great place for an early break. If you feel like exploring a little there's also an easy detour from here. Simply follow Fairy Hall Lane for less than a mile to reach the lakes, ponds and woodland of Great Notley Country Park where there are picnic areas.

Alternatively, stay on the old railway line and continue west through expansive farmland. The vast borage fields at Gatewoods Lane are the most attractive as they erupt in vivid purple flowers during summer. Gatewoods Pond is here, too, a pretty little nature haven where moorhens, dragonflies, newts and butterflies can be spotted.

The remainder of the ride is a pleasant mix of open countryside scenery and sheltered woodland riding. Leave the route just before Great Dunmow to follow the rough stony track and quiet country lane into Little Dunmow. This is an endearing little Essex village to end in, with a pretty priory chapel, thatched cottages and The Flitch of Bacon pub. The village holds the key to the route's unusual name, too; the Dunmow Flitch Trials originated nearby, a medieval ceremony introduced by Augustinian monks whereby a flitch of bacon would be awarded to any couple who could prove they had enjoyed a year and a day of marriage without argument! The trials are still held in the neighbouring market town of Great Dunmow every four years.

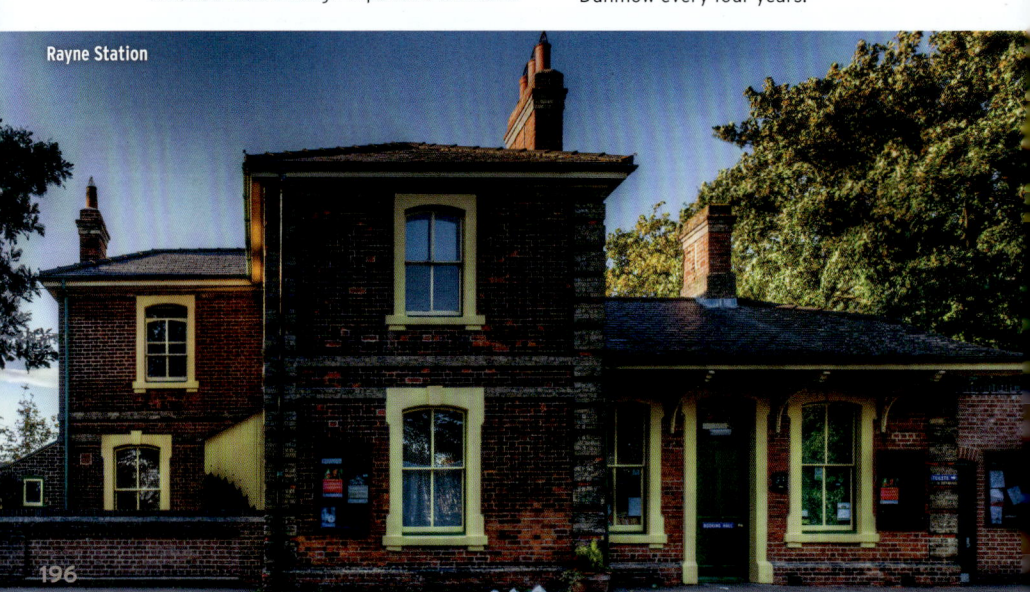

Rayne Station

Finish: Flitch of Bacon pub, Little Dunmow

RIDE 05

Train station: Braintree

Grade: Easy

Terrain, gradients and access: Very gently undulating along tarmac path and fine gravel track, with some road crossings and an on-road section at Little Dunmow.

Loops, links and longer rides: The Flitch Way is 15 miles in total. To ride the entire route, continue along the on-road section of NCN 16 through Great Dunmow, before rejoining traffic-free path all the way to the route's end at Tilekiln Green, or end a mile or so earlier at Hatfield Forest National Nature Reserve. The surface of the route is a little more rugged after Great Dunmow.

Stay: Mill House B&B, Rayne (01376) 320939
millhouse.webs.com

Eat and drink: Try the popular Eatons café in Braintree, Hoagies food truck (Sat only) beside the Flitch Way at Little Canfield, The Wooden Spoon café at Great Notley Country Park, or The Booking Hall Café at Rayne Station. The Flitch of Bacon pub is a traditional country pub at the route's end in Little Dunmow.

Wider area cycle map: Essex & Thames Estuary

Flitch Way

"A pleasant mix of open countryside scenery and sheltered woodland riding."

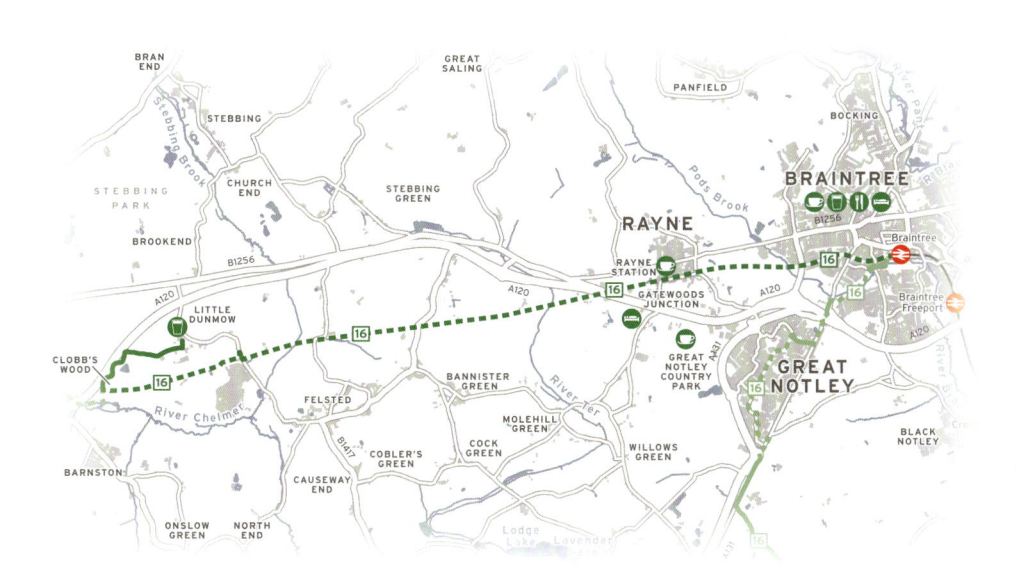

197

RIDE 06 — GREAT NORTH WAY

Start and finish: Fairlands Park, Stevenage

28 miles round trip with shorter rail return options

This is a fascinating ride for anyone interested in how you might design a cycle-friendly city and the different approaches two 'New Towns' took. Stevenage - designated the United Kingdom's first New Town under the New Towns Act in 1946 - took what many today would call a 'Dutch style' approach, with wide, high quality cycle lanes completely separated from motor traffic roads. These are simply a joy to cycle on and make up much of the start of the ride. It also has Fairlands Valley, 120 acres of beautiful rolling parkland, clearly much-valued by the residents of Stevenage. There's a pretty old centre and a very contrasting modern centre - the latter being the first purpose-built traffic-free shopping zone in Britain, apparently taking its inspiration from the Lijnbaan in Rotterdam, continuing the theme of Dutch inspiration.

The other theme of this ride is the way the Great North Road - better known as the A1 - has dominated the settlements hereabouts. Even the idyllic little village of Graveley that you visit just north of Stevenage has a pub that was clearly a coaching inn for north-south traffic. These days those who stop by often linger in the beer garden of the Waggon and Horse pub with its lovely view over the restored village pond. The Great North Way bike route used here clearly takes its name from the road of the same name.

By contrast Letchworth Garden City is an earlier take on how a New Town should look and harks back to the principles outlined in 1898 by social reformer Ebenezer Howard who strove to create a "garden city" in a belt of open countryside. It has a fascinating mix of buildings (including the amazing Spirella building which the route passes right by). NCN 12 loops right around the city to demonstrate just how close some attractive countryside is to the centre. There are frequent traffic calmed sections on the western part of the loop with more open, mountain or trekking bike style tracks to the east and a chance to hop off the route to visit the handsome market town of Baldock. Both wings of the route join south of Letchworth at the pretty village of Willian.

Using NCN 12 to head north of Letchworth you get the chance to visit the lower key but equally unusual attractions at Astwick and Stotfold, using the recently launched Etonbury Green Wheel route you will see signs for. Astwick hamlet is home to the tiny church of the little known Saint Guthlac, with a pretty green area with seating in front. In Stotfold you can follow signs to the lovely grade II listed watermill - currently open to the public with a tea room on alternate weekends in season.

Fairlands Valley Park

RIDE 06

Train Station: Regular trains from Letchworth to Stevenage (several trains every hour for the 10 minute hop down the line)

Grade: Moderate

Terrain, gradients and access: There are a few rolling hills in this area spanning northern Hertfordshire and southern Bedfordshire and there also a number of unsealed farm type tracks. Though the hills are moderate and the surfaces generally very good, they make a challenging enough combination to make this ride rank as moderate. Access controls are few and those that there are are not overly restrictive.

Loops, links and longer rides: This ride is part of NCN 12 which includes within it the Great North Way, from Potters Bar on the edge of London to Letchworth (the Great North Way is not to be confused with the Great North Trail or the Great North Cycle Way both of which are much further north). Currently NCN 12 finishes just north of Letchworth, as does this ride, but it extends south via the interesting sites of Old Knebworth village and the lovely Jacobean house at Old Hatfield, again using the Great North Way bike route.

Stay: Premier Inn Stevenage 0333 321 9027 premierinn.com

Eat and drink: Café at Fairlands Valley Park, plenty of choice along Stevenage's Old Town High Street next to the route and pubs at Graveley and Wilian villages. Letchworth centre has the traffic-calmed Eastcheap, a pleasant spot for sitting out especially at the excellent Simmons Bakers. The old flour mill at Stotfold makes a peaceful and scenic picnic location.

Wider area cycle map: South Cambridgeshire, Beds & North Herts

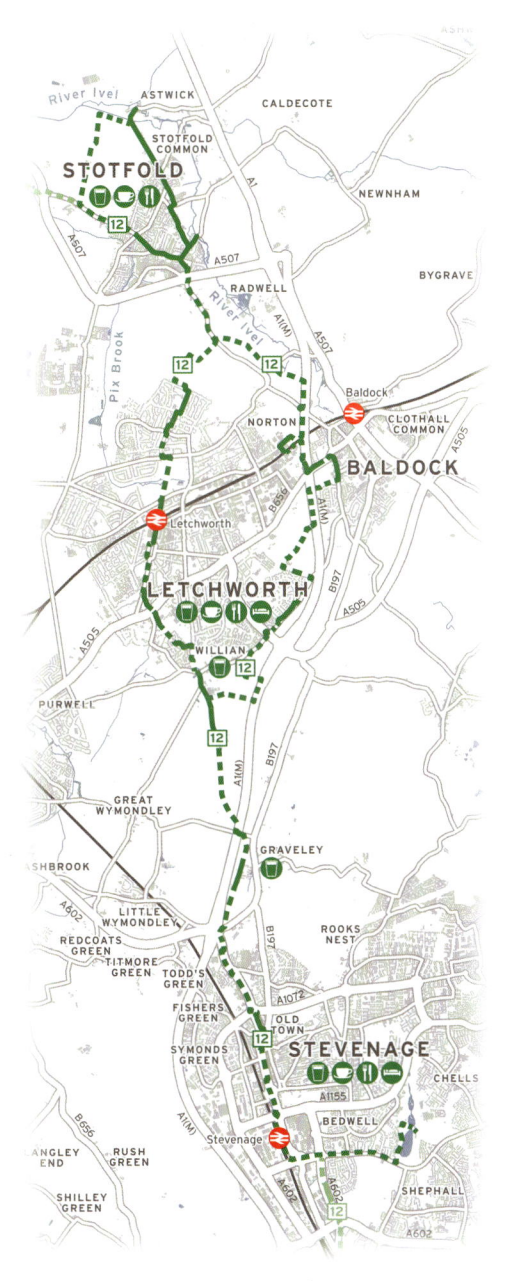

Village pond, Graveley

LUTON
& SOUTH BEDS WAY

This diverse route takes in some of Bedfordshire's most beautiful parkland and the dramatic chalk hills on the north eastern edge of the Chilterns.

Start at Luton train station and join the traffic-free path to Wardown Park, the finest of Luton's seven parks. The beautiful gardens, fountains and lakes of this Edwardian green space are an enticing distraction within the opening mile of the ride.

Duke of Burgundy, Totternhoe Nature Reserve

From here, climb through the residential edges of Luton, and link up with the River Lea to pass through Limbury and Leagrave. You'll soon reach Houghton Hall Park, an attractive area of grassland and woodland with a handsome old manor house visible at the north end of the park. More climbing follows and the views open up over treetops and the white chalk hills on the edges of the Chilterns. Dunstable is a good little market town to explore near the halfway point of the ride, and you'll cycle through the gorgeous Grove House Gardens in the centre of town, a perfect spot for a mid-ride picnic.

Quiet residential roads lead out of Dunstable and the route soon joins up with Sewell Greenway on the old Leighton Buzzard to Luton railway line where the Wildlife Trust-managed Sewell Cutting Nature Reserve is a stunning surprise. There's an opportunity at the western end to join NCN 574 and ride to the National Trust's Chilterns Gateway Centre. It's a three-mile ride that climbs steadily all the while, but is well worth the effort as you'll pass the Maiden Bower Ancient Monument on the way and get incredible windswept views across the chalk grassland of the Dunstable Downs.

Alternatively, simply stay on the Sewell Greenway to enjoy one of the highlights of the ride: a heavenly sweeping descent between the grassy, steep-sided banks of the Totternhoe Knolls. There are glimpses over the white chalk of Totternhoe Quarry along the way, too, and be sure to look for orchids and butterflies that thrive in the rich grassland in summer.

Leave the greenway at the old Stanbridgeford Station, now a private house with the former platforms in the garden, and be prepared for on-road riding all the way to Leighton Buzzard, passing little Bedfordshire villages on the way. Stanbridge is a particularly nice spot, and you'll ride past its 19th Century windmill, handsome church and country pub. Descend through the little village of Eggington into Leighton Buzzard, ending at the beautiful 15th Century market cross in the town centre, or continue into Linslade to reach the train station.

Finish: Leighton Buzzard train station

RIDE 07

Train stations: Luton and Leighton Buzzard
Grade: Moderate

Terrain, gradients and access: Tarmac path and fine gravel track with some road crossings, a short on-road section at Dunstable and a long on-road section between Stanbridge and Leighton Buzzard.

Loops, links and longer rides: An alternative at the start is to follow the traffic-free path beside the Luton to Dunstable Busway before joining up with the Luton to South Beds Way at Dunstable. From Leighton Buzzard, follow the Grand Union Canal south for a short distance to Tiddenfoot Lake, where a traffic-free route leads around the water, or continue further south to the Grove Lock pub. NCN 6 Grand Union Canal from Leighton Buzzard to Milton Keynes (**Ride 08**).

Stay: The White Horse, Leighton Buzzard (01525) 635739 whitehorsebandb.co.uk

Eat and drink: There's a National Trust café at the Chilterns Gateway Centre, or try the Five Bells pub at Stanbridge. Sorelli café, Espresso Head and The Black Lion in Leighton Buzzard are all popular.

Wider area cycle map: South Cambridgeshire, Beds & North Herts

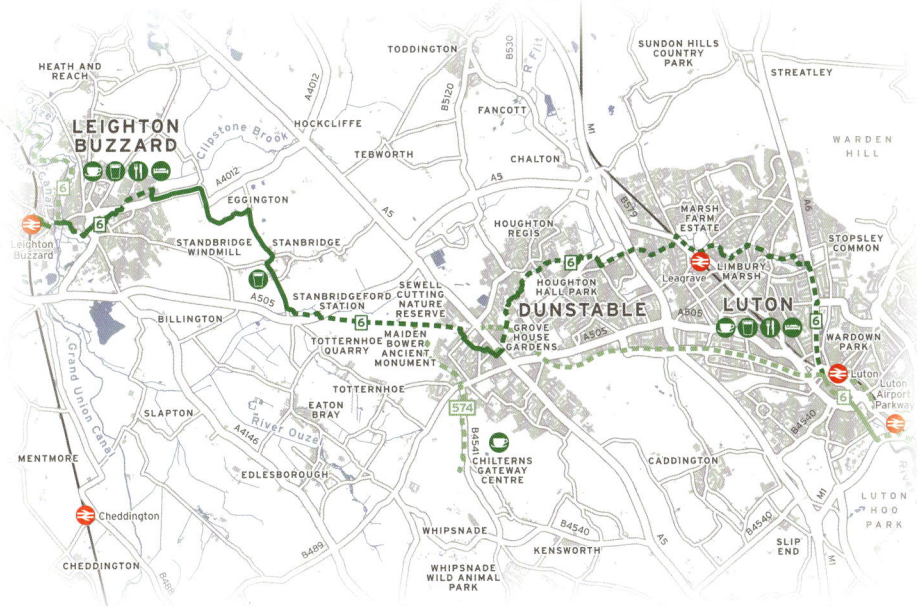

'The Course' by Michael Pinsky, Luton

201

RIDE 08 — 15.5 miles

Start: Leighton Buzzard train station

GRAND UNION CANAL

This is a gentle towpath ride through the parks and nature reserves of the Ouzel Valley, passing 'Britain's best kept secret' along the way.

Start at Leighton Buzzard train station and ride through the quiet residential streets of Linslade to join the Grand Union Canal. This is a popular and busy section of the towpath, and you'll soon be among other cyclists and walkers beside the attractive and nature-rich Ouzel Meadows, floodplains that run between the canal and River Ouzel.

After Leighton Lock the canal begins to snake around, so it's a meandering ride here through the pleasant Bedfordshire countryside, and you'll find the path becomes less populated after passing The Globe Inn. Three Locks at Stoke Hammond is a pretty spot to take a break, and there are good views over the Greensand Ridge to the east, where a long-distance walk along the sandstone escarpment stretches all the way to Gamlingay in Cambridgeshire.

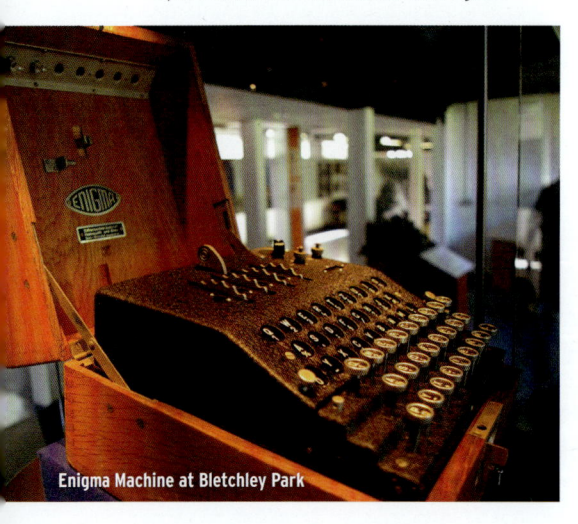

At Bletchley, the route leaves the water temporarily and takes you through quiet streets on the edge of the town. Here, there's an unmissable opportunity to visit Bletchley Park, once a top secret country estate where the codebreakers of World War II carried out their remarkable work.

Rejoin the canal at Caldecotte Lake, and now it's just beautiful parkland riding all the way to Milton Keynes. Caldecotte is a particularly nice spot, with a great view of the ornamental windmill at the entrance and an opportunity to complete a scenic traffic-free loop of the lake's shores. The southern end of the lake is the best for wildlife-watching, and there are two bird hides there for helping you to do just that.

Pass through the lovely hamlet of Simpson to enter Ouzel Valley Linear Park, dotted with medieval remains, ponds and grazing meadows. In the final miles, ride through Campbell Park, a divine mix of open pastures, woodland and gardens in the heart of Milton Keynes. It's a bit of a climb to reach the Light Pyramid artwork on top of the Belvedere, but it's worth it, as this is the highest point in the park and offers magnificent views across Bedfordshire and Buckinghamshire.

The park makes a very pleasant endpoint, or exit at the MK Rose memorial space and follow the wide and straight Midsummer Boulevard to reach Milton Keynes Central train station.

Enigma Machine at Bletchley Park

Finish: Milton Keynes Central train station

RIDE 08

Train stations: Leighton Buzzard, Bletchley or Milton Keynes Central

Grade: Moderate

Terrain, gradients and access: Flat tarmac and concrete path, fine gravel track and stony trail, a little rugged in parts. Some road crossings and on-road sections at Leighton Buzzard, Bletchley and Fenny Stratford, Simpson, Tinkers Bridge and Milton Keynes. Take extra care passing under low bridges on the towpath close to the water's edge. At Midsummer Boulevard in Milton Keynes you'll need to dismount and push around the shopping centre.

Loops, links and longer rides: The Milton Keynes Redways are a network of safer walking and cycling routes (usually surfaced with red tarmac) that criss-cross the city. At Willen Lake in Ouzel Valley Linear Park, take the traffic-free circular ride around the lake's shores and join up with NCN 51, an on-road and traffic-free route across Oxfordshire, Buckinghamshire, Bedfordshire, Cambridgeshire, Suffolk and Essex. NCN 6 Luton & South Beds Way leads from Leighton Buzzard to Luton (**Ride 07**).

Stay: National Badminton Centre Hotel (The Lodge), Milton Keynes (01908) 268422 **badmintonengland.co.uk**

Eat and drink: Try The Globe Inn at Leighton Buzzard, The Three Locks pub at Stoke Hammond, Hut 4 Café at Bletchley Park, The Plough at Simpson village and The Camphill Café at Willen Park.

Cycle hire: MK Motion Bike Hire, Caldecotte Lake 07761 658206 **letsgowiththechild.co.uk**, Santander Cycles 0208 166 9851 **santandercycles.co.uk** or Rutland Cycling, Milton Keynes 0330 5550080 **rutlandcycling.com**

Wider area cycle map: Warwickshire & The South Midlands

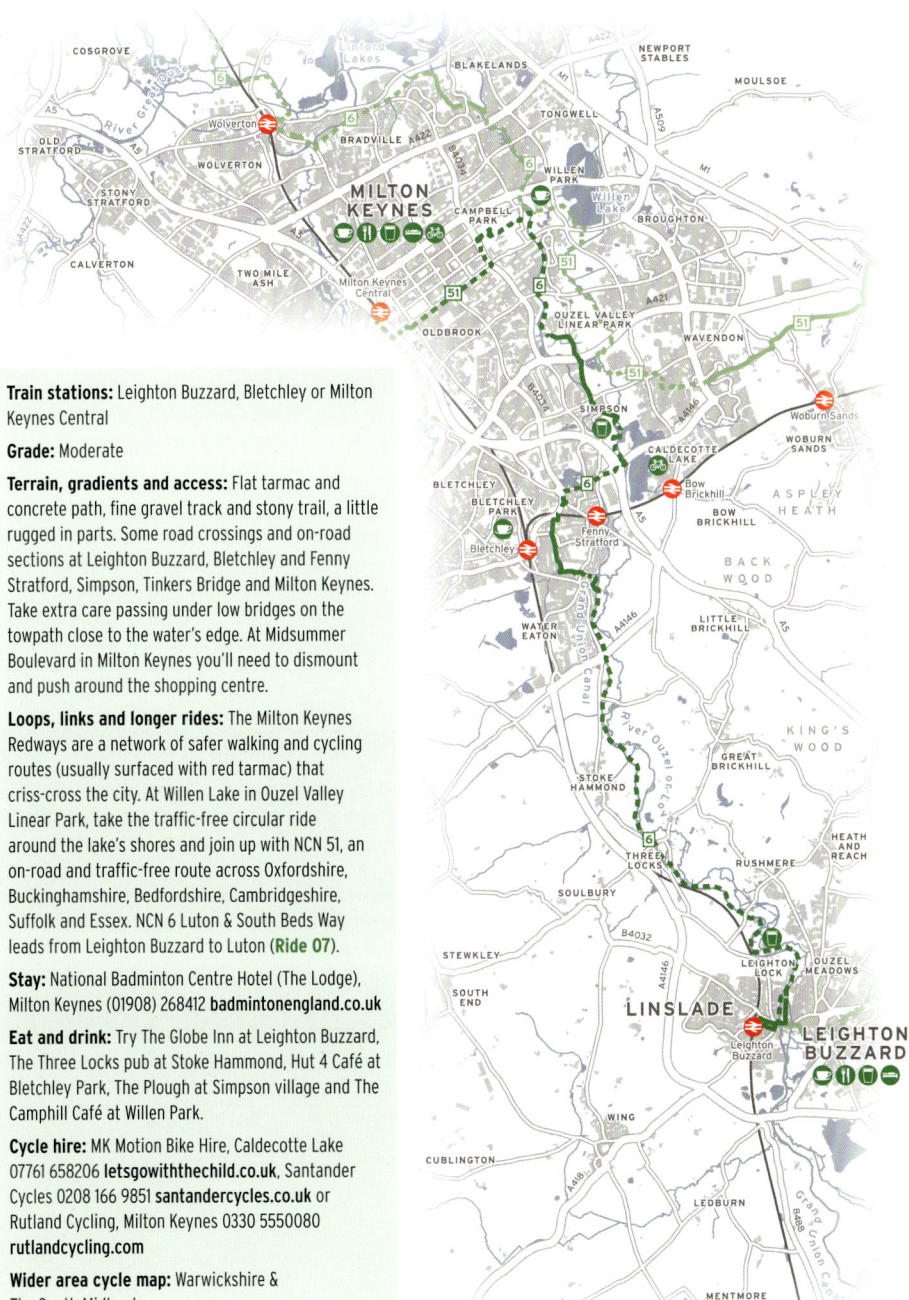

203

THE UNIVERSITY WAY

This gentle countryside route is called the University Way because it partly follows the course of the Varsity Line, a railway that once linked the famous university cities of Oxford and Cambridge, earning it the nickname 'The Brain Line'. The area has some enviable wildlife credentials, too. Sandy, at the route's beginning, is home to the headquarters of conservation charity The RSPB, and before setting off it's worth cycling the quiet country lane (Stratford Road) behind Sandy train station to reach The Lodge, its attractive nature reserve and headquarters.

Start the ride from Sandy's Market Square and quickly find yourself out in Bedfordshire's rich green countryside, where the flat arable landscape opens out beautifully in every direction. Blunham, once a station on the railway line, is now an important spot for nature, so look for the nodding blue heads of harebells dotted among the grassland here in summer, yellowhammers flitting across the farmland, or goldfinches picking at the teasel in autumn.

The grassy area at Willington Lock makes a good informal picnic spot at around the halfway point, and you can watch canoes and kayaks working their way up the river here. Alternatively, continue a short way to Danish Camp on the banks of the River Great Ouse. Vikings are believed to have used the moated site here to plan their attacks. Tours of this Scheduled Ancient Monument are by appointment only, but you can drop in to the welcoming visitor centre and café housed in a Norwegian log cabin.

Two beautiful country parks make the second half of the ride a complete delight, each boasting woodland, lakes and meadows. Bedford River Valley Park comes first and has a circular riverside cycling route around the Grange Estate that is worth exploring. Priory Country Park follows, with the huge Priory Lake at its centre, nestled in a sharp bend of the River Great Ouse.

In the ride's final miles, gently roll along the riverbank to end on the pretty Embankment in Bedford, a beautiful town park with manicured and colourful gardens, rowing boats slicing through the water, and people strolling along Mill Meadows, the islands in the centre of the river.

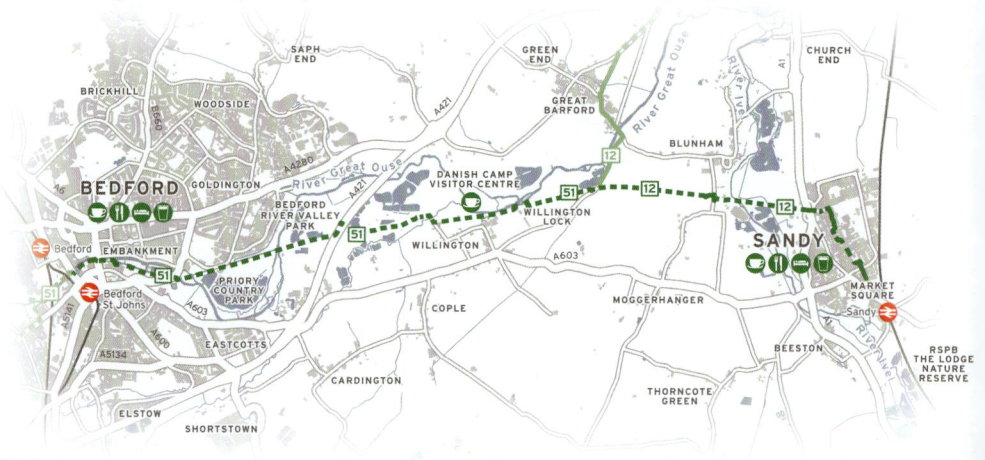

Finish: The Embankment, Bedford

RIDE 09

Train stations: Sandy, Bedford and Bedford St Johns

Grade: Easy

Terrain, gradients and access: Flat tarmac path, fine gravel track, some road crossings and short, on-road sections around Sandy and Blunham.

Loops, links and longer rides: The Bedford Green Wheel is a network of mostly traffic-free cycling routes around the towns of Bedford and Kempston. NCN 12 Grafham Water to St Neots (**Ride 10**).

Stay: Bedford Park House, Bedford (01234) 215100 befordparkhouse.co.uk

Eat and drink: Visit Gunns Bakery in Sandy for a famous Bedfordshire Clanger, or try Danish Camp Café at Willington. Bedford has many Italian restaurants and cafés that reflect the town's thriving Italian community; Amici is a particular favourite. Or, try The Embankment and The Park, popular pubs in Bedford.

Wider area cycle map: South Cambridgeshire, Beds & North Herts

Cycling in Bedford

Chiffchaffs are regular visitors to RSPB The Lodge

205

RIDE 10 — **Start:** Marlow Park, Grafham Water

10 mile circular ride around Grafham Water, or
15.5 miles from Marlow Park at Grafham Water to St Neots train station

GRAFHAM WATER
TO
ST NEOTS

This ride loops around the shores of the nature-rich Grafham Water and links to St Neots through the charming Cambridgeshire countryside. Marlow Park is the best place to start, with Rutland Cycling nearby in case you need any trail advice or have any repair needs. The route around Grafham Water doesn't always follow the shoreline, in fact, the trail leaves the reservoir almost immediately to follow quiet country lanes near Grafham village. However, the water soon surges into view again and you'll join it at Sanctuary Bay where the Wildlife Trust's Grafham Water nature reserve begins. There are wonderful opportunities for nature-watching here, especially in winter when huge flocks of water birds are attracted to the sheltered creeks of the reservoir.

Dinghies on Grafham Water

Leave the water again to climb up into the shelter of Savages Spinney, a small ancient oak and ash woodland that is carpeted with bluebells and primroses in spring. On this side of the reservoir there are a number of enticing little nature trails that lead off the main path. Take a break from your bike and wander along The Nightingale Trail through the plantation woodland, as it offers the best chance of hearing the secretive nightingale's famous song.

From the peaceful sanctuary of the nature reserve, head into the more populated area of Mander Park, where the views across the water are just lovely. If you're planning to circuit the reservoir then this is around the halfway point, so the picnic spots here are great for a mid-ride rest. From here, it's a gentle roll along the shoreline past the pretty boats of Grafham Water Sailing Club, through the little village of Perry and into the greenery of Plummer Park where the route splits.

To complete the loop back to Marlow Park, simply continue to follow the waterside trail for a further mile or so, crossing the long dam along the way for wonderful views back across the reservoir. Alternatively, head south on NCN 12 in Plummer Park and leave Grafham Water to ride into the flat farmland of Cambridgeshire. This is a pleasant, gentle descent on straight, rough farm tracks and quiet lanes. You'll pass between vast crop fields, where the well-known and distinctive 'little-bit-o-bread-and-no-cheeeeese' song of yellowhammers fills the air. Drop into Hail Weston village, taking particular care when crossing the ford here, before reaching the open grassy space of Riverside Park in St Neots, which stretches for a mile along the River Great Ouse. End here, among the huge weeping willow trees or at the park's Ambience Café. Alternatively, it's just half a mile to the lively Market Square in the centre of St Neots, and a further mile to the train station.

Finish: St Neots train station or Marlow Park, Grafham Water

RIDE 10

Train stations: St Neots or Huntingdon

Grade: Moderate

Terrain, gradients and access: Gently undulating around Grafham Water, then a gentle descent to St Neots. Stony trail, tarmac path and a short grassy section in Plummer Park. On-road sections at Grafham, Perry, Hail Weston and St Neots. There's a ford to cross at Hail Weston, or steps around it if needed.

Loops, links and longer rides: NCN 12 links Huntingdon and St Neots via Grafham Water so it is possible to start a ride at Huntingdon train station and head to Grafham Water. At St Neots, follow NCN 12 to just beyond Great Barford and join NCN 51 University Way (**Ride 09**).

Stay: The Eaton Oak, St Neots (01480) 219555 **theeatonoak.co.uk** or camping pods at Grafham Water Lodges, Perry 07732 186915 **grafhamwaterlodges.co.uk**

Eat and drink: Wheatsheaf pub in West Ferry. In St Neots, try The Eaton Oak pub or Ambience Café in Riverside Park.

Cycle hire: Rutland Cycling, Marlow Car Park at Grafham Water 0330 555 0080 **rutlandcycling.com**

Wider area cycle map: South Cambridgeshire, Beds & North Herts

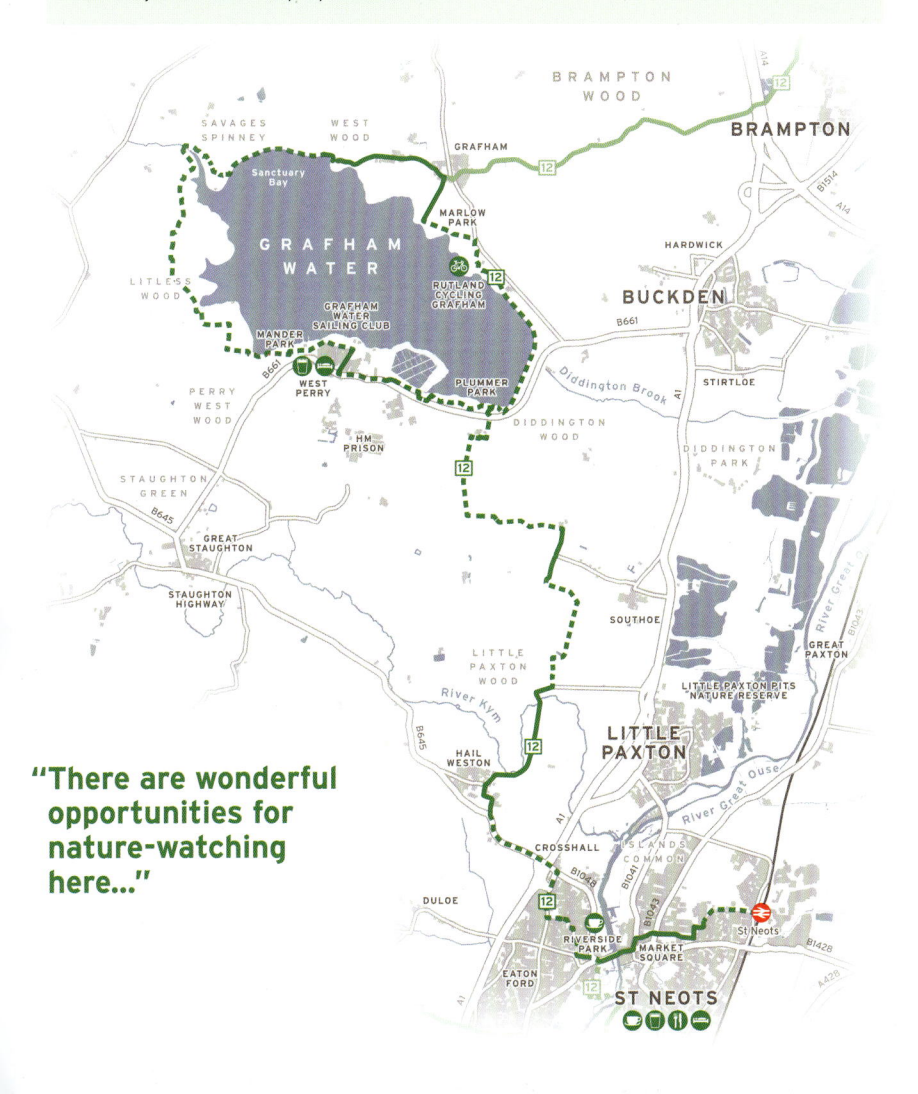

"There are wonderful opportunities for nature-watching here..."

RIDE 11
8.5 miles

Start: Cambridge train station

CAMBRIDGE
TO
WATERBEACH

This ride's opening miles are steeped in the scholarly splendour and tradition that defines Cambridge. Start at Cambridge train station and follow the local route to join NCN 11 and ride across the Commons to the grand buildings of St Catharine's College and King's College on King's Parade. It's worth taking a small diversion here to visit 'The Backs', where the colleges and their grounds back onto the River Cam to present one of the most recognisable, memorable and much-photographed Cambridge scenes.

Ride past the vibrant city market and beautiful 'Round Church', one of the oldest buildings in Cambridge, before joining the popular River Cam at Jesus Green, where the riverbank is studded with college boathouses. Rowing as a sport originated in Cambridge, where college rowing crews would chase each other during training, and today's varsity teams gliding powerfully through the water make for an impressive sight along this busy stretch of the river. Ride along the grassy and cattle-grazed Midsummer Common, before crossing the water on the Riverside Bridge, which takes you on the quiet roads through Chesterton to join the traffic-free towpath on the opposite bank of the River Cam.

Thatched Cambridgeshire cottages tucked among the greenery, and the glassy surface of the river, broken only by the occasional bird or boat, make for a deeply tranquil ride as you follow part of the Fen Rivers Way,

a long-distance footpath along the rivers Cam and Great Ouse from Cambridge all the way to King's Lynn.

Reach Baits Bite Lock in the route's final miles, which is the start point for the exciting Cambridge 'bumps' races that take place on the Cam each year, and where there's also a half-mile link route to Milton Country Park. If you don't feel like a diversion to this serene spot, then simply stick to the riverbank for two more miles to reach the hamlet of Clayhithe. Here you'll leave the water behind and head through the young trees of Cow Hollow Wood to the ride's endpoint at Waterbeach train station.

208

Finish: Waterbeach train station

RIDE 11

Train stations: Cambridge and Waterbeach

Grade: Easy

Terrain, gradients and access: Flat tarmac path and fine gravel track with some road crossings and on-road sections around Cambridge and Chesterton. At Brooklands Avenue (between Cambridge train station and NCN 11), use the road if confident in traffic or the shared-use path if less confident or cycling with children.

Loops, links and longer rides: Start the ride at Shelford train station for an additional four miles of traffic-free riding that takes in the 10,000th mile of the National Cycle Network. NCN 11 and 51 Cambridge to Wicken Fen via Anglesey Abbey (**Ride 12**).

Stay: YHA Cambridge, 0345 371 9728 **yha.org.uk**

Eat and drink: Make the most of the riverside pit stops on this route including The Mill pub overlooking the River Cam near the start, Basket Room Café at Jesus Green open air swimming pool and the highly-recommended Midsummer House, a riverside restaurant on Midsummer Common. At Clayhithe near the route's end, try The Bridge restaurant.

Cycle hire: City Cycle Hire, Cambridge (01223) 365629 **citycyclehire.com**, Rutland Cycling (at the station and Grand Arcade), 0330 555 0080 **rutlandcycling.com** or Grounds Cycle Centre, Milton Park 07869 469960 **groundscyclecentres.uk** Many more cycle hire outlets in Cambridge

Wider area cycle map: South Cambridgeshire, Beds & North Herts

"Steeped in the scholarly splendour and tradition that defines Cambridge."

Mathematical Bridge, Cambridge

CAMBRIDGE
TO
WICKEN FEN

Konik ponies at Wicken Fen National Nature Reserve

This is a ride of extremes, starting among the elegant and refined architecture in the culturally-rich city of Cambridge, and ending in the wild and atmospheric Fens at the National Trust's oldest nature reserve.

Start at the magnificent King's College and ride past Cambridge's popular open-air marketplace, before joining the south banks of the River Cam and passing through the city's remarkable riverside green spaces of Jesus Green, Midsummer Common, Stourbridge Common and Ditton Meadows. The city and river are soon left behind as you head into flat Cambridgeshire farmland. At Lode, just after you cross the main road at the ride's halfway point, it's worth following the short, traffic-free route to the National Trust's Anglesey Abbey, a Jacobean-style country house, and Lode Mill, a working water-powered mill that still grinds flour for visitors to buy.

Alternatively, continue along the route through Lode, a classic Cambridgeshire village of whitewashed thatched cottages and tall, colourful hollyhocks in summer. You're following The Lodes Way here, named after the manmade waterways that run through the Fens, and it's the linear paths between these waterways that lead you into a timeless, flat and marshy landscape under vast, moody skies. Flat they may be, but the fens provide no shelter from the wind, meaning cycling can be a battle on a blustery day. Take a rest on the benches at White Fen near Lode and Longmeadow Community Woodland, or a short while later alongside the steel figures of the 'portrait bench' near Reach Lode.

Pass through Burwell Fen, one of the lowest points in the Cambridgeshire Fens at nearly two metres below sea level, and climb up to the raised viewing point here to get the best view of the expansive scenery. The final miles are through Adventurers' Fen then Wicken Fen National Nature Reserve, one of the most important wetlands in Europe. Look out for the herds of grazing highland cattle and Konik ponies, before ending at the National Trust visitor centre. There are boat trips, a café and shop, wildlife viewing points and a cycle hire centre here, or it's a very short ride along a quiet road into Wicken village.

Finish: Wicken Fen National Nature Reserve

RIDE 12

Train station: Cambridge

Grade: Moderate

Terrain, gradients and access: Flat tarmac path, fine gravel track and stony trail. Several road crossings and on-road sections at Cambridge, Stow cum Quy, Bottisham, Lode and Wicken Fen. The bridge over Burwell Lode has nine steps on each side with a steep, narrow ramp for pushing bikes over, but there are plans for developing a cycling bridge here.

Loops, links and longer rides: From Wicken Fen, follow NCN 11 for a further seven miles along quiet country lanes and traffic-free paths to Ely. Ely's majestic Norman cathedral, 'the ship of the fens', is visible from the route and there is a train station at Ely for the return journey to Cambridge. Or, at Bottisham follow NCN 51 along a mostly on-road route to Newmarket and Bury St Edmunds.

Stay: YHA Cambridge 0345 371 9728 yha.org.uk or the National Trust has an area for wild camping at Wicken Fen (01353) 720274 nationaltrust.org.uk/wicken-fen

Eat and drink: Benet's café is the best place in Cambridge for ice cream, or eat at The Eagle pub on Bene't Street, where World War II airmen have scrawled messages on the ceiling. Mid-route, there are Elite Pizza, The Shed at Lode and The Dyke's End at Reach is a wonderful pub. The National Trust café at Wicken Fen is the best for fenland surroundings.

Cycle hire: City Cycle Hire, Cambridge (01223) 365629 citycyclehire.com Wicken Fen nature reserve (01353) 720274 nationaltrust.org.uk/wicken-fen (Easter to October), Rutland Cycling (at the station and Grand Arcade) 0330 555 0080 rutlandcycling.com or Grounds Cycle Centre, Milton Park 07869 469960 groundscyclecentres.uk Many more cycle hire outlets in Cambridge.

Wider area cycle map: South Cambridgeshire, Beds & North Herts

"A timeless, flat and marshy landscape under vast, moody skies."

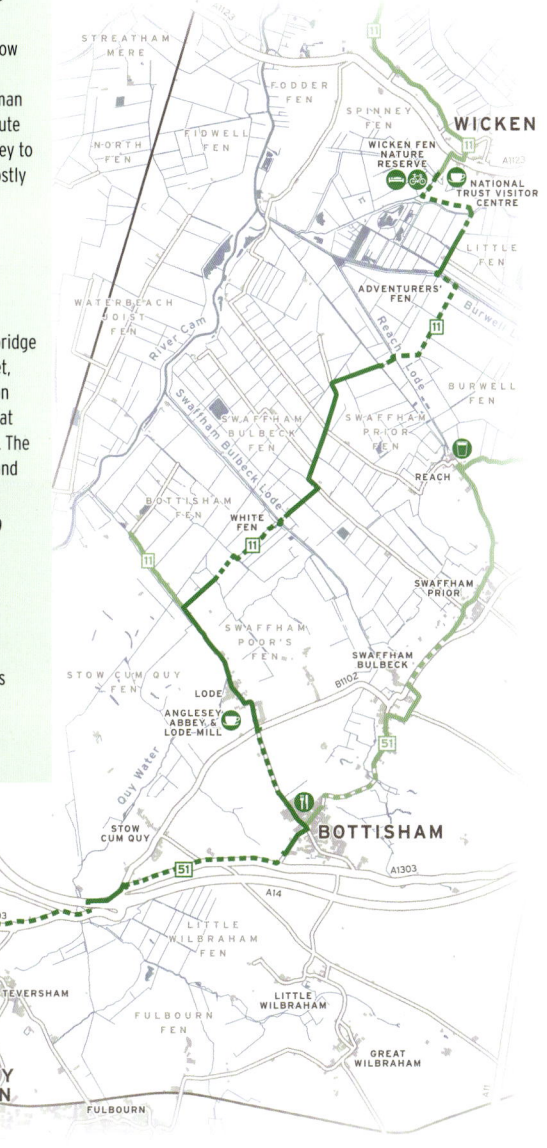

RIDE 13
6.5 miles — 53 63 — **Start and finish:** Viersen Platz, Peterborough

NENE PARK LOOP

Unhurried, carefree cycling is the best way to experience the serene Nene Valley. This gentle ride takes in the atmospheric wetlands west of Peterborough and the exceptional Nene Park.

Start from the walking and cycling bridge on Viersen Platz and join the south bank of the River Nene. Much of the ride's first half runs alongside the tracks of the Nene Valley Railway, so you may be passed by steam and diesel locomotives chugging along the popular heritage line. In the opening miles you'll also pass the tranquil lagoons and reedbeds of the Wildlife Trust's Woodston Ponds nature reserve. Originally, a British Sugar factory used the ponds in the sugar beet washing process, but since production stopped they've been enthusiastically recolonised by insects, newts, grey herons and reed warblers.

From here, ride along the edges of Orton Meadows, before joining the bridges and boardwalks that lead through woodland and marshy ground into Ferry Meadows Country Park at the heart of Nene Park. The park is the real highlight of the ride, and the pretty open water of the lakes, colourful spring flowers in Bluebell Wood, boating, birdwatching and gorgeous scenery are just some of the reasons why it attracts more than a million visitors each year.

At around the halfway point, ride along the shores of Overton Lake, where waterside picnic benches make a wonderful mid-ride stop. Ferry Meadows Café occupies an attractive spot here, too, where you can eat while watching swans and geese glide across the water. From here, enter a wilder part of the park at Ham Mere nature reserve, where there are secretive hides for getting a good look across the wetlands. Retrace your path back through Orton Meadows, before crossing the River Nene and following the straight line of the rowing course at Thorpe Meadows, beside dramatic open-air artworks in the sculpture park. The route joins up with the Workhouse Cycleway in the final miles, running through the birch, oak, maple and alder trees of Crightons' Wood, before ending back at the walking and cycling bridge.

Train station: Peterborough

Grade: Easy

Terrain, gradients and access: Flat tarmac path and fine gravel track. Some small road crossings and gated crossings over the heritage railway line.

Loops, links and longer rides: In Ferry Meadows Country Park, extend the ride by following the two and a half-mile Gunwade Trail around the meadows, woodland and Gunwade Lake. Peterborough Green Wheel is 45 miles of routes that circle the city following quiet roads and traffic-free paths, with 'spokes' leading into the city centre. NCN 12, 21 and 63 Celtic Causeway (**Ride 14**).

Stay: Ferry Meadows Caravan Club Site is open to members and non-members, and has tent pitches available (01733) 233526 **caravanclub.co.uk**

Eat and drink: In Ferry Meadows Country Park, Lakeside Kitchen and Bar is beside Gunwade Lake, while Ferry Meadows Café overlooks Overton Lake. The Boathouse pub is at Thorpe Meadows in the ride's second half.

Cycle hire: Rutland Cycling, Ferry Meadows Country Park 0330 555 0080 **rutlandcycling.com**

Wider area cycle map: The Fens

RIDE 13

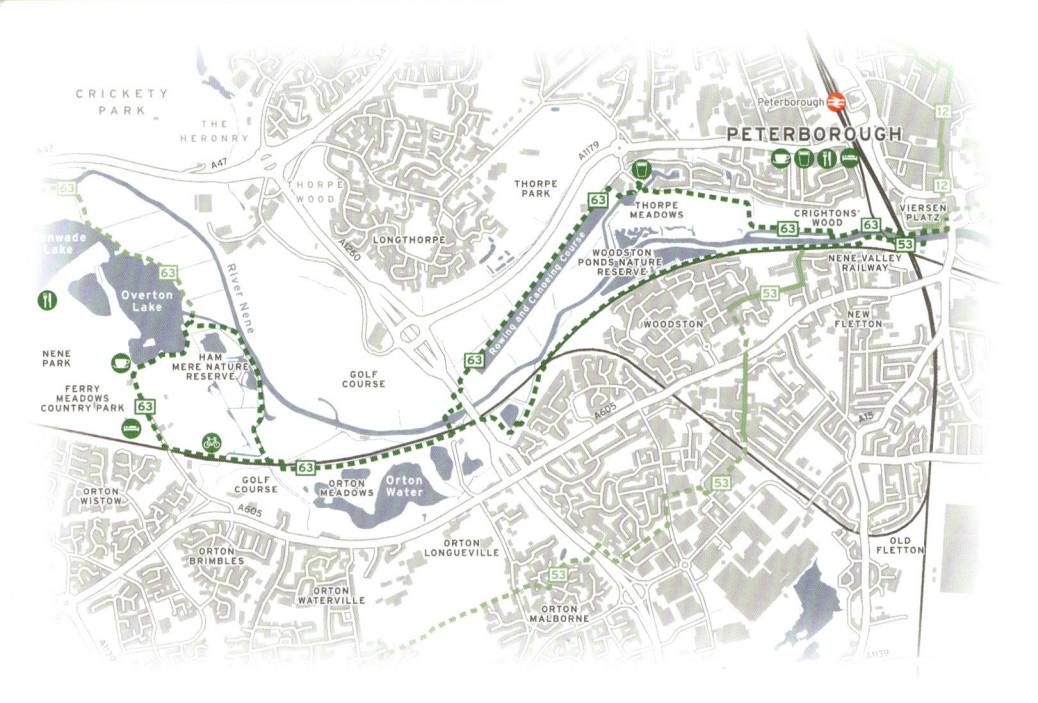

Peterborough waterways

213

CELTIC CAUSEWAY

Ride back into the Bronze Age on this loop through Peterborough's flat and fertile fenlands.

Start at Key Theatre and head east along the Embankment, past moored narrow boats, weeping willows dangling lazily into the water and swans, ducks and geese on the river bank. In the summer, take a tiny detour to the Lido, a popular outdoor swimming spot, for a dip.

Leave the city behind and ride along the very straight course of the River Nene, where the scenery quickly becomes remote and wild, and the raised trail offers great views over the washes. Just over two miles in, a signed half-mile trail off the main path leads you over a wooden footbridge and between crop fields to Flag Fen, where grass-roofed, reconstructed roundhouses sit among the farmland. Flag Fen is a fascinating archaeology park, and you can get a glimpse into how prehistoric people lived here, see original Bronze Age remains, or take a walk around the Roman herb garden and the mere.

Retrace the route back to the main trail, where the impressive curve of Shanks Millennium Bridge appears up ahead. Cross the bridge and turn right to follow the south bank of the River Nene back into Peterborough. The path is set a little lower down on this side, so the views are fairly limited as you ride back towards the city. Nevertheless, it's a pleasant leafy trail all the way to the attractive Stanground Lock.

Leave the water here to ride through the quiet residential area of Stanground, passing the beautiful St John the Baptist church along the way, before crossing back over the river. The final half mile is a repeat of the start along the Embankment, but this time you'll be able to see the spires of Peterborough's Norman cathedral, one of England's great cathedrals, poking out from between the trees up ahead.

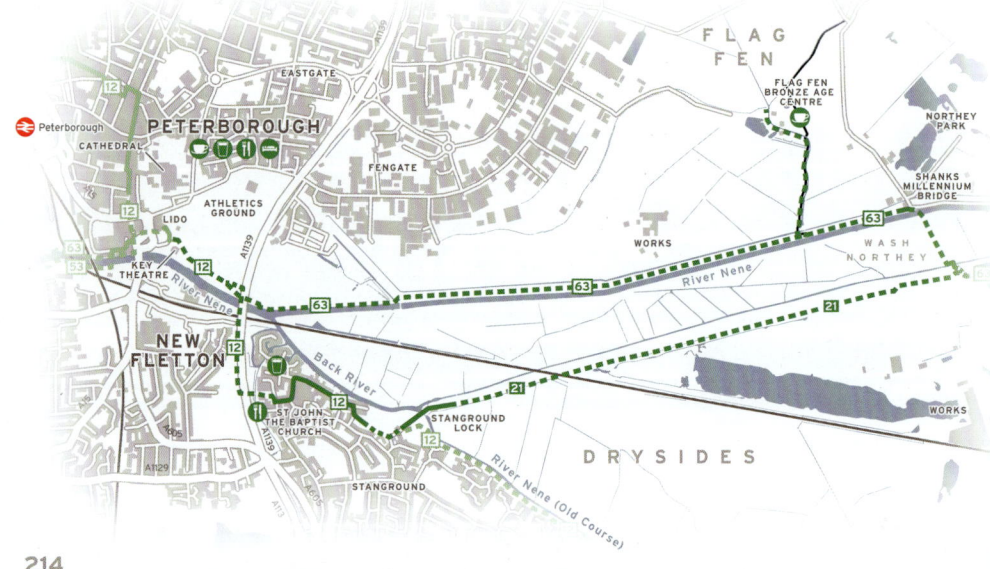

RIDE 14

"One of England's great cathedrals, poking out from between the trees up ahead."

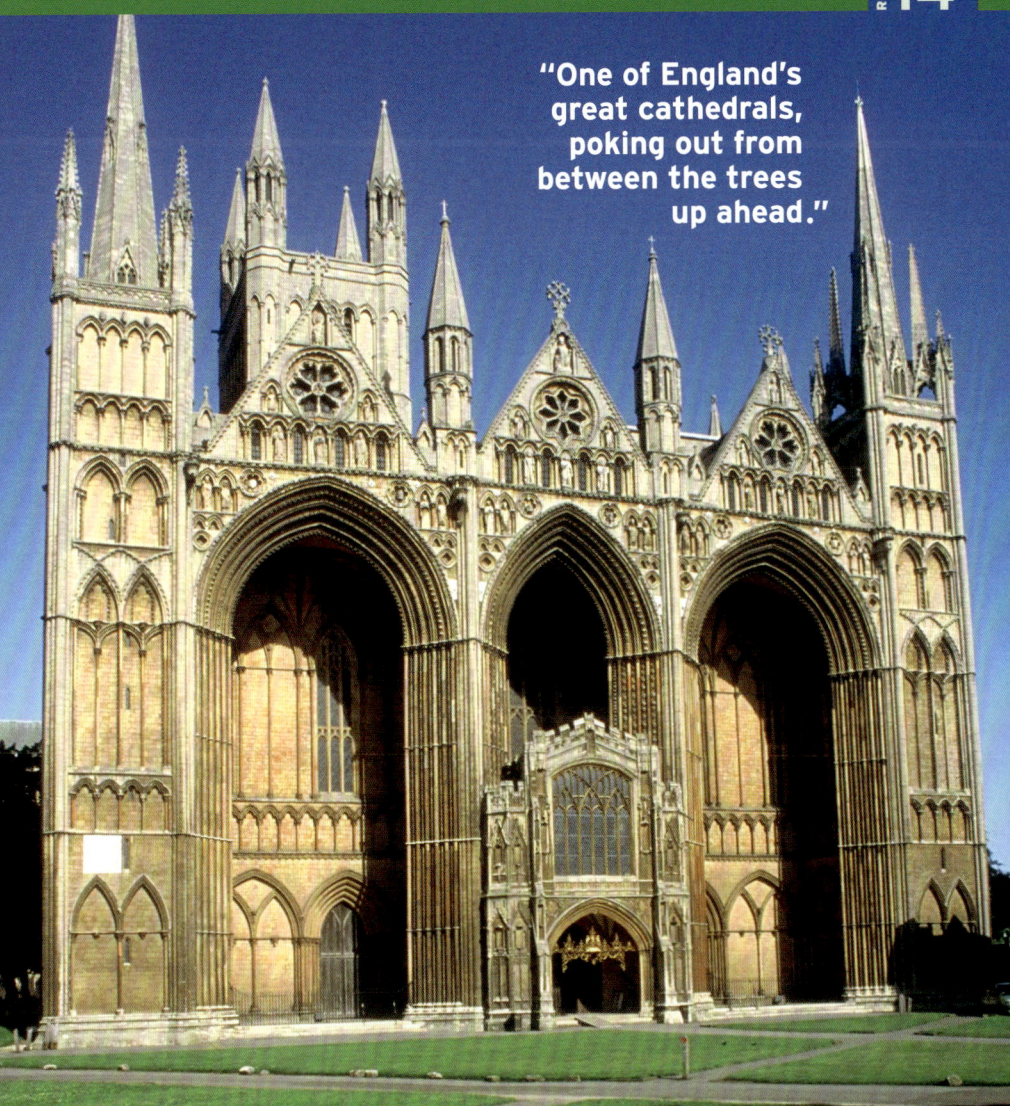

Train station: Peterborough
Grade: Easy
Terrain, gradients and access: Flat tarmac path and stony trail, with a short, on-road section at Stanground.
Loops, links and longer rides: Peterborough Green Wheel is 45 miles of routes that circle the city following quiet roads and traffic-free paths, with 'spokes' leading into the city centre. Nene Park Loop (**Ride 13**)

Stay: Clarks Guest House, Peterborough 0845 519 6521 peterboroughguesthouse.net
Eat and drink: Try The Chalkboard at Key Theatre at the start, or the café at Flag Fen mid-ride. There are plenty of cafés in Peterborough city centre, or try The Woolpack pub at Stanground.
Cycle hire: Rutland Cycling, Ferry Meadows Country Park, Peterborough 0330 555 0080 rutlandcycling.com
Wider area cycle map: The Fens

Peterborough Cathedral

RIDE 15
14 miles

Start: St Crispin's Road and Barker Street roundabout, Norwich

MARRIOTT'S WAY

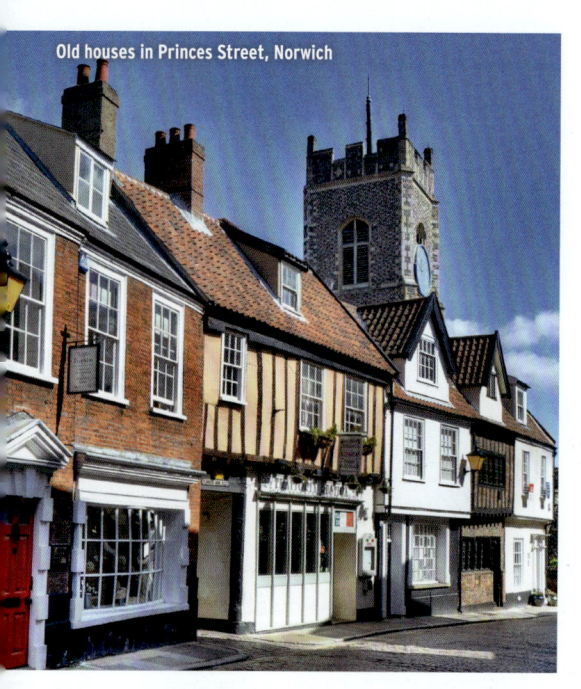

Old houses in Princes Street, Norwich

This ride through the Wensum Valley in Norfolk follows a section of one of the longest railway paths in the country. The medieval city of Norwich is a lovely start, and NCN 1 links the train station to the start of the Marriott's Way, passing close to the hilltop Norwich Castle on the way and Norwich Cathedral, voted as Norfolk's favourite building.

The Marriott's Way begins beside the River Wensum on the north west side of the city, following the path of the disused Midland and Great Northern Railway and named after William Marriott, the railway's Chief Engineer and Manager for more than 40 years. It's now a wildlife-rich green corridor of woodland, flowers and farmland, but its former life as a railway is recognised by sculptures along the path.

Leave the city behind, crossing the wriggling River Wensum and riding beside the grassland of Anderson's Meadow. In fact, the river twists and turns so sharply beside the route that you'll cross it five times in total, with good views across the water from each bridge. It's a great route for wildlife watching, and the species change with the seasons, so keep a particular watch for brown hares boxing on the farmland in spring, meadow brown butterflies in summer, and large flocks of redwings feeding on the berries in the plump hedgerows through autumn and winter.

The winding descent through thick trees to the village of Thorpe Marriott is a highlight of the ride's first half, and is followed by the deep forest plantations of Swannington Bottom and Mileplain, which make for cool, shady riding in the heat of summer.

In the second half, picnic at the site of the old Attlebridge station, before reaching the open water of the lagoons and fishing lakes at Lenwade. In the final miles, the beautiful wildflower meadows and grassland of Whitwell Common are beside the route as you ride into Whitwell and Reepham Station, which has been beautifully restored to the elegance of its 1930s-40s heyday. Steam and diesel engines operate from the station on running days, and there is a campsite should you wish to dally.

Finish: Market Place, Reepham

RIDE 15

"One of the longest railway paths in the country."

Train station: Norwich

Grade: Moderate

Terrain, gradients and access: Flat tarmac path, becoming crushed stone as the route gets more rural; mostly good but with some rough parts and with some gentle ascents and descents mid-route. Some road crossings throughout with on-road sections at Drayton, Attlebridge and Reepham, but otherwise traffic-free pretty much all the way.

Loops, links and longer rides: The Marriott's Way is 26 miles in its entirety, between Norwich and Aylsham. It is traffic-free all the way, but the surface of the path is more rugged between Whitwell Station and Aylsham so it can be difficult to ride in poor weather. From the route's start, follow NCN 1 for a short ride into the centre of Norwich.

Stay: Wedgewood House B&B, Norwich (01603) 625730 wedgewoodhouse.co.uk

Eat and drink: On the ride from Norwich train station to the route's start you'll pass many eateries, including Butterfly Café and The Café Club. Whitwell Station has a café, or in Reepham Market Place try the Kings Arms pub, The Dial House restaurant or Diane's Pantry.

Cycle hire: Beryl Bikes (020) 3003 5044 beryl.cc, Bicycle Links CIC, Norwich (01603) 631199 bicyclelinks.org.uk or Whitwell Station (01603) 871694 whitwellstation.com

Wider area cycle map: Norfolk

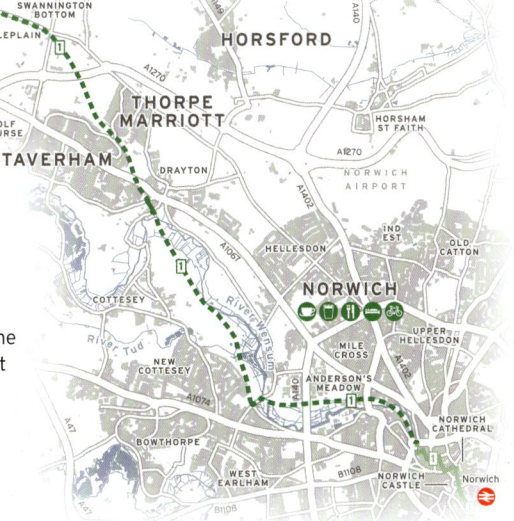

At Whitwell, the path continues along the Themelthorpe Curve, a famously sharp bend in the tracks. However, this ride ends in Reepham, so leave the railway path beyond Whitwell Station and follow the route signs to join Whitwell Road, a mile-long country lane into the pretty centre of the Georgian market town. It is a charming spot with thatched cottages and craft shops, a pretty church and a 16th Century coaching inn.

RIDE 16
10 miles

Start: Purfleet Place, King's Lynn waterfront

KING'S LYNN
TO
SANDRINGHAM

King's Lynn has a striking and historic area of docks by the river Great Ouse where we start our ride, including the remarkable Customs House. Heading south along the quay then left you pick up NCN 1 along Church Street, following signs to wend your way through the back streets of King's Lynn and into The Walks, an 18th Century park worth taking a little time off the route to explore – especially Red Mount chapel and the old entrance gates – originally part of the town's defences.

Once across the main rail line from London King's Cross and Cambridge into town you turn right onto the Sandringham Railway Path, leading you out of town through green spaces, passing between the Lynnsport leisure centre and the base of the local miniature railway society.

Towards the villages known as The Woottons (North and South) you share the pavement alongside the A1078 before entering South Wootton. Keep an eye out for NCN 1 signs that lead through more traffic-free open green space at Wootton Park.

Roads lead out of The Woottons and onto pretty Castle Rising village, dominated by the castle ruins with their huge Norman keep. The castle has been described as a combination of fortress and palatial hunting lodge. Originally it was probably reached by boat from King's Lynn up the marshy Babingley river. Today it's in the care of English Heritage and although you need to pay for a ticket to get a very close up look, the grassy car park is free and affords a good view of the site, making a nice picnic spot away from the traffic.

Heading away from the castle the route takes you past Trinity Hospital, an early 17th Century almshouse and onto a wonderful traffic-free section with great views over the Babingley River. Crossing the A149 you head into the Sandringham Royal Estate, with a huge variety of trees around you, following a quiet estate road to finish at the main entrance to Sandringham House itself. Even though you can't see the house from here, if you don't pay to venture in there is a beautifully located café and grassy picnic area here to enjoy. There are no trains from here back to King's Lynn, only buses.

Customs House, King's Lynn

Finish: Sandringham House entrance

RIDE 16

Train Station: King's Lynn

Grade: Moderate

Terrain, gradients and access: Some backstreet type roads and cycle lanes leaving King's Lynn on flat tarmac including a railpath. There are some road sections on the latter half of the ride and a few more ups and downs, though even on the roads other traffic is generally pretty light (care required on the short section of busier road through Castle Rising). Very few, if any access barriers en route.

Loops, links and longer rides: This route is mostly part of NCN 1 which runs from Dover to the Scottish Highlands for some 1,264 miles. In this area it heads into North Norfolk and around Suffolk before entering London along the Lea Valley.

A popular local ride at King's Lynn is to take the pedestrian and bike ferry across the Great Ouse river to West Lynn village and ride back to town along the river embankment, picking up NCN 1 at a road bridge downstream.

Stay: Fairlight Lodge, King's Lynn (01553) 762234
fairlightlodge.co.uk

Eat and drink: Lots of options in King's Lynn with a choice of spots for sitting out including the South Quay and by the Minster. Swan Inn just off the route at South Wootton serves food. Castle Rising Tearoom has a lovely location opposite the Castle and there is a café outside Sandringham House's main entrance.

Cycle hire: Wheel Travel 07940 497 093
wheel-travel.co.uk Bikes delivered to you – serving the north-west Norfolk area

Wider area cycle map: The Fens

Sandringham railpath

219

NORTH WEST

The North West is one of the most characterful parts of the country and this collection of rides takes in its most spirited cities and towns. Larger than life Blackpool is a highlight, and, going from the exuberant to the idyllic, so is the heart of the Lake District. Indeed, three rides in this collection show it at its very best; Whitehaven to Rowrah in Cumbria offers views over the remote Ennerdale Valley, one of the most secluded and scenic areas in the Lakes, whilst Keswick Railway Path leads through the thick woodland of Greta Gorge into the foothills of the magnificent Blencathra mountain. Both rides belong to the 140-mile Sea to Sea (C2C) route, the most popular challenge ride in the country. Finally the route taking in Lake Windermere and Langdale is a microcosm of the very best of Lake District scenery.

Mountainous views across Snowdonia and the Bowland Fells are just as impressive as the Lake District, creating a breathtaking backdrop for rides into the walled city of Chester and the Georgian architecture of Lancaster, whilst the magical estuaries of the Lune and Dee provide the setting for some of the most tranquil rides in this guidebook.

It's the stunning north west coastline that provides the biggest surprise, though. Rides along the Fylde Coast to Fleetwood, or beside the wide, sweeping curve of Morecambe Bay are a sheer delight, and the sunsets across the Solway Firth on the Maryport to Allonby ride cannot be bettered. But it's the Sefton Coastal Path from Crosby to Formby in Merseyside that really shines. You'll never be alone on this ride beside the wild, tufty dunes and wide beach; one hundred cast iron men are dotted across the foreshore to keep you company, part of the truly remarkable 'Another Place' artwork by Antony Gormley.

'Another Place', Crosby Beach

Routes overview

- **01** Burton Marsh Greenway & River Dee Path (14 miles)
- **02** Chester Railway Path (8 miles)
- **03** Wirral Way (12 miles)
- **04** Sefton Coastal Path (7 miles)
- **05** Leeds & Liverpool Canal (Burnley to Barnoldswick) (15 miles)
- **06** Blackpool to Fleetwood (11 miles)
- **07** Lune Estuary Path (6 miles)
- **08** Lancaster to Heysham via Morecambe Bay (6 miles)
- **09** Lune Valley Trail (5 miles)
- **10** Lancaster Canal (8 miles)
- **11** Bowness to Elterwater (12.5 miles)
- **12** Whitehaven to Rowrah (9 miles)
- **13** Keswick Railway Path (4 miles)
- **14** Maryport to Allonby (5.5 miles)
- ▬ Featured ride
- ▬ National Cycle Network (traffic-free and on-road)

RIDE 01
14 miles — 568 — **Start:** The Harp Inn, Little Neston

BURTON MARSH GREENWAY
&
RIVER DEE PATH

Suspension Bridge at Connah's Quay

The sprawling Dee Estuary and mountainous north Wales scenery at the beginning of this ride are a startling contrast to the stylish and compact walled city of Chester at the end.

Start at The Harp Inn in Little Neston, where the incredible views stretch right across the marshland to north Wales in the distance. The giant peak of Moel Famau and its neighbours in the Clwydian Range dominate the Welsh skyline, and the giant white suspension bridge at Connah's Quay can be seen spanning the estuary up ahead.

Within the opening miles there's a short, signed link route that will take you inland to Ness Botanic Gardens, or simply stay on the estuary edge and look across the water to Flintshire, where the tumbledown remains of Flint Castle can be seen.

Around three miles in, you'll approach the fenlands and reedbeds of RSPB Burton Mere Wetlands, straddling the border between England and Wales. This is the most enchanting spot on the entire ride, and wooden boardwalks lead you around wet meadows of grazing sheep, open pools and fat bulrushes. After this heavenly nature haven, the urban interruption of Deeside Industrial Estate is something of a surprise, but it's quickly passed and you'll soon be back on the banks of the River Dee, following its

Finish: Chester Cross   **RIDE 01**

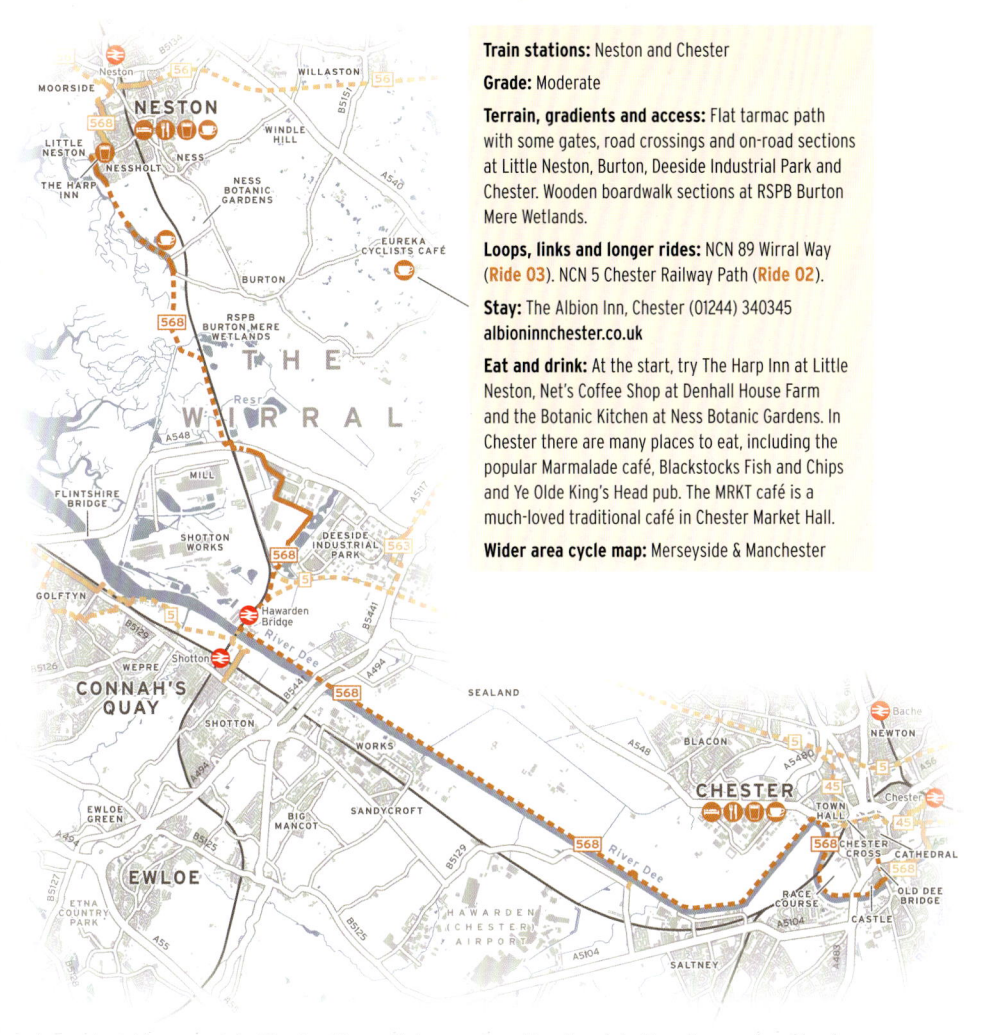

Train stations: Neston and Chester

Grade: Moderate

Terrain, gradients and access: Flat tarmac path with some gates, road crossings and on-road sections at Little Neston, Burton, Deeside Industrial Park and Chester. Wooden boardwalk sections at RSPB Burton Mere Wetlands.

Loops, links and longer rides: NCN 89 Wirral Way (**Ride 03**). NCN 5 Chester Railway Path (**Ride 02**).

Stay: The Albion Inn, Chester (01244) 340345
albioninnchester.co.uk

Eat and drink: At the start, try The Harp Inn at Little Neston, Net's Coffee Shop at Denhall House Farm and the Botanic Kitchen at Ness Botanic Gardens. In Chester there are many places to eat, including the popular Marmalade café, Blackstocks Fish and Chips and Ye Olde King's Head pub. The MRKT café is a much-loved traditional café in Chester Market Hall.

Wider area cycle map: Merseyside & Manchester

long, straight course into Chester. The path is gently raised along the waterside here, and it's often a wild and blustery ride with black-headed gulls patrolling the sandy banks of the river, and lapwings flying overhead in their distinctively lopsided way.

After a few miles, the spires of Chester Town Hall and Chester Cathedral become visible up ahead, and it's an easy, gliding ride along the river into the city, passing Chester Racecourse and the castle along the way. Leave the water behind at the Old Dee Bridge to enter the city walls and climb up the road into the city centre.

End at Chester Cross, the best spot for admiring the famous Chester Rows, ornate black and white medieval buildings that line the cobbled streets.

223

RIDE 02
8 miles

Start: Lime Wood Fields, Chester

CHESTER RAILWAY PATH

This ride from the charming city of Chester crosses the border into Wales along the former Mickle Trafford to Dee Marsh railway line, which used to transport steel to and from Hawarden Bridge Steelworks.

Start at Lime Wood Fields, a big grassy space on the north east side of Chester, and follow this popular green corridor along the top edge of the city. Just a short way along the route you'll reach Northgate Ponds Park, where there's a signed three quarters of a-mile link route into the heart of Chester, well worth following for the chance to explore the cathedral, Roman amphitheatre and medieval streets of one of England's finest walled cities.

Pass over the top of the Shropshire Union Canal, pausing to look down over the calm water and narrowboats gliding along it, before heading out into the open countryside.

Around the old railway station at Blacon, there are wide open views across the meadows and farmland in the foreground, while the Snowdonia Mountains loom large on the horizon.

After just a few miles you'll cross the border into Wales, riding through rich Flintshire farmland that surrounds the River Dee all the way to Hawarden Bridge. Rattling over the wooden planks of the huge old railway bridge across the water is an enlivening experience, and once across you'll join up with the Wales Coast Path through Wepre Riverside, a Site of Special Scientific Interest (SSSI).

End at Connah's Quay Wharf, where there are viewing points for watching the huge variety of wildlife on the Dee Estuary.

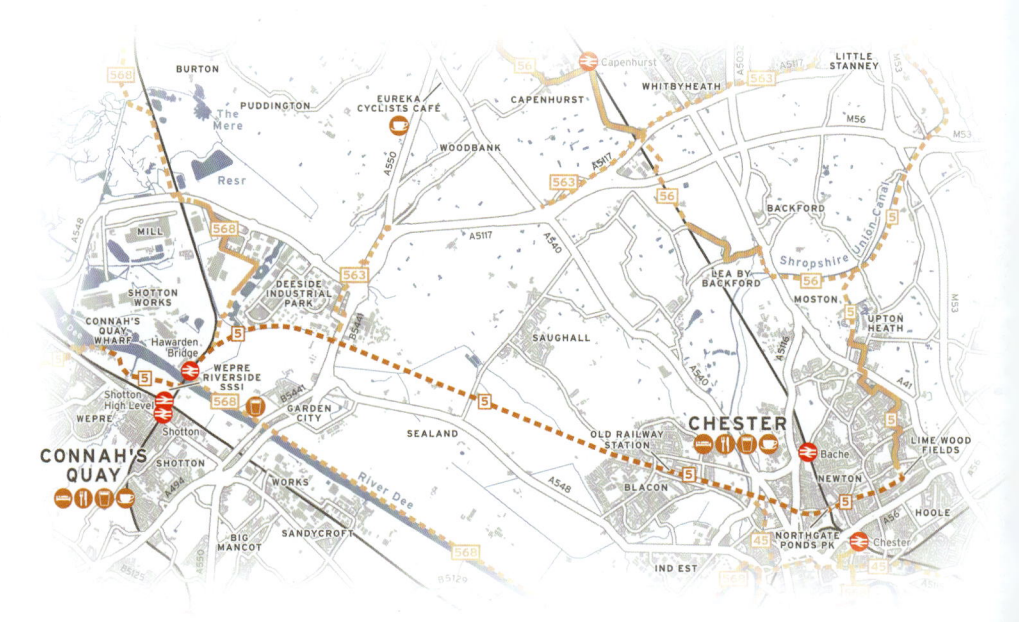

Finish: The Wharf at Connah's Quay

RIDE 02

Train stations: Chester, Hawarden Bridge and Shotton

Grade: Easy

Terrain, gradients and access: Flat tarmac path.

Loops, links and longer rides: Turn the route into a loop by following NCN 568 River Dee Path from Hawarden Bridge back into Chester (**Ride 01**). NCN 5 North Wales Coast Cycle Route (**Ride 25**).

Stay: The Bunkroom, Chester (01244) 325524 thebunkroom.co.uk

Eat and drink: There are lots of places to try in the centre of Chester. Alternatively, Sticky Walnut is near the start of the route at Hoole. There are lots of eating places around Shotton and Garden City near the route's end.

Wider area cycle map: Merseyside & Manchester

Eastgate Clock on Chester's old city walls

"The charming city of Chester...one of England's finest walled cities."

River Dee at Chester

225

WIRRAL WAY

The enduring beauty of the untamed and ever-changing Dee Estuary is a spectacular backdrop for this ride through the 12-mile Wirral Country Park, Britain's first ever country park. The importance of the estuary as a habitat for birds makes it a magnificent route for birdwatching by bike, and you'll traverse a cluster of wildlife-rich nature reserves along the way.

Start at the entrance to the country park on Grange Road, just a short distance from West Kirby train station, and pass immediately through the little Victorian Ashton Park. It's only a quick detour from here down Church Road to one of Europe's largest marine lakes, a lovely spot for watching dingy sailing and windsurfing.

Cubbins Green picnic site comes next, the first in a sequence of scenic spots on the route to rest or access the sandy beaches. A marvellous mix of woodland, farmland and saltmarsh features throughout the ride, but it's the sensational coastline that reigns in these opening miles; the raised aspect of the trail offers panoramic views across the wide mouth of the estuary to Flintshire in north Wales.

Pass between the meadows of Dawpool Nature Reserve and reach Wirral Country Park's Thurstaston Visitor Centre. It's worth locking up and heading to the beach to walk beneath the Dee Cliffs, where the handsome whitewashed Shore Cottage is perched on the edge of the sand. As you head south, the dark bulk of Moel Famau or 'the mother of mountains' can be seen across the estuary. It's the highest peak in Wales' Clwydian Range, and the crumbling remains of Jubilee Tower can be seen on its summit.

At around the halfway point, arrive at the renowned birdwatching spot of Parkgate, where there are excellent views across the saltmarsh from Old Baths Car Park. It's particularly good here at high tide, when birds of prey can be seen hunting over the water and the wading birds come closer to the shore. However, do venture beyond the car park into Parkgate village, Cheshire's only coastal resort, to roll beside the classic black and white Cheshire buildings that line The Parade and sample the village's famous ice cream.

After Parkgate, the path leaves the estuary behind and takes you inland, passing the village of Neston and gently climbing between the high walls of sandstone at Neston Rock Cutting. The attractive Hadlow Road Station at Willaston is the only old station remaining on this disused railway line and makes a nice late stopping point, before tackling the final miles of leafy park to end at Hooton train station.

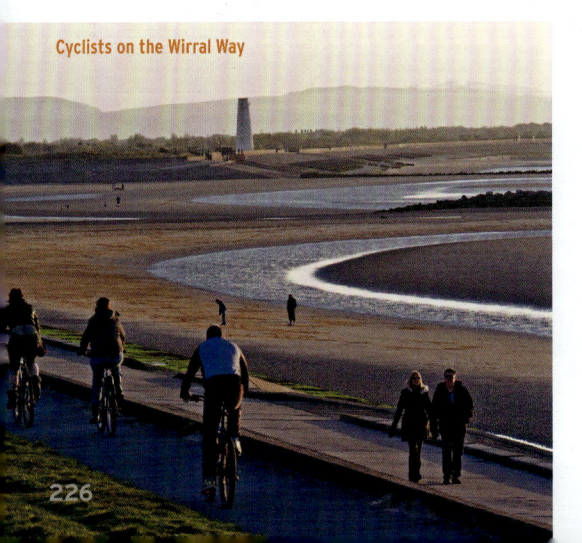

Cyclists on the Wirral Way

Finish: Hooton train station   RIDE **03**

Train stations: West Kirby and Hooton

Grade: Moderate

Terrain, gradients and access: Largely flat with a gentle climb in the second half. Fine gravel track with some road crossings and short, on-road sections around Gayton, Neston and Hooton.

Loops, links and longer rides: Turn the ride into a loop by joining NCN 56 at Parkgate and following a mix of on-road and traffic-free routes through the centre of the Wirral to Wallasey. At Wallasey, re-join NCN 89 to Hoylake and cycle back to the start at West Kirby. NCN 568 Burton Marsh Greenway & River Dee Path (**Ride 01**).

Stay: The Woodcote, Hooton (0151) 328 5730
thewoodcote.co.uk

Eat and drink: Aubergine Café in West Kirby is popular, or there are refreshments at Thurstaston Visitor Centre. In Parkgate, try the renowned ice cream at Nicholls Famous Ice Cream shop or The Parkgate Homemade Ice Cream Shop. Alternatively, eat at The Boat House pub or Mealors Seafood Shop for savoury food. Pollards Inn is at Willaston near the route's end.

Cycle hire: Bikes and Boards, West Kirby (0151) 6255533
bikeshopwestkirby.co.uk

Wider area cycle map: Merseyside & Manchester

227

RIDE 04 — 810 🚲 **Start:** Waterloo (Merseyside) train station

7 miles

SEFTON COASTAL PATH

A haunting open-air artwork and the astonishing natural beauty of the Sefton Coast set this apart as one of the country's most memorable routes.

Start at Waterloo (Merseyside) train station and ride the very short road into Crosby Coastal Park, where the marine lake, dunes and vast sands are incredibly popular and are a great start to the ride.

Rolling alongside the glorious, golden Crosby Beach is divine, and the opening two miles are spent in the company of 100 cast iron figures, known locally as the iron men. They are dotted across the foreshore gazing contemplatively out to sea; some are buried knee or thigh-deep in sand, whilst others stand on the surface, completely visible when the tide is out and up to their necks in water at high tide. This is the exceptional 'Another Place' artwork by renowned artist Antony Gormley, and it stays in the memory long after the ride is over.

Views across Liverpool Bay stretch right across to the Wirral Peninsula and the hills of north Wales, whilst a long belt of incredible tumbling dunes edges the path, and is one of the features that make the Sefton Coast so special.

Hall Road Coastguard Station marks the start of Hightown Dunes and Meadows nature reserve, a more wild and remote part of the route where the tufty, straw-coloured grasses are filled with clusters of purple wildflowers in summer.

At the halfway point of the ride, sit at the staggered white 'Pebble' sculpture to linger over the last views of the sea, before following the path away from the coast and into Hightown village. In the final miles the route follows the railway line where the path is fringed by tall rushes, and you'll cross over the River Alt as it winds its way to the sea.

At the end of the traffic-free path join Andrews Lane, turn right over the level crossing, then left into Formby Street to finish at Formby train station. Or, continue north for one mile to reach the National Trust Formby nature reserve and explore the beach, dunes and coastal pinewoods; you might spot rare native red squirrels or natterjack toads.

'Sardines' sculpture, Formby

Finish: Formby train station

RIDE 04

"One of the country's most memorable routes."

Train stations: Waterloo (Merseyside), Blundellsands & Crosby, and Formby

Grade: Easy

Terrain, gradients and access: Flat tarmac path and stony trail. Sand from Crosby Beach spills onto the path in the opening mile making it necessary to get off and push in parts. Short, on-road sections at Waterloo, Hightown and Formby.

Loops, links and longer rides: Sefton Coastal Path is part of the Trans Pennine Trail, a 215-mile coast to coast route from Hornsea to Southport. NCN 62 Liverpool Loop Line.

Stay: YHA Liverpool, near Albert Dock 0345 371 9527 www.yha.org.uk or Blundell B&B, Blundellsands (0151) 924 6947 blundellbandb.co.uk

Eat and drink: Try La Cafetiére Moroccan eatery or Moonlight Café in Crosby, The Pheasant at Hightown near the midway point or The Railway in Formby at the route's end. The Kitchen at Formby is a popular café.

Cycle hire: Citybike (0151) 233 3002 citybikeliverpool.co.uk

Wider area cycle map: Merseyside & Manchester

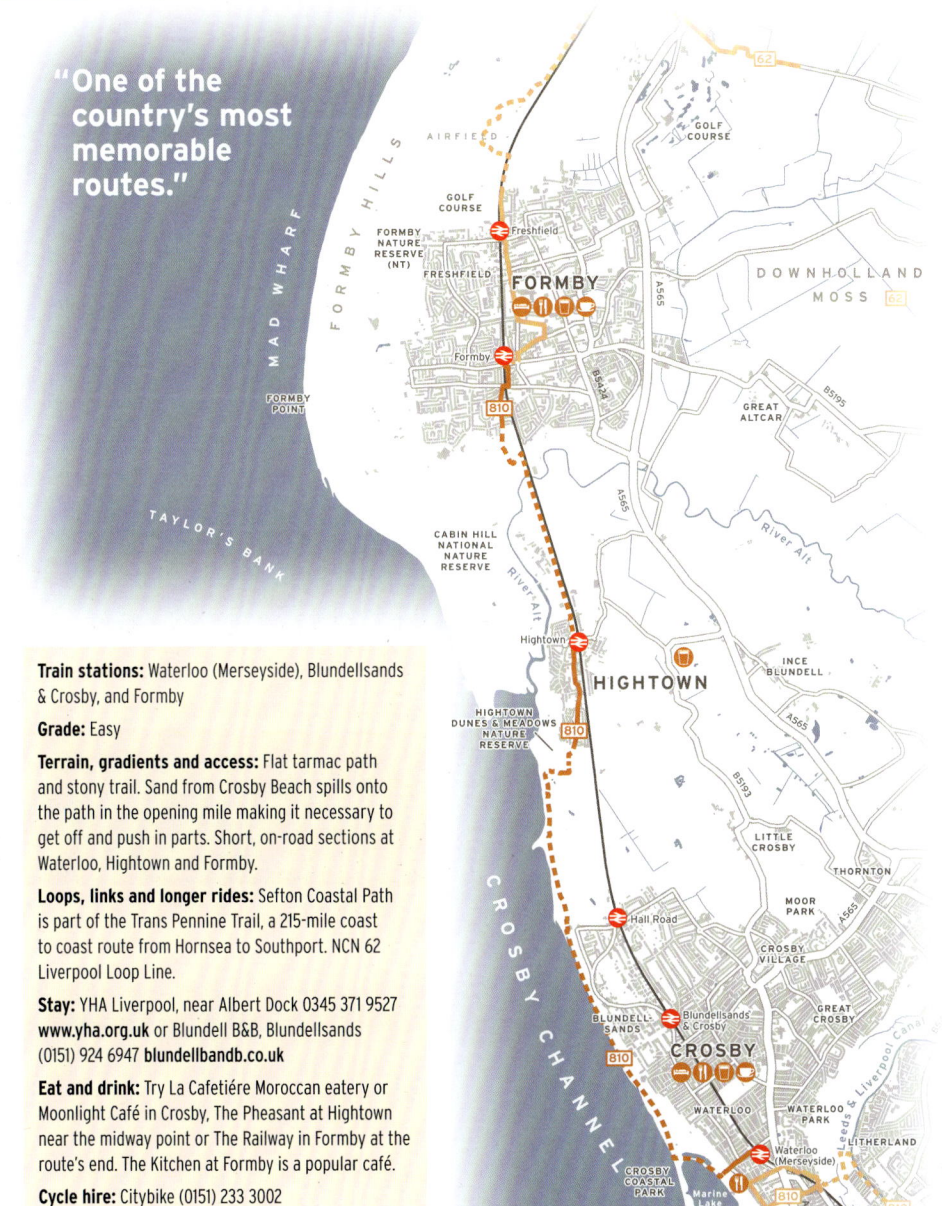

229

RIDE 05 — 15 miles — **Start:** Towneley Park, Burnley

LEEDS & LIVERPOOL CANAL

(BURNLEY TO BARNOLDSWICK)

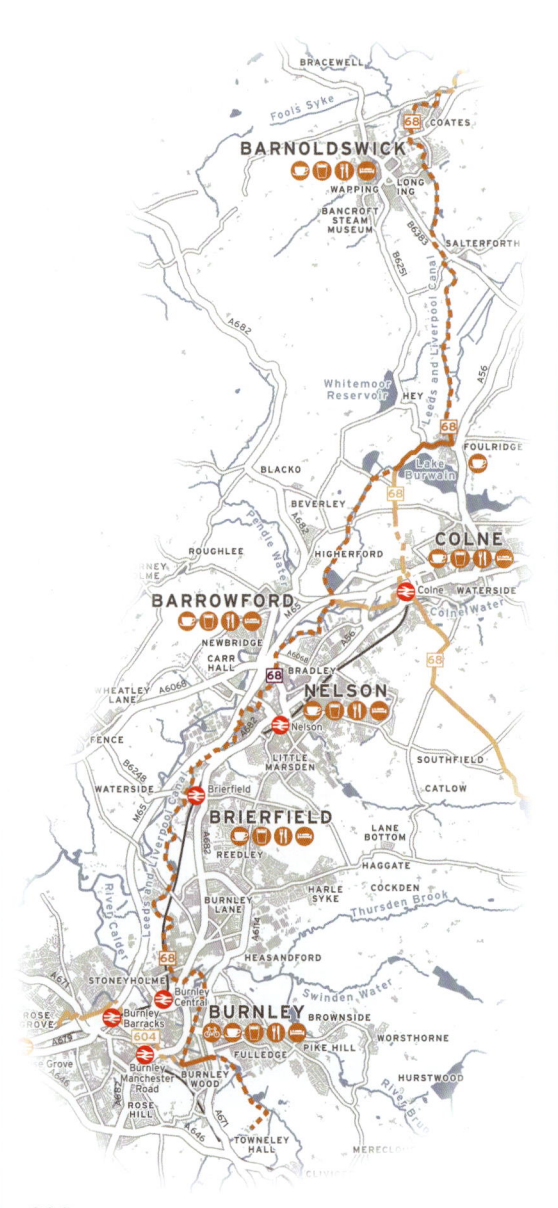

This is a ride of very different northern identities; imposing industrial architecture contrasts with sweeping Pennine views. Towneley Hall and its beautiful gardens, known as the jewel in Burnley's crown, date from the 14th Century and the hall is now an art gallery and museum.

Towneley Hall, Burnley

A short ride though parkland and down Parliament Street lets you join the Leeds and Liverpool canal. Head north along the so-called straight mile, a remarkable canal embankment with rooftop views. The Leeds and Liverpool canal is one of the most popular in the UK for leisure use, whether it's a gentle stroll or bike ride or messing about on boats. The leisure aspect, and the canal's delightfully rural character, gradually take over as you head north on the towpath, Burnley offers a delightfully green and leisure packed diversion right next to the canal in the form of the popular and beautiful Thompson Park.

Finish: Lock Stop Café, Greenberfield Locks, Barnoldswick

RIDE 05

Train Station: Burnley and Colne (Colne is around halfway along the route)

Grade: Easy

Terrain, gradients and access: One of the best quality UK canal towpath rides you could find in terms of surface; largely tarmac before Foulridge and largely well-maintained crushed stone after it. Access controls are minimal; there are A-frames along the way but they are often next to gates that remain unlocked or have been removed altogether.

Care is required at numerous bridges which can have a narrow towpath and so restricted sight of oncoming traffic and a low bridge arch.

Loops, links and longer rides: If you head west on joining the Leeds and Liverpool canal instead of north on NCN 68 then you will pick up NCN 604, currently open between Burnley centre and Rose Grove (when completed it will connect Church near Oswaldtwistle with Burnley via Clayton-Le-Moors). At Rose Grove Rail Station you can also pick up NCN 685, the Padiham Greenway. A nice local route that intersects the canal in Burnley is the Brun Valley greenway that heads towards Rowley Lake and the attractive village of Worsthorne in the Pennine foothills. At the northern end of the ride just north of Greenberfield Locks NCN 68 leaves the canal towpath for minor roads, to head into the Yorkshire Dales proper.

Stay: Higher Trapp House Hotel, Simonstone (01282) 772781

lavenderhotels.co.uk/hotels/higher-trapp-house

A little off the route but near the Padiham Greenway which gives direct cycle access to it.

Eat and drink: Right at the route start Towneley Hall has a café. Finsley Gate Wharf, Burnley lets you sit and watch canal life go by or at route's end try the very quaint and rural Lock Stop café. Foulridge also presents several opportunities including canalside Café Cargo.

Cycle hire: On Yer Bike Cycles, Queen Street, Burnley (01282) 438855 **onyerbike.com**

Wider area cycle map: Lancashire

Shortly after leaving the Burnley suburbs the long whale-like ridge of Pendle Hill comes into view to the northwest before a decidedly 19th Century industrial landscape at Nelson, with regimented rows of terraces backed by the enormous spire of St Mary's church. Throughout the canal towpath remains an oasis of nature and vibrant green corridor throughout the summer months.

After a short climb past the impressive Barrowford Locks you leave the canal towpath to follow minor roads and tracks over the top of the Foulridge tunnel. After, your surroundings are entirely rural all the way to Barnoldswick, with rolling pasture and an increasing number of canal boats forming the backdrop of the final few miles to the highest point on the Leeds and Liverpool canal at Greenberfield Locks. Having ridden from Lancashire into Yorkshire, you are now surrounded by the famed Yorkshire Dales countryside.

Near Foulridge

If you prefer to end the ride at Barnoldswick's pretty central square with its interesting selection of independent cafés and shops you can head off the canal at Salterforth's Blue Anchor pub and follow main road cycle lanes to the town centre.

231

RIDE 06 — 11 miles

Start: South Pier, Blackpool

BLACKPOOL
TO
FLEETWOOD

The razzmatazz of Britain's definitive bucket-and-spade destination provides a lively start to this ride, but is quickly superseded by the quiet, natural beauty of the attractive Fylde Coast.

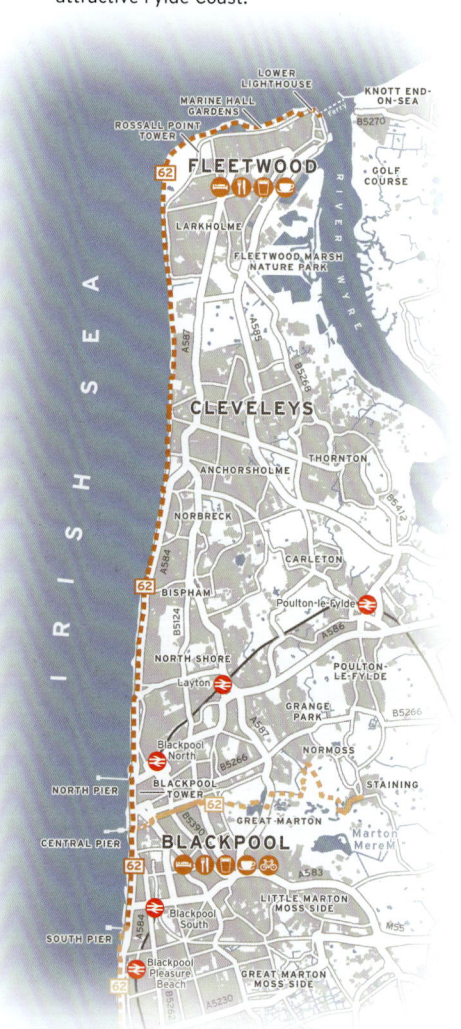

Start at Blackpool's South Pier and head north along the wide promenade. It's sensory overload in the opening miles, with the clatter of Blackpool trams alongside the route, the sweet candyfloss scent of the kiosks and a million bulbs lighting up the seafront during the famous Blackpool Illuminations each autumn.

The adrenalin-fuelled rides of the Pleasure Beach are left behind as you cycle towards one of England's most iconic landmarks: the unmistakable Blackpool Tower. In the opening miles, attractive and ornate Victorian shelters on the Promenade make great stopping points for taking in the scenery over the Irish Sea to north Wales, before you swoop between the curved, sandy-coloured layers of the promenade at Cleveleys, where the Isle of Man can be seen across the water on a clear day.

Beside the shingly, pebbly banks of Rossall Beach there are great views of the Lake District's peaks in the distance. However, the best views are in the final mile from Rossall Point Tower, a futuristic-style observation station that leans eagerly towards the sea. Go to the top deck to look over Fleetwood Beach, Morecambe Bay, the Lake District and the Forest of Bowland.

From here, roll past Fleetwood's Marine Hall Gardens and the little pastel-coloured beach huts on the seafront, before ending at the white sandstone Lower Lighthouse on The Esplanade. It's just a short ride from here to Fleetwood's ferry point for the 10-minute boat trip over the River Wyre to Knott End-on-Sea.

Finish: The Esplanade, Fleetwood

RIDE **06**

Promenade, Cleveleys

Train stations: Blackpool North, Blackpool South and Blackpool Pleasure Beach

Grade: Moderate

Terrain, gradients and access: Flat, wide concrete promenade with a very short and quiet on-road section at Rossall Beach (or dismount to push along this narrower part of the promenade).

Loops, links and longer rides: From Blackpool's South Pier, NCN 62 follows a mix of on-road and traffic-free route south to Lytham St Annes.

Stay: Premier Inn, Blackpool Beach 0333 777 3921 premierinn.com

Eat and drink: There are many places to eat in Blackpool, including 'Parks' Art Deco café overlooking the ornamental Italian gardens in Stanley Park, or Harry Ramsden's fish and chips near North Pier. At Fleetwood, try Beach Kiosk or Ferry Café on the waterside, or head into the town for popular Café Royal or the Granada Fish Bar and Restaurant.

Cycle hire: Blackpool Ebike Hire (01253) 622984 blackpoolebikehire.com

Wider area cycle map: Lancashire

"You swoop between the curved, sandy-coloured layers of the promenade at Cleveleys..."

RIDE 07
6 miles

Start: Lancaster train station

LUNE ESTUARY PATH

St George's Quay, Lancaster

This ride along the disused railway path to Conder Green and Glasson Dock offers great views over the attractive Lune Estuary and the rolling Bowland Fells. Lancaster, on the edge of the Lake District, is a very pleasing city to start from, and it's worth venturing into the centre to see its stunning hill-top castle and beautiful cathedral before setting off.

Start the ride from Lancaster train station and follow the short, mostly traffic-free link to the Millennium Bridge, before riding through St George's Quay along the banks of the wide River Lune. In the opening miles, you'll leave the waterside for a short while and enter Freeman's Wood to ride among black poplars, the UK's rarest native tree.

This is an excellent ride for birdwatching, so keep a lookout for skylarks over the wet grassland, and for wading birds on Freeman's Pool; the island in the centre is a breeding spot for oystercatchers and lapwings.

A very gentle climb follows the woodland, offering wonderful views over the fields and hills. Be sure to look inland and see the vast white Ashton Memorial dominating the Lancaster skyline from its raised position in Williamson Park on the east of the city. At Aldcliffe, prop up the gate whilst soaking up the peaceful surroundings of Aldcliffe Marsh, or stop a short while later at a pleasant picnic area around the ride's midway point.

Now the trail begins to widen, and you'll ride between little sheltered copses and woodlands before the estuary views open out beautifully. Cargo ships and pleasure boats navigate their way across the Lune, the trees and fields of the Heysham and Morecambe peninsula can

RIDE 07

Finish: Lock Keepers Rest, Glasson Dock

Train station: Lancaster

Grade: Easy

Terrain, gradients and access: Flat tarmac path, fine gravel track and stony trail. Some road crossings and a short, quiet on-road section at Lancaster.

Loops, links and longer rides: Bay Cycle Way is a 100-mile route along traffic-free paths and quiet roads from Walney Island to Glasson Dock, linking up the RSPB Leighton Moss nature reserve, Morecambe Bay and Lancaster city along the way. NCN 6 Lancaster Canal (Ride 10). NCN 69 Lancaster to Heysham, via Morecambe Bay (Ride 08). NCN 69 and 90 Lune Valley Trail (Ride 09).

Stay: The Stork Inn, Conder Green (01524) 751234 thestorkinn.co.uk

Eat and drink: Try the George and Dragon or Wagon and Horses pubs, both at St George's Quay in Lancaster at the start. The Green Finch café and The Stork Inn are at Conder Green. At Glasson Dock try the Dalton Arms, Lock Keepers Rest or visit the factory shop at The Port of Lancaster Smokehouse.

Wider area cycle map: Lancashire

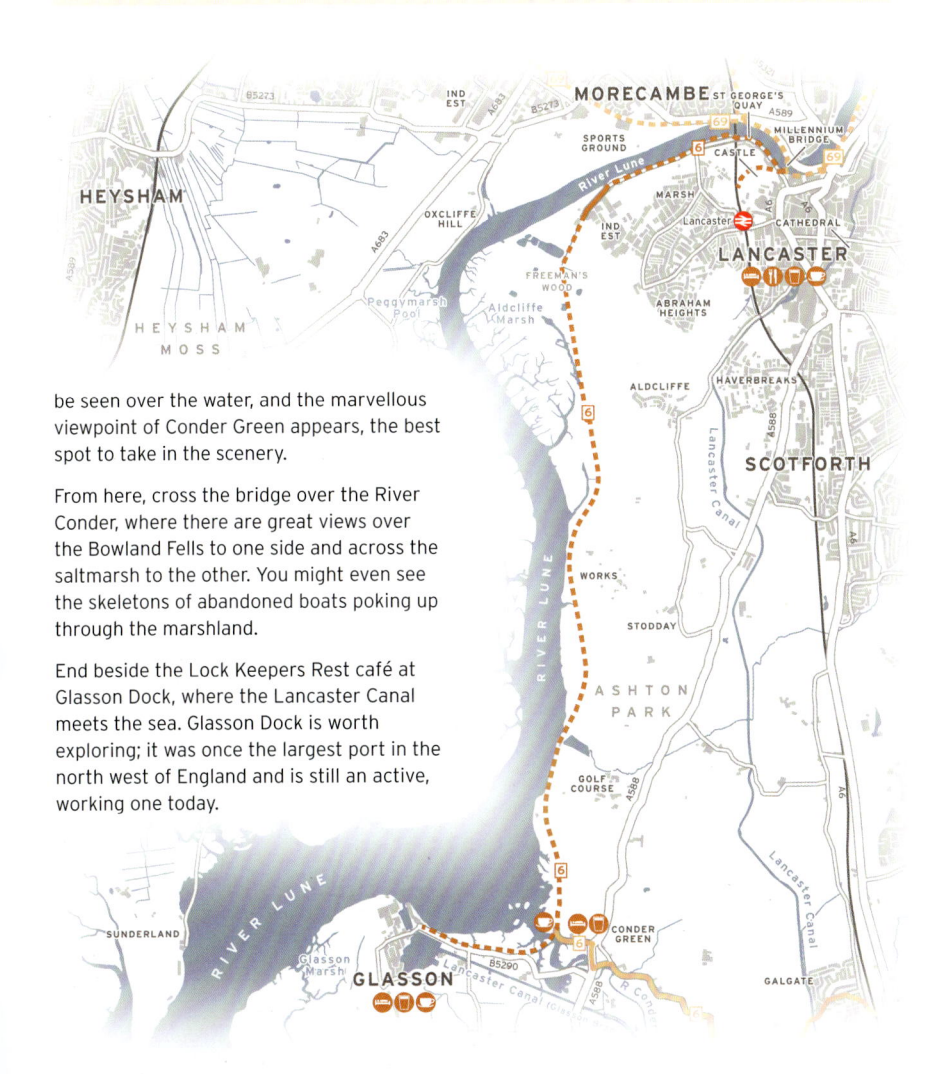

be seen over the water, and the marvellous viewpoint of Conder Green appears, the best spot to take in the scenery.

From here, cross the bridge over the River Conder, where there are great views over the Bowland Fells to one side and across the saltmarsh to the other. You might even see the skeletons of abandoned boats poking up through the marshland.

End beside the Lock Keepers Rest café at Glasson Dock, where the Lancaster Canal meets the sea. Glasson Dock is worth exploring; it was once the largest port in the north west of England and is still an active, working one today.

RIDE 08 — 6 miles | 69 | **Start:** Millennium Bridge, Lancaster

LANCASTER TO HEYSHAM
VIA
MORECAMBE BAY

The magnificent arc of Morecambe Bay makes this a classically English seaside ride.

Take in the views of Lancaster city from the Millennium Bridge across the River Lune at the start, then head along the river's north bank to join the straight and simple leafy link from Lancaster right to the seafront at Morecambe. You may encounter ambitious riders setting off on the 170-mile Way of the Roses, as this popular coast to coast route across Lancashire and Yorkshire starts from Morecambe Bay.

On the promenade, it's worth taking a short detour past the stone jetty and glamourous Art Deco Midland Hotel to reach the statue of national treasure Eric Morecambe on Central Promenade. He's been immortalised in his heel-flicking 'Bring me Sunshine' pose and is guaranteed to raise a smile.

From here, a three-mile ride south takes you along Morecambe Bay's gently curved promenade. The vast, exposed sandflats are a vital feeding habitat for wading birds, ducks and geese, so watch out for them as you ride.

On a clear day the views from the seafront are magnificent, and you'll see the Bowland Fells rolling away inland, the Lake District Fells rising up in the distance to the north, and the Furness Peninsula in Cumbria across the water.

In the final mile, the tree-covered mound of Heysham looms ahead, a delightful seaside village with whitewashed 17th Century cottages and St Peter's church emerging from the trees. There's a very short, steep climb to reach the village, but benches at the top give wonderful sea views.

End at Cliff Walk Tea Gardens and venture into the heart of the village on foot to see the colourful and tenderly cared-for gardens that have made Heysham a Britain in Bloom winner several times.

Or, take a look around the ruins of the eighth Century St Patrick's chapel on Heysham's sandstone headland, and walk around The Barrows, a stunning area of cliffs, coastal grassland and woodland. You could even catch a ferry from Heysham Harbour across the Irish Sea to the Isle of Man.

'Venus & Cupid' statue, Morecambe seafront

RIDE 08

Finish: Heysham

Train stations: Lancaster and Morecambe

Grade: Easy

Terrain, gradients and access: Flat tarmac path and wide promenade. Some small roads to cross and a couple of gates between Lancaster and Morecambe.

Loops, links and longer rides: NCN 69 Way of the Roses is a 170-mile route across Lancashire and Yorkshire from Morecambe on the west coast to Bridlington on the east. NCN 6 Lune Estuary Path (**Ride 07**). NCN 6 Lancaster Canal (**Ride 10**). NCN 69 and 90 Lune Valley Trail (**Ride 09**).

Stay: The Clifton, Morecambe (01524) 411573 hotel-clifton.co.uk

Eat and drink: In Morecambe, The Sun Terrace Restaurant and Rotunda Bar are both in The Midland Hotel, or try The Palatine in the town centre. Bells Cottage tearooms, The Royal Hotel and Half Moon Bay Café are all at Heysham.

Cycle hire: Morecambe Bay Partnership Ebike Hire exploremorecambebay.org.uk

Wider area cycle map: Lancashire

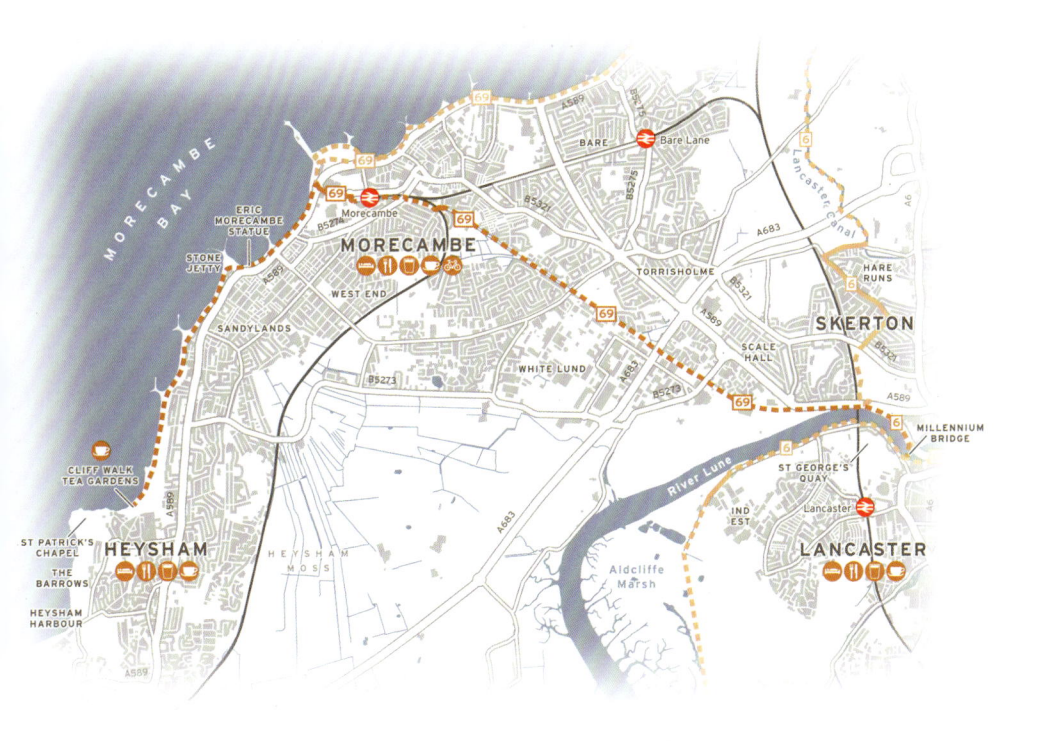

Start of the Way of the Roses, Morecambe Bay

RIDE 09
5 miles

Start: Millennium Bridge, Lancaster

LUNE VALLEY TRAIL

This short ride passes through the lush Lune Valley and into the western edges of the Forest of Bowland Area of Outstanding Natural Beauty, traversing landscape so beautiful that it became a source of inspiration for Romantic poet William Wordsworth and artist J M W Turner.

Start at Lancaster's Millennium Bridge over the River Lune and follow the leafy trail into the 15km linear River Lune Millennium Park, looking out for mute swans, herons, and cormorants on the water. Within the opening miles you'll pass beneath the stone arches of the spectacular Lune Aqueduct that carries the Lancaster Canal over the river, and there are steps leading up to the waterway for fine views of the river, canal and Lancashire landscape.

Around the halfway point, reach the former railway station at Halton, where there's bike parking and a chance to cross the bridge into the historic Halton village. Alternatively, continue along the path to reach the highlight of the route: the Crook O' Lune, a dramatic kink in the river shaped like a shepherd's crook. This is the spot captured in Turner's paintings and Wordsworth's poetry, and it's easy to see why the area seized them so.

Picnic beside rich pastures with terrific views over the Lune Valley, Yorkshire Dales and Ingleborough, one of the Yorkshire Three Peaks. Look out for leaping salmon in the river, or buzzards soaring over the ancient woodlands on the river's north bank upstream. Excellent views of the area can be enjoyed from the ancient viewpoint of Gray's Seat, too, which is reachable on foot from the picnic point.

From here, cross the river again and look to the right to see the elegant stone arches of Caton Lune Bridge. Then it's just a mile or so of gentle riding from Crook O' Lune to reach the route's end at Bull Beck picnic site.

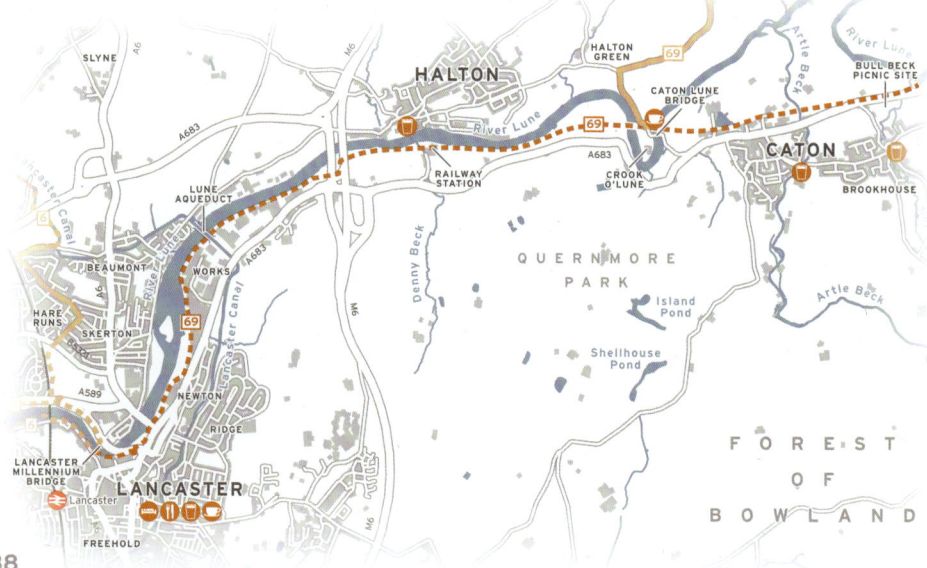

RIDE 09

Finish: Bull Beck picnic site

Train station: Lancaster

Grade: Easy

Terrain, gradients and access: A very gradual ascent along tarmac path with some road crossings. Take particular care crossing to Bull Beck picnic site at the route's end.

Loops, links and longer rides: Lune Valley Trail is part of NCN 69 Way of the Roses, a 170-mile coast to coast route across Lancashire and Yorkshire from Morecambe to Bridlington. NCN 69 Lancaster to Heysham via Morecambe Bay (**Ride 08**). NCN 6 Lancaster Canal (**Ride 10**). NCN 6 Lune Estuary Path (**Ride 07**).

Stay: Toll House Inn, Lancaster (01524) 599900 tollhouseinn.co.uk

Eat and drink: The Greyhound pub at Halton is popular. Woodies Café at Crook O' Lune is in a lovely spot but is open Wednesday to Sunday during July and August and Friday to Sunday from September to June. The Station and The Ship pubs are both at Caton, or The Black Bull pub is in Brookhouse.

Wider area cycle map: Lancashire

"A dramatic kink in the river shaped like a shepherd's crook."

Cycling the Crook O' Lune, Lune Valley

LANCASTER CANAL

Towpath cycling

The still and gentle waters of the Lancaster Canal on this towpath route are a wonderful contrast to the fast moving tides of Morecambe Bay and mountainous landscape of the Lake District, which are part of the far-reaching views along the way.

Start at Lancaster's Millennium Bridge over the River Lune, before climbing up through the city's Ryelands Park and along undulating country lanes to join the canal, locally nicknamed 'the black and white canal' thanks to its past cargoes of Lancashire coal and Cumbrian limestone. It's worth taking a short detour to the right here for fine views from the top of the spectacular Lune Aqueduct, before following the canal away from Lancaster and into deep countryside, passing beneath the arches of attractive stone bridges along the way.

Waterside benches feature after just a couple of miles, with a backdrop of gently crumpled hills making for a scenic and peaceful rest point. Alternatively, cycle a little further to reach Hest Bank, the route's halfway point, where there's a pretty picnic spot tucked into the canal bank near the moored barges and boats. From the towpath, the long view through the village streets down to Morecambe Bay is beautiful, and if you're here just before high tide you'll see huge flocks of wading birds gathering to roost.

In the second half of the ride, the commanding limestone mound of Warton Crag dominates the horizon. This is the highest point of Arnside and Silverdale Area of Outstanding Natural Beauty (AONB), with the famous Lake District fells just beyond it. The canal wriggles and bends in the final miles, making for pleasurable riding all the way to The Canal Turn pub.

Leave the water at a little play park just after the pub and join Market Street to ride through the centre of Carnforth, stopping at the cycling museum in Dyno Start Cycle Centre along the way.

End at Carnforth Station to visit the 1940s tearoom on the platform and experience a little bit of film history; this was the station used in Brief Encounter.

Finish: Carnforth train station

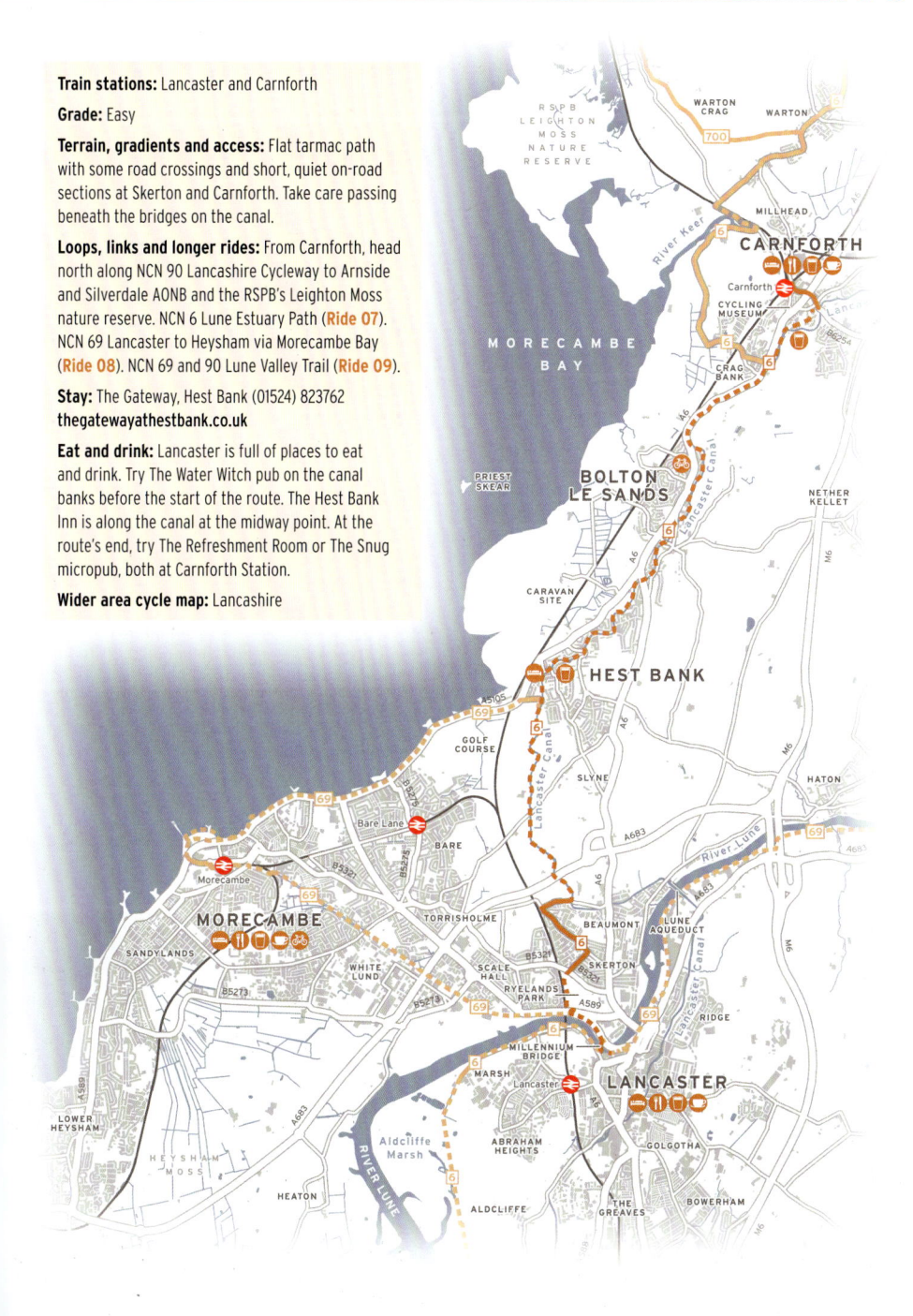

RIDE 10

Train stations: Lancaster and Carnforth

Grade: Easy

Terrain, gradients and access: Flat tarmac path with some road crossings and short, quiet on-road sections at Skerton and Carnforth. Take care passing beneath the bridges on the canal.

Loops, links and longer rides: From Carnforth, head north along NCN 90 Lancashire Cycleway to Arnside and Silverdale AONB and the RSPB's Leighton Moss nature reserve. NCN 6 Lune Estuary Path (**Ride 07**). NCN 69 Lancaster to Heysham via Morecambe Bay (**Ride 08**). NCN 69 and 90 Lune Valley Trail (**Ride 09**).

Stay: The Gateway, Hest Bank (01524) 823762 thegatewayathestbank.co.uk

Eat and drink: Lancaster is full of places to eat and drink. Try The Water Witch pub on the canal banks before the start of the route. The Hest Bank Inn is along the canal at the midway point. At the route's end, try The Refreshment Room or The Snug micropub, both at Carnforth Station.

Wider area cycle map: Lancashire

241

RIDE 11

12.5 miles
Ambleside option 10 miles

Start: Windermere train station

BOWNESS TO ELTERWATER

Certainly one of the tougher routes in this guide, but with spectacular rewards. The route links views over the watery playground of Windermere, the spectacular National Trust properties of Claife Viewing Station and Wray Castle before heading into the country of craggy peaks at the village of Elterwater, backed by the Langdale Pikes, a fell runners' and walkers' paradise. In any event any fear of off-road climbs should be banished as there is plenty of opportunity in the vicinity to hire a very high quality off-road e-bike if needed. There are also plenty of opportunities to catch 'Bike Boats' across the lake and make use of the extensive cycle network (both NCN and non-NCN) and devise other route options.

The tourist hordes of Windermere and Bowness soon fade away after you roll down the main streets and over the traffic-free link to the main car ferry across the lake (be aware the £2 fee for bike transit is card contactless only) with its own water's eye view of the multitude of islands and pleasure craft that populate England's largest and deepest natural lake, around 11 miles in length.

Once across you hug the western shore of the lake, past grassy picnic spots and boat launching areas before the tarmac ends and a track climbs and drops to a lovely lakeside section with all manner of sailing craft glimpsable through the trees. Another climb brings you directly to Wray Castle gate house – actually a Victorian Gothic style grand house in the style of a castle. It has extensive grounds including its own ferry terminal.

The route splits by the delightful cycle bridge over the River Brathay. West takes you along very quiet minor roads that climb steeply to a great viewpoint over the Langdale Pikes then to a descent to what becomes a very family friendly track approach to Elterwater village (after some rather more challenging off-road sections). Heading east is an easier and shorter option, following the Brathay valley to the tourist honeypot town of Ambleside with a short section on 'painted line' type cycle lanes on the A593.

View from Skelwith Fold

Finish: Elterwater village or Ambleside town centre

RIDE 11

Train Station: Windermere (end of branch line from Oxenholme Lake District station on west coast main line)

Grade: Challenging

Terrain, gradients and access: From Windermere train station NCN 6 rolls down Windermere's and Bowness's main streets where busy tourist traffic is often at safe crawling pace. Across the ferry it's a level waterside ride with a little slow moving leisure traffic that becomes traffic-free. Things get tougher after this as you climb and drop into woodland on the western shore of Windermere lake. Rolling tracks take over heading away from the lake and past Wray Castle entrance - generally good quality crushed stone but with plenty of small ups and downs. Be prepared for some narrower sections of single track, hopping on-road occasionally and for a very steep minor road climb to Skelwith Fold.

Loops, links and longer rides: The western sections of this ride are signed NCN 6, the northern end of the mammoth NCN 6 that in fullness of time will stretch all the way to London. Sections on the west coast of the lake will also be signed as NCN 6 but are currently well signed with wooden carved markers showing the good extent of the local off-road trail network. A track spur just after Wray Castle is signed to Hawkshead and the eastern spur after the route junction in the Brathay valley is NCN 37 (ultimately leading to Coniston). NCN 6 east of Windermere parallels both one of the main trunk roads into the Lakes and the only rail link, with stations at Staveley, Burneside and Kendal presenting plenty of opportunities for escaping the tourist crowds around the lake itself.

Stay: One Park Road, Windermere (015394) 42107 **1parkroad.co.uk**

Eat and drink: En route take your pick of the National Trust's Joey's Café inside the impressive Claife Viewing Station or at Wray Castle and the Britannia Inn or Maple Tree Café grouped around the village green at Elterwater.

Cycle hire: Country Lanes Cycle Hire, Windermere Train Station 07394 943 928 **countryaneslakedistrict.co.uk** Total Adventure Bike Hire 9 Church Street, Windermere (015394) 43151 **total-adventure.co.uk**

Wider area cycle map: South Cumbria & Lake District

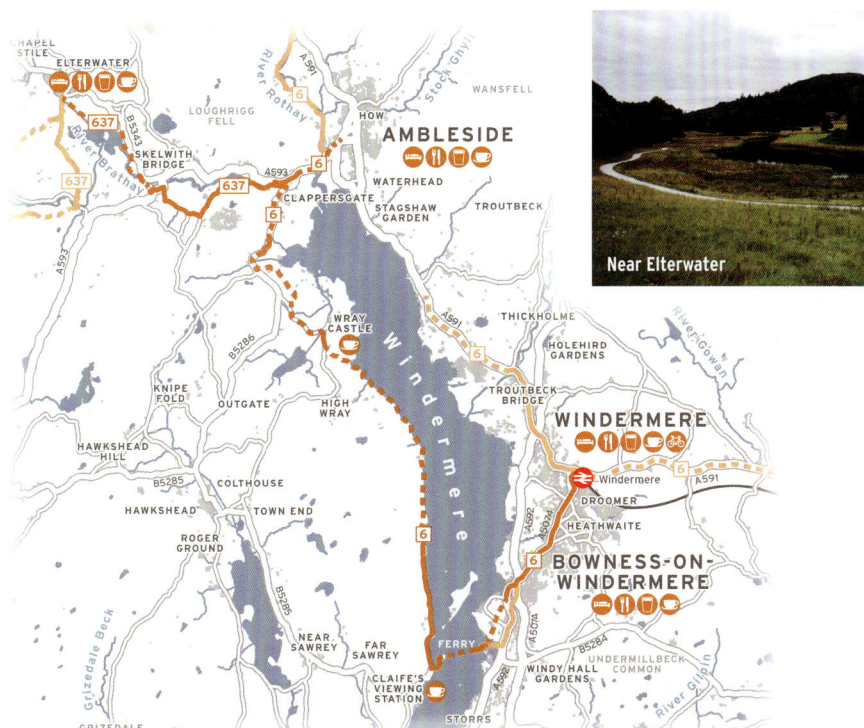

Near Elterwater

WHITEHAVEN
to
ROWRAH

As one of the start points for the UK's most popular challenge cycle route, the 140-mile Sea to Sea (C2C), Whitehaven Harbour is often abuzz with cyclists, each observing the tradition of dipping their wheels into the Irish Sea and posing for pictures alongside the giant C2C sculpture at the water's edge. Don't let the talk of challenge rides put you off though, this is one of the gentlest and most family-friendly sections of the entire route, and is ideal for experiencing the dramatic Cumbrian scenery without any of the testing hill climbs.

Start at the harbour and quickly leave the sea behind to ride through the edges of the town, before joining a beautifully smooth, tree-lined former railway path into the countryside. It's as popular with Lakeland walkers as it is with cyclists, so you're likely to have company as you weave alongside the lush meadows, yellow with buttercups in spring.

After just a few miles, the gaps between the trees reveal tantalising glimpses of the impressive Cumbrian fells, and in the route's second half the landscape opens up to reveal the incredible mountainous scenery of the Lake District. With just two miles to go, the views over the fells and the secluded Ennerdale Valley are out of this world.

Ennerdale is one of the most remote parts of the Lake District, and there are stone boulders and wide grassy verges beside the path for making an informal picnic spot to drink in this sensational setting.

The traffic-free route ends abruptly at the little hamlet of Rowrah, but carry on along a short section of road to reach the species-rich hay meadows of High Leys National Nature Reserve which are a sea of colour in June and July.

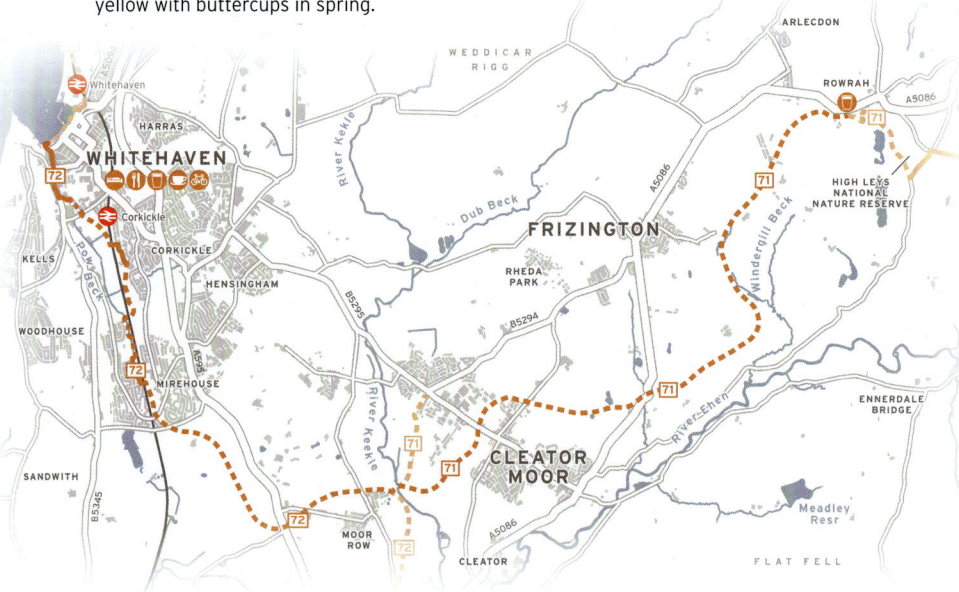

Finish: Rowrah

Train station: Whitehaven

Grade: Easy

Terrain, gradients and access: A very gentle ascent on tarmac path with some road crossings and short, on-road sections at Whitehaven and Rowrah.

Loops, links and longer rides: A three-mile ride along country lanes from Rowrah leads to the village of Ennerdale Bridge, with a further one and a half-mile ride to the shores of Ennerdale Water, the most remote lake in the Lake District (mountain bikes are recommended for tackling Ennerdale's forest roads). NCN 71 continues on-road from Rowrah to Whinlatter Forest, Keswick and beyond as part of the Sea to Sea (C2C), a 140-mile coast to coast ride across the North of England, from Cumbria to Tyne & Wear. From Whitehaven, follow NCN 72 up the Cumbrian coast on an eight-mile, traffic-free path to Workington.

Stay: The Corner House B&B, Whitehaven (01946) 696357 **thecornerhousebandb.co.uk**

Eat and drink: Whitehaven has many eateries, including the popular Zest Harbourside Café, or Café West on King Street. At the route's end, try The Stork Hotel at Rowrah.

Cycle hire: Haven Cycles, Whitehaven (01946) 63263 **havencycles-c2cservices.co.uk**

Wider area cycle map: South Cumbria & The Lake District

Foxgloves near Rowrah

RIDE 13 — 4 miles

Start: Old Railway Station Building

KESWICK RAILWAY PATH

All the romance of the Lake District is captured in this short and gentle ride from Keswick, a pretty town on the shores of Derwentwater that is a hub for outdoor activities.

Start at the former railway station and follow the former Cockermouth, Keswick and Penrith railway line. The path flirts with the pretty River Greta throughout, following it in parts and crossing it in others (eight times in total) using the old railway bridges.

The route follows the valley floor, passing through thick woodland close to the river's edge, where herons, dippers and wagtails may be spotted. There are some great spots for a riverside picnic beneath the trees in this second half of the ride. It's worth reflecting as you ride along that many of the bridges were rebuilt and a new tunnel opened following the devastating impact of Storm Desmond on the trail in December 2015.

At the end of the traffic-free path, take the short road into Threlkeld, a little village that sits in the shadow of the mighty Blencathra Mountain. There are a couple of charming, traditional Lakeland inns here, and a lovely coffee shop with superb mountain views.

Tunnel on the railway path

Finish: Threlkeld

RIDE 13

Train stations: Nearest are Aspatria and Penrith

Grade: Easy

Terrain, gradients and access: A very gentle ascent along stony trail. Several gates along the way and a short, on-road section into Threlkeld village.

Loops, links and longer rides: Take an alternative return route via Castlerigg Stone Circle if riding mountain bikes. This route includes some steep ascents and descents, on-road riding and unsurfaced track so isn't suitable for very young or inexperienced riders. Keswick Railway Path is part of the Sea to Sea (C2C), a 140-mile coast to coast ride across the North of England, from Cumbria to Tyne & Wear. From Threlkeld you can follow the C2C on a mix of traffic-free path and quiet roads to reach Penrith via the lovely Greystoke with an open air swimming pool and the characterful Boot & Shoe pub.

Stay: YHA Keswick 0345 371 9746 yha.org.uk or The Horse and Farrier Inn, Threlkeld (01768) 779688 horseandfarrier.com

Eat and drink: There are lots of good, hearty cafés in Keswick, but The Chalet Tearooms and Restaurant is particularly well-loved. At Threlkeld, eat at The Horse and Farrier Inn, The Sally Inn or Threlkeld Coffee Shop in the old village hall.

Cycle hire: Keswick Bikes (01768) 773355 keswickbikes.co.uk

Wider area cycle map: South Cumbria & The Lake District

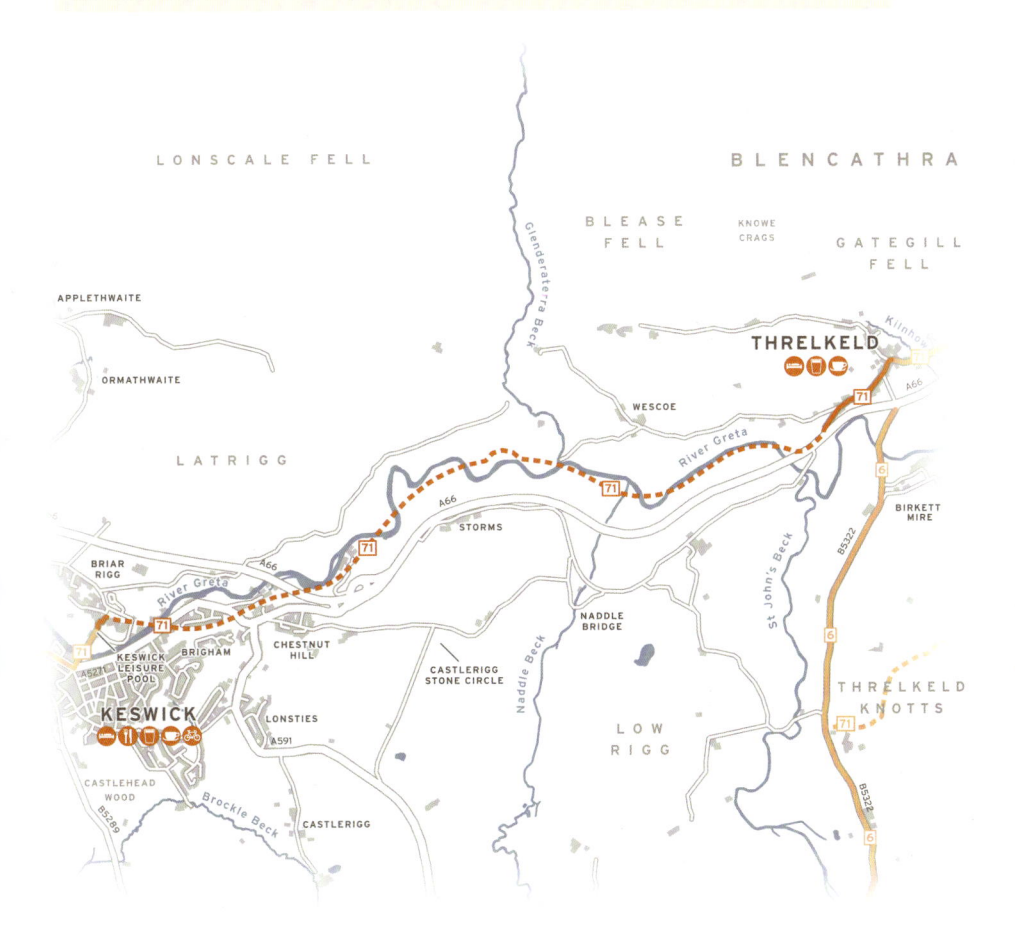

247

RIDE 14
5.5 miles

Start: Maryport Harbour

MARYPORT
TO
ALLONBY

This short and breezy promenade ride along the Cumbrian coast affords stunning views across the Solway Firth towards the mountains of southern Scotland. It traverses part of the World Heritage site of Hadrian's Wall, and offers some of the most captivating sunsets on the entire north west coast.

The town of Maryport has a proud seafaring history and was home to the Ismay family, famed for its involvement in the White Star Line shipping company that went on to build the Titanic. Before setting off it's worth visiting Maryport Maritime Museum on the harbour to discover more about the area's fascinating history, or venturing up the hill above the promenade to the large fort, part of the Roman Empire northern frontier.

Start the ride from Maryport Harbour and head out of the town on the mile-long promenade before turning off through Maryport Golf Course. The Solway Firth is a beautiful backdrop, and here the path is lined with wildflowers, from bluebells in the spring to crimson poppies in summer.

Around the midway point of the ride at Crosscanonby Road, take a break in the wetlands of Crosscanonby Carr Nature Reserve, a great spot for birdwatching. Here, you can cross the road on foot to see the Saltpans of Crosscanonby ancient monument, or take a short walk to the top of Swarthy Hill to investigate the Roman remains at Milefortlet 21.

Back on the trail, the village of Allonby can be seen nestled into the horseshoe-shaped bay ahead. A short ride will bring you to the Blue Dial Caravan Park where you take a stony trail through the dune grassland for a couple of miles to reach the Allonby Village south car park. Pause here to watch the kite surfers out in the bay, before continuing to the end of the ride in the village centre. There are marvellous views towards the Scottish mountains, Lake District fells and even the Isle of Man across the water on a clear day.

Sunset at Allonby beach

248

Finish: Allonby

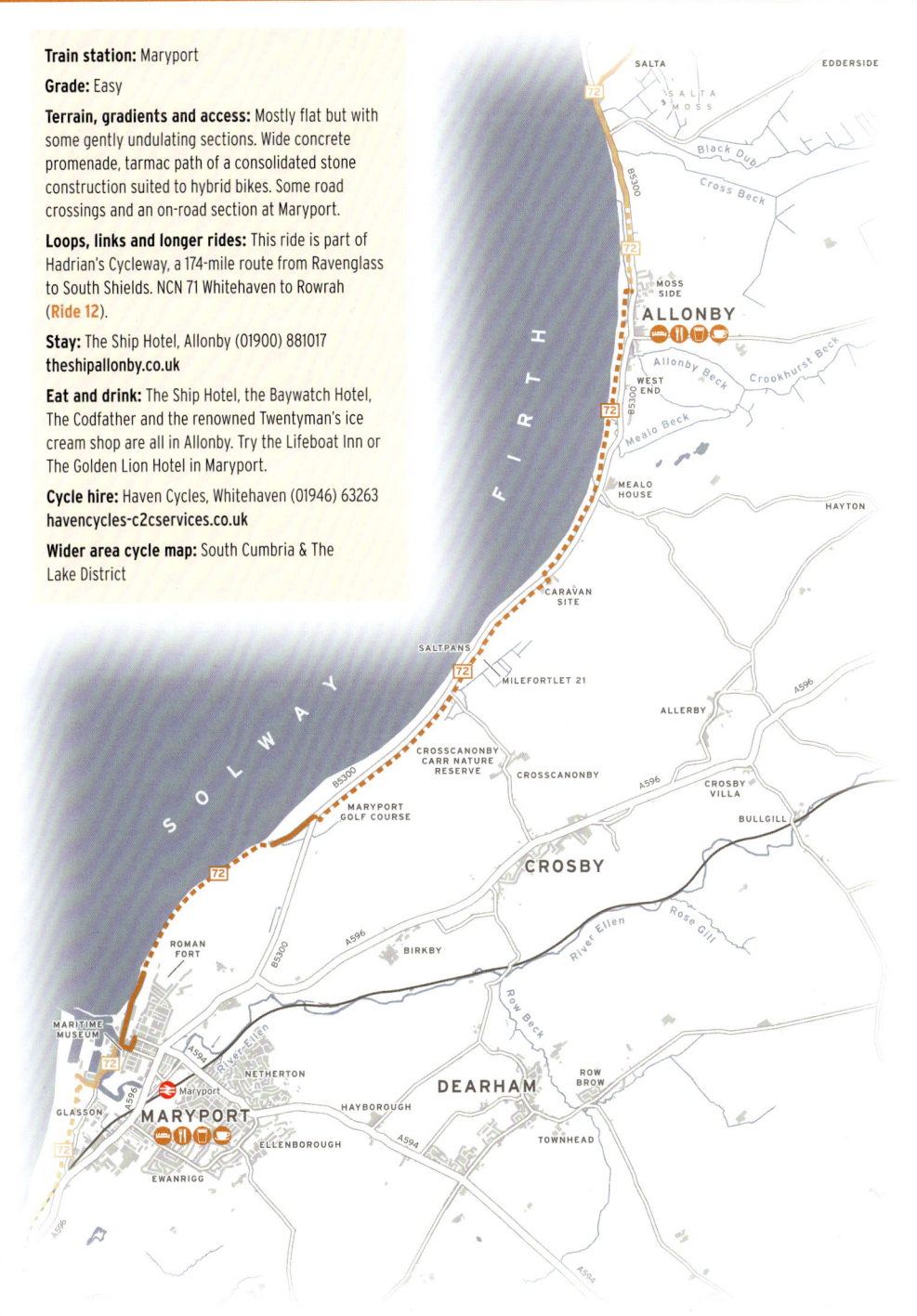

RIDE 14

Train station: Maryport

Grade: Easy

Terrain, gradients and access: Mostly flat but with some gently undulating sections. Wide concrete promenade, tarmac path of a consolidated stone construction suited to hybrid bikes. Some road crossings and an on-road section at Maryport.

Loops, links and longer rides: This ride is part of Hadrian's Cycleway, a 174-mile route from Ravenglass to South Shields. NCN 71 Whitehaven to Rowrah (Ride 12).

Stay: The Ship Hotel, Allonby (01900) 881017 theshipallonby.co.uk

Eat and drink: The Ship Hotel, the Baywatch Hotel, The Codfather and the renowned Twentyman's ice cream shop are all in Allonby. Try the Lifeboat Inn or The Golden Lion Hotel in Maryport.

Cycle hire: Haven Cycles, Whitehaven (01946) 63263 havencycles-c2cservices.co.uk

Wider area cycle map: South Cumbria & The Lake District

249

YORKSHIRE

England's largest county is also one of the most strikingly beautiful, renowned for winding cobbled lanes, steep hills and deep dales. This collection of rides takes in all the classic characteristics of Yorkshire; experience the peaks of the sheep-peppered Pennines, the deep limestone ravine of the Nidd Gorge and low-lying wildflower meadows in the Vale of York. Many of these rides enjoy a place in the 'Slow Tour of Yorkshire', 21 routes between 10 and 20 miles long that have been handpicked by Sustrans to showcase the best of the county by bike (discover them all at: **sustrans.org.uk**).

Interspersed among this heavenly rural landscape are some first-rate urban routes. Hull, Yorkshire's only maritime city, is the start point for a short and gentle ride to the coast along the Hornsea Rail Trail, whilst the walled city of York, the North's premier cycling city, provides a historic ending to one of the National Cycle Network's original walking and cycling routes.

Elsewhere, you'll have the chance to enter the World Heritage Site of Saltaire, encounter the dramatic Five Rise Locks on the Leeds & Liverpool Canal, and take a blustery ride over the Humber estuary on one of the longest cyclable suspension bridges in the world.

However, Yorkshire's real charm is not in its big and bold accomplishments, but in the many little-known gems that lie quietly waiting to be uncovered. That's why the simple, understated beauty of the Calder Valley Greenway is perhaps the most authentic experience of all. It will lead you through the Pennines and the 'valley of the rose hips' into the scenic, windswept borderlands, where the sprawling heather moorland of Yorkshire and Lancashire becomes knitted together.

Salts Mill

Routes overview

- **01** Poolsbrook Country Park to Rother Valley Country Park (7.5 miles)
- **02** Dove Valley Trail via RSPB Old Moor (13 miles)
- **03** Calder Valley Greenway (18.5 miles)
- **04** Castleford Greenway (21 miles)
- **05** Humber Bridge Route (6 miles)
- **06** Hornsea Rail Trail (15.5 miles)
- **07** Wyke Beck Way (6 miles)
- **08** Aire Valley Towpath (16 miles)
- **09** Riccall to York (10 miles)
- **10** York to Skelton (4.5 miles)
- **11** Wetherby Railway Path (6 miles)
- **12** Nidderdale Greenway (3 miles)
- **13** The Cinder Track (Scarborough to Whitby) (23 miles)
- ▬ Featured ride
- ▬ National Cycle Network (traffic-free and on-road)

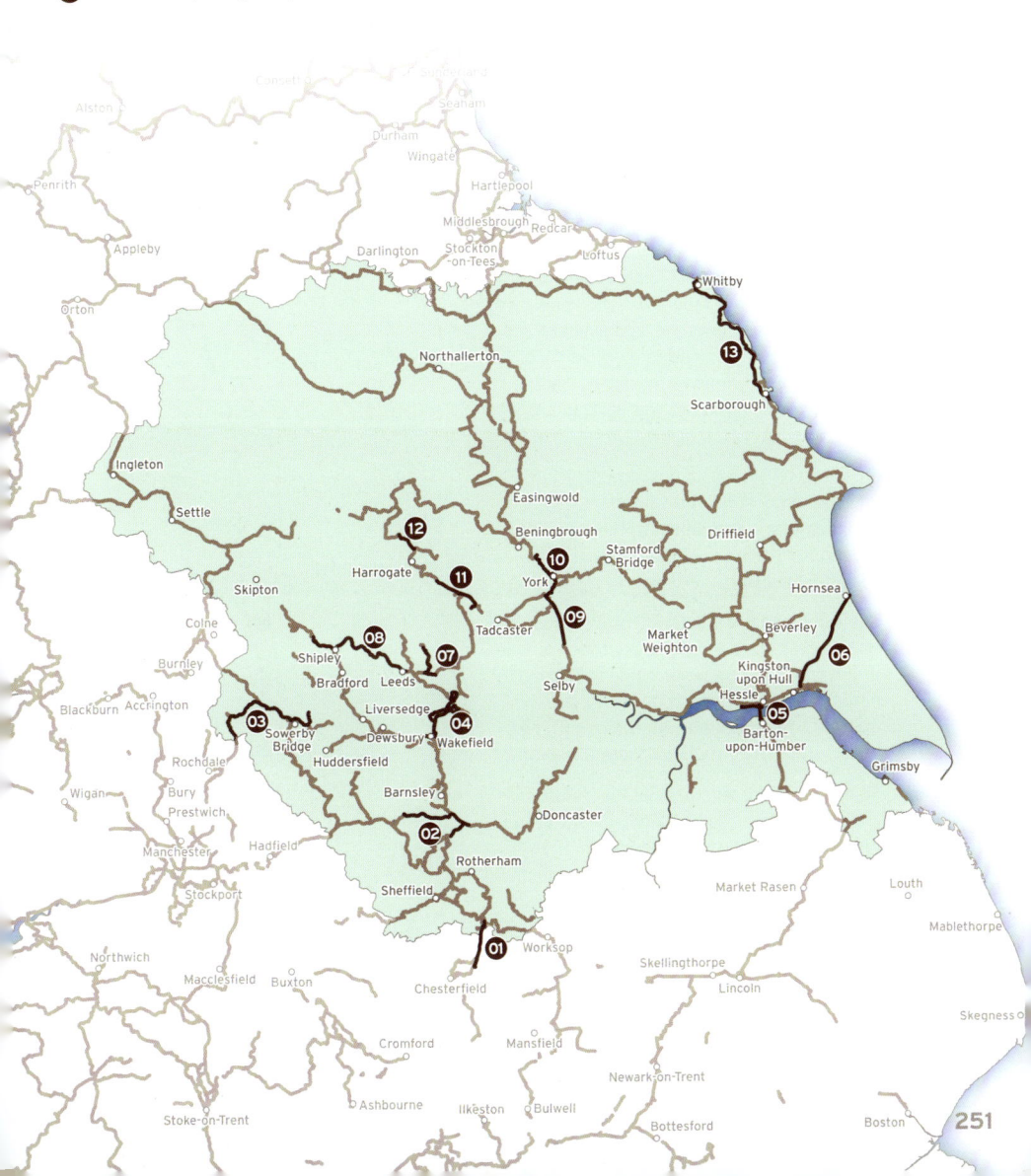

RIDE 01
7.5 miles

Start: Poolsbrook Country Park

POOLSBROOK COUNTRY PARK
TO
ROTHER VALLEY COUNTRY PARK

This ride between former collieries in Derbyshire and Yorkshire is a pleasant, gentle descent from one popular country park to another.

Start on the shores of the water at Poolsbrook, a country park created on the site of the old Ireland colliery. It has huge areas of open water, grassland and woodland, plus four miles of walking and cycling trails to explore before setting off.

Leave the park and join up with the long-distance Trans Pennine Trail to head north. In the opening miles there are wide open views across the farmland, and over the wet grassland and reeds beside the River Doe Lea. You'll also glimpse Slittingmill Viaduct over the farmland to the west, arching its way across the River Rother.

From here, it's a mix of open countryside and sheltered woodland, and there's a good secluded picnic spot beneath the trees at around the halfway point of the ride for a peaceful break.

The woodland and grassland of Westthorpe Hills stretch up to the right, another example of the area's old collieries being reclaimed by nature, before you reach the old Killamarsh Station, a reminder that this quiet path was once part of the busy Great Central Railway.

Shortly afterwards, cross the River Rother and enter Rother Valley Country Park at the southern end of the lake. There are often waterskiers bouncing across this stretch of water, so it's a good place to pause and watch the action, before heading into the heart of the park to the visitor centre, housed in an 18th Century mill. There are five lakes within the park and a number of different cycling trails to tackle, including a gentle loop of the nature reserve, or a tougher, hillier route for experienced mountain bikers.

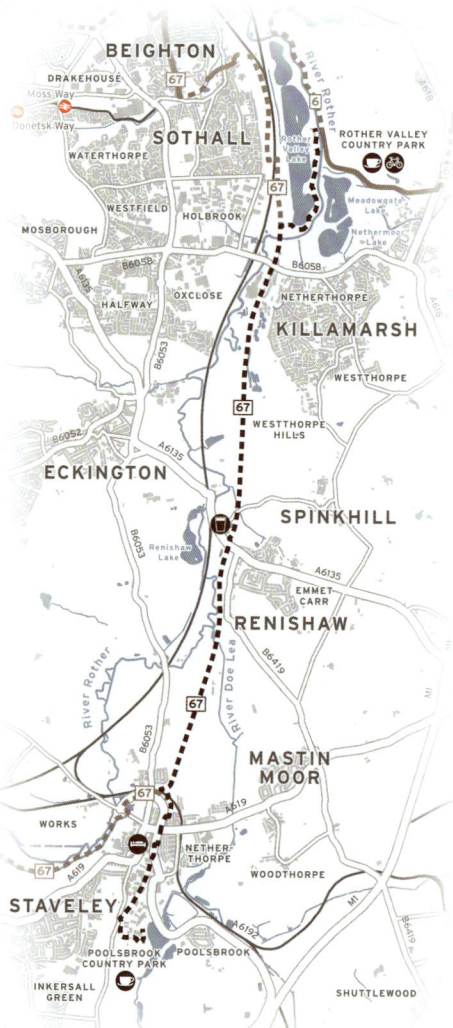

Finish: Rother Valley Country Park

RIDE 01

Train station: Nearest are Chesterfield and Woodhouse

Grade: Easy

Terrain, gradients and access: Very gently descending on fine gravel track and stony trail. Some road crossings.

Loops, links and longer rides: At Rother Valley Country Park there are several gentle, family-friendly trails around the lakes, and a more challenging mountain bike trail, or leave the park and follow NCN 67 and 6 for around eight miles to Sheffield. From Staveley, follow part of NCN 67 Cuckoo Way on a flat, five and a half-mile, traffic-free route along the canal towpath to Chesterfield, passing through Bluebank Pools Local Nature Reserve on the way. NCN 6 Sheffield to Rotherham.

Stay: Old Rectory Guest House, Staveley (01246) 473307 oldrectoryguesthouse.co.uk

Eat and drink: Try Poolsbrook Park Café, The Sitwell Arms in Renishaw or Stables Café at Rother Valley Country Park.

Cycle hire: Rother Valley Watersports and Activity Centre, Rother Valley Country Park (0114) 247 1452 rvcp.co.uk

Wider area cycle map: South Yorkshire & The Peak District

Rother Valley Lake

RIDE 02
13 miles | 62 | 67 | 🚴 > **Start:** Elsecar Heritage Centre

DOVE VALLEY TRAIL
VIA
RSPB OLD MOOR

This little section of the popular long-distance Trans Pennine Trail crosses the nature-rich washlands of the Dearne Valley in South Yorkshire. Elsecar Heritage Centre is an attractive start, and the restored stone buildings of its old ironworks and colliery workshops are now studios and shops that are open to visitors.

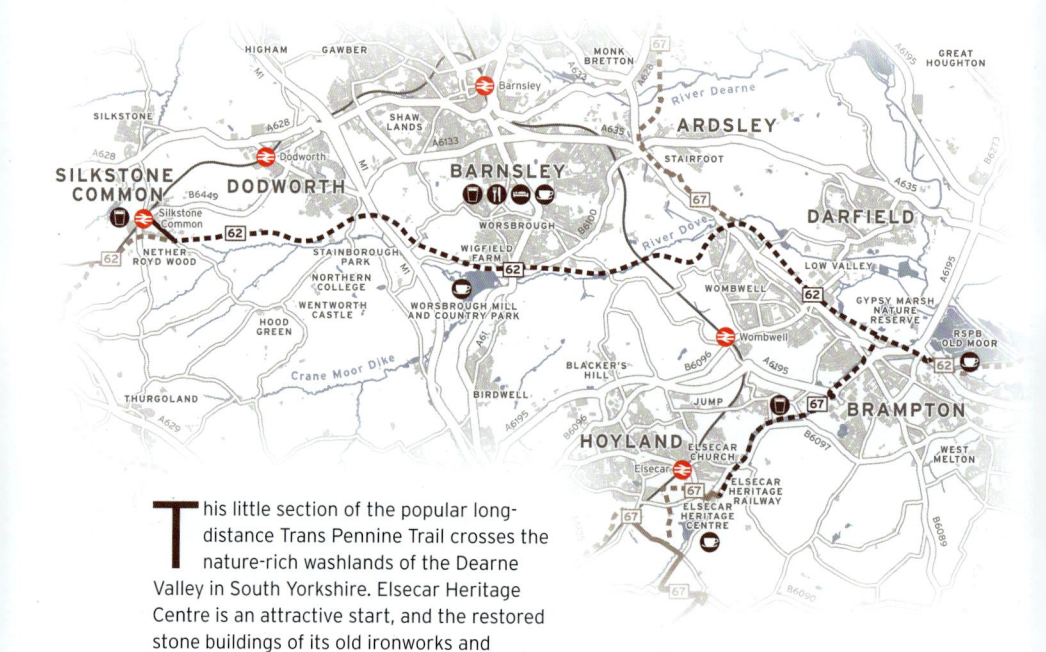

Leave these behind and join Elsecar Canal, with the smoke-blackened spire of Elsecar church looming to the left and the tracks of the heritage steam railway stretching off to the right. The path is surrounded by thick greenery and woodland in the opening miles, and you'll ride deep into the Lower Dearne Valley to reach two of the RSPB's fine Yorkshire nature reserves.

The lowland heath and fens of RSPB Gypsy Marsh nature reserve come first, a colourful oasis of heather and wild orchids in summer, with yellowhammers and green woodpeckers flitting between the trees. The bigger RSPB Old Moor nature reserve follows less than a mile later, and positively teems with birdlife, especially in winter when thousands upon thousands of wading birds are drawn to the mosaic of open water, fens, wet grassland and reedbeds. Take a stroll around Old Moor's viewing hides, or have a tea break in the popular café here.

From here, a mixture of woodland and farmland surrounds the route all the way to Worsbrough Mill and Country Park. This is a

Finish: Silkstone Common train station RIDE **02**

Train stations: Elsecar and Silkstone Common
Grade: Moderate

Terrain, gradients and access: A steady ascent for most of the way along fine gravel track and stony trail. Some gates, road crossings and a short, on-road section at Silkstone Common.

Loops, links and longer rides: From RSPB Old Moor, follow the Trans Pennine Trail east on a 13-mile, traffic-free route to Doncaster. At Silkstone Common, follow the Trans Pennine Trail for a further three and a half miles to Penistone train station to join the six and a half-mile, traffic-free trail to Dunford Bridge, one of Sustrans' Greener Greenways. The Trans Pennine Trail is a 215-mile coast-to-coast route from Hornsea to Southport.

Stay: Wortley Cottage Guest House (0114) 288 1864 wortleycottage.co.uk

Eat and drink: Brambles Tearoom and The Pantry café and shop are at Elsecar Heritage Centre. Try The Elephant and Castle pub at Hemingfield, the café at RSPB Old Moor, Wigfield Farm Café, or The Millers Tea Room at Worsbrough Country Park.

Cycle hire: Nearest is Wortley Cycles, Wortley (0114) 288 2179 wortley-cycles.co.uk

Wider area cycle map: South Yorkshire & The Peak District

Elsecar Band Stand

fabulous place to explore, with a 17th Century working water mill, huge reservoir and some great picnic spots. Alternatively, Wigfield Farm is alongside the trail here too, an open farm and visitor centre where young children will take great delight in meeting the animals.

Back on the trail, look to the horizon to see Stainborough Park, South Yorkshire's only Grade One listed landscape, which surrounds Wentworth Castle. The handsome Northern College can be seen clearly within the park, and then a mile later the columns and dome of Wentworth Castle's Rotunda, an Italian-inspired temple, appear on the skyline to the left. There's a signed link from the Dove Valley Trail to Wentworth Castle if you feel like taking a closer look; it's less than a mile away but the route climbs steadily all the way.

The ride's final miles are among lush green pastures with views over the sprawling Yorkshire hills. On the edges of Nether Royd Wood, leave the trail and climb up the short road to end at Silkstone Common train station.

CALDER VALLEY GREENWAY

The verdant Calder Valley in the starkly beautiful Pennines is one of the most desirable areas of Yorkshire but is delightfully little-known, making this scenic route a genuine hidden gem. Cobbled streets, former cloth mills and heather clad moorland give a wonderful sense of history along the way and make for a characterful ride.

Start at Halifax train station near The Piece Hall, Halifax's historic cloth trading hall, before heading towards the Shay Stadium. Ride down the cobbled Shaw Lane and traffic-free path to Salterhebble where you'll join the Calder and Hebble Navigation through the densely wooded Calder Valley. Salterhebble Locks and the arches of the magnificent Copley Viaduct all feature in the opening miles, and as you cross the River Calder at Sowerby Bridge there is a great view of Wainhouse Tower, one of Calderdale's most eye-catching landmarks.

From here, join the banks of the Rochdale Canal to ride between lush woodland and the steep sides of the valley, with rich green meadows and rugged Pennine hillsides rising up around the trail. At Mytholmroyd, you'll pass the bottom of Cragg Vale, the longest continuous gradient in England, and hill-lovers won't be able to resist this climb of almost 1,000 feet over five and a half miles.

For a more sedate ride, however, stick to the gentle contours of the greenway and watch the smoke-stained stone chimneys and old textile mills of Hebden Bridge or 'valley of the rose hips' come into view. This spirited and independent little town is an absolute delight, and is a great place for a break. Don't leave without visiting the National Trust's Hardcastle Crags just outside the town; it's nicknamed 'Little Switzerland' because of its sensational scenery, steep river valley woodland, rippling streams and waterfalls.

Further along the canal, reach Todmorden and stop to glance behind at the imposing Stoodley Pike monument perched high on the Pennines, before passing through the friendly little market place. From here, the landscape becomes craggier and more remote, and you'll climb steeply past Gauxholme Locks to Walsden. This is a good place to end and make the return journey to Halifax by train. Alternatively, continue along the towpath to reach the highest point of the highest broad canal in England and cross the border into Lancashire. It's worth going these few extra miles as the increasingly wild and dramatic landscape is just breathtaking, and is swathed with purple heather moorland in summertime.

Hebden Bridge

Finish: The Summit pub, near Littleborough

RIDE 03

Train stations: Halifax and Walsden

Grade: Moderate

Terrain, gradients and access: Tarmac path and stony towpath with some short, cobbled sections. Some road crossings and short, on-road sections at Halifax, Sowerby Bridge, Luddenden Foot, Mytholmroyd and Todmorden. A gentle ascent throughout, with a steeper climb following Todmorden. Take care passing beneath low bridges that run close to the water's edge.

Loops, links and longer rides: From Salterhebble, follow the Calder Valley Greenway in the opposite direction for four and a half miles to reach Brighouse, via Cromwell Bottom Local Nature Reserve. At Sowerby Bridge, Mytholmroyd and Hebden Bridge, Calder Valley Greenway intersects with NCN 68 Pennine Cycleway, a long-distance route between Derby and Berwick-upon-Tweed. NCN 66 Spen Valley Greenway is one of the routes that pioneered the NCN.

Stay: Holdsworth House, Halifax (01422) 240024 holdsworthhouse.co.uk

Eat and drink: Try the real ales at The Puzzle Hall Inn or Hollins Mill, both in Sowerby Bridge, or Whistle Stop Takeaway at Sowerby Bridge train station. Jo's Kitchen is at Mytholmroyd, while Park Life Café, Organic House Café and Stubbing Wharf pub are all cyclists' favourites in Hebden Bridge. In the route's final miles, try The Café on Water Street at Todmorden, Gordon's Garden Tea Room at Walsden or The Summit pub at the route's end near Littleborough.

Cycle hire: Juiced Up Bikes, Sowerby Bridge 07766 693246 juicedupbikes.co.uk

Wider area cycle map: West Yorkshire

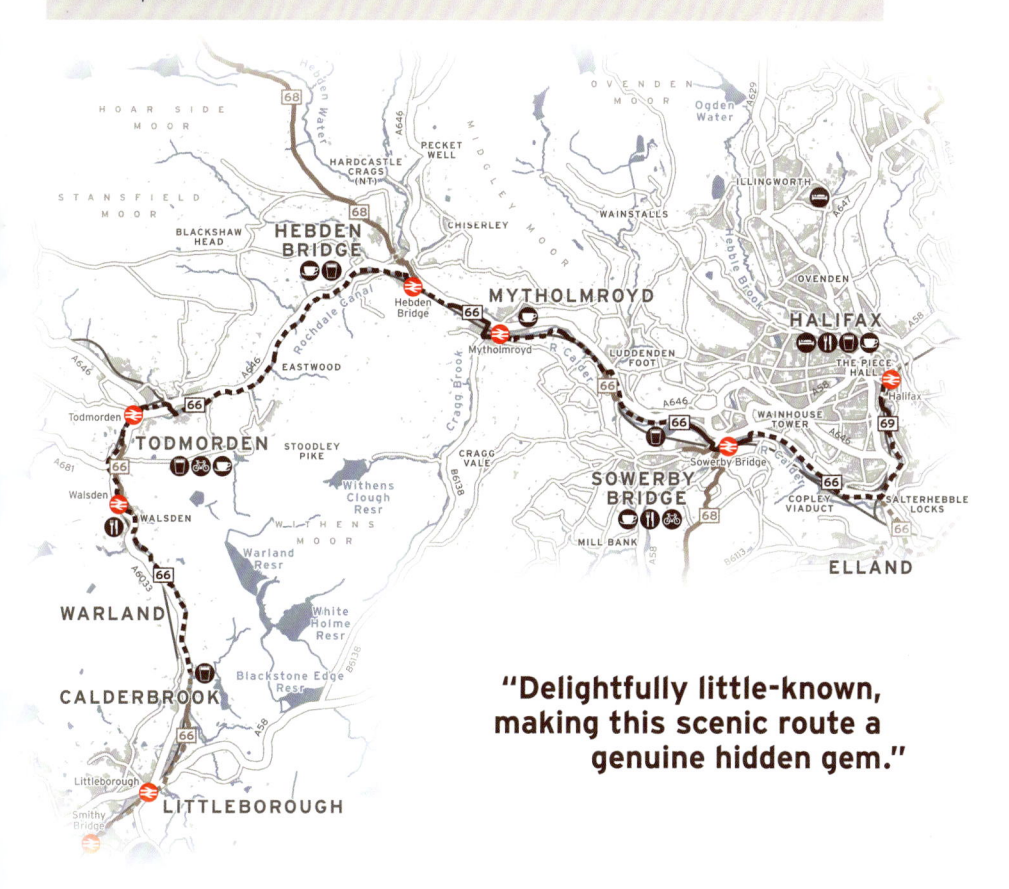

"Delightfully little-known, making this scenic route a genuine hidden gem."

257

CASTLEFORD GREENWAY

The Hepworth in Wakefield is an impressive starting point in its own right but will also thrill lovers of modern art, being named after sculptor Barbara Hepworth who was born in Wakefield. From its commanding riverside setting you pick up the signed Wonders of Wakefield (WoW) cycle route. There are some light-signalled crossings and a small pavement section across a busy road intersection at the start to find the lovely old packhorse bridge, just down from the impressive Chantry Chapel on a medieval bridge.

From here you leave the modern world behind, following WoW signs to head over the Calder and Hebble Canal, with birds' eye views of it from an impressive ramped bridge. Then head alongside the River Calder before diving off into woodland. At a route intersection it's worth a there-and-back detour to see lovely little Heath village, set in expansive common land. It's also this junction where you pick up signs for the Trans Pennine Trail which uses NCN 67 hereabouts.

After a ramp push over the 'Blue Bridge' back over the Calder keep following TPT North signs to touch the canal by the Stanley Ferry pub and keep climbing through the Stanley area of Wakefield on road. You soon leave roads behind again to pick up a good quality tarmac railpath into the Leeds area, proclaimed by an entrance gateway above your head.

Whilst the main route carries straight on the railpath leaving the TPT/NCN 67 and becoming the Castleford Greenway, another worthwhile diversion is to keep following

National Cycle Network 69

TPT signs through Methley village to reach the river Aire. Here there is a fantastic loop around RSPB St Aidan's bird and nature reserve using signed bridleways.

The main route uses a brief section of roads through Methley village, before picking up NCN 69 at Methley Junction to head back over the river Calder on a wonderfully wide tarmac path. Drop down to your right here and head along the riverside path (canal on your right). Signs take you onto the canal towpath at the picturesque Fairies Hill Moorings and it's now simply a case of following the towpath (part of the Castleford-Wakefield Greenway network) all the way back to the Stanley Ferry pub and retracing your route back to The Hepworth.

RIDE 04

Train Station: Wakefield Kirkgate

Grade: Moderate

Terrain, gradients and access: Usually flat riverside tracks and railpath with occasional linking road sections with a moderate amount of traffic. Generally few access barriers though there are a number of A-frames. The biggest obstacle to easy access is the so-called 'blue bridge' over the river Calder, just a couple of miles into the ride. This has two large flights of pretty steep steps but they do have access ramps at the sides to wheel your bike up.

Loops, links and longer rides: NCN 67 follows the canal all the way to Leeds centre and is the northern end of the Wakefield to Leeds Trans Pennine Trail spur option. The Castleford-Wakefield Greenway NCN 69 also provides a link into Castleford centre via a riverside path and there is a railpath link to the Cutsyke area too.

Stay: Bootique, Stanley Road, Wakefield (01904) 375035 bootique.ltd

Eat and drink: The Hepworth has its own café, Heath village has Kings Arms pub, Stanley Ferry (pub) on the Aire & Calder navigation and the Green House takeaway café near the TPT on the St Aidan's loop option.

Wider area cycle map: West Yorkshire

Castleford Greenway

259

RIDE 05

6 miles

Start: Barton-upon-Humber train station

HUMBER BRIDGE ROUTE

Humber Bridge

Bridge rides don't come much better than this blustery and exhilarating crossing over the Humber, one of the longest cyclable suspension bridges in the world. The views of the bridge from either end are marvellous, but the scenery across the estuary from its centre is the most memorable.

Start at Barton-upon-Humber train station and head for the south shore of the Humber Estuary. Waters' Edge Country Park is beside the southern end of the bridge, and its woodlands, wetlands, wildflower meadows and visitor centre are certainly worth a visit. However, leave time to cycle just a short distance further west to Far Ings National Nature Reserve (NNR), where the vast swooshing reedbeds and open pools in the former clay pits on the estuary banks are very special indeed. You'll need to look carefully to spot the reserve's shy bearded tits, bitterns and water rails among the reeds, but the ducks and wildfowl on the open pools and islands are easy to see.

Head back to rejoin the trail and start the long ride over the gently curving Humber Bridge, one of the most iconic features of the east Yorkshire and north Lincolnshire landscape. At over a mile long, it may take a little while to complete, especially allowing for an estuary breeze and midway pauses to enjoy the far-reaching views.

Finish: Ferriby train station

RIDE 05

Train stations: Barton-upon-Humber, Hessle and Ferriby

Grade: Easy

Terrain, gradients and access: Flat tarmac path with some road crossings and short, on-road sections at Barton-upon-Humber, Hessle and North Ferriby.

Loops, links and longer rides: Yorkshire Wolds Cycle Route is a 146-mile circular route along quiet roads around the Wolds in East Yorkshire. Trans Pennine Trail begins in the nearby seaside town of Hornsea, and is a 215-mile coast to coast route ending in Southport, Merseyside. NCN 65 Hornsea Rail Trail (**Ride 06**).

Stay: West Wold Farm House, Barton-upon-Humber 07889 532937

Eat and drink: On the south side of the bridge, try Fig Tree Café or Harrisons @ The George Inn in Barton-upon-Humber. On the north side, Ferriby's Coffee House in North Ferriby is popular.

Cycle hire: Nearest is Grimsby Cycle Hub (01472) 354986 cyclehublincs.org.uk

Wider area cycle map: Yorkshire Wolds, York & The Humber

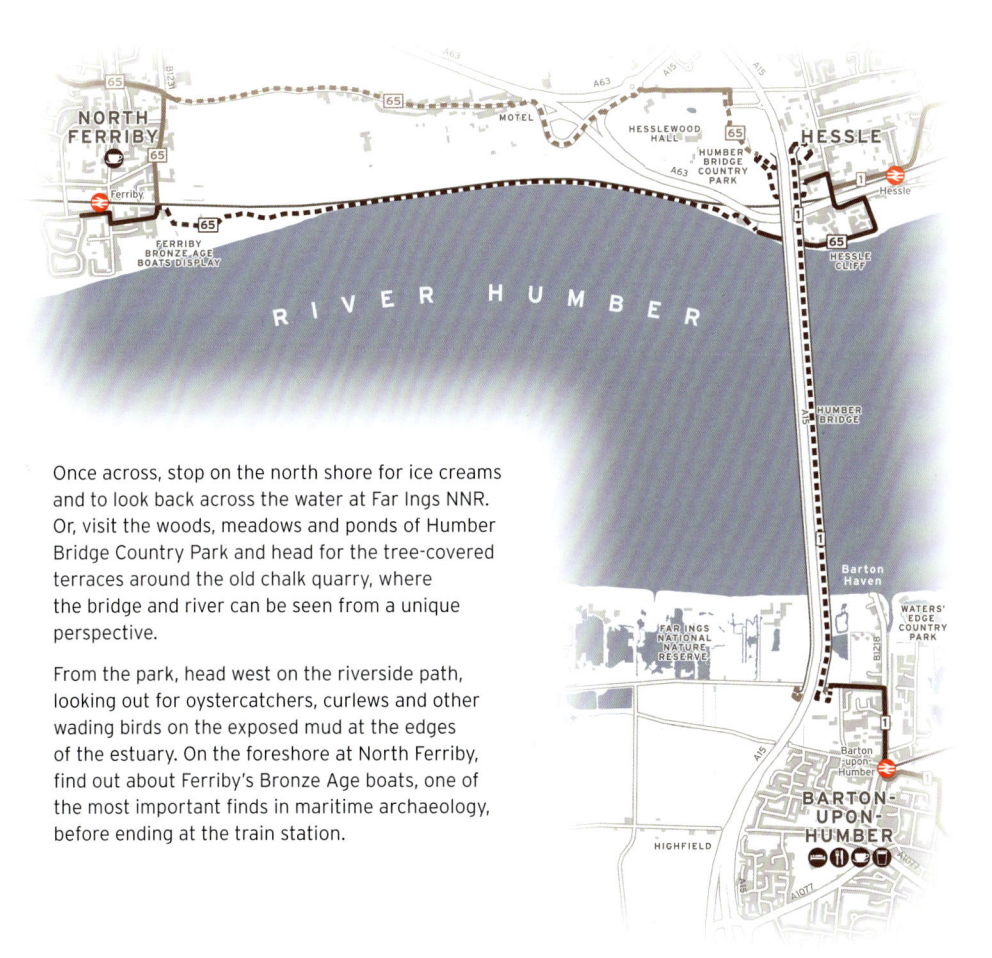

Once across, stop on the north shore for ice creams and to look back across the water at Far Ings NNR. Or, visit the woods, meadows and ponds of Humber Bridge Country Park and head for the tree-covered terraces around the old chalk quarry, where the bridge and river can be seen from a unique perspective.

From the park, head west on the riverside path, looking out for oystercatchers, curlews and other wading birds on the exposed mud at the edges of the estuary. On the foreshore at North Ferriby, find out about Ferriby's Bronze Age boats, one of the most important finds in maritime archaeology, before ending at the train station.

261

RIDE 06

15.5 miles | 65 | **Start:** Hull Paragon Interchange station

HORNSEA RAIL TRAIL

This gentle and diverse ride features city, coast and countryside as it crosses the flat and fertile landscape of East Yorkshire. Hull is a wonderful start and is Yorkshire's only maritime city, so it's worth exploring before setting off.

Start the ride from the train station and head through Hull's Old Town, cycling past some of the city's finest architecture along the way. You'll pass the beautiful City Hall and the Maritime Museum, both with vast domed towers on top, and the elaborate building of the Guildhall. Cross the River Hull, weaving its way to the Humber Estuary, and reach the start of the traffic-free path at Garden Village.

This is where the urban outskirts of the city start to be left behind, and you'll soon enter the remote, marshy grassland of Holderness Plain. It's a flat and exposed ride from here. Wide open views stretch out in every direction across the low-lying arable land, and the vast East Yorkshire sky creates an overwhelming sense of space.

At New Ellerby, there's an opportunity to follow a short, signed link route along country lanes to the Elizabethan manor house of Burton Constable Hall, which makes a pleasant mid-ride diversion. Alternatively, continue along the Rail Trail and make a pub stop a few miles later in the little village of Great Hatfield.

A tiny detour in the final mile leads to the shores of Hornsea Mere, Yorkshire's largest freshwater lake, or simply follow the trail all the way to Hornsea seafront. End on South Promenade for a breezy walk along the sandy and shingly beach, where there are far-reaching views across the choppy North Sea.

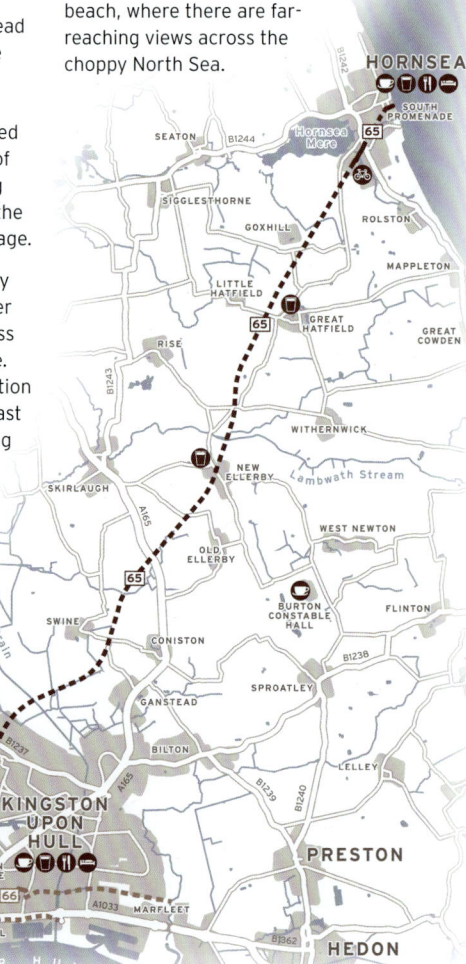

262

Finish: South Promenade, Hornsea

RIDE 06

"End on South Promenade for a breezy walk along the sandy and shingly beach..."

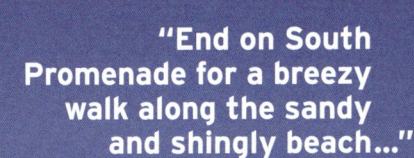

Train station: Hull Paragon Interchange

Grade: Moderate

Terrain, gradients and access: Flat tarmac path and gravel track with some road crossings and on-road sections at Hull and Hornsea.

Loops, links and longer rides: Hornsea Rail Trail is the eastern end of the popular Trans Pennine Trail, a 215-mile coast to coast route from Hornsea to Southport. Yorkshire Wolds Cycle Route is a 146-mile circular route along quiet roads around the Wolds in East Yorkshire. NCN 1 and 65 Humber Bridge Route (**Ride 05**).

Stay: Beachside B&B, Hornsea (01964) 534653 beachsidehornsea-bedandbreakfast.co.uk

Eat and drink: Tasty or Thieving Harry's café are both popular at Hull Marina. Along the route, try The Railway Inn at New Ellerby, Stables Tearoom at Burton Constable Hall or Wrygarth Inn at Great Hatfield. At Hornsea, try Hornsea Mere Café, Café Chocolat or Sullivans fish and chips.

Cycle hire: Switchback Cycles, Hornsea Freeport (01964) 537231 **switchbackcycles.co.uk**

Wider area cycle map: Yorkshire Wolds, York & The Humber

The Trans Pennine Trail starts on Hornsea Promenade

RIDE 07
6 miles | 66 | 677 | 🚲 | **Start:** Temple Newsam House, Leeds

WYKE BECK WAY

This green corridor through the Wyke Beck Valley in Leeds links up meadows, woodland and ponds between two magnificent country parks. Temple Newsam Park at the start is vast and wonderful, and its raised position gives lovely views over the area. Take a look around the farm, woodland and parkland landscaped by Capability Brown in the 18th Century, but leave plenty of time to go inside the giant red Tudor-Jacobean mansion house: it's one of the best historic houses in the country.

Start the ride from the gates of the house and immediately join the tree-lined road for a smooth, long descent beside Temple Newsam grounds and Halton Moor, with the city of Leeds visible beyond. From here, the ride becomes a patchwork of green spaces interspersed with urban areas, and you'll leap from one to the other. Halton Moor Wood is quickly followed by the residential streets of Halton, followed in turn by the greenery of Primrose Valley Local Nature Reserve (LNR), and so the pattern continues.

Killingbeck Fields LNR is the most countrified of all, and its nature-filled wildflower meadows are home to shy roe deer which you're most likely to spot around dusk and dawn. It's a climb from here to the green spaces of Fearnville Fields and Arthur's Rein, but the ride through Wykebeck Woods LNR, a very pretty ancient wet woodland, is particularly enjoyable, and a real highlight of the ride.

Moments after leaving the woodland, enter Roundhay Park, one of Leeds' most popular open spaces. Climb the trail to meet Carriage Drive and glide along the banks of the huge Waterloo Lake, ending at the café on the shores of the water. Alternatively, follow the cycle route past the mansion house to the smaller Upper Lake. Deeper within the park is an enchanting wooded ravine and gorge, an attractive sham castle on the grassy slopes, and the exotic rainforest of Tropical World.

264

Finish: Waterloo Lake, Roundhay Park, Leeds

RIDE 07

Train stations: Nearest are Leeds and Cross Gates

Grade: Easy

Terrain, gradients and access: Descending at the start, then gently climbing along tarmac path and fine gravel track. Some road crossings and on-road sections at Temple Newsam, Halton and Killingbeck.

Loops, links and longer rides: From Temple Newsam, there is a mostly traffic-free route into Leeds centre, via the Royal Armouries Museum. From the Royal Armouries Museum in Leeds, follow NCN 67 Aire & Calder Navigation for a nine-mile, traffic-free ride to Mickletown. NCN 66 and 696 Aire Valley Towpath (**Ride 08**).

Stay: The Beechwood B&B, Leeds (0113) 266 2578 beechwoodhotelleeds.com

Eat and drink: Temple Newsam Tea Rooms is at Temple Newsam Park, while Lakeside Café and Tropical World Café are both at Roundhay Park. Preston café bar or Tasty Kitchen & Coffee are both good at Oakwood, next to Roundhay Park.

Cycle hire: Leeds Urban Bike Park (0113) 277 2413 leedsurbanbikepark.com

Wider area cycle map: West Yorkshire

Roundhay Park

265

RIDE 08

16 miles | 66 696 | **Start:** Granary Wharf, Leeds

AIRE VALLEY TOWPATH

Lovely locks feature all the way along this 17-mile stretch of the Leeds & Liverpool Canal but the best are saved to last: Bingley Five Rise Locks. They elevate the canal up an impressively steep hill and are deservedly among the 'seven wonders of the waterways', with sensational views from the top lock.

Start at Granary Wharf, a lively city centre spot on the banks of the Leeds & Liverpool Canal. It can be reached directly from Leeds train station. West Yorkshire was the wool capital of the world at one time, and the vast, many-windowed textile mills and towering chimneys that line the towpath as you leave Leeds are testament to this once great industry. In the opening mile, stop for an over-the-shoulder look at the city as the route begins its transformation from urban to rural and the old mill buildings are gradually replaced by rich green pastures and pretty stone bridges spanning the water.

Around three miles in, get great views of Kirkstall Abbey peeping out from among the thick trees across the valley to the right of the trail, and pause on the well-positioned benches to enjoy a lingering look at these medieval remains. A short while later, reach Rodley Nature Reserve, a wildlife-rich wetland in the bottom of the Kirkstall Valley, before climbing steadily between the river and the canal, with the Aire Valley scenery opening out beautifully in some spots, and thick woodland closing around you in others.

The final miles of the ride are packed with fascinating features. Saltaire comes first, an astonishingly attractive spot where the

Bingley Five Rise Locks

Finish: Five Rise Locks, Bingley

RIDE 08

Train stations: Leeds and Bingley

Grade: Moderate

Terrain, gradients and access: A gentle ascent with pronounced climbs around some of the locks, particularly Five Rise Locks at the route's end. Tarmac path, stony trail and fine gravel track, with some road crossings and a short, on-road section at Calverley Bridge. Take care passing under low bridges on the towpath close to the water's edge.

Loops, links and longer rides: From Bingley, continue along the towpath for a further two and a half miles to the National Trust's East Riddlesden Hall. From the Royal Armouries in Leeds, follow NCN 67 Aire & Calder Navigation for a nine-mile, traffic-free ride to Mickletown. NCN 66 and 677 Wyke Beck Way (**Ride 07**).

Stay: Five Rise Locks Hotel, Bingley (01274) 565296 five-rise-locks.co.uk

Eat and drink: In Leeds, Laynes Espresso near the station is popular plus there are waterside cafés and restaurants at the route's start in Granary Wharf including The Hop. On the route, try The Tiny Tearoom at Calverley Bridge, Are-Jay-Bargie café boat at Saltaire, or Salts Diner and Café into the Opera in Salts Mill. Five Rise Locks Café and Five Rise Locks Hotel are both at the route's end.

Cycle hire: Leeds Urban Bike Park (0113) 277 2813 leedsurbanbikepark.com

Wider area cycle map: West Yorkshire

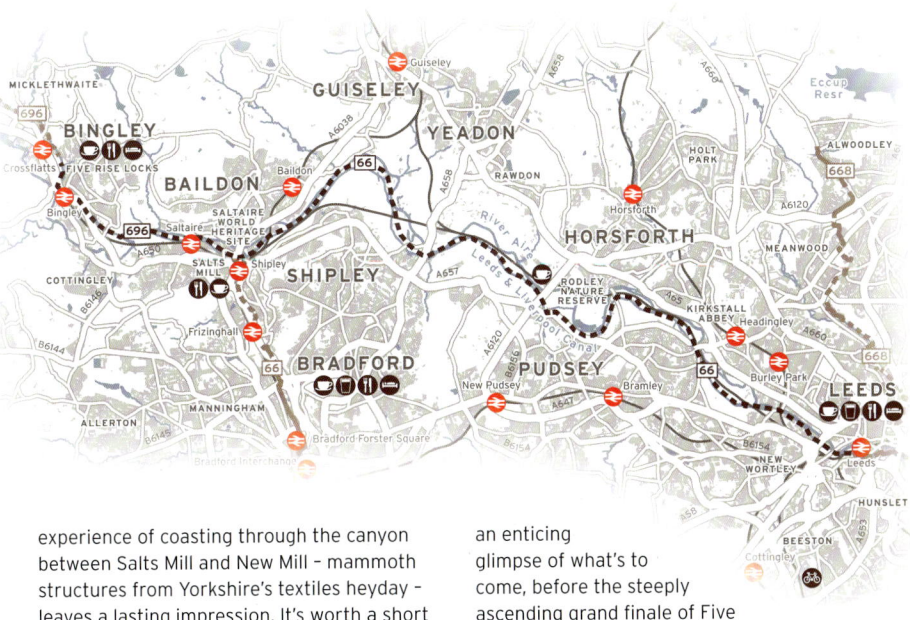

experience of coasting through the canyon between Salts Mill and New Mill – mammoth structures from Yorkshire's textiles heyday – leaves a lasting impression. It's worth a short deviation off the towpath here to explore the World Heritage Site of Saltaire, a beautifully preserved Victorian model village created for the mill workers.

Back on the canal, cross the water near Bingley to complete the ride on the opposite bank. Three Rise Locks soon emerges, giving an enticing glimpse of what's to come, before the steeply ascending grand finale of Five Rise Locks appears a short while later. It's an intensely sharp, heart-hammering climb alongside them, but the sweeping Yorkshire scenery from the top lock is a perfect ending.

267

RIDE 09
10 miles

Start: Millennium Green, Riccall

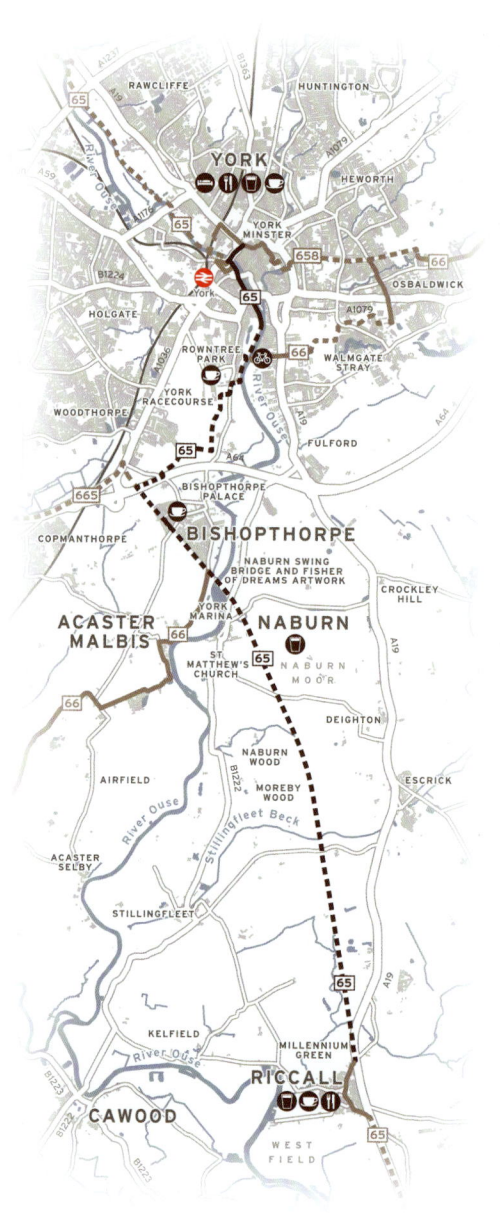

RICCALL
TO
YORK

This is one of the original walking and cycling routes on the National Cycle Network and remains one of the finest, leading from fertile farmland and North Yorkshire villages into the historic heart of York, once the capital of the North. Along the way, look out for the scale model of the solar system that extends along much of the route; it's built at a scale that makes it possible to cycle ten times the speed of light without breaking a sweat.

Start among the meadows and wild flowers of Millennium Green on the edge of the pretty village of Riccall, before riding north between fields of stubbly crops and deep green brassicas. Giant oak trees overhang the path in parts, heavy with acorns in late summer, and you'll enter deeper woodland as you ride along the edge of Moreby and Naburn woods. The spire of St Matthew's church poking out from among the trees signals the little village of Naburn, and there's a short, signed route from the trail that leads into the centre of the village where The Blacksmith's Arms pub can be found for a good halfway stop.

In the second half of the ride, pass the yachts of York Marina and cross the River Ouse on the old Naburn swing bridge. Look up to see the wonderful 'Fisher of Dreams' artwork perched on top of the bridge: a giant steel sculpture of an expectant fisherperson dangling their line into the water. A section of tree-lined trail follows, where there's a chance of spotting bee orchids, harvest mice and delicate long-tailed tits, before reaching Bishopthorpe village.

Finish: York Minster

RIDE 09

'Fisher of Dreams' sculpture

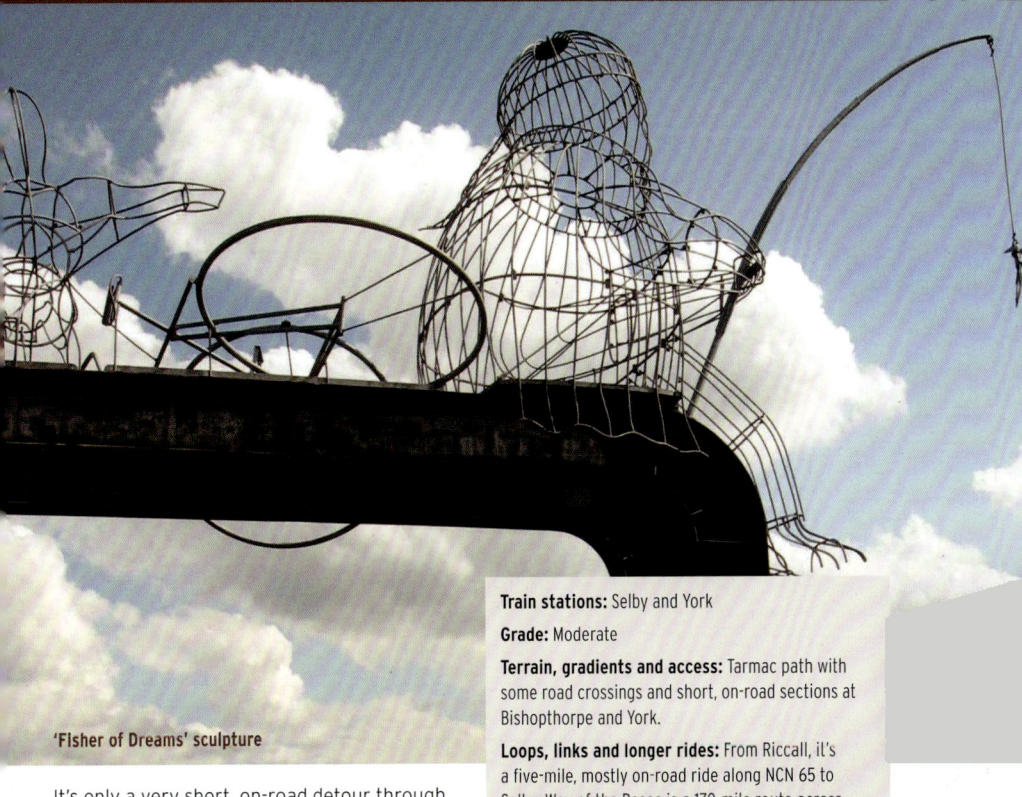

It's only a very short, on-road detour through the village to the gothic gatehouse of Bishopthorpe Palace, the official residence of the Archbishop of York. Alternatively, simply stick to the path to pass the track and grandstands of York Racecourse, before joining the banks of the River Ouse at Rowntree Park. This is an elegant city park, and it's a lovely ride along the riverbank here, watching pleasure boats cruise leisurely along the water.

Leave the river at Lendal Bridge to ride the final quarter of a mile through the city streets to end in the shadow of the mighty York Minster. Leave lots of time to explore because, along with being fabulously historic and fetchingly beautiful, York is also one of the country's top cycling cities.

Train stations: Selby and York

Grade: Moderate

Terrain, gradients and access: Tarmac path with some road crossings and short, on-road sections at Bishopthorpe and York.

Loops, links and longer rides: From Riccall, it's a five-mile, mostly on-road ride along NCN 65 to Selby. Way of the Roses is a 170-mile route across Lancashire and Yorkshire, via York. NCN 65 York to Skelton (**Ride 10**). NCN 665 and 67 Wetherby Railway Path (**Ride 11**).

Stay: YHA York 0345 371 9051 yha.org.uk

Eat and drink: The Hare and Hounds is at Riccall, as is The Burro restaurant, housed in the village's old brick windmill. Along the route, try The Blacksmiths Arms at Naburn, Brunswick Organic Nursery and Farm Shop in Bishopthorpe and Rowntree Park Café. Cycle Heaven café is just over the Millennium Bridge. Bettys, York Cocoa House and the Blue Bell pub are all in lovely positions close to York Minster.

Cycle hire: Cycle Heaven, York (01904) 622701 cycle-heaven.co.uk or Get Cycling (01904) 636812 getcycling.org.uk

Wider area cycle map: Yorkshire Wolds, York & The Humber

269

YORK
TO
SKELTON

RIDE 10 — 4.5 miles — Start: York Minster

York Minster

This short ride leads from the heart of one of England's top cycling cities into the flat, low-lying land in the Vale of York. York Minster, one of the world's greatest cathedrals, is a magnificent start, and an impressive line-up of distinguished and beautiful buildings line the route as you leave the city: Theatre Royal, King's Manor and City Art Gallery are among them.

Pass through the famous city walls at the Bootham Bar toll booth and join the banks of the wide River Ouse within the opening mile. If arriving by train there is a wonderful signed traffic-free link to the route, directly from inside the station near the York Tap pub, with great views over the river from a newly constructed bridge. The river is swiftly left behind though, and the vast green space of Rawcliffe Meadows on the city's floodplain takes over. Traverse wildflower-rich grassland and little copses, whilst taking in gentle views over the flat green fields and red brick farmsteads that typify the Vale.

Rejoin the banks of the River Ouse in the ride's final mile, before turning right onto Stripe Lane. The lane meets the busier A19 at Skelton, but dismount here and push a very short distance along the pavement to end at

RIDE 10

Finish: Skelton

Train station: York

Grade: Easy

Terrain, gradients and access: Flat, tarmac path with short, on-road sections at York and Skelton.

Loops, links and longer rides: This is part of the Way of the Roses route, a 170-mile coast to coast route across Lancashire and Yorkshire from Morecambe to Bridlington. NCN 65 Riccall to York (**Ride 09**). NCN 665 and 67 Wetherby Railway Path (**Ride 11**).

Stay: YHA York 0345 371 9051 yha.org.uk

Eat and drink: There are lots of places to eat and drink in York. Bettys, York Cocoa House and the Blue Bell pub are all in lovely positions close to York Minster. At Skelton, try Maple Leaf Café at Skelton Garden Centre. There is also a restaurant in the walled garden of Beningbrough Hall.

Cycle hire: Cycle Heaven, York (01904) 622701 cycle-heaven.co.uk or Get Cycling (01904) 636812 getcycling.org.uk

Wider area cycle map: Yorkshire Wolds, York & The Humber

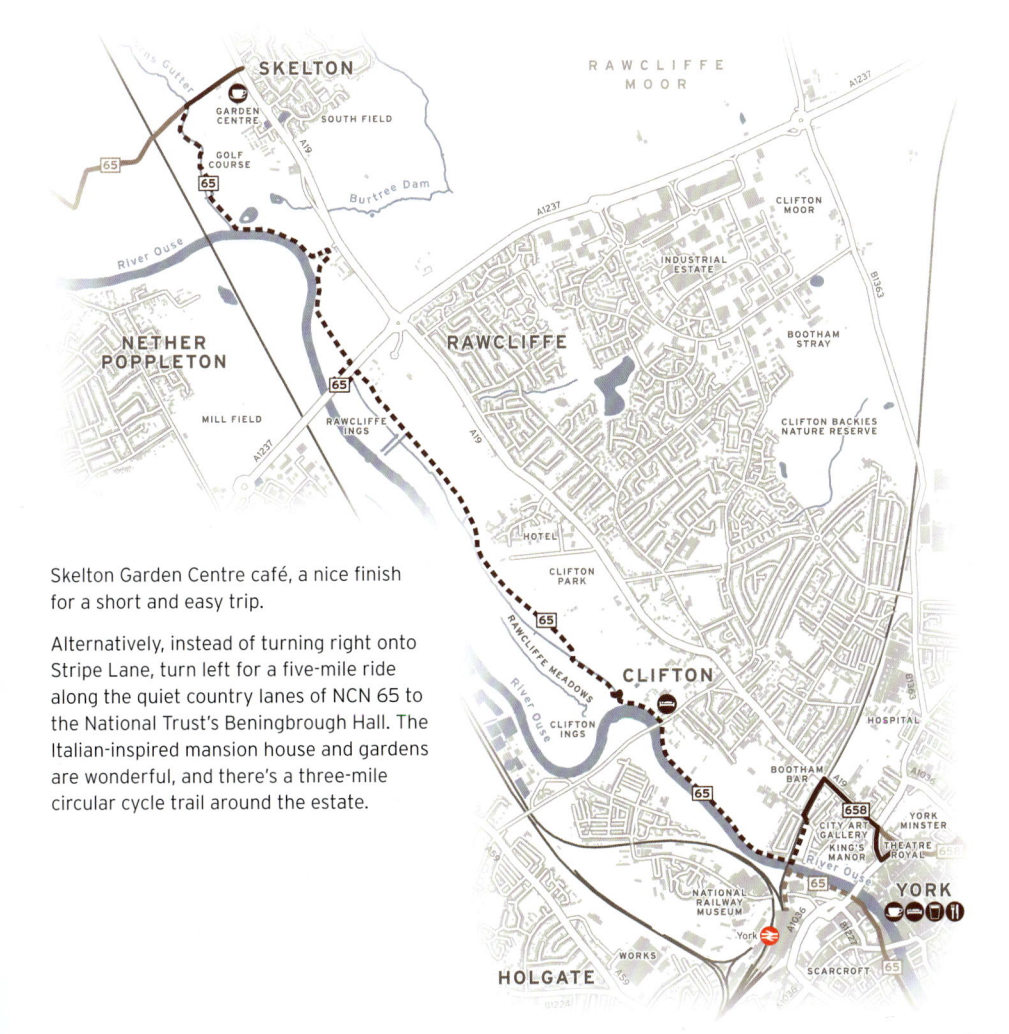

Skelton Garden Centre café, a nice finish for a short and easy trip.

Alternatively, instead of turning right onto Stripe Lane, turn left for a five-mile ride along the quiet country lanes of NCN 65 to the National Trust's Beningbrough Hall. The Italian-inspired mansion house and gardens are wonderful, and there's a three-mile circular cycle trail around the estate.

RIDE 11
6 miles

67 | 665 | 🚲 | ➤ **Start:** Thorp Arch Retail Park

WETHERBY RAILWAY PATH

This gentle trail follows a former railway path through the Yorkshire countryside, passing through the historic market town of Wetherby along the way.

Start among the shops of the retail park and immediately join the old Thorp Arch railway cutting, thick with foxgloves, cowslips and crab apples. It's a flat and easy ride past the edges of Leeds United's training ground and into the tree cover of Jackson Wood. Lovely views over the farmland follow, with traditional hedgerows of spiky burdock and colourful red campion lining the path on the way to Spring Wood, where the ponds are a good place to pause and look for damselflies, common frogs and great crested newts.

Ride past Wetherby Racecourse, regarded by many as the finest jump course in the north of England, before joining the road into the market town of Wetherby. This is the midway point of the ride, and it's worth a little detour here to explore the town. The River Wharfe winds sharply through the centre, indeed Wharfe is a Celtic name meaning 'twisting' or 'winding', and there are some lovely riverbank picnic spots, particularly beside the gushing weir and attractive arches of Wetherby Bridge.

Or, take a look around the historic buildings of the market place, including The Shambles and the Classical Town Hall. You're certain to get a warm welcome wherever you go; thanks to its special position, equidistant between Edinburgh and London, Wetherby became a vital stopping point for 18th Century mail coaches, so it has a long history of playing host to weary travellers.

Leave Wetherby behind and link up with the Harland Way, riding the final miles through a mixture of sheltered tree cover and wide open arable farmland. The traffic-free path comes to an end at the High Street in Spofforth, so join the road here for a short ride to the ruins of Spofforth Castle, manor house of the powerful Percy family for more than 200 years.

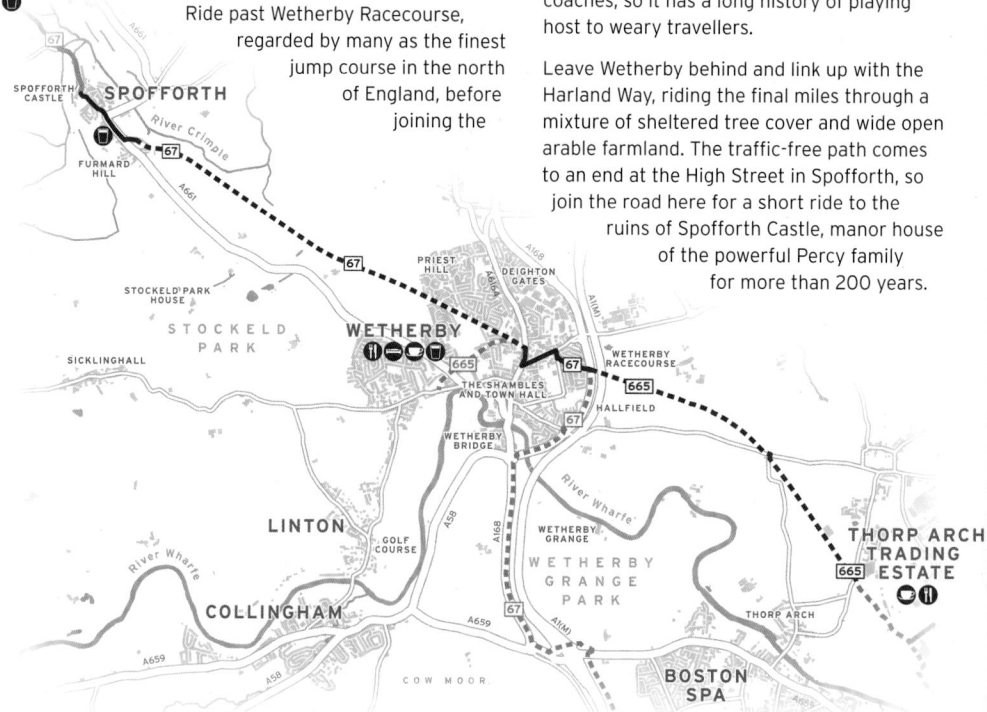

272

RIDE 11

Finish: Spofforth Castle

Train station: Nearest is Harrogate
Grade: Easy
Terrain, gradients and access: Mostly flat tarmac path and stony trail, with some road crossings and on-road sections at Wetherby and Spofforth.
Loops, links and longer rides: Follow NCN 67 for a further seven miles along an on-road and traffic-free route through Follifoot and the Great Yorkshire Showground into the centre of Harrogate. NCN 67 Nidderdale Greenway (**Ride 12**).

Stay: Wharfe House, Wetherby (01937) 588819 wharfe.house
Eat and drink: The Café and Bistro is at Thorp Arch Retail Park. North Street Deli and Wetherby Whaler fish and chips are both popular in Wetherby. The Railway Inn and The Castle Inn are both at Spofforth, whilst Radcliffe Arms is at the nearby village of Follifoot.
Wider area cycle map: West Yorkshire

"There are some lovely riverbank picnic spots, particularly beside the gushing weir..."

Wetherby weir

RIDE 12 — 3 miles | 67 | **Start:** The Gardeners Arms, Bilton

NIDDERDALE GREENWAY

Spring cycling on the Nidderdale Greenway

On this short and gentle ride, the North Yorkshire countryside is golden with wheat fields in the summer and ablaze with the amber leaves of the surrounding ancient woodland in autumn. However, it's the remarkable views from the top of Nidd Viaduct near the route's start that are the real highlight, and they are wonderful no matter what time of year.

Start at The Gardeners Arms pub in Bilton and climb the short road to the start of the traffic-free path in the beautiful Nidd Gorge. Within the opening mile you'll reach the River Nidd, crossing it on the beautiful seven-arch viaduct. This is the best spot for soaking up glorious views over the fields and the thick, dark coniferous forest that spreads across the hillside to the right.

It's a meandering ride through sublime woodland from here, with bluebells erupting up the steep valley sides in spring, and pretty yellow and purple wildflower meadows visible beyond the trees in summer.

In the final mile, join the shady shores of the river to look for kingfishers, listen for woodpeckers, or find a spot for a waterside picnic, before climbing gently towards the route's end at Ripley village. Finish in the cobbled market square among the pretty ivy-covered buildings and traditional shops. The entrance to the distinguished Ripley Castle is here, too, and a walk around its grand walled gardens, lake and deer park is a thoroughly enjoyable ending to this short but memorable ride.

274

Finish: Ripley Castle

RIDE 12

Train stations: Nearest are Starbeck and Harrogate

Grade: Easy

Terrain, gradients and access: Tarmac path, largely flat with a very short, climb from the river near the end. A very short on-road section at Bilton and one road crossing near Ripley.

Loops, links and longer rides: From Bilton, follow a further two miles of mostly traffic-free route into the centre of the pretty spa town of Harrogate, or join NCN 636 Beryl Burton Way to Knaresborough, named after the legendary Leeds-born cyclist. At Ripley, continue along NCN 67 on a traffic-free path through Hollybank Wood.

Stay: Sophie's B&B, Hampsthwaite (01423) 779219 sophiesbedandbreakfast.co.uk

Eat and drink: Betty's Café Tea Rooms overlooking The Stray in Harrogate is renowned. Try The Gardeners Arms pub at Bilton where the route starts or Sophie's Café in Hampsthwaite. In Ripley, visit Ripley Ice Cream, Ripley Castle Tearoom or The Boar's Head.

Cycle hire: Vern Overton Cycling, Darley 07595 460465 voc.bike, Nidderdale Cycle Hire, Summerbridge (also at Boars Head, Ripley) 07821 463853 nidderdalecycles.co.uk or Harrogate Electric Bikes (01423) 313571 harrogateelectricbikes.co.uk

Wider area cycle map: West Yorkshire

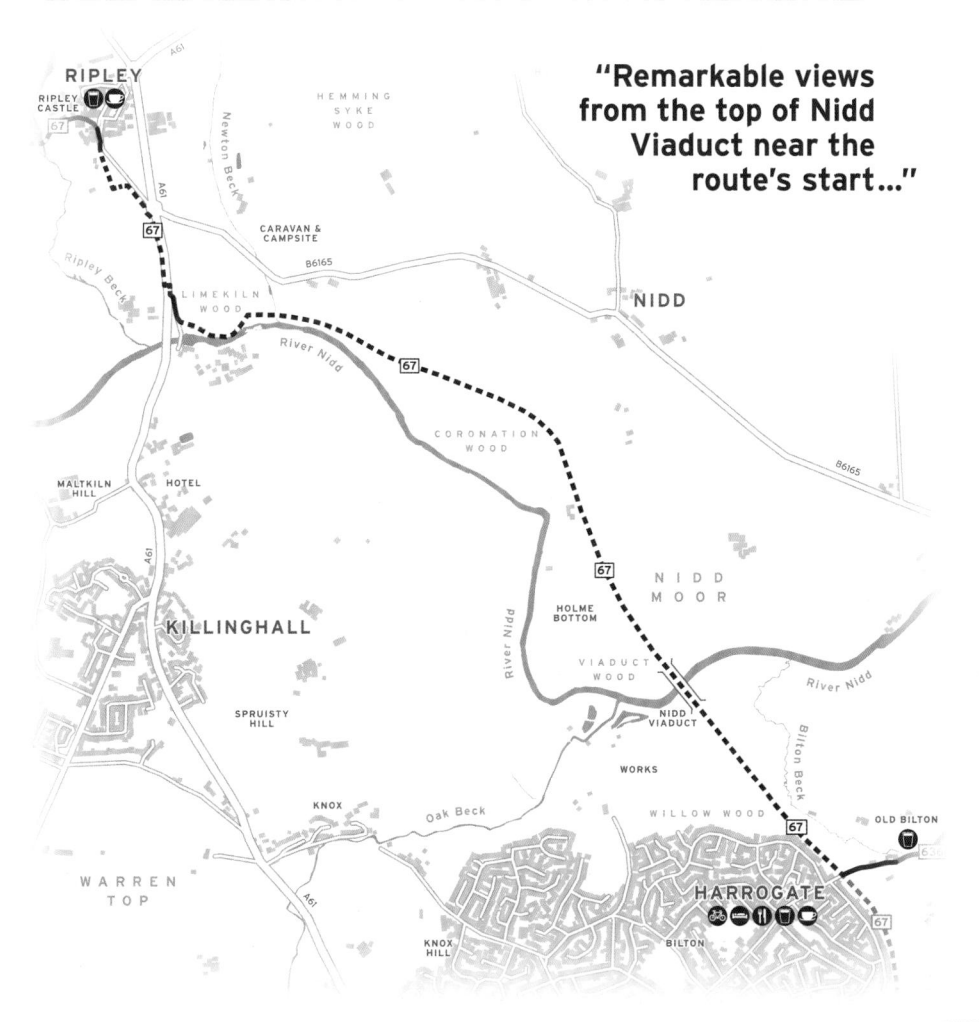

> "Remarkable views from the top of Nidd Viaduct near the route's start..."

275

RIDE 13 — 23 miles

Start: The Esplanade, Scarborough

THE CINDER TRACK

(SCARBOROUGH TO WHITBY)

For sheer traffic-free trail spectacle The Cinder Track has few rivals. Looking at the North Yorks Moors National Park with hills tumbling towards the North Sea, it's hard to believe a railway through this landscape was ever contemplated. The Scarborough to Whitby ride follows the trackbed of an old railway line that ran for 80 years between 1885 and 1965.

This is a long there and back ride and a train back takes several hours as there is no direct line. You might want to tackle only a portion of it unless you want a pretty long day in the saddle or an overnight stop halfway.

We start the ride above Scarborough's south bay on NCN 1. You can take in the magnificent views across the graceful curve of sand backed by many fine buildings, including the enormous Victorian Grand Hotel and Scarborough Castle. NCN 1 threads its way on roads past the train station to pick up the traffic-free trail itself, rather incongruously, at the back of Sainsbury's car park.

Despite the 20th Century start you could easily be riding into the past as you skirt the edges of Scalby and Burniston villages, with an accompanying backdrop of wheat fields, pasture and glimpses of the sea. After passing Cloughton you enter the National Park and the surrounding terrain becomes more challenging. The gradient remains steady, despite a long ride to the clifftops of Ravenscar, where it emerges by the village tearooms.

Seaviews are much more the order of the day north of Ravenscar, passing under the steep-sided ridge of Stoupe Brow. Coastal views open up back to Ravenscar and across the rocky bay to the one-time smugglers' haunt of Robin Hood's Bay, rivalling Scarborough and Whitby for the character of its buildings and its attractiveness as a tourist honeypot – albeit on a smaller scale.

The famed abbey at Whitby comes into view on the horizon before a steep crossing of the river Esk on the old viaduct and a road descent to the busy Whitby harbour, backed by a jumble of ancient red-tiled buildings that once looked down upon shipyards where Captain Cook's Endeavour was built.

View from Ravenscar

Finish: Whitby harbour

RIDE 13

Train Station: Stations at both Scarborough and Whitby though there is no direct line between the two

Grade: Challenging

Terrain, gradients and access: Certainly one of the more challenging railpaths you are likely to encounter. The steepest gradient comes on the pull up to Ravenscar - it's only moderately steep compared to the surrounding hills but steep for a railpath. The surface is unsealed and as the name suggests quite loose in places, as the cinder moniker suggests. Occasional muddy sections in the woodland, especially in winter.

Loops, links and longer rides: If you want a more challenging off-road route then the Cinder Track is part of the larger regional Moor to Sea cycle network whose signing appears alongside the Cinder Track's in places. A few road crossings and some road sections on NCN at either end. A small minority of access points along the way are steps only.

Stay: Hayburn Wyke B&B - right on the trail. (01723) 870202 hayburnwykeinn.co.uk

Eat and drink: Lots of pubs and cafés a short ride off the trail, at Burniston, Cloughton Newlands, Robin Hood's Bay and Hawsker (but be aware some involve steep climbs). Two of the prettiest eateries are the Hayburn Wyke pub (en route) and the Youth Hostel café at Boggle Hole (around a mile off the trail down a very steep minor road).

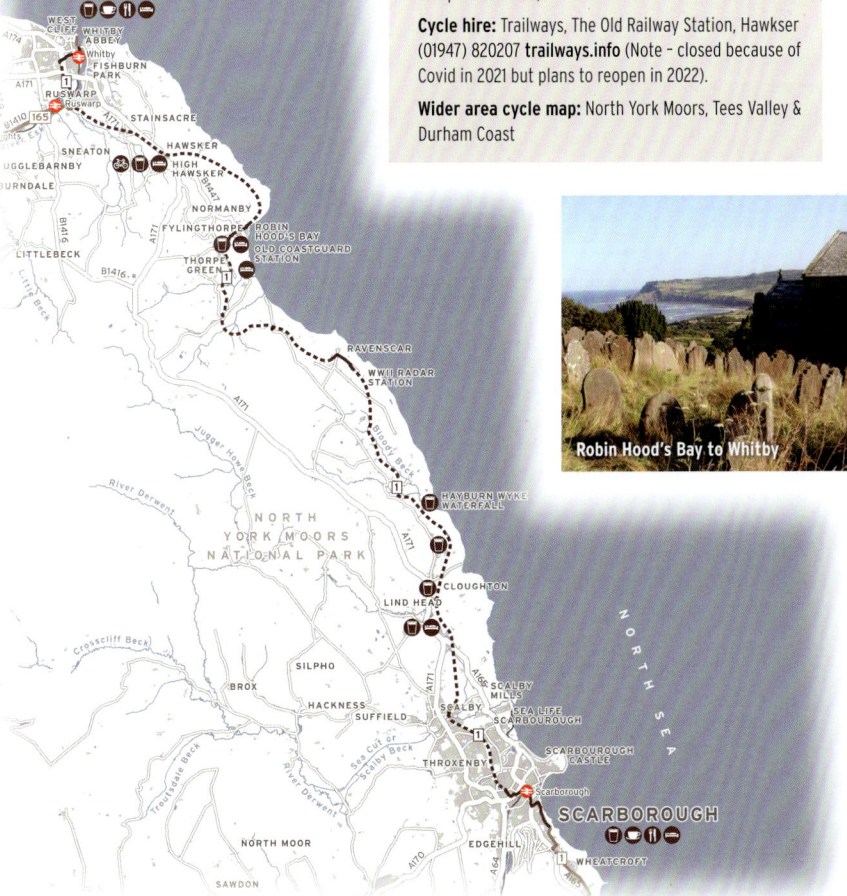

Cycle hire: Trailways, The Old Railway Station, Hawkser (01947) 820207 trailways.info (Note - closed because of Covid in 2021 but plans to reopen in 2022).

Wider area cycle map: North York Moors, Tees Valley & Durham Coast

Robin Hood's Bay to Whitby

277

NORTH EAST

At the midway point of the Consett & Sunderland Railway Path, the iconic 'Angel of the North' appears on the skyline, offering an open-armed welcome that captures the warmth, pride and creativity of the North East in a single moment. This is easily one of the most spirited and characterful parts of the country to cycle around.

Many of this region's traffic-free routes follow fine former railway paths, leading through the stunning moorland landscape of Northumberland, the Durham Dales and wild North Pennines. Several paths link together to form part of the country's most popular challenge cycle route, the Sea to Sea (C2C), and it's quite possible that tackling these short and scenic sections might ultimately persuade you to attempt all 140 miles across the North East and Cumbria.

The most northerly route in this collection brings you to the Scottish borders to follow a lakeside trail through the enchanting woodland of Kielder, England's largest forest, whilst the most easterly experience is a refreshing seaside ride beside the sandy beaches, noisy seabird colonies and majestic lighthouses of the Tyneside coast. In between, the city cycling is exceptional and you'll have the chance to ride into Durham, one of England's most attractive cathedral cities, or beneath the colossal bridges spanning the River Tyne in the heart of Newcastle, where you're guaranteed an unforgettable time on the 'Toon'.

The routes offer a glimpse into the North East's fascinating history too, from the humble home of the great railway pioneer George Stephenson, to the former collieries, steelworks and shipyards that were once the biggest and most productive in the world. But for sheer breathtaking scale there is nothing to match Hadrian's Wall, the country's greatest Roman monument, and you'll encounter it more than once on your cycle journey across this incredible region.

'Angel of the North'

Routes overview

- **01** Middlesbrough to Darlington (17 miles)
- **02** Brandon & Bishop Auckland Walk (9.5 miles)
- **03** Waskerley Way (9 miles)
- **04** Derwent Walk (11 miles)
- **05** Souter Lighthouse to St Mary's Lighthouse (10.5 miles)
- **06** Newcastle to Tynemouth (11 miles)
- **07** Newcastle to Prudhoe (13 miles)
- **08** South Tyne Trail (5.5 or 10 miles)
- **09** Lakeside Way (26.5 miles)
- **10** Berwick-upon-Tweed to Holy Island (15 miles)
- —— Featured ride
- —— National Cycle Network (traffic-free and on-road)

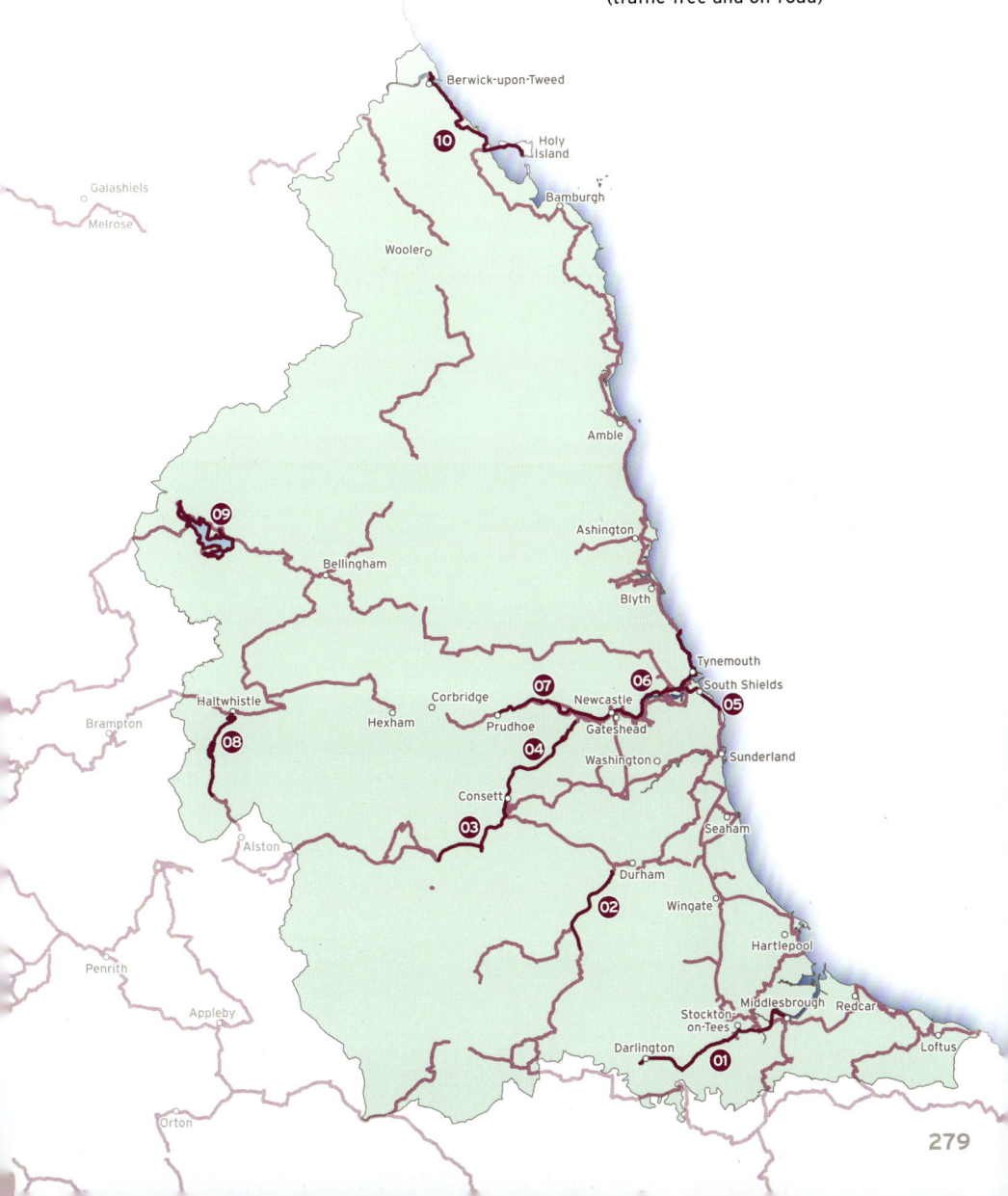

RIDE 01
17 miles

Start: Middlesbrough Transporter Bridge

MIDDLESBROUGH
TO
DARLINGTON

This route combines spectacular bridges, handsome market towns and quirky local visitor attractions to make a truly memorable ride.

Middlesbrough's historic Transporter Bridge is a true icon of the city and until recently the 'gondola' suspended beneath its metal towers shuttled back and forth daily. Sadly the working future of the bridge is in doubt but it's still an awe-inspiring sight and a magnificent landmark to start your journey from.

You shortly dive away from NCN 1 through Teessauras Park, with nicely crafted metal dinosaurs lurking at various points around the greenery. Head west alongside a wide section of the river Tees, past an industrial but pretty impressive backdrop on the opposite bank, soon rejoining NCN 1. The twin towers of the Newport Bridge loom large and it's worth taking a short ride up the access ramps to take a closer look at this 1930s built bridge. The middle section, once upon a time, was able to be raised up between the two giant towers to allow ships to pass underneath.

Heading further upstream to the Tees Barrage at Stockton, though built in the 1990s, has an art deco feel to it. The barrage regulates the upstream river to stop flooding. The construction of it also bought the opportunity to build an internationally-rated white water sports centre. The adrenaline thrills continue here in the form of the Airtrail climbing attraction. Sight of the amazing curves of the traffic-free Infinity Bridge means you are now just a stone's throw from the handsome centre of Stockton-on-Tees.

After passing through Stockton centre NCN 14 uses a mix of back streets, parkland and railpath to pass out into open countryside. Quiet roads and tracks give way to a longer section of rural railpath approaching Darlington. Once you hit the edge of town fine quality and well-signed cycle lanes take over, with local destinations being helpfully marked as so many minutes away by bike.

Infinity Bridge, Stockton

Finish: Darlington town centre

Train Station: 30 min direct service from Darlington to Middlesbrough (you can cut the route short at Thornaby and Dinsdale stations too).

Grade: Easy

Terrain, gradients and access: Mainly good quality, flat tarmac paths and some minor roads. There are a couple of extended sections of crushed stone path, after Teessaurus Park in Middlesbrough and heading towards Darlington, both wide and in good condition. There are few access controls but you will need to push up the very shallow steps of the traffic-free bridge that takes you over a busy road and into Stockton centre. Be aware that a short section of road after Longnewton village has very fast traffic - though it's wide and cycling is actually reasonably safe on it for that reason - but special care must be taken crossing it to head onto a much quieter minor road to continue on NCN 14.

Loops, links and longer rides: East of your start at Middlesbrough's Transporter Bridge NCN 1 continues its journey in the North-East by passing through the suburbs to meet the coast at Redcar then heading down to Staithes via Saltburn-by-Sea. Just under 4 miles along the route the Tees Barrage is where you leave NCN 1 and pick up NCN 14, but NCN 1 and 14 can also be followed to the north from here, the former paralleling the coastline hereabouts and the latter snaking in a huge S-shape via Hartlepool and Durham to South Shields. You will also see signs for the local Eight Bridges Way, linking many of the spectacular local river crossings in a loop starting at the Transporter Bridge.

Stay: Premier Inn, Stockton-on-Tees 0333 321 9054 premierinn.com Nice location right by the Tees Barrage.

Eat and drink: Middlesbrough centre is a short ride from the Transporter Bridge and has plenty of choice. En route the Tees Barrage has regular visits from the San Seb coffee and snack van. The lovely wide main street in Stockton has handsome buildings befitting its status as a sizeable market town, and the pedestrianised area around the town hall is particularly attractive for sitting out for to eat and drink. There's also the Shambles, an old market hall. Pride of place in Darlington has to go to the covered market, recently redeveloped with many exotic food options on offer. The pedestrianised area around the historic market building also hosts a market and is a great place to sit and eat.

Cycle hire: Yorkshire Bike Hire, Northallerton (around 20 miles from the route start but delivery possible depending on min hire charge) 07734 979 029 yorkshirebikehire.co.uk

Wider area cycle map: County Durham & North Yorks

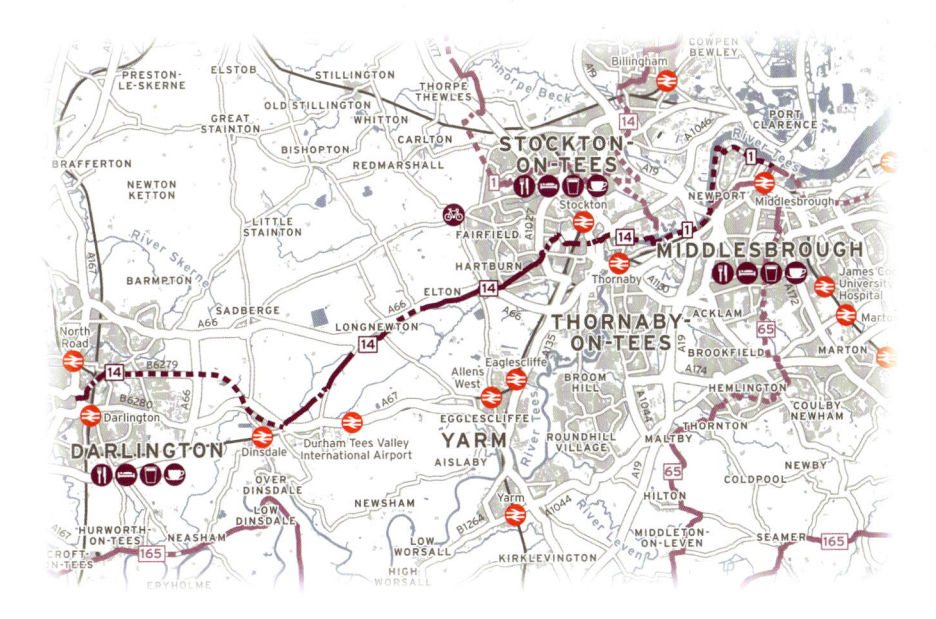

RIDE 02 — 9.5 miles

Start: Newton Cap Viaduct, Bishop Auckland

BRANDON
&
BISHOP AUCKLAND WALK

Sweeping scenery, fine castles and former colliery towns make this a fascinating and attractive ride across the Wear Valley along the route of an old coal railway line.

Start from the northern end of Newton Cap Viaduct, a magnificent 11-arch bridge spanning the River Wear, and in the opening mile get great over-the-shoulder views of the splendid palace of Auckland Castle, former home to the Bishop of Durham. Enter a wooded corridor where a sequence of trailside benches offer vast views over rolling hills and farmland, before reaching the former mining town of Willington.

It's a gentle climb out of the town, weaving beside grassy banks and meadows on the way to the old railway station at Brancepeth. The picnic spot at the station is a lovely place to take a break, and there's an option to follow the short country lane into the very pretty village centre, home to Brancepeth Castle and the attractive St Brandon's Church.

From here, ride into deeper countryside between crop fields and trees to The Ponderosa, a wildlife haven of hay meadows, heather and grassland where nature has enthusiastically reclaimed the site of the old Brandon Colliery. In the final mile, drop down steeply to cross the River Deerness, keeping a keen watch along the way for the otters that are occasionally spotted flitting furtively across the water here.

A short but steep climb from the river takes you up into Broompark picnic area, an important junction for Durham's former railway lines. From here, the views over the Deerness Valley are superb, and it's just a short ride into the heart of Durham, unquestionably one of the most beautiful cities in the UK.

Newton Cap Viaduct, Bishop Auckland

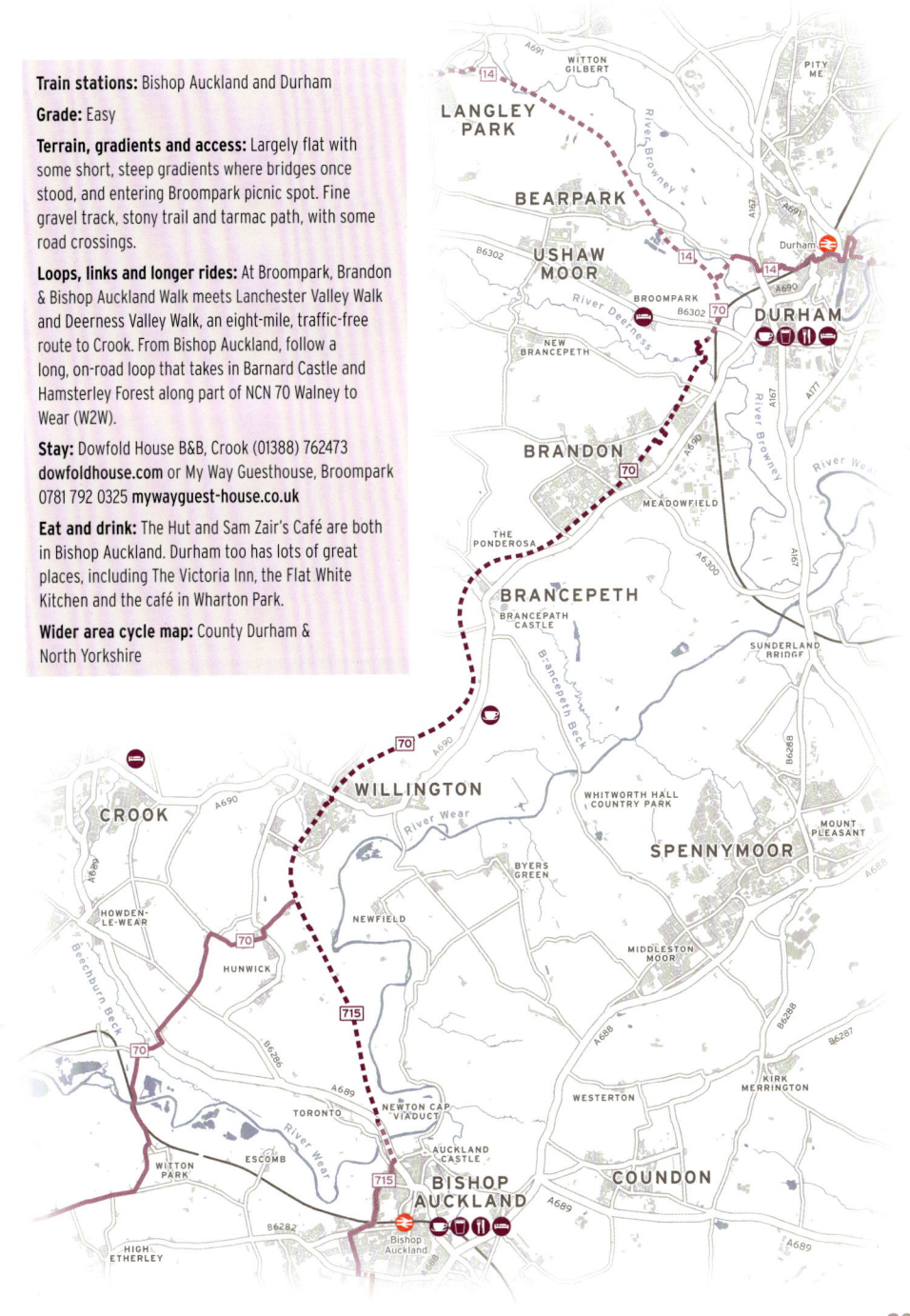

Finish: Broompark picnic area, Durham

RIDE 02

Train stations: Bishop Auckland and Durham

Grade: Easy

Terrain, gradients and access: Largely flat with some short, steep gradients where bridges once stood, and entering Broompark picnic spot. Fine gravel track, stony trail and tarmac path, with some road crossings.

Loops, links and longer rides: At Broompark, Brandon & Bishop Auckland Walk meets Lanchester Valley Walk and Deerness Valley Walk, an eight-mile, traffic-free route to Crook. From Bishop Auckland, follow a long, on-road loop that takes in Barnard Castle and Hamsterley Forest along part of NCN 70 Walney to Wear (W2W).

Stay: Dowfold House B&B, Crook (01388) 762473 dowfoldhouse.com or My Way Guesthouse, Broompark 0781 792 0325 mywayguest-house.co.uk

Eat and drink: The Hut and Sam Zair's Café are both in Bishop Auckland. Durham too has lots of great places, including The Victoria Inn, the Flat White Kitchen and the café in Wharton Park.

Wider area cycle map: County Durham & North Yorkshire

283

RIDE 03
9 miles

Start: Parkhead Station, Stanhope Moor

WASKERLEY WAY

Incredible views over the North Pennines and an effortless roll all the way from Stanhope Moor to Lydgetts Junction make Waskerley Way one of the most exhilarating short rides in the country.

Start at the warm and sheltered oasis of Parkhead Station in the heart of the Durham Dales but come prepared for a chilly, fresh breeze out on the exposed and rugged heather moorland. Watch out for sheep skittering across the path in the opening miles, and keep a lookout for the area's birdlife; lapwings can be spotted in the summer months and the loud, complex song of skylarks fills the air as these little birds hover over the heather.

Waskerley Reservoir looms into view on the right and the delightfully named Muggleswick Common tumbles away to the left before the lush, green fields of the Derwent Valley come into view, stretching off into the distance below.

The route was once a working railway line, and its former stations have been turned into scenic picnic spots. Waskerley Station picnic area is nearest to the halfway point, so it's a good place to rest among grassy meadows that are bejewelled with colourful orchids in summer. Shortly afterwards, the path hairpins sharply at Burn Hill and the second part of the ride becomes more sheltered and leafy in parts, with the wildlife-rich mixed woodland around Whitehall Station providing another excellent chance to pause awhile.

You'll encounter the real gem of this ride in the final mile, Hownsgill Viaduct, known locally as Gill Bridge. It is one of the North East's most magnificent railway structures and it's a beautifully blustery ride across its top, with magnificent views over the treetops of Hown's Wood, Knitsley Wood, and the sprawling pastures and moorland of the Derwent Valley. End at the rust red smelt wagon at Lydgetts Junction, the crossroads of four excellent traffic-free walking and cycling trails.

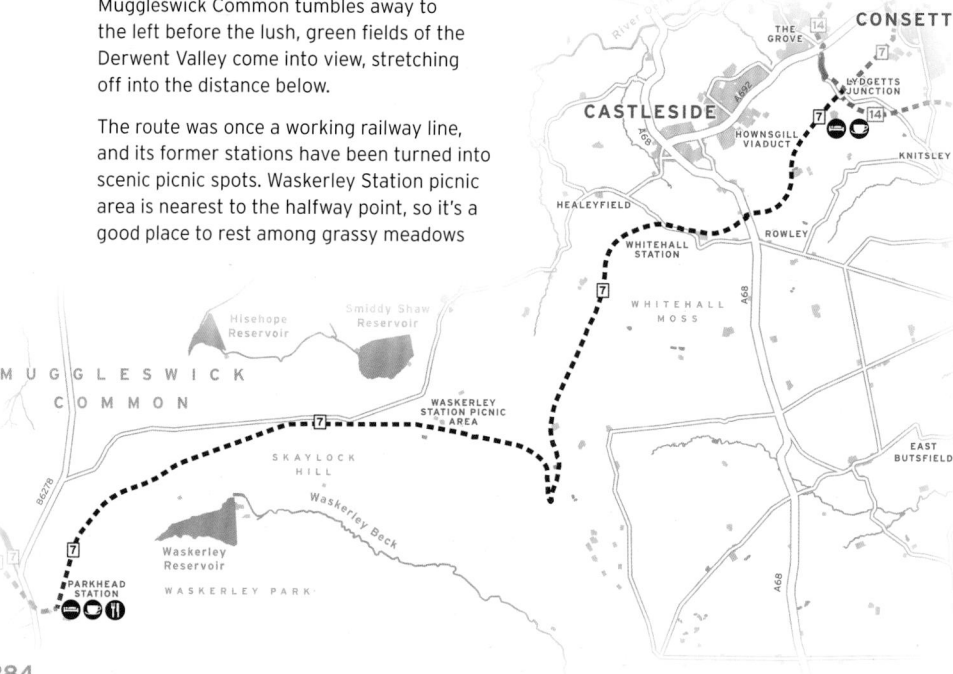

RIDE 03

Finish: Lydgetts Junction, Consett

Train station: Nearest is Durham

Grade: Easy

Terrain, gradients and access: Gently descending along fine gravel path. Several gates and a couple of road crossings along the way.

Loops, links and longer rides: At Lydgetts Junction four traffic-free walking and cycling routes meet: Waskerley Way, Consett & Sunderland Railway Path, Lanchester Valley Walk and Derwent Walk (**Ride 04**). Waskerley Way is part of the Sea to Sea (C2C), a 140-mile coast to coast ride across the north of England, from Cumbria to Tyne & Wear.

Stay: Parkhead Station B&B (01388) 526434 parkheadstation.co.uk

Eat and drink: Durham Dales Centre Tea Room is in Stanhope, whilst Parkhead Station Tea Rooms is a welcoming haven at the route's start. At the route's end, try Hownsgill Farm Tea Rooms near Lydgetts Junction.

Wider area cycle map: Sea to Sea (C2C)

"One of the most exhilarating short rides in the country."

Cyclists on the Waskerley Way

RIDE 04
11 miles — **Start:** Lydgetts Junction, Consett

DERWENT WALK

Viaducts and views are the most memorable features of this ride along a scenic and richly historic railway path through the Derwent Valley.

Start at the smelt wagon at Lydgetts Junction and ride into the edges of Consett, once a bedrock of the industrial North East. Brittle brown moorland stretches away on the horizon during the opening mile, before you reach the pretty, manicured gardens of Blackhill and Consett Park. This is a particularly good park to visit in summer, when the gardens are in full bloom and colliery bands play on the Victorian-style bandstand.

In the ride's first half, you'll pass two fine old railway stations: Shotley Bridge, where part of the old platform remains intact, and Ebchester, close to the ruins of the Roman fort Vindomora. Both stations make excellent picnic spots and there are trail-side benches at each, offering astounding views over the Derwent Valley.

From here, ride along the tops of the neighbouring Pontburn and Fogoesburn viaducts in quick succession. There is incredible scenery over the treetops from both, and a good chance of seeing red kites circling overhead as the species has been reintroduced to the area by the Northern Kites project.

Derwent Park at Rowlands Gill comes next, an excellent family-friendly pitstop with a café, toilets and ice cream kiosk, before you enter the marvellous mix of woodland, wetland, meadows and riverside space at Derwent Walk Country Park. Crossing over Nine Arches Viaduct within the park is the ride's real highlight, and this is by far the finest of the three viaducts on the route, with dramatic views across the valley and over the Georgian grandeur of Gibside Estate. Gibside is now a National Trust property and its enormous Column of Liberty monument is the most striking feature here, standing proudly on the skyline.

In the final miles, pass the edges of pretty Clockburn Lake and stay close to the River Derwent, following it all the way to Swalwell. Near Blaydon Tennis Club, cross the river and follow the gravelly trail to end by Bladon Rugby Club.

Lilypond at Gibside

Finish: Blaydon Rugby Club, Gateshead

RIDE 04

Train station: MetroCentre, Gateshead

Grade: Easy

Terrain, gradients and access: Gently descending but with some short, undulating sections. A mixture of tarmac path, stony trail and dirt track. Several road crossings, particularly around Consett and Rowlands Gill. One step to lift bikes up near the start.

Loops, links and longer rides: At the River Tyne, Derwent Walk joins up with Keelman's Way, a 14-mile, largely traffic-free route along the south of the Tyne from Wylam to Hebburn. Derwent Walk forms part of NCN 14 Three Rivers, 80 miles of cycling routes around the North East between Middlesbrough and South Shields. At Lydgetts Junction four traffic-free cycle routes meet: Waskerley Way (**Ride 03**), Consett & Sunderland Railway Path, Lanchester Valley Walk and Derwent Walk.

Stay: Hownsgill Farm Tea Rooms and Bunkhouse 07904 050120 c2cstopoff.co.uk

Eat and drink: Derwent Walk Inn at Ebchester and Maguire's Fish and Chips at Rowland's Gill. Thornley Woodlands Visitor Centre in Derwent Walk Country Park has a pop-up café. On finishing the ride, head to Pedalling Squares, a retro cycling coffee bar at The Old Brassworks, Gateshead.

Cycle hire: Newburn Activity Centre, Newburn (0191) 264 0014 newburnactivity.co.uk or It's All About the Bike (0191) 276 7250 thecyclehub.org

Wider area cycle map: Sea to Sea (C2C)

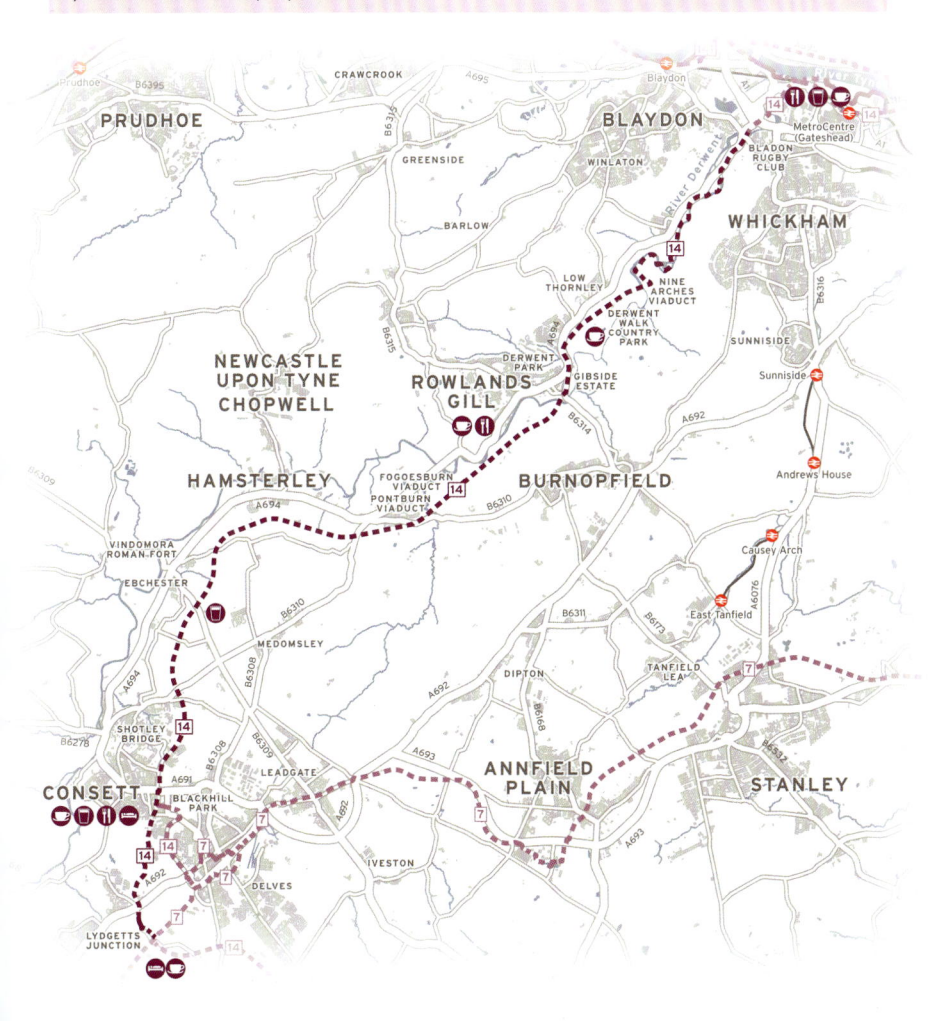

RIDE 05 — 10.5 miles

Start: Souter Lighthouse

SOUTER LIGHTHOUSE
TO
ST MARY'S LIGHTHOUSE

Two fine lighthouses keeping a dignified watch over the North Sea bookend this ride along the North and South Tyneside coasts. It takes in spectacular seabird colonies and golden bays, and has the added pleasure of a ferry trip midway.

Start at the National Trust's Souter Lighthouse, a bold and beautiful structure classically striped in red and white. The white bulk of St Mary's Lighthouse, the ride's endpoint, can be spotted in the far distance from here too. Ride beside the limestone cliffs of The Leas and past the jagged limestone lump of Marsden rock, alive with cormorants, kittiwakes and fulmars during the breeding season.

At Bents Park you'll leave the sea momentarily to ride through the streets of South Shields to the ferry point. The seven-minute trip across the Tyne on the Shields Ferry is a nice chance to rest, before reaching dry land again at North Shields and rolling beside the market and renowned restaurants of Fish Quay.

It's a short, steep climb past the endpoint of the long-distance Sea to Sea (C2C) route, a significant cyclists' milestone, to reach Tynemouth at around the ride's halfway point. This is such a pretty little village and definitely worthy of exploration. The tumbledown Tynemouth Castle and Priory are perched on the rocky headland here, and the café-lined streets are criss-crossed with flapping bunting. Alternatively, cycle a short distance further to reach Tynemouth's charming neighbouring village Cullercoats, once a thriving artists' colony.

Glorious beaches and bays abound alongside the route but if you want quiet seclusion then King Edward's Bay at Tynemouth is the best, whereas the one-mile stretch of golden sands and dunes at Tynemouth Longsands is ideal for families, with a lifeguard patrol in summer and a growing reputation among surfers.

In the final miles, the long, latte-coloured sands of Whitley Bay Beach stretch northwards to the tiny St Mary's Island at the route's end, with its white lighthouse perched on the shores. End at Curry's Point Local Nature Reserve (LNR) overlooking the lighthouse. The lively history of smuggling and violent shipwrecks here is a perfect contrast to the present day peace of the beautiful nature haven.

Souter Lighthouse

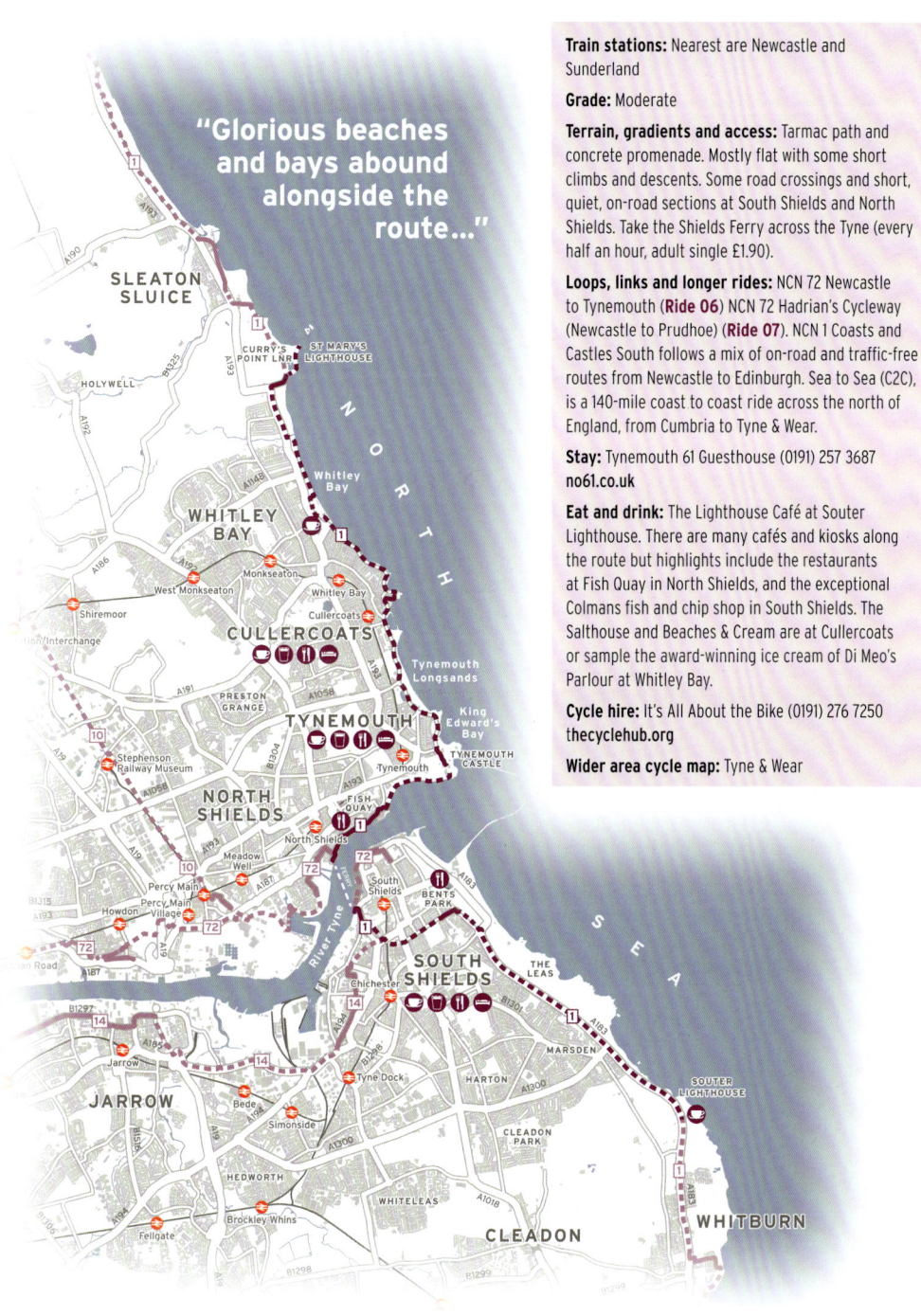

Finish: St Mary's Lighthouse   **RIDE 05**

"Glorious beaches and bays abound alongside the route..."

Train stations: Nearest are Newcastle and Sunderland

Grade: Moderate

Terrain, gradients and access: Tarmac path and concrete promenade. Mostly flat with some short climbs and descents. Some road crossings and short, quiet, on-road sections at South Shields and North Shields. Take the Shields Ferry across the Tyne (every half an hour, adult single £1.90).

Loops, links and longer rides: NCN 72 Newcastle to Tynemouth (**Ride 06**) NCN 72 Hadrian's Cycleway (Newcastle to Prudhoe) (**Ride 07**). NCN 1 Coasts and Castles South follows a mix of on-road and traffic-free routes from Newcastle to Edinburgh. Sea to Sea (C2C), is a 140-mile coast to coast ride across the north of England, from Cumbria to Tyne & Wear.

Stay: Tynemouth 61 Guesthouse (0191) 257 3687 no61.co.uk

Eat and drink: The Lighthouse Café at Souter Lighthouse. There are many cafés and kiosks along the route but highlights include the restaurants at Fish Quay in North Shields, and the exceptional Colmans fish and chip shop in South Shields. The Salthouse and Beaches & Cream are at Cullercoats or sample the award-winning ice cream of Di Meo's Parlour at Whitley Bay.

Cycle hire: It's All About the Bike (0191) 276 7250 thecyclehub.org

Wider area cycle map: Tyne & Wear

289

RIDE 06
11 miles · 72 · Start: Gateshead Millennium Bridge, Newcastle

NEWCASTLE
TO
TYNEMOUTH

This is a deeply diverse route taking in the contemporary, stylish city of Newcastle and its lively Quayside, as well as a remarkable ancient fort once at the heart of the Roman Empire.

Start at the sleek Gateshead Millennium Bridge and roll past the outdoor terraces of the waterfront cafés and bars that overlook the River Tyne. It's worth pausing to look behind: once at Newcastle's many magnificent bridges spanning the river, and again a short while later at the wise words "it's all about the bike" emblazoned in giant letters on the wall of The Cycle Hub, a buzzy café, bar, bike workshop and all-round affable spot for cyclists to meet and chat.

Leaving the Quayside behind, you'll join a leafy trail alongside the River Tyne and glimpse the moored boats at St Peter's Marina to the right of the trail, before passing through Walker Riverside Park. This was once a place of heavy industry, but now it's a sanctuary of birdsong, woodland, wildflower meadows and great views of the Tyne.

Just a few miles later reach Wallsend, a name derived from the fact that Britain's greatest Roman monument, Hadrian's Wall, ends right here. Segedunum is beside the path and it's well worth stopping here to explore what was once the easternmost fort on Hadrian's Wall. An 80-metre section of original wall can still be seen, plus there's a museum, reconstructed Roman bath house and 35-metre tall observation tower.

From here, head to Redburn Dene, a park artistically spiked with timber staithes as a reminder of the area's industrial past, before joining the waterside at Royal Quays and riding around the vast white yachts.

In the final miles, pass through the restaurant-lined Fish Quay, renowned for great fish and chips, and along the mouth of the Tyne. It's a short, steep climb to Tynemouth, passing its North Pier and the little sailing and rowing clubs in the sandy bay, before ending at the entrance to Tynemouth Castle and Priory on the rocky headland of Pen Bal Crag. The gorgeous sand of King Edward's Bay sits beneath the castle and the charming Tynemouth village is to the left.

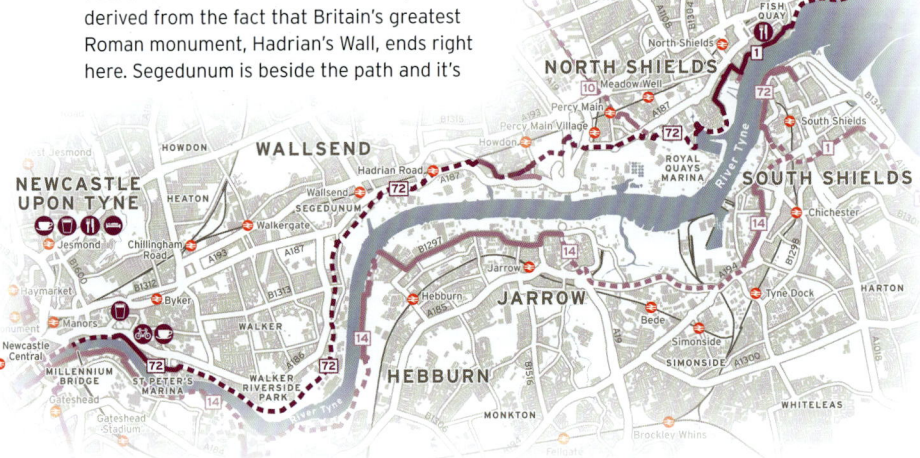

Finish: Tynemouth Castle and Priory

RIDE **06**

Train station: Newcastle

Grade: Easy

Terrain, gradients and access: Mostly flat along tarmac path with several road crossings and short, on-road sections at Newcastle Quayside, Willington Quay, North Shields and Tynemouth.

Loops, links and longer rides: This ride is part of the Sea to Sea (C2C), a 140-mile coast to coast ride across the north of England, from Cumbria to Tyne & Wear. NCN 72 Newcastle to Prudhoe (**Ride 07**). NCN 1 Souter to St Mary's (**Ride 05**).

Stay: Tynemouth 61 Guesthouse (0191) 257 3687 no61.co.uk

Eat and drink: The Cycle Hub on Newcastle's Quayside serves great food, including exceptional fruit scones and coffee. Fish Quay at North Shields has many popular fish and chip shops and restaurants. Tynemouth Surf Café is popular among cyclists.

Cycle hire: It's All About the Bike, Newcastle Quayside (0191) 276 7250 thecyclehub.org

Wider area cycle map: Hadrian's Cycleway

Cyclist at the Ouseburn Viaduct, Byker

RIDE 07 — 13 miles

Start: Gateshead Millennium Bridge, Newcastle

NEWCASTLE
TO
PRUDHOE

This ride along a section of the long-distance Hadrian's Cycleway blends bold Newcastle architecture with the tranquil, natural beauty of Tyne Riverside Country Park, a jewel on the banks of the River Tyne.

The elegant Gateshead Millennium Bridge is a lovely start and is a great spot to look for the UK's only urban colony of kittiwakes, or view the glassy bulges of the unusual Sage Gateshead building. From here, roll along the north bank of the Tyne beneath six magnificent bridges spanning the water, before reaching the site of the Elswick shipyard, one of the many shipyards that once lined the Tyne. This was a particularly productive spot, producing 84 warships in just three decades, but it's now a far more peaceful part of the river with views stretching across the trees and hillsides of Gateshead.

Leave the waterside temporarily and ride up into the wooded slopes of Paradise, a conservation site of mature woodland where many species of butterflies and birds can be spotted. However, the real nature haven of the ride starts a few miles later at Newburn where you'll enter Tyne Riverside Country Park, an astoundingly beautiful sanctuary of splendid thick woodland, chalk grassland known as 'The Spetchells' and wide river views stretching all the way to Prudhoe. Newburn is around the halfway point of the ride, so take a break at the waterside terrace of The Boathouse, now the Branzino Italian restaurant, on the edges of the park, or picnic on the riverbank a little further along the trail.

At Wylam the route joins up with the Wylam Waggonway, and you'll follow this old horse-drawn coal route for a while, before crossing the river on the wooden planks of the impressive Points Bridge at Hagg Bank to join the Tyne's southern shores for the final miles. Short, steep climbs, swift descents and thick woodland all add a little adventure to the ride on this side of the river, and in spring the intoxicating scent of wild garlic drifts up from the forest floor for most of the way.

A short, stony track leads away from the main trail to the route's end at Prudhoe train station, or it's just a very short, on-road ride from the station to the fine Northumberland fortress of Prudhoe Castle.

River Tyne, Newcastle

Finish: Prudhoe train station

RIDE 07

Train stations: Newcastle, Wylam and Prudhoe

Grade: Moderate

Terrain, gradients and access: Paved and tarmac path, fine gravel track and stony trail. Some road crossings and short, quiet on-road sections from the station to the fine Northumberland fortress of Prudhoe Castle.

Loops, links and longer rides: This route follows part of the long-distance NCN 72 Hadrian's Cycleway, a 174-mile route from Ravenglass to South Shields. NCN 14 Keelman's Way is a 14-mile, largely traffic-free route along the south bank of the Tyne from Wylam to Hebburn.

Stay: Ovington House B&B, Ovington (01661) 832442 ovingtonhouse.co.uk

Eat and drink: Newcastle has many great places to eat including Pink Lane Coffee near Newcastle train station and The Cycle Hub at Newcastle Quayside. Branzino's Italian restaurant or Hedley's riverside coffee shop are both mid-route at Newburn. Prudhoe Castle serves snacks and drinks.

Cycle hire: It's All About the Bike, Newcastle Quayside (0191) 276 7250 thecyclehub.org or Newburn Activity Centre, Newburn (0191) 264 0014 newburnactivity.co.uk

Wider area cycle map: Hadrian's Cycleway

Cyclist near Gateshead Millennium Bridge, Newcastle

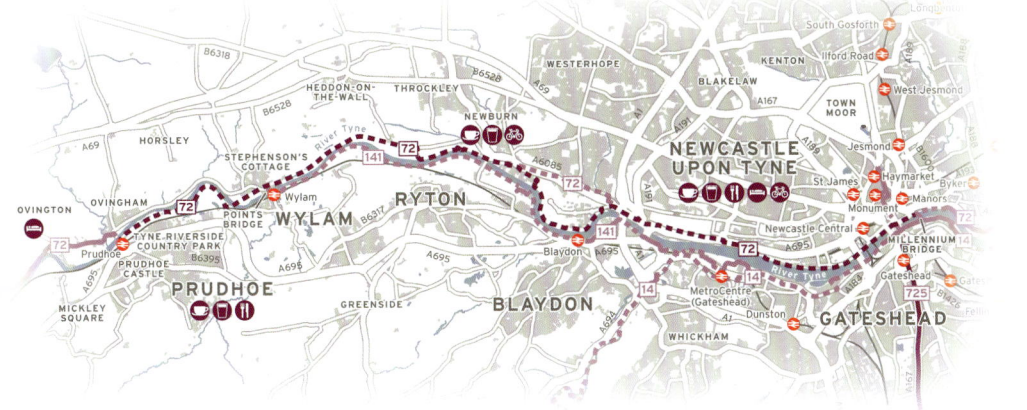

293

RIDE 08 | 68 | Start: Haltwhistle

5.5 miles to Lambley Viaduct or
10 miles to Slaggyford

SOUTH TYNE TRAIL

> "This route weaves through the stunningly scenic South Tyne Valley..."

Alston Arches, Northumberland

Starting in the heart of Hadrian's Wall Country, this route weaves through the stunningly scenic South Tyne Valley in Northumberland across some of the most remote and unspoilt landscape in England.

Start from the train station in Haltwhistle, a town hailed as the geographical 'Centre of Britain'. There are visible remains of Hadrian's Wall, the country's greatest Roman monument, just to the north of the town which make a nice detour before setting off on the ride.

Head south from the station, immediately crossing over the wide River Tyne and looking east to see the beautiful curves of Alston Arches, a viaduct that spans the water downstream. The remote and wild sheep-grazed hills of the North Pennines begin to appear, creating a beautiful backdrop for the ride. You're sure to see oystercatchers and golden plover on the tufty and tumbling hillsides in summer. However, the most satisfying birds to spot are curlews, the emblem of Northumberland National Park, with their elegant curved beaks and haunting call.

As the railway path cuts through the steep hillside, the open scenery is replaced by high-sided banks, thick greenery and deep woodland. At the old platform of Featherstone Park station there's an option to turn left for a very short, on-road ride to the Wallace Arms at Rowfoot, a good midway pub spot.

Further along reach Coanwood Station where there are two options for continuing. For a shorter and entirely traffic-free ride, follow signs for the South Tyne Trail through thick and shady woodland, before reaching the magnificent nine-arch Lambley Viaduct. The

Finish: Lambley Viaduct or Slaggyford

RIDE 08

Train station: Haltwhistle

Grade: Haltwhistle to Lambley Viaduct - Easy
Haltwhistle to Slaggyford - Moderate

Terrain, gradients and access: A steady climb all the way, with a steeper descent and ascent around Lambley. Tarmac path and fine gravel track with some road crossings, a very short on-road section at Haltwhistle, and a much longer on-road section at Lambley. There are many gates along the route.

Loops, links and longer rides: From Slaggyford, follow NCN 68 for a further five miles on-road to cross the border into Cumbria and reach Alston. South Tyne Trail is part of The Pennine Cycleway, 354 miles of routes that cross the Northumberland, Yorkshire Dales and Peak District National Parks.

Stay: Herding Hill Farm, Haltwhistle (01434) 320175 herdinghillfarm.co.uk or YHA, Alston 0345 260 2489 yha.org.uk

Eat and drink: In Haltwhistle, try The Black Bull pub. The Wallace Arms is at Rowfoot.

Cycle hire: Hadrian Cycling Ltd, Haltwhistle 0745 695 3114 hadriancyclingltd.co.uk

Wider area cycle map: North Cumbria & Scottish Borders

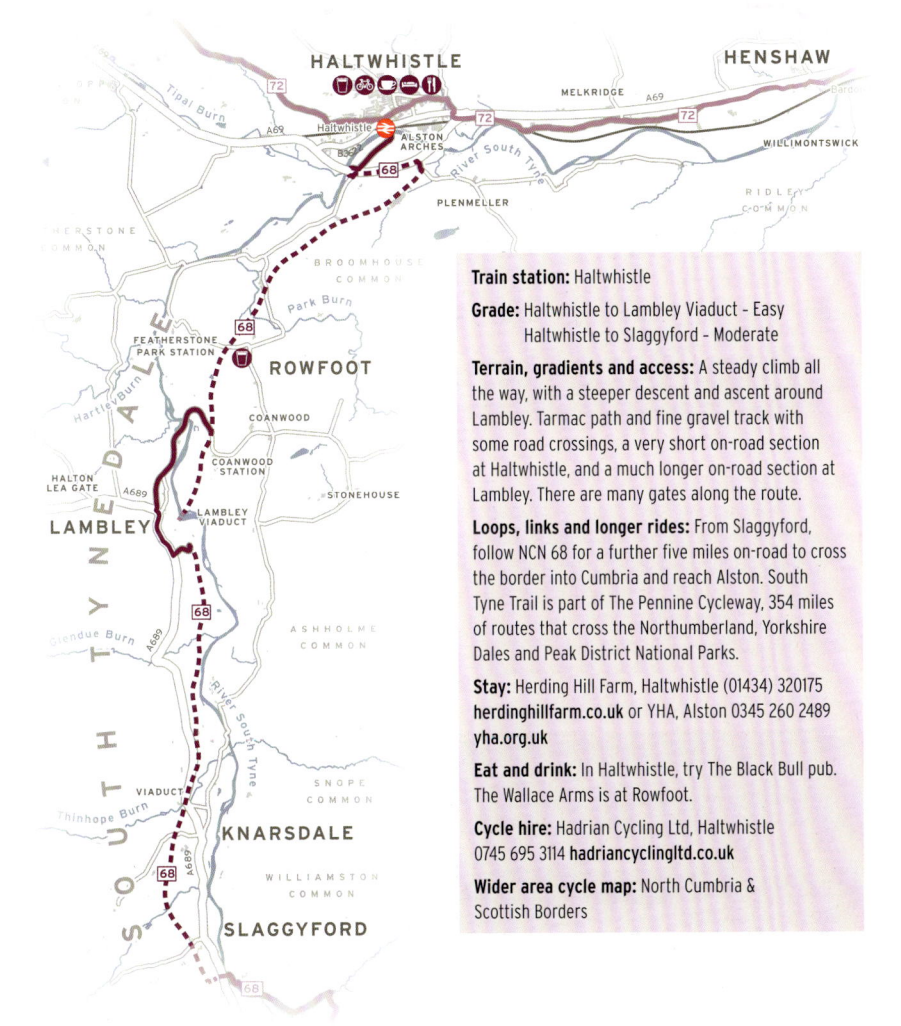

views across the valley and wide, shingly shores of the river are breathtaking from the top of the viaduct, but there's no access from the far end so you'll have to retrace the route back from here.

Alternatively, from Coanwood Station follow the road through Lambley village and around the viaduct. There are some steeper gradients here, but the views from the top of the climb are some of the best on the ride, and the top of the viaduct can be seen in the east, poking out from between the trees.

From here, it's flat all the way to Slaggyford, passing beneath the trees of Softley Low Wood along the way and crossing another, smaller viaduct at Burnstones. End at the old railway station at Slaggyford, or drop down on the quiet road into the pretty little village.

295

RIDE 09 — 26.5 miles

Start and finish: The Bike Place, near Kielder Castle

LAKESIDE WAY

Kielder Water and Forest Park in Northumberland, nudging at the edges of the Scottish border, is simply sensational. Cycle it by day and stay into the evening to experience the star-studded magnificence of the darkest night skies in England and the largest expanse of protected night sky in the whole of Europe.

Around 3,000 feet of climbing on this tumbling trail around the irregular contours of the reservoir mean it is no easy ride. However, it offers outstanding views and there are fascinating sculptures to discover along the way; the giant forest head, 'Silvas Capitalis', is a favourite. Look out for some of the 'Kielder Super Six' too: pipistrelle bats, ospreys, red squirrels, otters, roe deer and salmon.

Start the ride at The Bike Place near Kielder Castle and simply follow the 'Lakeside Way' signs all the way. Water views are captivating from the moment you cross over Kielder Viaduct and join the north shore of the reservoir in the ride's opening miles. But it's a tantalisingly mixed route, and you'll frequently leave the water to climb steeply or descend dramatically through the heavily-scented conifers that make up part of England's largest forest.

Kielder Dam is visible for miles before it is reached, and the ride across its top leads to the lovely Lakeside View picnic spot on the water's edge. A mile later, reach Tower Knowe Visitor Centre, the halfway point of the route, and take a detour up the hill to Elf Kirk viewpoint for the most iconic view of Kielder. Classic vistas await on the route itself, too, including one of the most picture-perfect panoramas of the ride from a lone bench perched at the 15-mile point, which overlooks the yachts of Whickhope Anchorage.

In the final miles, pedal over the elegantly curved suspension bridge across Lewis Burn and seek out Patterson's Pause, one of the area's most tranquil spots. It's testament to the magical diversity of Kielder that this sedate setting is immediately followed by the rugged and infinitely less restful 'Lonesome Pine', one of the routes that makes up the country's largest network of mountain bike trails. Don't worry, you won't need to join this challenging trail, just ride past the start of it. In the final mile, follow the signs for Kielder Castle to finish back at The Bike Place.

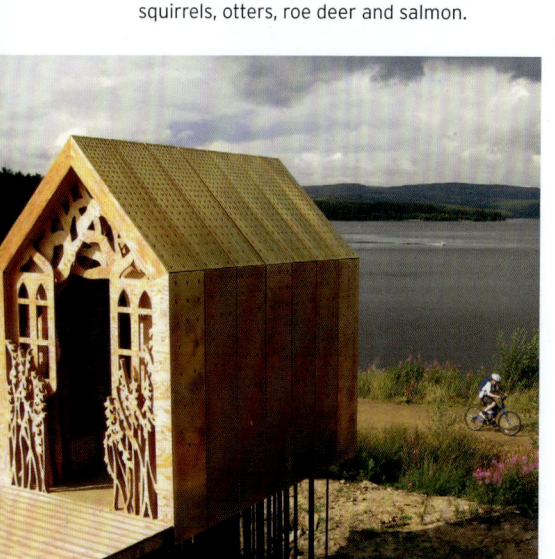

'Freya's Cabin', Kielder Water

RIDE 09

Train station: Nearest is Hexham. Bus service runs twice daily from Kielder (1hr 20mins).

Grade: Challenging

Terrain, gradients and access: Fine gravel track and stony trail with very short and quiet on-road sections and road crossings near Kielder Castle, Kielder Dam and Hawkhirst Scout Activity Centre. There are several gates in the final miles and steep, twisting ascents and descents throughout. Follow in a clockwise direction for an easier ride.

Loops, links and longer rides: NCN 10 Reivers Route is a 173-mile route from Whitehaven in Cumbria to Tynemouth in North Tyneside, via Northumberland National Park and Kielder Forest.

Stay: Kielder Campsite (01434) 239257 kieldercampsite.co.uk or The Pheasant Inn, Stannersburn (01434) 240382 thepheasantinn.com

Eat and drink: Kielder Castle Café, The Anglers Arms pub and Tower Knowe Café are all on the route. At the dam, head into Falstone village for Falstone Old School tearoom and The Blackcock Country Inn, or try The Pheasant Inn at nearby Stannersburn.

Cycle hire: The Bike Place, Kielder and Leaplish (01434) 250457 thebikeplace.co.uk

Wider area cycle map: Reivers Cycle Route

> "It offers outstanding views and there are fascinating sculptures..."

297

BERWICK-UPON-TWEED
TO
HOLY ISLAND

Berwick-upon-Tweed is dramatically located; sandwiched between the wide Tweed estuary and the North Sea, highlights include massive Elizabethan defensive walls and Georgian barracks. The old port area has great views of the Tweed estuary and the three magnificent bridges over it.

Your route leaves across the lowest level Old Bridge to give impressive views across the bay. Heading out of town takes you to a dramatic clifftop track to arrive at the popular local beauty spot of Cocklawburn beach, one of the highlights of the Northumberland Coast Area of Outstanding Natural Beauty.

A brief road section leads to a track behind the sand dunes with evidence of WWII defences here in the form of Scremerston gun emplacement. Quiet roads lead through tiny Cheswick and across a lovely open section through Goswick Golf course.

Probably the roughest track section follows across wide open salt flats grazed by sheep before arriving at the massive expanse of Goswick sands, an amazing sight at low tide, as Holy Island (also known as Lindisfarne) comes into view. Eventually you head across a sluice bridge and left onto the track that leads to the causeway over to the island. Here you can explore the roads and tracks and wonder at the dramatically ruined priory and the magnificently located castle-cum-country house atop the remains of an extinct volcano. The story of the founding of the priory here, the shrine of St Cuthbert, the Lindisfarne gospels and the invasion of the island by Vikings is as dramatic as any in British history and is told at the Lindisfarne centre.

South of Spittal

Finish: Holy Island

RIDE 10

Signs on the route

Train Station: Berwick-upon-Teed

Grade: Moderate

Terrain, gradients and access: There are no really steep gradients here, just a few moderate climbs, but some of the off-road sections certainly require a bit more riding skill and fitness – especially those grassier sections leaving Cocklawburn beach and approaching Holy Island. There are a small number of access gates, but overall access is easy.

Loops, links and longer rides: NCN 1 heads south of Holy Island along the Northumberland coast using mainly quiet minor roads and taking in such scenic highlights as Bamburgh and Dunstanburgh castles (it is actually part of the long distance Coast and Castles route). When complete, NCN 1 will continue all the way to Dover in the south and to the north coast of Scotland. You may also see signs for the Sandstone Way which is a 120 mile local mountain biking route linking Hexham and Berwick-upon-Tweed.

Stay: Eat & Sleep Lindisfarne, Beal (01289) 381827
eatandsleeplindisfarne.co.uk

Eat and drink: Plenty of choice in Berwick with a couple of very nicely located cafés on the quay area a highlight. The only option en route is the Goswick Golf Club clubhouse which does meals in a nice location and has outside seating. On Lindisfarne itself there are several options including Pilgrims Coffee and the Ship Inn.

Wider area cycle map: North Northumberland & Scottish Borders

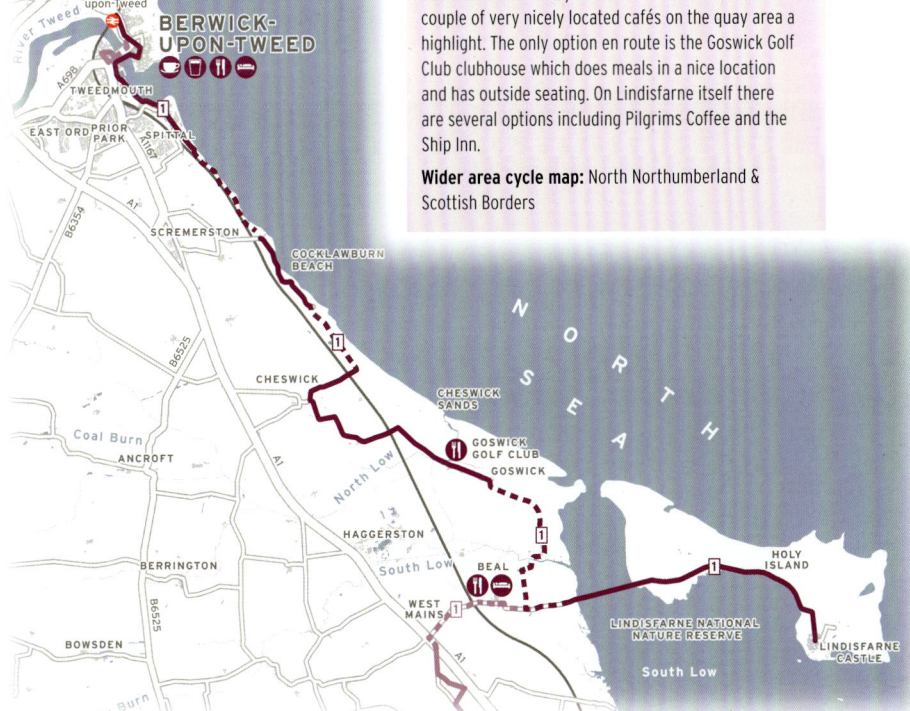

299

SCOTLAND

Scotland's dramatic scenery has to be seen to be believed, and this collection of rides shows it at its very best, from stunning coasts and lochs to breathtaking glens and mountains.

Two of the most attractive rides in Scotland feature in this collection; Benderloch to Appin offers sweeping west coast views and ends overlooking Castle Stalker in its remote and enchanting position on Loch Laich, whilst a ride along part of the Great Glen Way in the Highlands begins in the shadow of Ben Nevis, Britain's highest mountain, and ends on the shores of the world famous Loch Ness.

Scotland's finest cities, art and architecture feature, too, from the flinty grey buildings of Aberdeen, 'the Granite City', to the cultural centre of Glasgow and the handsome, historic capital city of Edinburgh. Indeed, there's a truly astounding variety of iconic structures to be seen along the routes, from the longstanding landmark of the Forth Rail Bridge, to the more recent landmark features of the river Clyde in Glasgow.

However, it is Scotland's remote, unspoiled countryside and sensational wildlife that set these rides apart. The country's two national parks – Loch Lomond & The Trossachs, and the Cairngorms – are highlights, and both feature in this collection. Loch Lomond's shores are the endpoint for a lovely canal and riverside ride from Glasgow, whilst the Deeside Way will take you through the Cairngorms on a regal route once used by the Royal family to visit their summer retreat at Balmoral. Nowadays you're far more likely to spot the area's other famous summer residents, the ospreys, and a ride along the scenic Speyside Way leads to Boat of Garten, known as 'The Osprey Village' after the majestic birds of prey that breed nearby.

Forth Rail Bridge

Routes overview

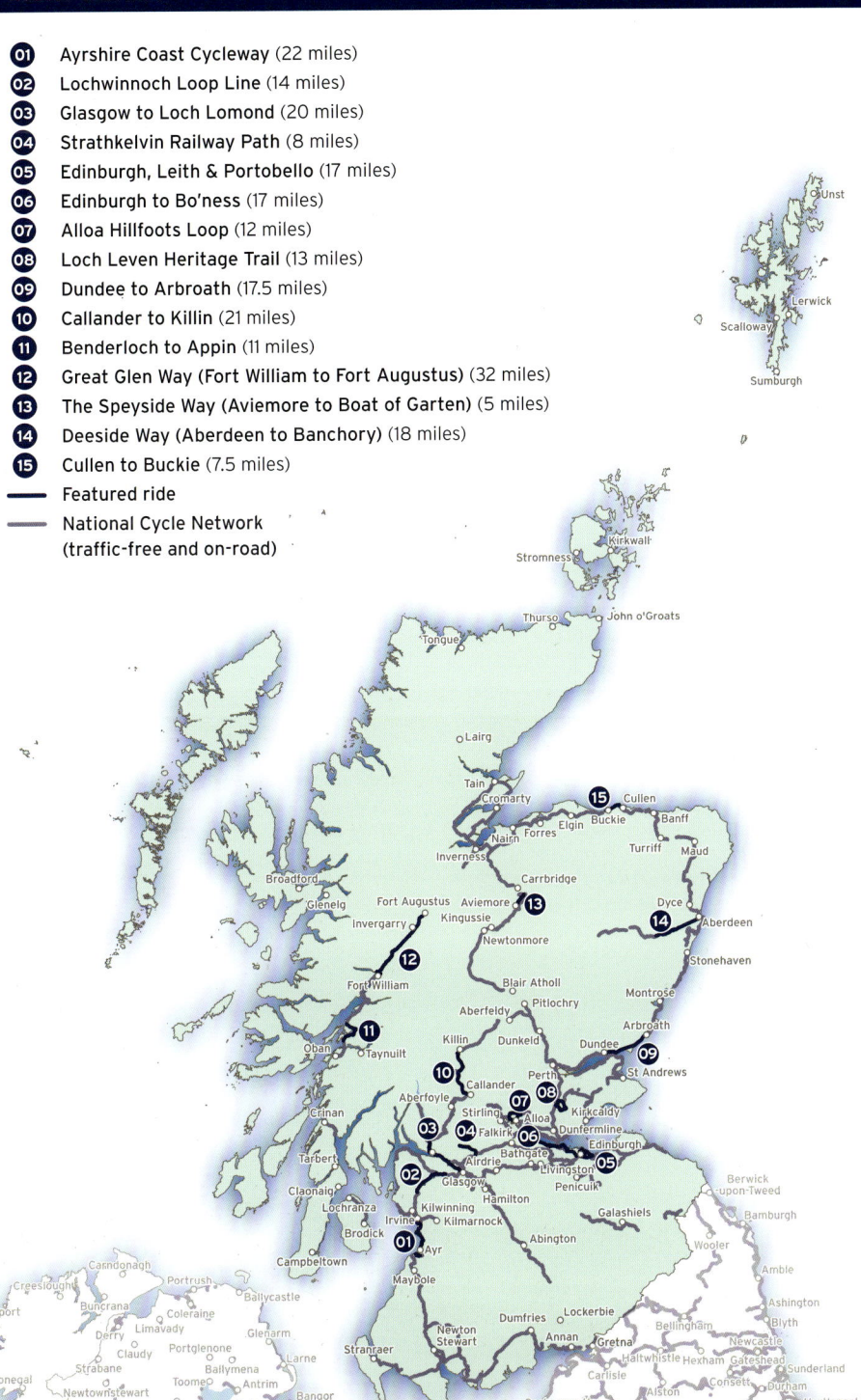

- **01** Ayrshire Coast Cycleway (22 miles)
- **02** Lochwinnoch Loop Line (14 miles)
- **03** Glasgow to Loch Lomond (20 miles)
- **04** Strathkelvin Railway Path (8 miles)
- **05** Edinburgh, Leith & Portobello (17 miles)
- **06** Edinburgh to Bo'ness (17 miles)
- **07** Alloa Hillfoots Loop (12 miles)
- **08** Loch Leven Heritage Trail (13 miles)
- **09** Dundee to Arbroath (17.5 miles)
- **10** Callander to Killin (21 miles)
- **11** Benderloch to Appin (11 miles)
- **12** Great Glen Way (Fort William to Fort Augustus) (32 miles)
- **13** The Speyside Way (Aviemore to Boat of Garten) (5 miles)
- **14** Deeside Way (Aberdeen to Banchory) (18 miles)
- **15** Cullen to Buckie (7.5 miles)
- — Featured ride
- — National Cycle Network (traffic-free and on-road)

AYRSHIRE COAST CYCLEWAY

The attractive little village of Alloway draws Rabbie Burns fans from far and wide; the Burns Birthplace Museum and the fine Burns Monument and gardens pay homage to the widely loved Scottish Bard and Scotland's literary heritage. The lovely Brig O' Doon bridge here also famously features in Burns' works. Being in Alloway also presents a good opportunity to visit Rozelle House in 96 acres of expansive landscaped parkland. Opposite is similarly impressive Belleisle Park which also has its own café.

Opposite the museum you can head down access slopes onto a fine tarmac railpath which takes you all the way to the coast. You will reach the Heads of Ayr, where there are are fine clifftop walks and picnic areas around the ruined tower of Greenan Castle and magnificent views of Arran, Ailsa Craig and Kintyre.

Hugging the beach, the route crosses the River Doon on an elegant traffic-free bridge and approaches Ayr along the side of the huge grassy open space known as Low Green, offering a fine view of Ayr. The centre itself boasts an unusual 126ft high Wallace Tower and the towering spire of the Town Hall. It's worth a stroll around as it is only a few minutes ride from the NCN route that runs along the coast.

Some wiggling through backstreets are linked by an impressive bridge crossing of the river Ayr. You are soon enjoying more seaside prom riding at Prestwick then passing right by Glasgow Prestwick airport. There's then a fine section across the golf links of Troon, with the path crossing the links themselves (look out for flying golf balls...) with great views seaward to the magnificent Marine Hotel.

More spectacular beach scenery awaits as you round the promontory that sits in front of Troon town before heading away from the coast directly past Barassie train station, soon entering the tranquillity of Shewalton Wood wildlife reserve. The final run in to Irvine gives you the chance to visit the harbour area (just off the NCN route), the most attractive part of town, housing the Scottish Maritime Museum.

Troon beach

Finish: Irvine train station

RIDE 01

Train Station: Ayr and Irvine (20 minute return trip) with Prestwick, Troon and Barassie stations right by the route if you want to head back early. Regular trains from Glasgow Central.

Grade: Easy

Terrain, gradients and access: Lots of lovely tarmac promenade riding, though wind and blown sand coming off the many fine beaches en route might be an occasional bother in strong weather. Few access controls. The few street sections are generally backstreets. Very few access barriers. Generally flat.

Loops, links and longer rides: This ride uses part of NCN 7 which when complete will link Sunderland to Inverness. It also uses the local railpath known as the Burton cycle track on the southern edge of Alloway.

Stay: Doonbank Cottage Bothy, Alloway (01292) 441825 doonbankcottage.co.uk

Eat and drink: Plenty of seafront opportunities as you roll along the many seaside promenades (Remedy café - Ayr, Mancinis @ the Beach - Prestwick). There is a village coffee shop in Alloway and a tearoom at the fine Rozelles House just north of the village and at nearby Belleisle Park. Plenty of choice at Irvine's attractive harbour area.

Cycle hire: Irvine Cycles (01294) 272712 irvinecycles.co.uk or Harbour Cycle Hire, Harbour Street, Irvine 07759 299288

Wider area cycle map: Aryshire, Lanark & Arran

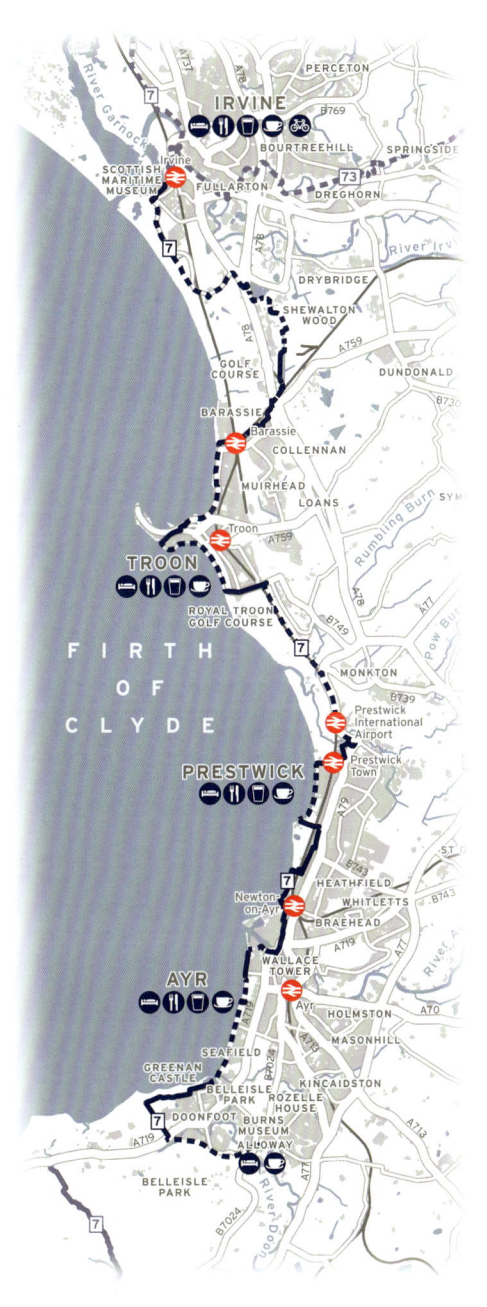

Rozelle Park, Ayr

303

RIDE 02 — 7 75 🚲 **Start:** Paisley Canal train station
14 miles

LOCHWINNOCH LOOP LINE

This ride along the former route of the Lochwinnoch Loop Line is a diverse, wildlife-rich mix of sheltered cuttings and railway embankments giving views over open farmland, hills and two beautiful lochs. It runs parallel to the Glasgow to Ayrshire coast railway line throughout, so there are many opportunities to hop on or off the train.

Paisley is a historic and beautiful town to start from, so it's a good idea to head into the centre to see the stunning Town Hall, ornate Grand Fountain and Paisley Abbey before setting off. Start the ride on the platform of Paisley Canal train station and follow the path under the bridge, heading west through the residential areas until Elderslie, where a ramp leads down to a half-mile, on-road ride through the town. Before rejoining the railway path you might want to continue straight on for a short distance to the Wallace Memorial beside Main Road in Elderslie, said to be sited near the birthplace of William Wallace.

Back on the railway path, reach the junction of NCN 7 and 75, marked by the impressive giant pencil sculpture, before looping over the A737. On the outskirts of Kilbarchan there's an opportunity to take a very short detour into the village to visit the restored 18th Century Weaver's Cottage and discover more about local handloom weavers, or simply continue along the path, looking out for the hilltop temple and Castle Semple collegiate church as you ride.

You are now in Clyde Muirshiel Regional Park and quickly reach the first loch on the ride, Castle Semple. The banks of the loch are great for picnicking whilst watching windsurfers out on the water, or follow the signed, traffic-free Semple Trail to RSPB Lochwinnoch nature reserve, one of the few wetlands left in west Scotland. It's a perfect spot to look for otters, or watch the elaborate courtship display of great crested grebes in spring.

Back on the trail, the final miles are gentle and scenic, with fine views over Barr Loch and the remains of Barr Castle. Pass the edges of the small town of Kilbirnie and, near the end of the railway path, take the path to the right across the Ladeside playing fields, from where it's a short, on-road ride beside the River Garnock to end at Glengarnock train station.

Walkers on the Lochwinnoch path

RIDE 02

Finish: Glengarnock train station (near Kilbirnie)

Train stations: Paisley Canal or Glengarnock

Grade: Moderate

Terrain, gradients and access: Largely flat along a tarmac path, with short, on-road sections in Elderslie and Glengarnock.

Loops, links and longer rides: This ride follows part of NCN 7 Lochs and Glens South, a 214-mile route from Carlisle to Glasgow. At the pencil sculpture near Johnstone, join NCN 75 along a railway path to Port Glasgow and then down to Greenock and Gourock on the Firth of Clyde, with views across to Ben Lomond and the Southern Highlands. At Gourock, take a ferry to Dunoon and continue to Portavadie, where another ferry connects with NCN 78 on the Kintyre peninsula. NCN 7 and 754 Glasgow to Loch Lomond (**Ride 03**).

Stay: Dryesdale Guesthouse, Paisley (0141) 889 7178 dryesdale.co.uk

Eat and drink: The Lord Lounsdale pub in Paisley is a cyclists' favourite, or try Paisley Abbey café. Castle Semple Café is in a lovely spot beside the loch, try RSPB Lochwinnoch Tearoom for drinks and snacks. For something more substantial try Junction Café on Lochwinnoch high street.

Cycle hire: R T Cycles at Glengarnock (01505) 682191 cyclerepairman.co.uk and at Castle Semple Visitor Centre (seasonal and weather dependent) 07867 790889.

Wider area cycle map: Lochs & Glens South

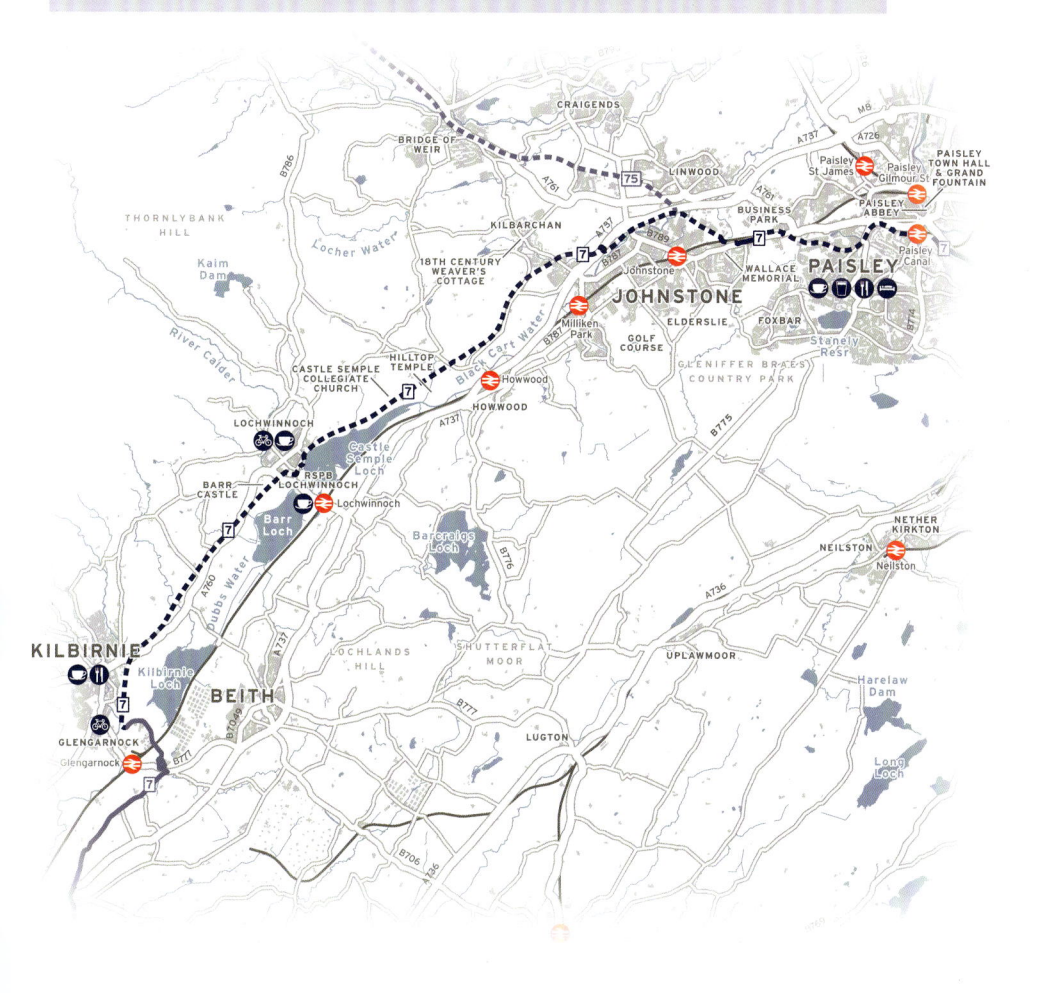

RIDE 03
20 miles | 7 754 | **Start:** Bell's Bridge, Glasgow

GLASGOW
TO
LOCH LOMOND

This incredibly varied ride leads from the handsome city of Glasgow along the banks of the River Clyde, the Forth & Clyde Canal and a former railway path to the village of Balloch, near the sublime shores of Loch Lomond.

Start at Bell's Bridge where you'll be surrounded by dramatic waterside structures, including the distinctive curves of the Scottish Exhibition and Conference Centre, affectionately known as 'the armadillo', the new SSE Hydro concert hall and the mighty Finnieston Crane. Head west along the north bank of the River Clyde, passing the Riverside Museum along the way. It's worth a detour from here to visit Kelvingrove Art Gallery and Museum and to see one of UK's finest collections of paintings.

A couple of miles later there's a great opportunity to take another detour at Primrose Street and follow the short, traffic-free link to the fascinating Fossil Grove at Victoria Park, home to the remains of a prehistoric forest. Or, just stay on the main trail and cycle through areas where there used to be major shipyards and now much redevelopment, with the heather-covered Kilpatrick Hills becoming visible in the distance.

Continue through Clydebank and look out for the huge blue Titan Crane at the river's edge, before joining the towpath of the Forth & Clyde Canal. Passing under the towering Erskine Bridge, you then arrive at Bowling, where the canal joins the River Clyde. Here you can

> "To the village of Balloch, near the sublime shores of Loch Lomond."

306

Finish: Balloch, Loch Lomond

RIDE 03

Train stations: Exhibition Centre or Balloch

Grade: Moderate

Terrain, gradients and access: Tarmac path with some road crossings and on-road sections at Clydebank, Dumbarton, Renton and Balloch; a few narrower gated openings.

Loops, links and longer rides: This ride is part of Lochs and Glens North, a 217-mile route from Glasgow to Inverness. At Bell's Bridge, join NCN 7 and 75 to Paisley and join the Lochwinnoch Loop Line (**Ride 02**), or on joining the Forth & Clyde Canal at Clydebank, follow the towpath east back into Glasgow to create a circular ride. At the ride's end in Balloch, join West Loch Lomond Cycle Path for a 17-mile, mostly traffic-free route (NCN 40) along the west side of Loch Lomond to the village of Tarbet.

Stay: Gowanlea Guesthouse, Balloch (01389) 752456 hotelatlochlomond.co.uk

Eat and drink: Glasgow has many places to eat; try Clydebuilt Bar and Kitchen in the Scottish Exhibition and Conference Centre, or Riverside Café at Riverside Museum. The Balloch House country pub is at the route's end in Balloch, as is The Tullie Inn. At Loch Lomond Shores there are cafés, bars and restaurants, a beach kiosk and a farmers' market every first and third Sunday of the month.

Cycle hire: Gear Bikes, Glasgow (0141) 339 1179 gearbikes.com or Nextbike Glasgow has several docking stations in and around the city nextbike.co.uk/en/glasgow

Wider area cycle map: Lochs & Glens North

see the varied and colourful houseboats and the old railway swing bridge.

Continue to Dumbarton, the ancient fortress-capital of Strathclyde, where a diversion will take you to the stunning volcanic plug of Dumbarton Rock with the castle dramatically positioned upon it. In Dumbarton, cross the River Leven to join the path along its west bank, following the water through the Vale of Leven. Along the way you'll pass the village of Renton and the town of Alexandria before reaching Balloch village at the edge of Scotland's first National Park, Loch Lomond & The Trossachs.

End at Balloch train station, which is very close to the riverside path, or continue along NCN 7 for a short, on-road ride to the beautiful Balloch Castle Country Park. Alternatively, join West Loch Lomond Cycle Path for half a mile to reach the 'Bonnie Banks o' Loch Lomond', made famous in traditional Scottish song. From here there are views up the length of the loch and of Scotland's southernmost Munro, Ben Lomond.

Picnic area on the Clyde

307

RIDE 04
8 miles | 755 | Start: Kilsyth Road, Kirkintilloch

STRATHKELVIN RAILWAY PATH

Strathkelvin Railway Path

This wonderful former railway path leads from Scotland's urban central belt into remote countryside, featuring Scotland's gently rolling Campsie Fells along the way. The volcanic plug of Dunglass is a striking feature of the route's end.

Start at Eastside or Kilsyth Road in Kirkintilloch, quickly crossing the River Kelvin and riding close to Glazert Water, where there are some lovely spots to pause and look out for kingfishers. The route is edged with trees and wildflowers as you head north to Milton of Campsie and then swing west, riding parallel to the Campsie Fells, an impressive range of volcanic hills.

Pass through trees around Lennoxtown and consider taking an interesting detour, turning left at the crossing of Station Road and following the route into Lennox Forest, where there are wide forest roads through the conifer trees. Look out for crossbills in the trees and enjoy long views down to Glasgow city. Or, simply stay on the path from Lennoxtown. After a few miles you'll have the chance to take a very short detour to Clachan of Campsie, where there's a popular coffee shop, gallery and an opportunity to lock up and take a short, scenic walk up Campsie Glen.

Back on the path, ride along the northern edge of Bank Wood. Soon, the craggy rocks of Dunglass appear on your left, a dramatic volcanic plug signalling the end of the ride. The traffic-free path finishes on Strathblane Road – turn left here to cycle a very short distance on-road to The Kirkhouse Inn.

Finish: The Kirkhouse Inn, Strathblane

RIDE 04

Train stations: Nearest are Lenzie and Milngavie
Grade: Easy
Terrain, gradients and access: Flat, tarmac path with some road crossings.
Loops, links and longer rides: The Strathkelvin Railway Path can be picked up again on the B757 in Kirkintilloch, opposite the Gallowhill Road junction, and runs for a further four miles south to Moodiesburn. Also at Kirkintilloch, join NCN 754 Forth & Clyde Canal for a 16-mile, traffic-free ride east to the Falkirk Wheel or a 16-mile, traffic-free ride west to Bowling.

Stay: Kirkhouse Inn, Strathblane (01360) 771771 kirkhouseinn.com
Eat and drink: At Kirkintilloch, try Café Mariana or Ghiloni's Café and Ice Cream Parlour. Sonas Café Bistro at Clachan of Campsie is very popular, or try The Kirkhouse Inn at Strathblane.
Cycle hire: Gear Bikes, Glasgow (0141) 339 1179 gearbikes.com or Nextbike Glasgow has several docking stations in and around the city
nextbike.co.uk/en/glasgow
Wider area cycle map: Glasgow, Stirling and Argyll & Bute

Cyclists on the Strathkelvin Railway Path

309

RIDE 05 — Start and finish: Royal Scottish Academy, Princes Street, Edinburgh

17 miles including an optional 3.5 mile loop of Holyrood Park

EDINBURGH, LEITH & PORTOBELLO

This magnificent ride encompasses internationally known attractions such as Princes Street, Holyrood Park and the Royal Yacht Britannia plus lesser-known but equally spectacular sights like Portobello beachfront.

Starting at the Royal Scottish Academy on Princes Street, use cycle lanes along George Street to come to St Andrews Square and the imposing Melville monument. Drop down through Edinburgh's handsome New Town area to King George V park, to head under Rodney Street Tunnel and pick up the Warriston Path, now following signs for Leith along NCN 75.

The Warriston Path ends in Leith at Sandport Place bridge. The there-and-back spur to Royal Yacht Britannia heads off to the left along NCN 75. It is well-signed through backstreets and along the attractive Commercial Quay to arrive at the large shopping centre on Ocean Drive, an unlikely access point for Royal Yacht Britannia (bike racks out front).

Back at Sandport Place the onward route continues over the bridge, picking up local route 10 signs to Leith Links and Portobello. Just over the bridge it's worth exploring the attractive quayside area with many seafood eateries. You are soon heading along the edge of the beautiful wide open space of Leith Links onto the Restalrig railway path. A brief interlude on a pavement cycle lane brings you to another glorious traffic-free section along Portobello seafront with wonderful views across the Firth of Forth and plenty of attractive café stops.

Out of Portobello join the road at Joppa, still on local route 10, but shortly look out for the Brunstane Burn Walkway signs on the opposite side of the road. Newhailes House is signed off the route (open at weekends viewings of the house by appointment, café open in stables even if house is closed). This path joins NCN 1 just over the very shallow steps (easily pushed) at Brunstane station and there follows a magnificent approach back to Edinburgh centre on the Innocent railpath. Just under the magnificent tunnel there is a signed cycle link to Holyrood Park where you can take the option of circling Holyrood Park on a road that is only open to motor traffic on selected days of the week.

The final leg back to Princes Street is well signed, weaving through handsome backstreets before it skirts the lovely Meadows parkland area, taking to on-street cycle lanes to through the heart of Edinburgh Old Town.

Innocent railpath into Edinburgh

RIDE 05

Train Station: Edinburgh Waverley

Grade: Moderate (challenging if you include the optional loop of Holyrood Park)

Terrain, gradients and access: Generally nice quality tarmac cycle paths with many surprisingly leafy ones only a stone's throw from Edinburgh centre. Generally good access at crossings though some shallow steps to cross over the railway line at Brunstane station. Mainly flat but some notable hills through Edinburgh centre and a sustained climb on the optional circuit of Holyrood Park. Some busy motor traffic on the short NCN section through central Edinburgh where you use on-street cycle lanes but this soon drops away to leave the overwhelming majority of the ride traffic-free.

Loops, links and longer rides: NCN 75 connects Leith to Portavadie on the Cowall Peninsula in Argyll – the section you use on this ride takes you through central Edinburgh and out to Leith. After using local route 10 to leave Leith to the east and head through Portobello you join NCN 1 at Brunstane to re-enter the city. NCN 1 continues north over the Forth Bridge whilst NCN 76 is a fine ride out of Edinburgh along the south coast of the Firth of Forth.

Stay: Jurys Inn, Jeffrey Street, Edinburgh (0131) 2003300 jurysinn.com

Eat and drink: Options in Edinburgh are countless but there are nice cafés in Princes Street gardens. Leith Commercial Quay is a mix of offices, cafés and bars attractively restored and a nice place to sit out. If you visit Royal Yacht Britannia there is an on board café and the attractive area around the Water of Leith in the centre has plenty of varied options too. Just off the route near the start of the Brunstane path at Newhailes House there is an attractive café in the old stable block.

Cycle hire: Cycle Scotland, Blackfriars Street, Edinburgh (0131) 556 5560 or 07796 886899 cyclescotland.co.uk

Wider area cycle map: Edinburgh, Sterling & Forth

311

RIDE 06
17 miles

EDINBURGH
TO
BO'NESS

Start: Haymarket train station, Edinburgh

This wonderful ride from Scotland's capital follows the Firth of Forth to the historic town of Bo'ness, passing the impressive Forth Rail Bridge along the way. Edinburgh is one of the UK's finest cities and well worth exploring before setting off. The castle, Royal Mile and labyrinth of cobbled lanes through the Old Town are particularly attractive.

Start the ride from Haymarket train station and head down Haymarket Yards onto the Roseburn Path, following the line that was once part of the Caledonian Railway. After a mile, take the left fork to Davidson's Mains, riding beside the neat greens of two golf courses and through the leafy streets of Edinburgh's affluent Barnton district to arrive at historic Cramond Brig.

Head into the parklands of the Dalmeny Estate on NCN 76 to take the scenic coastal path, pausing near the water to look back at Cramond Island, just off the mainland. You'll ride under the mighty Forth Rail Bridge, along the High Street of South Queensferry and under the Forth Road Bridge. This is a good spot to take a mid-ride break whilst admiring the sensational setting. Or, push up the ramp and take an exhilarating ride across the bridge to get sweeping views up and down the Forth and over the famous Forth Rail Bridge, before ending at North Queensferry train station.

However, to complete the second half of the ride continue along NCN 76 to the gates of the stunning Hopetoun House, often named as Scotland's finest stately home. Ride through the estate's deer park, particularly good in autumn when the male red deer are rutting and barking, before taking the quiet road to handsome Abercorn church and riding down the dizzying zig-zag ramp to Nethermill Bridge.

From here, it's a two-mile scenic trail close to the water's edge through the trees of Wester Shore Wood to Blackness, where the 15th Century Blackness Castle can be seen jutting out into the water. It's often called 'the ship that never sailed' due to its vessel-like shape and seafront position, surrounded by water at high tide. At Blackness, turn left to join the two-mile, windswept seafront path to the coastal town of Bo'ness. End at the Bo'ness & Kinneil Railway Museum or head into the town centre, an Outstanding Conservation Area full of listed buildings and views across the Forth to the Ochil Hills.

Finish: Bo'ness and Kinneil Railway Museum, Bo'ness

RIDE 06

Train stations: Edinburgh Haymarket, Dalmeny, North Queensferry and Linlithgow

Grade: Moderate

Terrain, gradients and access: Mostly flat on tarmac path and fine gravel track. Some road crossings and short, on-road sections through Barnton and between South Queensferry and Hopetoun. Take care cycling around the tramlines at Haymarket Yards. There are some restrictive gates in Hopetoun House Estate.

Loops, links and longer rides: This ride partly follows NCN 76 Round the Forth route following both shores of the Forth. At Linlithgow, there is an option to join NCN 754, which runs along the canal towpaths between Edinburgh and Glasgow. Or, across the Forth Road Bridge join NCN 1 to Fife. Edinburgh is the northern end of Coasts and Castles South, a 200-mile route between Newcastle-upon-Tyne and Edinburgh.

Stay: Brooks Hotel, Edinburgh (0131) 228 2323 brooksedinburgh.com

Eat and drink: Edinburgh is full of great places. Try the Miller & Carter pub at Cramond Brig, or The Hawes Inn in South Queensferry, linked to Robert Louis Stevenson's novel *Kidnapped*. The Stables Tearoom is at Hopetoun House or visit Hopetoun Farm Shop. Corbie Inn in Bo'ness is popular, or have afternoon tea on a steam train at Bo'ness and Kinneil Railway Museum during summer weekends.

Cycle hire: Leith Cycle Co, Edinburgh (0131) 467 7775 leithcycleco.com or Bike Trax, Edinburgh (0131) 228 6633 biketrax.co.uk

Wider area cycle map: Round the Forth

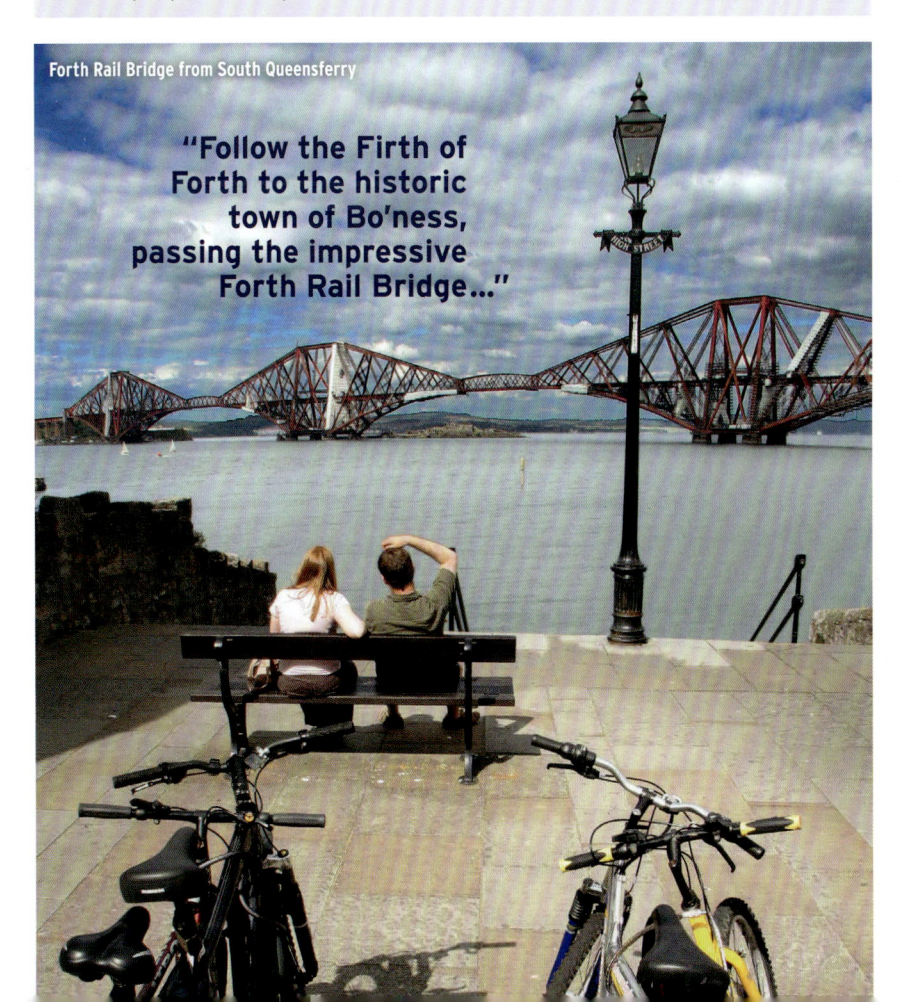

Forth Rail Bridge from South Queensferry

"Follow the Firth of Forth to the historic town of Bo'ness, passing the impressive Forth Rail Bridge..."

313

RIDE 07 — 12 miles | 76 767 768 | **Start and finish:** Alloa train station

ALLOA HILLFOOTS LOOP

This loop starts in Alloa, once the brewery capital of Scotland, and passes through the Hillfoots Villages along the southern base of the Ochil Hills. The landscape of open farmland and towering hills along the way is wonderful, and you'll pass whisky cooperages and bonded warehouses, with their distinctive, heady aroma.

Start at Alloa train station, following NCN 767 across the road and along a former wagon path to join NCN 76 at Lime Tree House, the old council offices. Here is an opportunity for an early detour, as it's just a very short traffic-free ride to the east to reach the medieval Alloa Tower, Scotland's largest and oldest keep, and a childhood home to Mary Queen of Scots. Or, continue along the main trail by following the route west to the hamlet of Cambus, where you'll pass working whisky warehouses to the right, the River Devon to the left and a large ruined dovecot.

Near Tullibody, continue northwards on NCN 768 along the old railway path towards Menstrie, crossing the River Devon on the way. At Menstrie, you'll join a more rugged, but quiet road, rolling along the pleasant, gentle gradients beneath the towering Ochil Hills.

There are many footpaths that lead up into the hills, the most notable being through the stunning gorge of Alva Glen. The start of this walk is at Alva Glen car park beside the cycle route, so if you fancy an on-foot adventure then lock up near here and head into the hills. It's around a mile and a half to the viewpoint and be prepared for a steeper ascent near the end.

Alternatively, simply continue along the road behind Alva village. The only challenging hill climb of the ride is around here, but it's mercifully short and followed by an effortless descent (take care as there are some blind corners to negotiate).

East of Alva, it's just over a mile to Tillicoultry, where you'll head through the park and the quiet residential streets to join the Devon Way route (NCN 767). Turn left here for a detour to the lovely village of Dollar three miles further east, or complete the loop by carrying straight on, crossing the river and following the railway path past Sauchie. In the final miles there are wonderful views back over the Ochil Hills and the route just taken, giving a satisfying sense of scale to the trip, before ending back at Alloa train station.

View towards the Ochil Hills

RIDE 07

Train station: Alloa

Grade: Moderate

Terrain, gradients and access: A mixture of flat tarmac paths and some hill climbs along the edge of the Ochil Hills. The most notable climb is at Alva, followed by a descent that needs extra care as there are blind corners. Some road crossings and on-road sections between Alloa and Cambus, Menstrie and Alva, and at Tillicoultry.

Loops, links and longer rides: Alloa is on NCN 76 Round the Forth route following both shores of the Forth. At Alloa, follow NCN 76 a short distance east to Clackmannan and join the traffic-free NCN 764 West Fife Way to Dunfermline. Also from Clackmannan, follow NCN 76 on a speed-reduced road to Kincardine and then a high-quality, four-mile, traffic-free path to the historic village of Culross on the shores of the Forth.

Stay: Taigh Lusnambansith B&B, Clackmannan (01259) 722063
taighlusnambansith.webeden.co.uk

Eat and drink: Hot drinks are available at Alloa Tower. A short detour into Tullibody brings you to Cafelicious. Number 5 Inn is at Alva and there are plenty more options just south of this on the main street. In Tillicoultry, try Tilly Tearoom or the cafés at Affinity Sterling Mills outlet shopping village.

Cycle hire: Nextbike, docking stations around Stirling
nextbike.co.uk

Wider area cycle map: Round the Forth

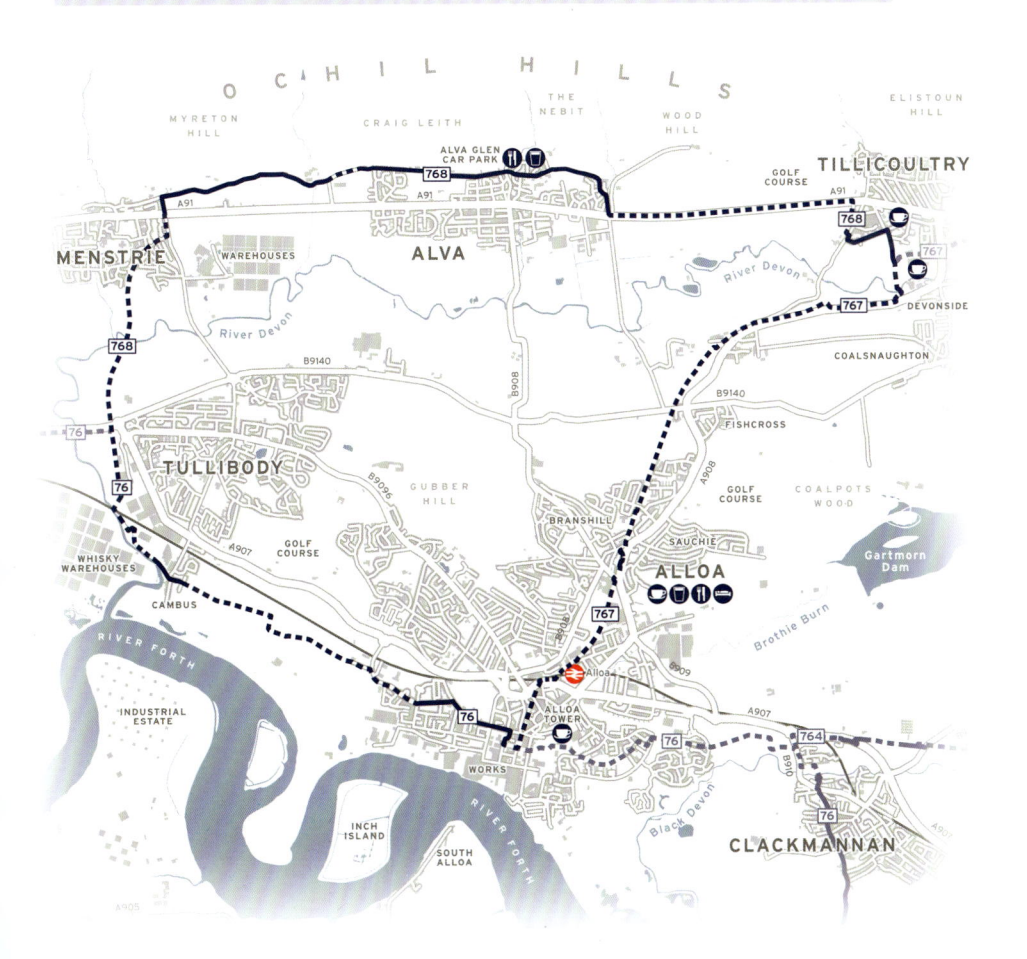

RIDE 08 — 13 miles

Start and finish: Kinross Pier

LOCH LEVEN HERITAGE TRAIL

This attractive, family-friendly loop of Loch Leven offers a classic Scottish experience, from the twinkling waters of the loch to deep birch and pine woodland, native wildlife and views over the rolling Ochil and rugged Lomond hills.

Start at Kinross Pier and ride through Kirkgate Park, pausing at the end of the churchyard to look across to Castle Island and Loch Leven Castle where Mary Queen of Scots was imprisoned and forced to abdicate, before escaping in 1568. Interestingly, the key to her prison door was dropped in the loch during the escape, found many years later, and is still in the possession of a local family.

Head through marshy wetland and willow trees, against the backdrop of the Ochil Hills, to reach Burleigh Sands, where there's a popular picnic area and a small stretch of sandy shoreline. Tall Scots Pine trees line the trail from here and Green Isle can be seen offshore, a small refuge for swans and other water birds. Continuing round the loch, you reach the reedbeds of Carsehall Bog, a great place for wildlife-watching.

On the south east end of the loch, gliders may be seen soaring silently overhead above the Scottish Gliding Centre at Portmoak. Cross over the River Leven and enter the RSPB's Loch Leven nature reserve. This is around the midway point of the ride and there are picnic benches overlooking St Serf's Island and the wildflower meadows which provide a pleasant fuel-stop, or, further on, take a tiny detour through the subway (watch out for the steps) to reach the RSPB Loch Leven visitor centre and eat lunch in the café.

Alternatively, simply stay on the path to access the nature reserve's viewing hides that offer fine panoramas over the water. In fact, a mile and a half further west you'll have climbed to the highest point of the trail, a wonderfully scenic spot.

The path heads down a zig-zag before rejoining the shores of the loch to return to the start point at Kinross Pier. There are boat trips from the pier to Castle Island between April and October.

Train stations: Nearest is Lochgelly

Grade: Moderate

Terrain, gradients and access: Fine gravel track throughout, mostly flat but with some gentle gradients. At peak times the route is very busy with walkers and cyclists, so cycle carefully, particularly at Kinross.

Loops, links and longer rides: The Heritage Trail from Kinross to Wester Balgedie is part of NCN 1, which heads south to Dunfermline over the Cleish Hills, or north towards Falkland and St Andrews. At Kinross, join NCN 775 north to Perth.

Stay: The Kirklands Hotel & Restaurant, Kinross (01577) 863313 thekirklandshotel.com

Eat and drink: At Kinross, try The Kirklands Hotel & Restaurant. Loch Leven's Larder at Channel Farm near Wester Balgedie is very popular and situated on NCN 1 slightly north of the loch, while Lochend Farm Shop & Café is located about two miles from the trail at the east of the loch, near to the Scottish Gliding Centre. RSPB Loch Leven café offers lovely water views or Loch Leven Lodges Coffee Shop is on the shores at Findatie.

Cycle hire: Loch Leven Cycles at Loch Levens Larder (01577) 862839

Wider area cycle map: Round the Forth

RIDE 08

317

RIDE 09
17.5 miles

Start: Dundee train station

DUNDEE
TO
ARBROATH

This wonderful, family-friendly ride never strays far from the waterside as it follows the River Tay from the industrial heritage of Dundee docks to the fishing town of Arbroath. You'll pass castles, sandy beaches, rocky shorelines and a championship golf course along the way.

Start at Dundee train station and immediately pass RRS Discovery, used in the 1901 Antarctic Expedition led by Captain Scott. Ride beneath the Tay Road Bridge to reach the Victoria Dock, home to the historic frigate HMS Unicorn. From here, you'll head along the north of the dock area past warehouses and industrial units, but these are soon exchanged for fine views of Broughty Castle as you ride the promenade along the bay. At Broughty Ferry, it's worth taking a very short, on-road detour to reach Claypotts Castle, a little-known but outstanding 16th Century Scottish tower house.

Alternatively, simply stay on the route to ride past handsome Broughty Castle, built in the 15th Century to defend Dundee from attack, the award-winning sandy beach and pretty Barnhill Rock Garden. From here, it's just a couple of miles to Monifieth, where there's a great play park for children, before you join the path beside the railway line to Carnoustie.

There are some great views over the famous championship golf course as you enter Carnoustie, and the path runs close to the town's sandy and rocky beach here, making it easy to pause for a mid-ride paddle. Leave Carnoustie at West Haven and quickly reach the charming fishing village of East Haven, one of the oldest known fishing villages in Scotland.

From here, pass another golf course at Elliot Links before entering Arbroath. Finish at the striking, white Arbroath Signal Tower Museum near the picturesque harbour, where you can end in a suitably traditional coastal manner by sampling the renowned Arbroath Smokies (wood-smoked haddock).

Picturesque Arbroath Harbour

RIDE 09

Finish: Arbroath Harbour

Train stations: Dundee and Arbroath

Grade: Moderate

Terrain, gradients and access: Almost entirely flat along tarmac path and fine gravel track. Some road crossings and short, quiet on-road sections at Dundee, Broughty Ferry, Carnoustie and Arbroath. Photo ID may be required at the gated entrance to Dundee's working docks. Alternatively, start the ride from the east side of the docks or pass around them on Broughty Ferry Road.

Loops, links and longer rides: At the north end of the Tay Road Bridge, take the lift up and follow NCN 1 south across the bridge on traffic-free path to Tayport and Tentsmuir Forest in Fife. Or, follow NCN 77 The Salmon Run, a 54-mile, mostly on-road route that leads west from the Tay Road Bridge to Invergowrie, Perth and Pitlochry. At Balmossie, join the Dundee Green Circular Route, a mainly traffic-free loop round Dundee.

Stay: Premier Inn Dundee Centre 0333 777 4656 premierinn.com

Eat and drink: There are many places to eat at Victoria Docks in Dundee and in the towns of Monifieth and Carnoustie along the way. Try The Ship Inn at Broughty Ferry or the Old Brewhouse restaurant and bar at Arbroath Harbour. Fish and chip restaurants and Arbroath Smokies can be found around the harbour.

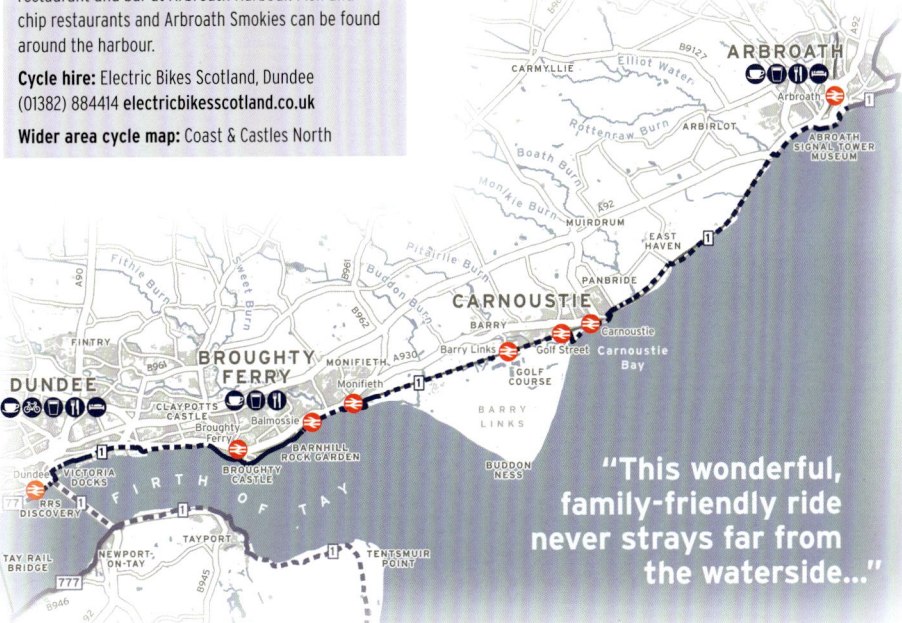

Cycle hire: Electric Bikes Scotland, Dundee (01382) 884144 electricbikesscotland.co.uk

Wider area cycle map: Coast & Castles North

Broughty Ferry promenade

"This wonderful, family-friendly ride never strays far from the waterside..."

CALLANDER TO KILLIN

Loch Earn

This route through The Trossachs is simply spectacular, and is one of the highlights of the classic Lochs and Glens North long-distance route from Glasgow to Inverness. The scenery is outstanding, from deep forests and fine lochs to the steep slopes of Glen Ogle, the Gateway to the Highlands, which Queen Victoria once described as "Britain's Khyber Pass".

Start from the car park at Callander Meadows and quickly leave the bustling tourist town behind as you follow the line of the old Callander and Oban Railway. Cross open countryside to Kilmahog before climbing up the narrow wooded Pass of Leny, where it's worth taking a break to walk the small footpath to the gushing waters of the Falls of Leny, before continuing along the trail to join the western shores of Loch Lubnaig.

The landscape starts to open out beautifully near the northern end of the loch, where there is a short, steep zig-zag climb from the old railway to the forest road, and then a descent from Keip Farm into Strathyre village. Take a mid-ride break here before the exertion that follows through Glen Ogle.

Then it's a wonderful ride along the valley of the meandering River Balvag, where there's a chance of spotting otters in the water. At Kingshouse there are fine views down Balquhidder Glen toward Loch Voil, and you can detour from the route here into Balquhidder village to see Rob Roy's grave by the ruins of the old church. Or, simply stay on the path, winding through wood and moorland, and then zig-zagging up to join the old railway line that cuts through Glen Ogle. This is the most spectacular part of the ride

Finish: Bridge of Dochart, Killin

RIDE 10

Train stations: Nearest are Dunblane, Balloch and Pitlochry

Grade: Challenging

Terrain, gradients and access: A mix of tarmac path, fine gravel track and stony trail, suitable for all but lightweight road bikes. Some road crossings and on-road sections at Loch Lubnaig, Strathyre and Killin. A couple of steep zig-zag paths, a gentle climb up Glen Ogle and steeper drop down the forest trail to Killin. There's a narrow gate on Glen Ogle.

Loops, links and longer rides: From Callander, follow NCN 7 to ride along the southern shores of Loch Venachar. At the west end of Loch Venacher, follow the local route to Loch Katrine and Inversnaid on Loch Lomond, or continue along NCN 7 to Achray Forest, Aberfoyle, Balloch and Glasgow (**Ride 03**). From Killin, NCN 7 continues on an undulating road for 16 miles to Kenmore.

Stay: Auchenlaich Farmhouse, Callander (01877) 331683 **auchenlaichfarmhouse.co.uk** or Mhor 84 Motel, Balquhidder (01877) 384646 **mhor.net**

Eat and drink: Mhor Bread Tearoom and Bakery in Callander is very popular, or try the coffee shop at Trossachs Woollen Mill, Kilmahog or the nearby Lade Inn. In Strathyre, Broch Café is in the Forestry Commission car park. Mhor 84 at Balquhidder is recommended, or there is often a mobile snack bar in the car park at the top of Glen Ogle. In Killin, The Old Smiddy and Shutters Coffee Shop are both popular.

Cycle hire: Wheels Cycling Centre, Callander (01877) 331100 **scottish-cycling.com** or Killin Outdoor Centre, Killin (01567) 820652 **killinoutdoor.co.uk**

Wider area cycle map: Lochs & Glens North

as you head gently up the glen, crossing two magnificent viaducts, with Loch Earn and the traffic on the A85 visible down below.

At the head of Glen Ogle, cross the road before beginning the exciting forest descent into Killin village at the western end of Loch Tay. End at the Bridge of Dochart in Killin, over the Falls of Dochart, where the water rages after a downpour, and where there are wonderful views over the Tarmachan ridge and Ben Lawers range.

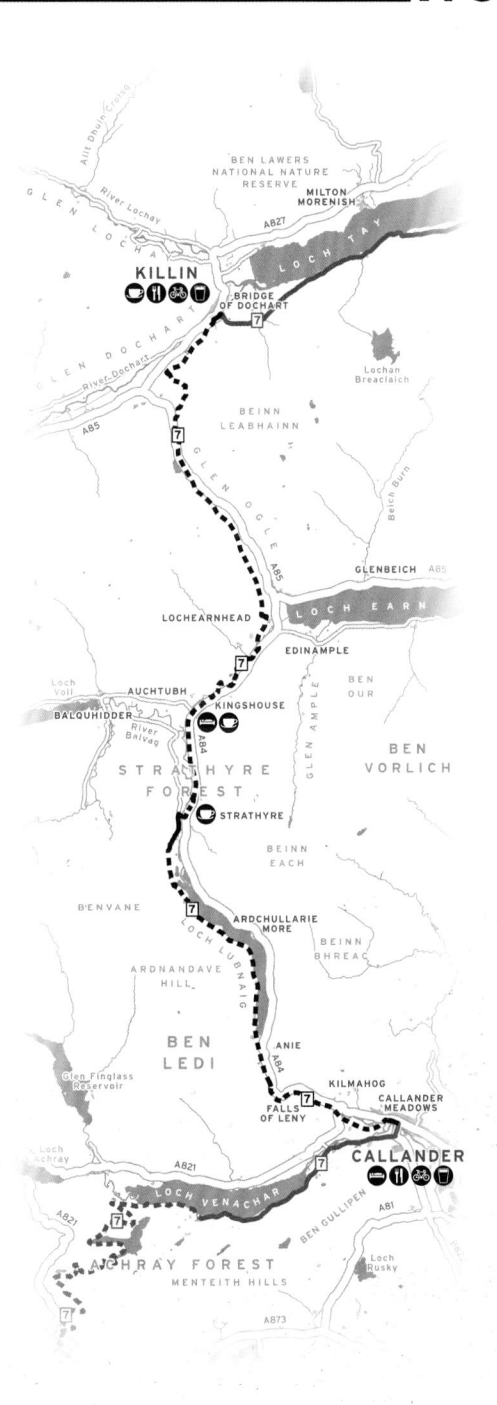

BENDERLOCH
TO
APPIN

Ride 11 — 11 miles — Start: Benderloch (NCN 78)

This fabulous route offers one of the newest and most scenic rides on the National Cycle Network in Scotland. It closely follows the stunning west coast and the shores of Loch Creran along the way, before ending with spectacular views over the iconic Castle Stalker.

Start on the old railway path by the car park in Benderloch village and head north to enter the dense forestry plantations around Barcaldine. After rounding the circular walled garden that used to belong to Barcaldine House (it's now a campsite), ride between the towering Douglas fir trees at Sutherland's Grove, where there is access to the exciting mountain bike trails through the forest.

Soon you are back on the old railway line, heading through woodland high above the road. Look down to the left to see old lookout points built by the Home Guard during World War II. Winter is a better time for spotting them, when the trees are bare. Also notice the large cut stones strewn around the sides of the path, deposits from the Creagan Bridge when it was converted from a rail to a road bridge in 1999.

Ride through a steep-sided railway cutting and emerge above the bridge itself where the beautiful views stretch over glistening Loch Creran and along the Strath of Appin. Cross the bridge to the other side of the loch where the path runs alongside the road before rejoining the old railway line through open farmland, past Appin village and the site of the old Appin railway station.

Reach a seat which overlooks the magnificent 14th Century Castle Stalker perched on its island in Loch Laich, an inlet of Loch Linnhe. End here, and enjoy the staggering backdrop of mountains on the Morvern Peninsula and on Mull, or ride for a further quarter of a mile to end at Linnhe Marina.

Castle Stalker

RIDE 11

Finish: Appin, overlooking Castle Stalker

Train stations: Nearest are Oban, Connel Ferry and Fort William

Grade: Moderate

Terrain, gradients and access: Mostly flat tarmac path, with a couple of short climbs and descents. Some road crossings and a section on minor roads and forest trail through Barcaldine.

Loops, links and longer rides: This ride is part of NCN 78, the Caledonia Way, which runs for 228 miles from Campbeltown to Inverness. At Benderloch, follow NCN 78 south to Oban, mainly on-road. From Appin, NCN 78 continues north for another five miles on traffic-free path and very quiet roads. Near Appin, cross the estuary by pushing over the narrow, wooden Jubilee Bridge to reach Port Appin and catch a ferry to the Isle of Lismore. NCN 78 Great Glen Way (**Ride 12**).

Stay: SHYA Oban (01631) 562025 syha.org.uk or The Pierhouse Hotel and Seafood Restaurant, Port Appin (01631) 730302 pierhousehotel.co.uk

Eat and drink: The award-winning Tralee Bay Fish and Chips is at Tralee Bay holiday park, while the Ben Lora Café and Bookshop is at Benderloch. Creagan Inn at Creagan and The Pierhouse Hotel and Seafood Restaurant in Port Appin. The Old Inn on the A828 at Portnacroish is one of the oldest Highland Inns in Scotland.

Cycle hire: Appin Electric Bikes (non-electric bikes also available), Appin (01631) 730426 or Oban Cycles (01631) 566033 obancyclesscotland.com

Wider area cycle map: Oban to Campbeltown

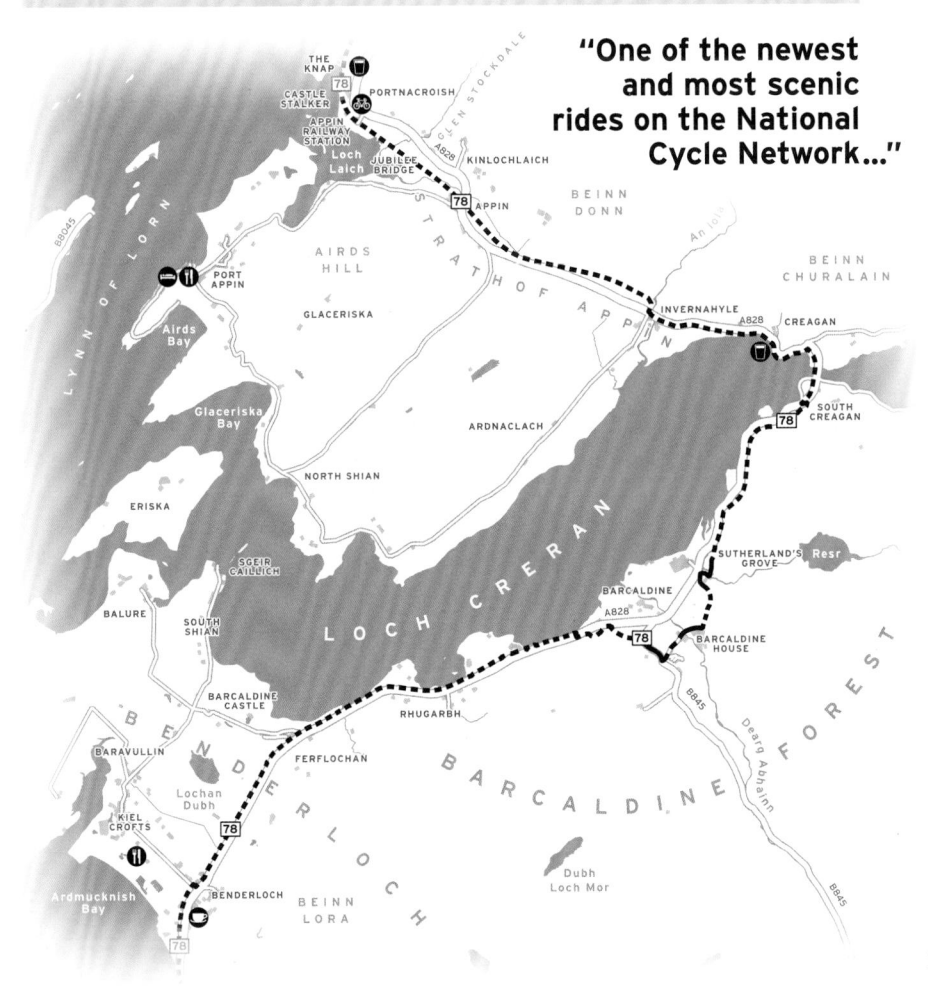

"One of the newest and most scenic rides on the National Cycle Network…"

RIDE 12
32 miles

Start: Fort William train station

GREAT GLEN WAY

(FORT WILLIAM TO FORT AUGUSTUS)

Mountains and lochs make a stunning backdrop to this beautiful ride through the Great Glen in the Highlands. It leads from Fort William, known as the outdoor capital of the UK, to Fort Augustus on the southern shores of the world-famous Loch Ness. The Great Glen Way's walking and canoeing routes also run through the glen.

Start at Fort William train station and follow the signs to Corpach on a mix of roads and traffic-free paths through the residential areas. Cross the River Lochy near the remains of Old Inverlochy Castle before joining the towpath of the Caledonian Canal at Corpach. You can head along to Corpach Sea Lock to see the western end of the canal which juts into Loch Linnhe, then set off along the towpath to Banavie. This is one of the highlights of the canal, as you climb up alongside the eight interconnected locks that make up Neptune's Staircase. Not only is this a historic site, but it's also the best spot for views of Ben Nevis, Britain's highest mountain. If you're lucky you may see it on one of the 70 days a year when the summit is not shrouded in cloud.

From here, it's a straightforward ride along the towpath to Gairlochy with wide open views across the mountains and treetops. Part designed by Thomas Telford, the Caledonian Canal was built between 1802 and 1822, partly as a job-creation scheme. Look out for the series of information panels along the way that explain its interesting history.

Finish: Fort Augustus

Train station: Fort William
Grade: Challenging

Terrain, gradients and access: Fine gravel canal towpath, tarmac path and forest roads alongside Loch Lochy, where there are also some gradients. Mostly flat. Some road crossings and on-road sections at Fort William, between Gairlochy and Clunes, Kilfinnan and Laggan, near the Great Glen Water Park and in Fort Augustus.

Loops, links and longer rides: This ride is part of the Caledonia Way, which runs for 228 miles from Campbeltown to Inverness. Continue to Inverness from Fort Augustus, following B-roads on the south side of Loch Ness for another 32 miles to end at Inverness Castle. From Fort William, there is a signed cycle path up to Torlundy and the World Championship mountain bike trails, or follow NCN 78 southwards, using the Camusnagaul and Corran Ferries and eventually joining the traffic-free Benderloch to Appin route (**Ride 11**).

Stay: Huntingtower Lodge, Druimarbin, Fort William (01397) 700079 **huntingtowerlodge.com** or SYHA Glen Nevis, Fort William (01397) 702336 **syha.org.uk**

Eat and drink: Long sections of this ride are remote with no food outlets, so it's a good idea to take snacks along. There are lots of places to eat at the start in Fort William; try The Light Garden Café at The Nevis Centre. Along the canal, try the Moorings Hotel at Banavie, The Eagle Barge at Laggan Locks. The Lock Inn at Fort Augustus is popular, or try The Boathouse Lochside Restaurant on Loch Ness.

Cycle hire: Offbeat Bikes, Fort William (01397) 704 008 **offbeatbikes.co.uk** or Nevis Cycles, Inverlochy (01397) 705555 **neviscycles.com**

At Gairlochy, cross over the swing bridge and follow the road along the western shores of Loch Lochy. There are some sensational views across the water before reaching the hamlet of Clunes, where the route joins a road through the thick trees of Clunes Forest. There are a few challenging gradients on this section, taking you high above the loch at points, before you descend again to rejoin the canal at Laggan Locks, a pleasant place to rest where there is a barge converted into a café.

From here, it's a pleasant ride along the towpath through the tall trees of Laggan Avenue to reach Laggan Swing Bridge. Leave the canal behind, cross the main road and join the quiet road into Great Glen Water Park, where the activity centre offers everything from river rafting to gorge walking. Here, join the four-mile path along a former railway line, passing through mixed woodland on the eastern side of Loch Oich (the Great Glen Way walking route follows a rougher trail along General Wade's military road close to the loch's edge for some of the way). At the end of the loch at Aberchalder, cross the road again onto the towpath and cycle all the way to the attractive town of Fort Augustus. You'll discover another series of lock gates marking the point where the canal flows into famous Loch Ness. End here, locking up your bike to take a walk around the town or a boat cruise on the loch, looking out for the mythical monster of course.

Locks at Fort Augustus

RIDE 13 — 5 miles | **Start:** Aviemore train station

THE SPEYSIDE WAY

(AVIEMORE TO BOAT OF GARTEN)

Cycling on the Speyside Way

This ride in the Scottish Highlands follows part of the scenic Speyside Way, a long-distance trail running from the heart of the Cairngorms National Park to the Moray Firth. As you thread your way through the native birch woodland, scented pine forests and heather moorland, the panoramic views of the mighty Cairngorm Mountains to the east are sensational, matched by gorgeous glimpses of the immaculately restored steam trains running along the Strathspey Railway.

Start at Aviemore train station, home to the Strathspey Steam Railway Company which runs heritage steam trains and rolling stock between Aviemore, Boat of Garten and Broomhill. It's worth taking a moment before setting off to admire these gleaming machines from a bygone age. From here, follow the road north and take the path beneath the railway before joining the quiet residential streets heading northwards out of the town. You'll pass the steam railway marshalling yards and join a traffic-free path near the golf course and the banks of the pretty River Spey.

Views over the Cairngorms' impressive northern mountains unfold as you ride across the moorland and forests. Keep a lookout overhead for ospreys, as this is a hotspot for these magnificent birds of prey. They are known to fish on the area's rivers and lochs.

The final mile is a gentle, on-road ride through the giant Scots pine trees and detached houses of Boat of Garten, known as 'The Osprey Village'. End at The Boat Hotel for afternoon tea, or in summer take the steam railway back to Aviemore (bikes are permitted).

Finish: Boat of Garten

RIDE 13

Train station: Aviemore

Grade: Easy

Terrain, gradients and access: Gently undulating along fine gravel track with some road crossings and on-road sections at Aviemore and Boat of Garten.

Stay: Ardlogie Guest House, Aviemore (01479) 810747 ardlogie.co.uk

Eat and drink: Aviemore is full of cafés and restaurants; try Mountain Café or La Taverna Ristorante. At Boat of Garten, The Boat Hotel is great for afternoon tea and cakes, and Anderson's Restaurant is highly recommended.

Cycle hire: Bothy Bikes, Aviemore (01479) 810111 bothybikes.co.uk or Ride Scotland, Boat of Garten (01497) 831729 ridescotland.com

Wider area cycle map: Lochs & Glens North

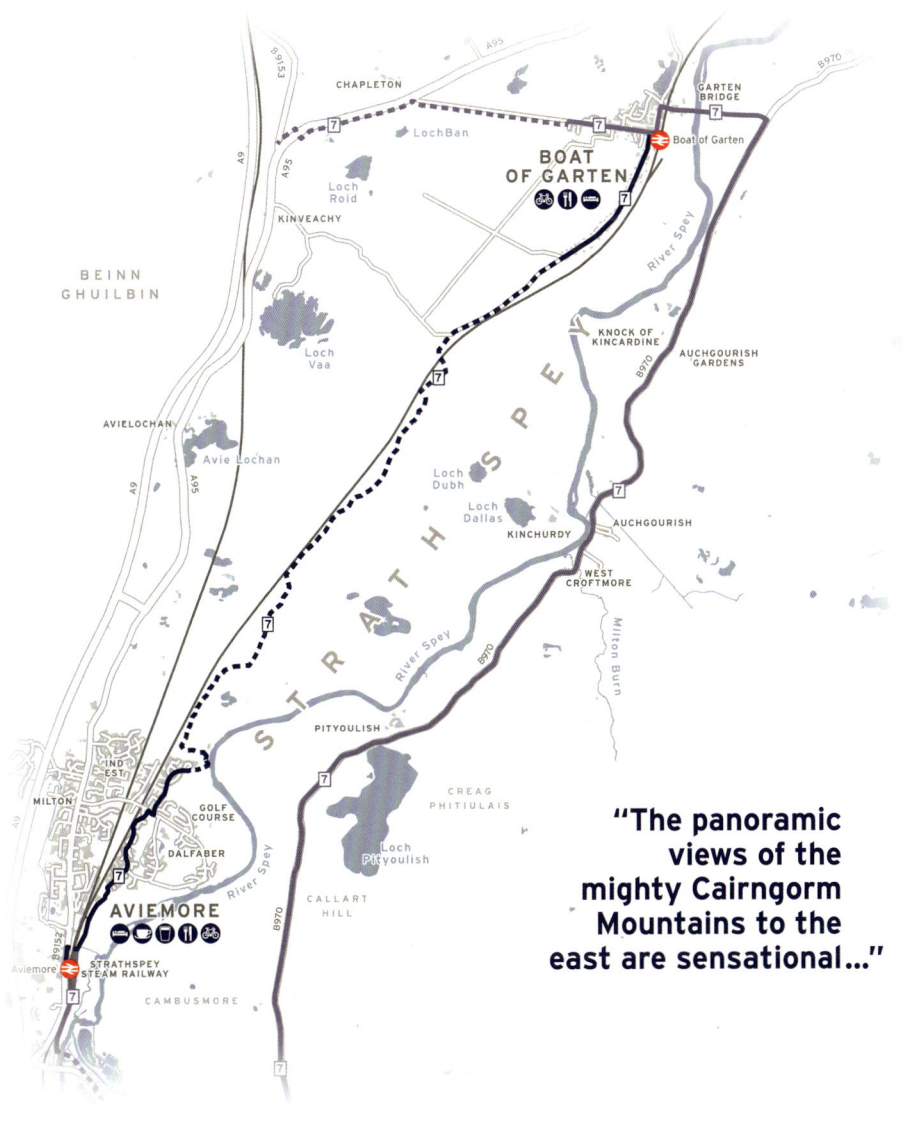

"The panoramic views of the mighty Cairngorm Mountains to the east are sensational..."

327

RIDE 14
18 miles

Start: Duthie Park, Aberdeen

DEESIDE WAY

(ABERDEEN TO BANCHORY)

This incredibly scenic route takes you to Banchory, the gateway to Royal Deeside, largely following the old Deeside Railway line, used at one time by the Royal family when visiting their sensational summer home at Balmoral.

River Dee near Banchory

Start at Duthie Park, behind the famous David Welch Winter Gardens which are free to enter and well worth a visit before setting off. In the opening miles you'll pass the fine millennium bridge over Holburn Street as you ride through the suburbs of Aberdeen, often called 'the Granite City' because of its many flinty grey buildings made from the locally quarried stone.

Before long the city is left behind and the landscape transforms into beautiful green countryside, with wonderful views of the distant, heather-covered Highlands. Approaching Peterculter, locally known as Culter (pronounced Cooter), soak up the attractive views over the River Dee and take a mid-ride break at the little picnic area beside the route. Or, head into the village to visit the Heritage Centre.

From here, it's a mix of railway path and quiet lanes through the tall conifers of Cairnton Wood into Drumoak, where it's worth walking across the recreation park to the picnic tables and more pretty views over the River Dee and Park Bridge. Alternatively, take a pleasant, hilly detour north of the village to Drum Castle, one of Scotland's oldest tower houses and one of the finest historic spots in Deeside.

On the outskirts of Drumoak, join the old railway path once more. All along the route are old station platforms from the railway's glory days, often with information points and pictures to help you imagine it. However, the Royal Deeside Railway station at Milton of Crathes craft village is the best spot for getting a glimpse of the old railway's past, or for taking a ride on a steam or diesel engine along a mile of the track. The driveway to Crathes Castle leads off from here, too; ride along it to reach the enchanting 16th Century tower house and estate, once part of the Royal Forest of Drum.

In the final mile, you'll reach Banchory churchyard where there's an option to dismount and take a walk down to the 'Platties', a concrete path originally built out over the riverbank for fishermen, where the water views are delightful (don't cycle along this stretch, though, as there are steep steps at the Banchory end and the path can sometimes be under water).

Continue along the trail to King George V Park and Pavilion, then follow the road to the High Street to end in Banchory's charming town centre.

RIDE 14

Finish: High Street, Banchory

Train station: Aberdeen

Grade: Moderate

Terrain: Flat tarmac path and fine gravel track with some road crossings and on-road sections between Peterculter and Drumoak, and into Banchory.

Loops, links and longer rides: From Banchory, The Deeside Way continues over the Bridge of Dee and through Blackhall Forest. At the west side of the forest there is a traffic-free path to Kincardine O'Neil, from where the trail continues through farm and woodland to just east of the Loch of Aboyne. From Aboyne, it continues for 11 miles on railway path to the village of Ballater, with the crags of Lochnagar visible in the distance. Aberdeen is the most northerly point of NCN 1 Coasts and Castles North long-distance route.

Stay: SYHA Aberdeen (01224) 646988
syha.org.uk

Eat and drink: At the start, try Duthie Park Café or Newton Dee café. In Peterculter centre there is a good selection of eateries. Milton Brasserie is at Crathes, as is The Royal Deeside Railway tearoom or Crathes Castle Courtyard Café. The Douglas Arms hotel in Banchory is recommended.

Cycle hire: Empowering Ebikes, Peterculter 07378 301567

Wider area cycle map: Coast & Castles North

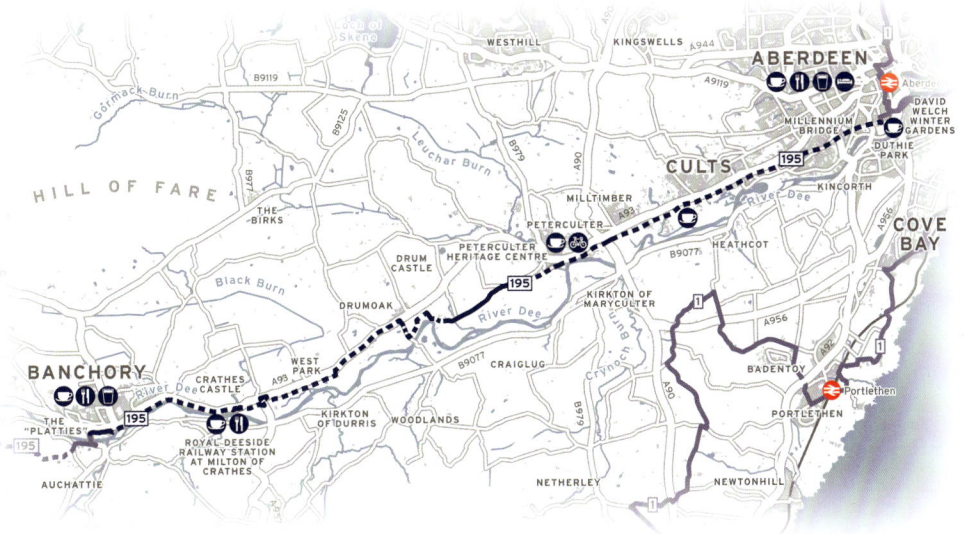

Holburn Street, Aberdeen

RIDE 15
7.5 miles

Start: North Deskford Street, Cullen

CULLEN
TO
BUCKIE

The dramatic cliffs and coastline of Moray are the star of this ride, which takes in exceptional beaches and pretty fishing towns and villages.

Start at the northern end of North Deskford Street in Cullen and immediately join the old path of the Moray Coast Railway over the impressive viaduct, one of three such structures that carried the railway through the town.

It's an incredibly scenic start, as you find yourself elevated above Cullen and riding along the cliff tops with magnificent views across the Moray Firth. The Firth is home to the world's most northerly population of bottlenose dolphins, so keep a lookout for these enchanting creatures as you ride.

Follow the path around the curve of Cullen Bay, pausing just before the headland for a great view back over the town, golf course and sandy beach, before reaching Portknockie. Here, you'll head along one of the straight Victorian streets typical of the villages on this coast. They came about during the boom in herring fishing during the late 19th and early 20th Centuries, but now only a few working fishing boats remain in the harbours. It's worth taking a short detour to the low cliffs to see the village's most visited attraction: Bow Fiddle Rock, an offshore rock carved into an unusual shape by the sea.

Alternatively, simply continue west through Portknockie to rejoin the coastal path, winding along to Findochty with its church standing proudly above the sea. Take a detour to the old harbour, or ride through the residential streets on NCN 1, climb the hill and cross the road to rejoin the old railway line. From here it's a straight and simple trail, edged with yellow gorse in summer, which leads all the way to the historic fishing town of Buckie.

End among the shops and cafés in the centre of Buckie, or ride through the town and follow signs to Buckpool Harbour, finishing at the official endpoint of the Speyside Way, a long-distance route to Aviemore on the edge of the Cairngorm Mountains.

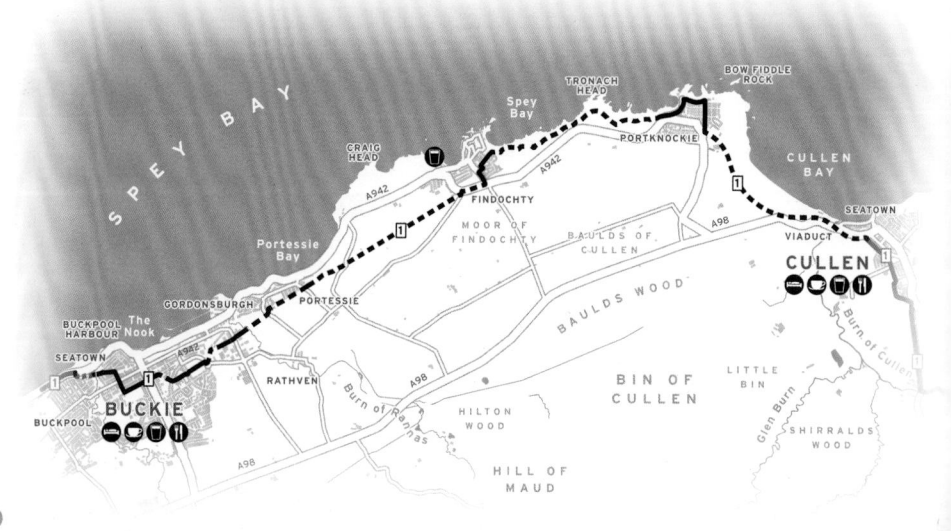

Finish: Buckpool Harbour, Buckie

RIDE 15

"It's a straight and simple trail, edged with yellow gorse in summer..."

Train stations: Nearest are Huntly, Keith and Elgin.

Grade: Easy

Terrain, gradients and access: Mostly flat but with one notable climb leaving Findochty. Tarmac path and fine gravel track with some road crossings and quiet, on-road sections throughout.

Loops, links and longer rides: Also try the Speyside Way, which leads to Boat of Garten and Aviemore (**Ride 13**). NCN 1 is part of the North Sea Cycle Route (Eurovelo Route 12) that spans eight different countries: Belgium, the Netherlands, Germany, Denmark, Sweden, Norway, Scotland and England.

Stay: Kintrae B&B, Buckie (01542) 839755 morayguesthouse.co.uk

Eat and drink: In Cullen, try the popular Rockpool Café and Restaurant, The Three Kings pub or Cullen Ice Cream Shop. Be sure to seek out Cullen Skink, a local dish of thick soup made from smoked haddock, potato and onion. Along the way, try The Admirals Inn, Findochty. At Buckie there is plenty of choice including Sandisons café.

Cycle hire: Outfit Moray, Lossiemouth (01343) 549571 outfitmoray.com

Wider area cycle map: Aberdeen to Shetland

Cyclists on path between Buckie and Findochty

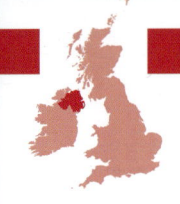

NORTHERN IRELAND

Mountainous views, lush greenery and historic cities make cycling in Northern Ireland a complete joy. There's a waterside theme to this small collection of rides, as they feature some of Northern Ireland's beautiful loughs, docks, rivers and canals.

The Connswater Greenway is one of latest and most impressive traffic-free rides in Northern Ireland, linking two highlights of the city, the Castlereagh Hills and Victoria Park, just a stone's throw from the world-famous Titanic Quarter.

Rich history and water views are the highlight of the short and simple Foyle Valley ride, an award-winning route starting from the elegant Peace Bridge in Londonderry/Derry, one of Europe's finest walled cities, and following the banks of the River Foyle. It also offers an irresistible option of riding through villages in the Republic of Ireland to the border town of Strabane with its magnificent 'Let the Dance Begin' bronze and steel sculptures.

A scenic towpath ride beside the Newry Canal takes you through County Armagh to end at the fine Newry Town Hall, with Camlough Mountain looming impressively in the distance. But it's the Lagan & Lough ride that offers the most outstanding scenery of all. Divis Mountain dominates the skyline as you ride through the Lagan Valley to the magnificent city of Belfast, and the final miles offer stunning views across the Belfast Lough to the County Down coast.

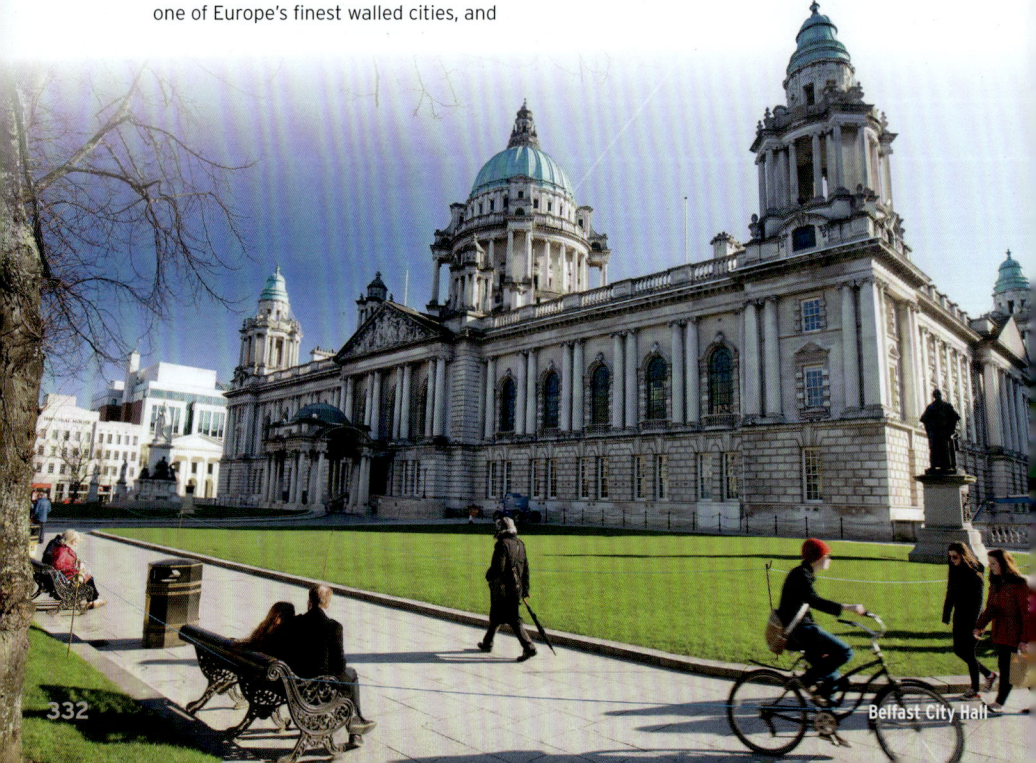

Belfast City Hall

Routes overview

- **01** Newry Canal Towpath (20 miles)
- **02** Lagan & Lough (20 miles)
- **03** Connswater Greenway (5 miles)
- **04** Foyle Valley Cycle Route (4.5 miles)
- — Featured ride
- — National Cycle Network (traffic-free and on-road)

North Foreshore path, Newtownabbey

RIDE 01
20 miles

Start: Bann Bridge, Portadown

NEWRY CANAL TOWPATH

This pretty ride through County Armagh follows the western bank of the Newry Canal, a busy waterway for more than 200 years and the first summit level canal in Britain and Ireland. It was constructed to take coal from the County Tyrone coalfields to Dublin via the Irish sea. The canal is no longer navigable and its towpath is now a peaceful and popular cycling and walking route.

Start at Bann Bridge in Portadown and follow the banks of the River Bann for a mile to the Point of Whitecoat. This is where the rivers Bann and Cusher meet under a modern bridge and where you'll join the towpath of the Newry Canal to ride beside the pools and peatland of Brackagh Nature Reserve.

Moneypenny's Lock appears just a mile later, where the attractively restored 18th Century lock keeper's cottage is a pretty spot to pause and watch for kingfishers, and a small museum in the old stables reveals the history of life on the Newry Canal. Continue six miles south to the popular tearooms at Scarva. This is a particularly beautiful spot in summer when concerts take place on the attractive bandstand and colourful, prize-winning floral displays fill the village. It also makes a good turn around point for families desiring a shorter ride.

From here, continue south to Acton Lake, also known by the more intriguing local name of Lough Shark, where buzzards can be spotted soaring overhead, while coots and swans glide over the water. The lake is the summit of the canal and the restored cottage here was the home of the sluice gate operator. At the halfway point, take a break in the little village of Poyntzpass, before joining the quiet Canal Bank road through lush green farmland.

The rural scenery in the second half of the ride is beautiful, and you'll pass several attractive stone bridges including Gambles Bridge, also known as Crack Bridge because of a giant crack in its stonework and, some suggest, because it was once a meeting place for local folk to share the craic (fun).

The traffic-free route comes to an end on the northern edges of Newry, so join the road for the final half mile to end in front of the beautiful red brick Newry Town Hall with views of the distant Camlough Mountain behind. Or, cross the river and head to the city's main shopping area of Hill Street, home to the handsome, granite Newry Cathedral.

Sunny countryside cycling

RIDE 01

Finish: Town Hall, Newry

Train stations: Portadown and Newry

Grade: Moderate

Terrain, gradients and access: Tarmac path and fine gravel towpath. Some road crossings and on-road sections at Scarva, Poyntzpass, Jerrettspass and Newry.

Loops, links and longer rides: Loops, links and longer rides: From Portadown, either follow NCN 9 on a three and a half-mile, mostly traffic-free ride to the shores of Craigavon Lake, or the Loughshore Trail, a 113-mile loop of quiet lanes around Lough Neagh, the largest freshwater lake in Britain. From Newry, continue along the cycle route on a six-mile, on-road ride to Camlough Lake.

Stay: Canal Court Hotel, Newry (028) 3025 1234 canalcourthotel.com

Eat and drink: Try Chimes Coffee House or Zio restaurant in Portadown, Hollie Berry Tearooms at Scarva, Rice's Hotel in Poyntzpass or Al Forno and Art Bar Funkel in Newry.

Cycle hire: Ring of Gullion Cycles, Newry (028) 3088 8352 or Cloughmor Extreme, Rostrevor 077068 75394 **cloughmorextreme.com**

Wider area cycle map: Strangford Lough

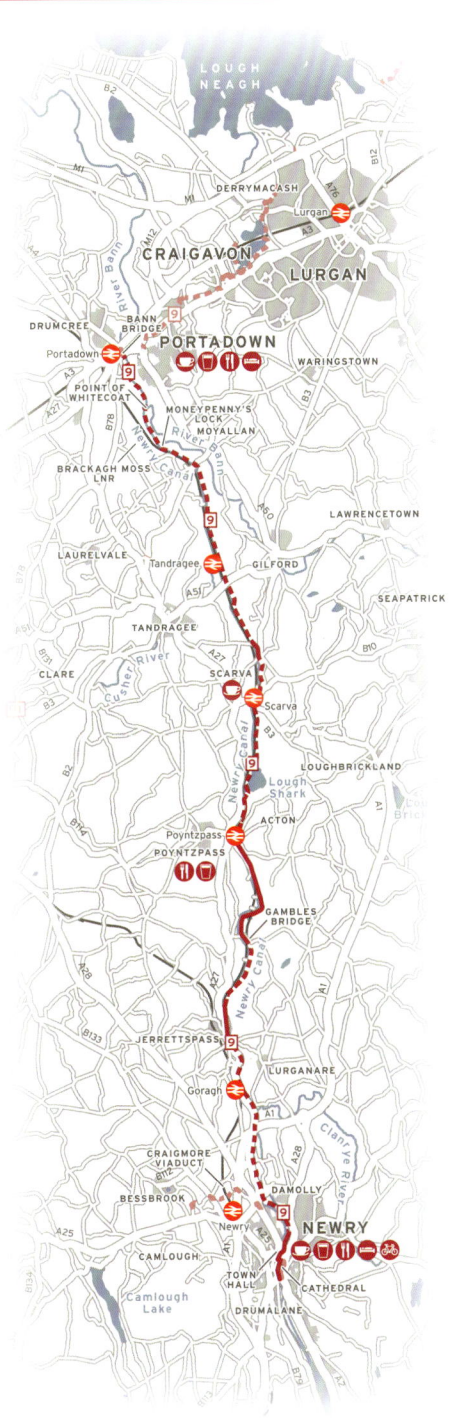

Craigmore Viaduct

335

RIDE 02
20 miles | 9 93 | **Start:** Lagan Valley Island, Lisburn

LAGAN
&
LOUGH

'The Big Fish', Donegall Quay

This towpath ride through the peaceful Lagan Valley Regional Park also takes in the magnificent scenery along the River Lagan through central Belfast and alongside the beautiful Belfast Lough.

Start at the impressive white buildings of Lagan Valley Island and immediately pass beneath the arc of 'Concentric Twist', one of the route's renowned artworks. In the opening mile you'll enter Lagan Valley Regional Park, 11 miles of stunning riverside parkland and woodland to enjoy all the way to Stranmillis on the outskirts of Belfast.

Around six miles in reach Shaw's Bridge, where it's worth leaving the path to cross the river into the National Trust's Minnowburn. The Terrace Hill Rose Garden here offers incredible views across the Lagan Valley, and a path through the open meadows and beech trees leads to the Giant's Ring, an early Bronze Age stone monument.

Back on the trail, reach Lagan Meadows Local Nature Reserve (LNR), the halfway point of the ride and a lovely spot for a mid-ride rest among glades of wildflowers, wetlands and marshes. Alternatively, cross the river again here to picnic among the heavily-scented pine trees of Belvoir Park Forest, where there's a good chance of seeing some of the resident red squirrels. There is a café overlooking the towpath a mile beyond Shaw's Bridge.

In the second half of the ride join the Stranmillis cycle track into the heart of Belfast. Leave plenty of time to explore this vibrant and cultural capital city; the City Hall, St Anne's Cathedral and the Crown Bar are among the exquisite buildings here.

At Donegall Quay you'll ride past the city's ornate Albert Memorial Clock and 'The Big Fish', easily the most striking artwork on the route. As you pause to admire the sheer scale of this bright blue 32-foot salmon, you'll be able to see two more giants across the water: Samson and Goliath, huge yellow cranes in Belfast's docks. Leave the busy docklands behind and follow the North Foreshore Path on a peaceful waterside route, looking out for wading birds or even the silky heads of seals in Belfast Lough.

In the final miles, pause at Hazelbank Park for some of the best views on the ride across the Lough, Cave Hill and the County Down coast, before continuing north to end at Loughshore Park in Jordanstown.

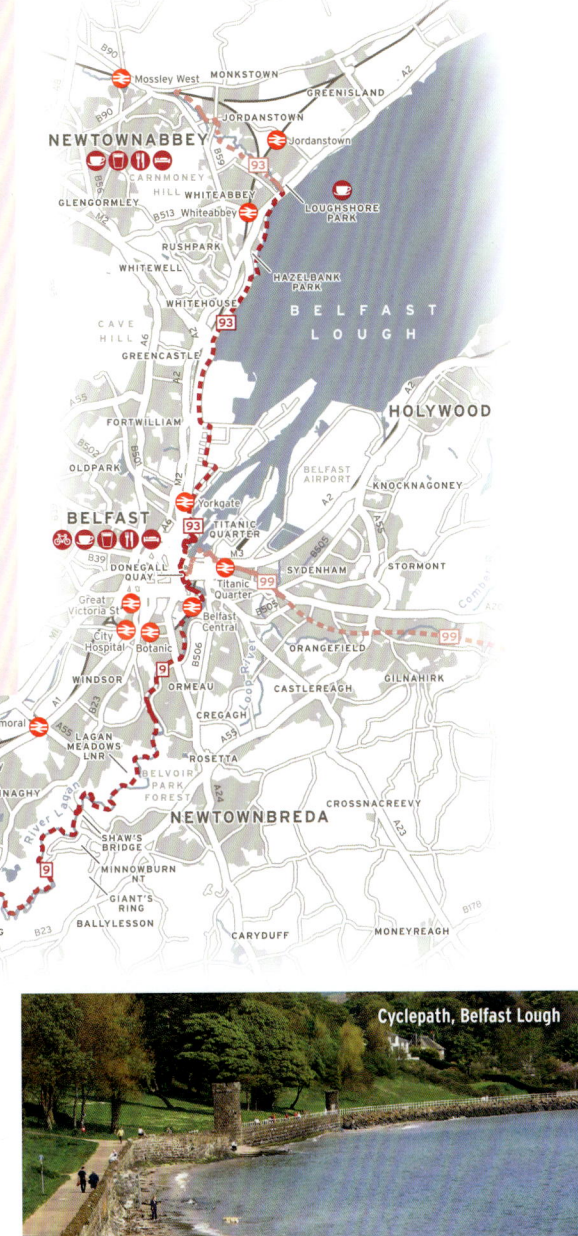

Finish: Loughshore Park, Jordanstown

RIDE 02

Train stations: Lisburn, Belfast Lanyon Place and Jordanstown

Grade: Moderate

Terrain, gradients and access: Flat tarmac path with some road crossings and short, on-road sections at Stanmillis Embankment and Belfast Harbour.

Loops, links and longer rides: From Lisburn, follow NCN 9 along an on-road route to link up with NCN 94 Loughshore Trail, a 113-mile loop of quiet lanes around Lough Neagh, the largest freshwater lake in Britain. NCN 99 Comber Greenway.

Stay: Ravenhill House, Belfast (028) 9028 2590 ravenhillhouse.com

Eat and drink: The Coffee Dock is at Lagan Valley Island at the ride's start, or the Piccolo Mondo coffee and pizza van in the car park at the National Trust's Minnowburn mid-way. There are many excellent places to try in Belfast, including The Crown, a pub owned by the National Trust. Barista Coffee House is at Loughshore Park at the ride's end.

Cycle hire: Belfast City Bike Tours, Belfast 0785 033 7336 belfastcitybiketours.com, Belfast Tandems (not just tandems!) (028) 9080 6666 belfasttandems.business.site or Belfast Bikes (034) 3357 1551 belfastbikes.co.uk

Wider are cycle map: Belfast to Ballyshannon

Cyclepath, Belfast Lough

337

RIDE 03
5 miles

Start: Cregagh Glen

CONNSWATER GREENWAY

The Connswater Community Greenway is a 5 mile linear park through east Belfast, following the course of the Connswater, Knock and Loop Rivers, connecting some lovely open, green spaces. The Greenway has been lauded for creating vibrant, attractive, safe and accessible parkland offering leisure, recreation, community events and activities.

Although your start point of Creagh Glen is not really suitable for cyclists (with narrower unpaved paths) it is worth exploring on foot, the glen leading to Castlereagh Hills and superb views of Belfast. Cycle parking can be found outside Cregagh Road shops.

An initial short section of route passes through the Creagh housing estate area where George Best – undoubtedly east Belfast's most sporting son - was born and raised and all football fans will be well acquainted with his legendary status.

You soon leave the road and head along the banks of the Loop River – the creation of the greenway not only benefitted active travel but also allowed the flood alleviation works here. Crossing Castlereagh Road, move through the Orby area to Dixon playing fields where you have a choice; continue north towards Victoria Park or explore the eastern spur through Orangefield Park, following the banks of the Knock River.

There are a variety of trails to follow within Orangefield Park. It has an interesting history as World War II saw it used as an American Army training facility with a German Prisoner of War camp set up nearby. Today the park's features include horticultural displays and a children's playground. Pride of place here goes to the Orangefield Velodrome's outdoor banked oval track, the only surviving facility of its kind in Northern Ireland. Popular in the 1950s and 1960s, it continues to be used today.

A track leads from the park to Knock Burial Ground which is one of the most ancient sites in Belfast. The oldest gravestone dates from 1644. This spur of the trail concludes at the Knock Carriageway from where you can retrace your route to Dixon playing fields.

Rejoining the main route and heading north now, pass the Hollow at Elmgrove, the 'green' heart of the Greenway. At this point the Connswater meets the two tributaries, the Knock and Loop Rivers where you also find the Conn O'Neill Bridge. The O'Neills were great warriors in Ulster and Conn O'Neill was the last of these great O'Neill chieftains (giving his name to the Connswater River). This area is also synonymous with singer Van Morrison whose eponymous song turned tree-lined Cyprus Avenue into the most famous street in east Belfast.

Soon comes one of the trail highlights, C.S. Lewis Square, named after the Belfast-born author. The square boasts seven bronze sculptures from his most famous work 'The Lion, The Witch and The Wardrobe'. The Square is at the intersection of the Connswater and Comber Greenways beside the EastSide Visitor Centre, where visitors can access information on the city's attractions.

As the Greenway heads north it stays close to the Connswater River passing the Oval football stadium. It finally heads into the spectacular Victoria Park with lots of wildlife here including a large variety of birdlife in the winter months.

RIDE 03

Finish: Victoria Park

Train Station: Titanic Quarter and Sydenham are the nearest stations to the route end at Victoria Park

Grade: Easy

Terrain, gradients and access: Mostly flat, a few gradients but nothing dramatic other than one short sharp gradient leaving 'The Hollow' to get to Beersbridge Road. All paths are sealed and of good quality. No barriers of note.

Loops, links and longer rides: The Greenway intersects with the Comber Greenway (NCN 99) which heads east into the rolling green scenery of County Down and west to Belfast's internationally-acclaimed Titanic Quarter. From route's end, Victoria Park, you can also head along Airport Road to join segregated cycle lanes and NCN 93 into the Titanic Quarter too.

Stay: Fitzwilliam Hotel is a fine five star option (02890) 442080 fitzwilliamhotelbelfast.com but there are also cycle-friendly Jurys Inn, Premier Inn and Holiday Inn Express options that are centrally located. Also the Stormont Hotel in East Belfast is very close to NCN 99.

Eat and drink: Mauds Ice Cream on Creagh Road is a fond favourite for locals. Lazy Claire Patisserie on Castlereagh Road is worth a stop for the macrons and coffee. JACK Coffee Bar in the Eastside Centre at CS Lewis Square features locally sourced produce and showcases products from local artists and food producers. Shopping centres by the intersection with the Comber Greenway have lots of choice.

Cycle hire: Belfast City Bike Tours, Belfast 0785 033 7336 belfastcitybiketours.com, Belfast Tandems (not just tandems!) (028) 9080 6666 belfasttandems.business.site or Belfast Bikes (034) 3357 1551 belfastbikes.co.uk

Wider area cycle map: Belfast, Newcastle & Strangford Loch

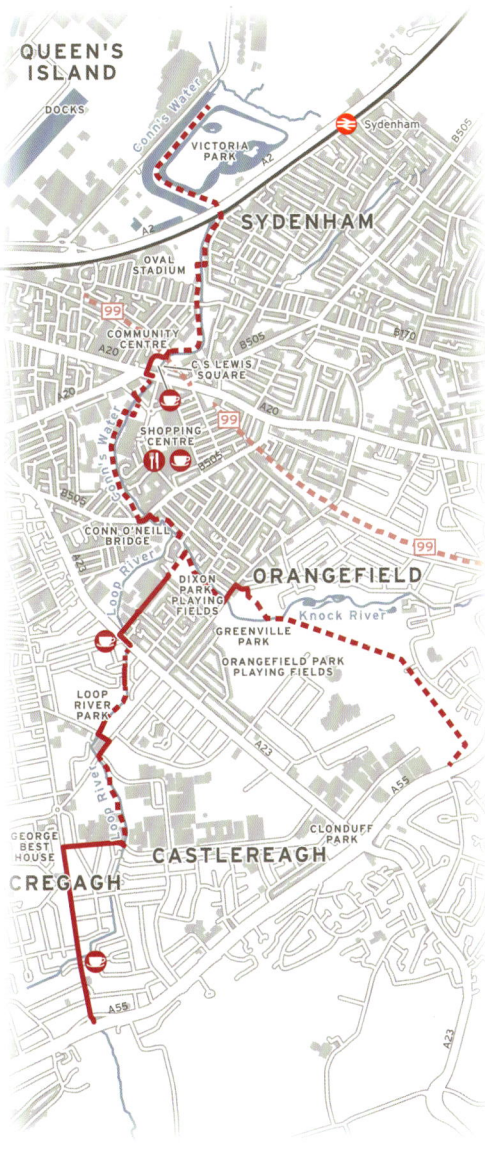

Connswater Greenway

339

RIDE 04
4.5 miles | 92 | **Start:** Peace Bridge, Londonderry/Derry

FOYLE VALLEY CYCLE ROUTE

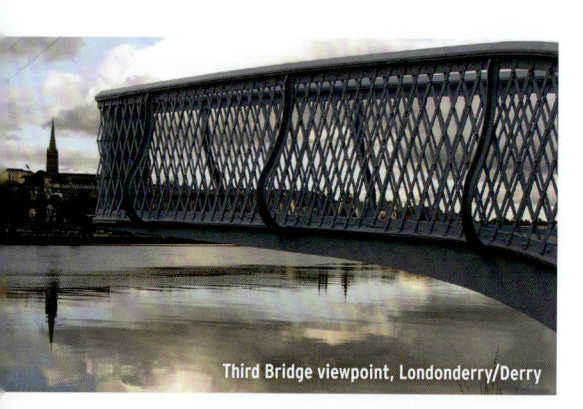

Third Bridge viewpoint, Londonderry/Derry

This short and gentle riverside route starts in the historic walled city of Londonderry/Derry and follows the former track of the Great Northern Railway along the west bank of the beautiful River Foyle. Before setting off, take a ride across the elegant curves of the Peace Bridge from where you'll get great views up and down the river, and visit the attractive St Columb's Park on the east bank. Alternatively, stay on the west bank for a walk around the 17th Century walls that surround the city. They dominate the skyline and are studded with more than twenty original cannons, including the famously powerful 'Roaring Meg'.

Start the ride at Londonderry/Derry Peace Bridge and head south along the Foyle Embankment, looking to the west to see the beautiful red sandstone Guildhall and the stone archway of Shipquay Gate, one of the four original entrances through the city walls. Moments later reach Craigavon Bridge, an unusual double-decker road bridge spanning the river. At the end of the bridge's upper deck is the iconic 'Hands Across the Divide' sculpture, two bronze men reaching out to one another in a symbol of reconciliation after division, you'll be able to see it over your shoulder as you continue along the path.

Next comes the Foyle Valley Railway Museum where you can pause to wander along the reconstructed station platform and discover the rich railway history of the area. From here, the city starts to recede and countryside scenery takes over. The elegant, Georgian Prehen House can be seen poking out from the ancient trees of Prehen Woods across the water, and the rounded green hills of Corrody, Slievekirk and Gortmonly create a striking backdrop.

After four and a half miles the path leaves the water's edge to meet Ballougry Road, so for a completely traffic-free ride turn around here and retrace the route back to the Peace Bridge. Alternatively, join Ballougry Road for a one and a half-mile ride that takes you into the Republic of Ireland, ending in the quiet little Donegal village of Carrigans at The Carrig Inn or village shop.

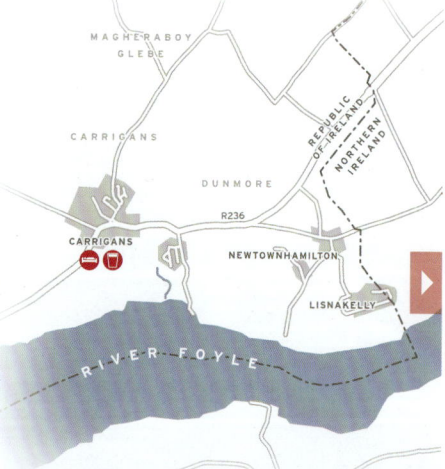

Finish: Ballougry Road, near Carrigans

RIDE 04

Train station: Londonderry/Derry
Grade: Easy

Terrain, gradients and access: Flat tarmac path. If continuing to Carrigans village there is a hill climb and a one and a half-mile on-road section.

Loops, links and longer rides: You can continue along the Foyle Valley from Londonderry/Derry to Strabane, some 21 miles. The 16.5 miles from the riverside path to Strabane are all on-road and include several hill climbs, but there are great views over the River Foyle and distant hills in Donegal. The Inis Eoghain Cycleway is a 34-mile, traffic-free and on-road loop starting and ending in Londonderry/Derry, taking in the Foyle Valley and Lough Swilly along the way.

Stay: Mount Royd Country Home, Carrigans +353 (0)74 914 0163 **mountroyd.com**

Eat and drink: Try the popular Primrose On The Quay or Peader O'Donnell's traditional Irish music bar, both in Londonderry/Derry. The Carrig Inn is at Carrigans where The Milk Bar also offers milkshakes.

Cycle hire: Nearest is Claudy Cycles, Claudy (028) 7133 8128 **claudycycles.com**

Wider area cycle map: Ballyshannon to Ballycastle

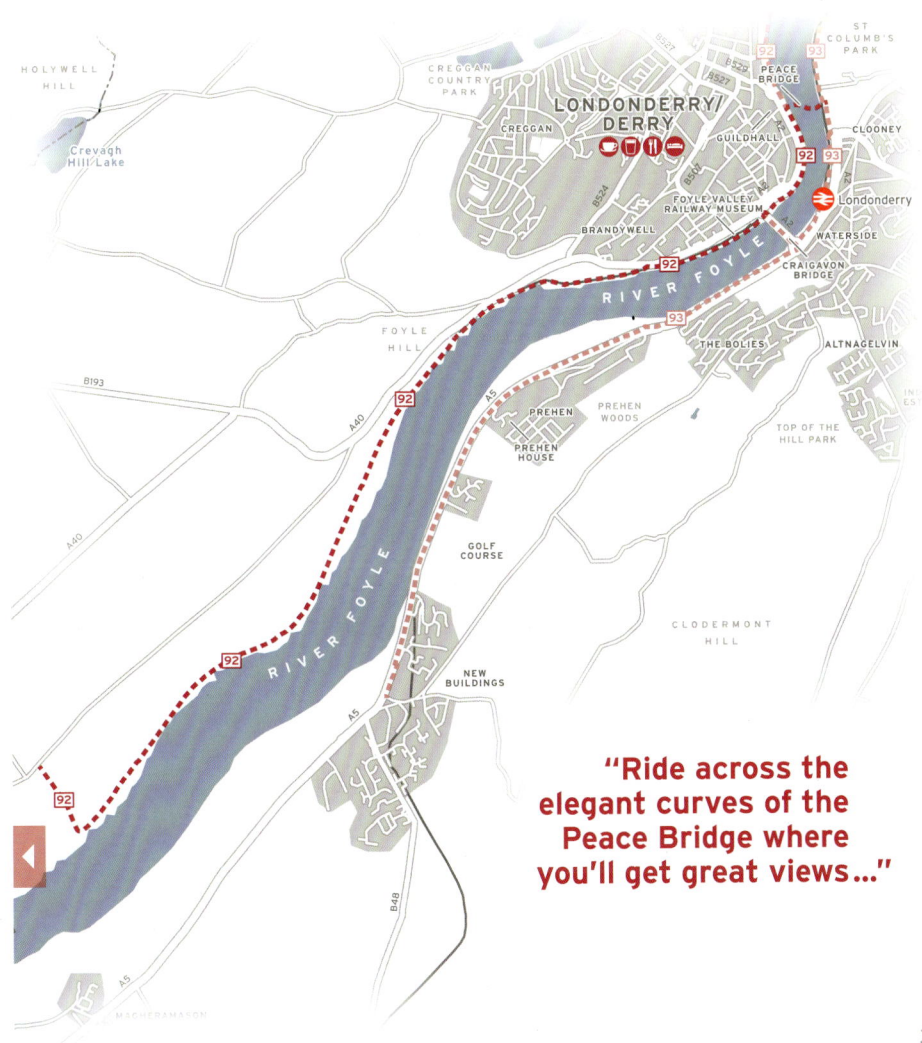

"Ride across the elegant curves of the Peace Bridge where you'll get great views…"

341

PHOTOGRAPHY

Sustrans would like to thank the following for kindly allowing the use of their images in this guide

Route name	Picture caption	Credit	Website
Introduction pages			
Page 1	Exploring National Cycle Network Route 7 and the Lochs and Glens Way	Andy McCandlish / Sustrans	
Page 3	Taking a break at Littlehaven, South Shields	Paul Kirkwood	getpedalpower.info
Page 5	The Taff Trail Cardiff (National Route 8)	J Bewley / photojb	photojb.co.uk
Page 6	Near Foulridge	Richard Peace	
Page 7	Xavier Brice	J Bewley / photojb	photojb.co.uk
Page 8	'Terris Novalis' by Tony Cragg	Barry Wilson / Sustrans	
	Ely summer workcamp, Wicken Fen	David Martin / Sustrans	
Page 9	'Genome stripes' by Katy Hallett	Katy Hallett / Sustrans	
	Chris Smith	Julia Bayne	
	Lunch stop on the Nidderdale Greenway	Dean Smith / Sustrans	
	York Cathedral	Chandra Prasad / Sustrans	
Page 10	Forth & Clyde Canal	Jim Hall	
	Sustrans Connect2 'Paul Cully Bridge'	J Bewley / Sustrans	
	Paths for Everyone	Sustrans	
Page 11	There are now over 14,000 miles of the National Cycle Network	J Bewley / Sustrans	
Page 12	Mangotsfield Bristol & Path Railway Path	J Bewley / Sustrans	
Page 14	Strawberry Line	J Bewley / Sustrans	
Page 15	The Peregrine Path	Dave Pearsons	
Page 16	Family-friendly cycling	Chas Thursfield	
Page 17	Collier's Way	Chas Thursfield	
	Granite Way	J Bewley / Sustrans	
	Millennium Coastal Path	Sustrans	
Page 18	Volunteers updating signs on the Network	Tony Moon / Sustrans	
	Signage at Stover Valley Country Park	Richard Peace	
Page 20-21	Dundas Aqueduct Kennet & Avon Canal	Chandra Prasad / Sustrans	
South West			
Introduction	Glastonbury Tor	Visit Britain / Martin Brent	
Coast to Coast Trail	Boats moored at Devoran	Axel Schneegass	www.flickr.com/photos/axelschneegass
Pentewan Valley Trail	Mevagissey harbour	Baz Richardson	www.flickr.com/photos/32424281@N07/
Clay Trails	Clay Trail with a 'Cornish Alp'	Lindley Owen / Sustrans	
Camel Trail	Padstow Harbour	Robert Davies	www.flickr.com/photos/grandetour/
Drake's Trail	Gem Bridge	Sam Howard / Beds for Cyclists	
Stover & Wray Valley Trails	Countryside views near Lustleigh	Richard Peace	
	Railpath near Moretonhampstead	Richard Peace	
The Granite Way	Lake Viaduct near Sourton	J Bewley / Sustrans	
Tarka Trail	Cyclists on the Tarka Trail	Sam Howard / Beds for Cyclists	
Stop Line Way	Donyatt Halt	South Somerset District Council	
Dorchester to Weymouth	Portrait Bench in Weymouth	Chandra Prasad / Sustrans	
North Dorset Trailway	Cyclists on the Trailway	Chandra Prasad / Sustrans	
Two Tunnels Greenway	Tucking Mill Viaduct fishing lake	J Bewley / Sustrans	
The Strawberry Line	Strawberry Line at Winscombe	J Bewley / Sustrans	
Bristol & Bath Railway Path	Cycling into the sunset near Fishponds	J Bewley / Sustrans	
Kennet & Avon Canal	Evening ride along the Kennet & Avon Canal towpath	Nick Turner / Sustrans	
Swindon to Marlborough	Grade II listed diving board at Coate Water National Cycle Route 45	www.visitwiltshire.com www.visitwiltshire.com	
Stroud Valleys Trail & Stroud Water Canal	Stroudwater Canal near Ebley Mill	Richard Peace	
South East			
Introduction	Brighton Pier	Visit Brighton	
Red Squirrel Trail	Sandown Pier	Abhijeet Vardhan	www.flickr.com/photos/abhijeetv/
Centurion Way	Mosaic floor at Fishbourne Roman Palace	dg	www.flickr.com/photos/dgeezer/
Shoreham Promenade	Cyclists on Worthing promenade	Dawn Reid / Sustrans	
Downs Link North	Cyclist near Christ's Hospital	Richard Peace	
	Guildford Castle	Richard Peace	

342

Sustrans' Traffic-free Cycle Rides

Midlands

Leicester to Watermead Park	Bulrushes at Watermead Park	J Bewley / Sustrans	
Derby Canal & The Cloud Trail	Trent & Mersey Canal near Swarkestone	Jackie Petrie	www.flickr.com/photos/jaybeepea
Mickleover Trail	Gate to the trail in the sun	Andrew Johnston	www.flickr.com/photos/genghis_man/
Nutbrook Trail	Cycling along the Nutbrook Trail	Peter Foster / Sustrans	
Biddulph Valley Way	Chatterley Whitfield headgear	Nigel Bowers	www.flickr.com/photos/advancedbiker/
Tissington Trail	Railway cutting on the Tissington Trail at Heathcote	Paul Kirkwood	getpedalpower.info
Monsal Trail	View of houses from Monsal Trail	Merseyside Young Walkers	www.fillyaboots.co.uk
Clumber Park & Sherwood Forest	Newstead Abbey	Richard Peace	
Water Rail Way	'The Lady of Shalott' by Anwick Forge	David Martin / Sustrans	
Longdendale Trail	The Longdendale Trail in Upper Longdendale	Richard Peace	

East of England

Introduction	Cyclist in Cambridge	Phil Mynott Photography	www.philmynottphoto.co.uk
The Alban Way	Hatfield House	Hatfield House	www.hatfield-house.co.uk
Cole Green Way	River Lea at Hertford	Mina Waters	www.flickr.com/photos/minaphotos/
	Mid-summer on the River Lee	Kevin Hurst	www.flickr.com/photos/110864385@N05/
The Ayot Greenway	Fountain in Welwyn Garden City	John Phillips	www.flickr.com/photos/26774111@N00/
	Ayot Greenway in the sunshine	Lee Henderson	www.flickr.com/photos/lorddexter/
Flitch Way	Rayne Station	Mark Seton	www.markseton.co.uk
	Flitch Way	Chas Thursfield	
Great North Trail	Fairlands Valley Park	Richard Peace	
	Village pond, Graveley	Richard Peace	
Luton & South Beds Way	Duke of Burgundy, Totternhoe Nature Reserve	Wildlife Trust BCN	wildlifebcn.org
	'The Course' by Michael Pinsky, Luton	Michael Pinsky, artist and photographer	www.michaelpinsky.com
Grand Union Canal	Enigma Machine at Bletchley Park	Tim Gage	www.flickr.com/photos/timg_vancouver/
The University Way	Cycling in Bedford	Chandra Prasad / Sustrans	
	Chiffchaffs are regular visitors to RSPB The Lodge	Brian Savidge	
Grafham Water to St Neots	Dinghies on Grafham Water	Anglian Water	
Cambridge to Waterbeach	Mathematical Bridge, Cambridge	Visit Britain / Britain on View	
Cambridge to Wicken Fen	Konik ponies at Wicken Fen National Nature Reserve	Brian Taylor	www.flickr.com/photos/35857078@N05/
Nene Park Loop	Peterborough waterways	Geoff Harman	www.flickr.com/photos/uplandsgeoff/
Celtic Causeway	Peterborough Cathedral	Visit Britain / Britain on View	
Marriott's Way	Old houses in Princes Street, Norwich	Baz Richardson	www.flickr.com/photos/bazrichardson/
King's Lynn to Sandringham	Customs House, King's Lynn	Richard Peace	
	Sandringham railpath	Richard Peace	

North West

Introduction	'Another Place', Crosby Beach	Sefton Council	
Burton Marsh Greenway & River Dee Path	Suspension Bridge at Connah's Quay	Stephen O'Brien	www.flickr.com/photos/34352063@N05/
Chester Railway Path	Eastgate Clock on Chester's old city walls	Chester West and Chester Council	
	River Dee at Chester	Peter Foster / Sustrans	
Wirral Way	Cyclists on the Wirral Way	Wirral Council	
Sefton Coastal Path	'Sardines' sculpture, Formby	John Grimshaw	
Leeds Liverpool Canal	Towneley Hall, Burnley	Richard Peace	
	Near Foulridge	Richard Peace	
Blackpool to Fleetwood	Promenade, Cleveleys	Paul Kirkwood	getpedalpower.info
Lune Estuary Path	St George's Quay, Lancaster	Visitlancashire.com	
Lancaster to Heysham via Morecambe Bay	'Venus & Cupid' statue, Morecambe seafront	J Bewley / Sustrans	
	Start of the Way of the Roses, Morecambe Bay	Rupert Douglas / Sustrans	
Lune Valley Trail	Cycling the Crook O' Lune, Lune Valley	Visitlancashire.com	
Lancaster Canal	Towpath cycling	John Grimshaw	
Bowness to Elterwater	View from Skelwith Fold	Richard Peace	
	Near Elterwater	Richard Peace	
Whitehaven to Rowrah	Foxgloves near Rowrah	Hannah Roberts / Sustrans	
Keswick Railway Path	Tunnel on the railway path	Phil Cheatle / Sustrans	
Maryport to Allonby	Sunset at Allonby beach	Nikki Wingfield / Sustrans	

Yorkshire

Introduction	Saltsmill	Saltsmill	

344

Picture credits

South East

Downs Link North	Cyclist near Christ's Hospital	Richard Peace	
	Guildford Castle	Richard Peace	
Downs Link South	Estuary Shoreham-by-Sea	Richard Peace	
Brighton Seafront	Man with bike, Brighton beach	Visit Brighton	
	Hut on Brighton beach	Sarah Gardiner / Sustrans	
Forest Way	Signs along the way	David Young / Sustrans	
	Forest Way near Groombridge	David Young / Sustrans	
Tudor Trail	Penshurst Place and Gardens	Visit Britain / Rod Edwards	
Crab & Winkle Way	Canterbury Cathedral	David Young / Sustrans	
Oyster Bay Trai	Local oysters	Ben Sutherland	www.flickr.com/photos/bensutherland/
	Whitstable Harbour	Richard Enfield	www.flickr.com/photos/smudge9000/
Viking Coastal Trail	View over Broadstairs	David Young / Sustrans	
Thames Path	Thames riverside at Staines	J Bewley / Sustrans	
	Cyclist on riverside path	J Bewley / Sustrans	
Jubilee River Path	Dorney landscape	John Ashford / Sustrans	
Two Palaces	Buckingham Palace	Oleg Brovko	www.flickr.com/photos/belboo/
Lee Navigation (South)	Cyclist in Lee Valley Nature Reserve	Lee Valley Regional Park	
Phoenix Trail	Sculpture by Lucy Casson	Katy Hallett / Sustrans	
	Red kite	Brian Savidge	

Wales

Introduction	Looking down on Talybont Reservoir	Sam Howard / Beds for Cyclists	www.bedsforcyclists.co.uk
The Brunel Trail	Haverfordwest Castle	David Oldman	www.flickr.com/photos/46503273@N00/
Millennium Coastal Path	Millennium Coastal Path	Tim Snowdon / Sustrans	
	Millennium Coastal Path	Tim Snowdon / Sustrans	
Swiss Valley Trail	Swiss Valley Trail	Peter Knowles / Sustrans	
Clyne Valley Country Park	Clyne Gardens	Gareth Lovering	www.flickr.com/photos/swansealocalboy/
Swansea Bike Path	Swansea Bay	Craig Williams	www.flickr.com/photos/12678461@N08/
Afan Valley Trail	Afan Valley	Richard Szwejkowski	www.flickr.com/photos/68112440@N07/
Three Parks Trail	'The Wheel of Drams' sculpture	John Grimshaw / Sustrans	
Taff Trail (South)	Cardiff Bay	J Bewley / Sustrans	
Taff Trail (North)	Pontsticill Reservoir	Tim Knifton	www.flickr.com/photos/timster1973/
Abergavenny to Pontypool	Above Blaenavon	Richard Peace	
Monmouthshire & Brecon Canal (Newport to Pontypool)	Canalside riding	J Bewley / Sustrans	
	Canal bridge near Pontymoile Basin	J Bewley / Sustrans	
Monmouthshire & Brecon Canal (Pontypool to Abergavenny)	Canal route view	J Bewley / Sustrans	
Peregrine Path	The Peregrine Path	Dave Pearson	www.flickr.com/photos/elhawk/
Elan Valley Trail	Garreg-ddu Reservoir	Martin Turner	www.flickr.com/photos/martinturner/
Ystwyth Trail	Aberystwyth Promenade	Pru Comben / Sustrans	
Montgomery Canal	Powis Castle gardens	National Trust	
	Powis Castle	National Trust	
Dogellau to Tywyn	Snowdonia views from the route	Richard Peace	
	Views across Barmouth Bay	Richard Peace	
Mawddach Trail	Mawddach Trail	Sam Howard / Beds for Cyclists	www.bedsforcyclists.co.uk
Llangollen Canal	Pontcysyllte Aqueduct	John Crickmore	www.flickr.com/photos/29712319@N02/
Lôn Eifion	Lôn Eifion	Julian Cram / Sustrans	
Lôn Las Menai	Caernarfon Castle	Sam Howard / Beds for Cyclists	
Lôn Las Ogwen	Llyn Ogwen	Rory Trappe	www.caeclyd.com/
Lôn Las Cefni	Cefni Reservoir	Ian Thomas	www.flickr.com/photos/53335906@N03/
North Wales Coast Cycle Route	Colwyn Bay	Dave Archer / Sustrans	
	Rhyl Promenade	Ian Wilson	www.flickr.com/photos/8752701@N08/

Midlands

Introduction	Thomas Telford's bridge at Ironbridge with poppies	John Horton	www.flickr.com/photos/9258223@N05/
Stratford Greenway	Thatched houses and St Peter's church in Welford-on-Avon	Visit Britain / Lee Beal	
The Brampton Valley Way	Brampton Valley Way	J Bewley / Sustrans	
Grand Union Canal (Market Harborough Arm)	Bridge in Market Harborough	Sustrans	
	Welland Park	J Bewley / Sustrans	
Rea Valley Cycle Route	Cannon Hill Park, Birmingham	Michele Moroni	www.flickr.com/photos/calim1974/
Birmingham to Sandwell Valley	'The Golden Boys' statue in Birmingham's Centenary Square	Ben Abel	www.flickr.com/photos/benbobjr
Silkin Way	Ironbridge Village	Steve Paskin	www.flickr.com/photos/111442785@N04/
Rutland Water	Rutland Water and Normanton church	Visit Britain / Tony Pleavin	
Leicester to Watermead Park	Bulrushes at Watermead Park	J Bewley / Sustrans	
Derby Canal & The Cloud Trail	Trent & Mersey Canal near Swarkestone	Jackie Petrie	www.flickr.com/photos/jaybeepea

Picture credits

Yorkshire

Poolsbrook Country Park to Rother Valley Country Park	Rother Valley Lake	Simon Dell Photography	www.flickr.com/photos/sheffieldcity/
Dove Valley Trail via RSPB Old Moor	Elsecar Band Stand	John Simpkins	www.flickr.com/photos/jrs1967_1/
Calder Valley Greenway	Hebden Bridge	Paul Kirkwood	getpedalpower.info
Castleford Greenway	National Cycle Network 69 Castleford Greenway	Richard Peace Richard Peace	
Humber Bridge Route	Humber Bridge	Steve Babb	www.flickr.com/photos/stevebabb/
Hornsea Rail Trail	Trans Pennine Trail starts on Hornsea Promenade	Anthea Truby / Sustrans	
Wyke Beck Way	Roundhay Park	Rory Prior	www.lightpriority.net/
Aire Valley Towpath	Bingley Five Rise Locks	Barry Wilson / Sustrans	
Riccall to York	'Fisher of Dreams' sculpture	Paul Kirkwood	getpedalpower.info
York to Skelton	York Minster	Chandra Prasad / Sustrans	
Wetherby Railway Path	Wetherby weir	Alan Dingwall	www.flickr.com/photos/16125468@N05/
Nidderdale Greenway	Spring cycling on the Nidderdale Greenway	Dean Smith / Sustrans	
Cinder Track	View from Ravenscar Robin Hood's Bay to Whitby	Richard Peace Richard Peace	

North East

Introduction	'Angel of the North'	Peter Joss	www.flickr.com/photos/60720263@N07/
Middlesbrough to Darlington	Infinity Bridge, Stockton	Richard Peace	
Brandon & Bishop Auckland Walk	Newton Cap Viaduct, Bishop Auckland	Paul Bradley	www.paulbradleyphotography.co.uk www.flickr.com/photos/pcbradley
Waskerley Way	Cyclists on the Waskerley Way	Wendy Johnson / Sustrans	
Derwent Walk	Lilypond at Gibside	National Trust Images / John Millar	
Souter Lighthouse to St Mary's Lighthouse	Souter Lighthouse	Paul Kirkwood	getpedalpower.info
Newcastle to Tynemouth	Cyclist at the Ouseburn Viaduct, Byker	Cog + Wheel	
Newcastle to Prudhoe	River Tyne, Newcastle Cyclist near Gateshead Millennium Bridge, Newcastle	Richard Peace Sustrans	
South Tyne Trail	Alston Arches, Northumberland	William Nicholson	
Lakeside Way	'Freya's Cabin', Kielder Water	Sustrans	
Berwick-upon-Tweed to Holy Island	South of Spittal Signs on the route	Richard Peace Richard Peace	

Scotland

Introduction	Forth Rail Bridge	Joe Cornish / Visit Britain	
Ayrshire Coast Cycleway	Troon beach Rozelle Park, Ayr	Richard Peace Richard Peace	
Lochwinnoch Loop Line	Walkers on the Lochwinnoch path	Donald Reid / Sustrans	
Glasgow to Loch Lomond	Picnic area on the Clyde	Scottish canals	
Strathkelvin Railway Path	Strathkelvin Railway Path Cyclists on the Strathkelvin Railway Path	Peter Griffiths / Sustrans K Taylor / Sustrans	
Edinburgh, Leith & Portobello	Innocent railpath into Edinburgh	Richard Peace	
Edinburgh to Bo'ness	Forth Rail Bridge from South Queensferry	Jason Patient	
Alloa Hillfoots Loop	View towards the Ochil Hills	Clackmannanshire Council	
Dundee to Arbroath	Picturesque Arbroath harbour Broughty Ferry promenade	K Taylor / Sustrans K Taylor / Sustrans	
Callander to Killin	Loch Earn	K Taylor / Sustrans	
Benderloch to Appin	Castle Stalker	K Taylor / Sustrans	
Great Glen Way	Locks at Fort Augustus	K Taylor / Sustrans	
The Speyside Way	Cycling on the Speyside Way	Paul Davison	
Deeside Way	River Dee near Banchory Holburn Street, Aberdeen	K Taylor / Sustrans David Gold	
Cullen to Buckie	Cyclists on path between Buckie and Findochty	K Taylor / Sustrans	

Northern Ireland

Introduction	Belfast City Hall North Foreshore path, Newtownabbey	Northern Ireland Tourist Board Robert Ashby / Sustrans	
Newry Canal Towpath	Sunny countryside cycling Craigmore Viaduct	Robert Ashby / Sustrans Robert Ashby / Sustrans	
Lagan & Lough	'The Big Fish', Donegall Quay Cyclepath, Belfast Lough	Robert Ashby / Sustrans Robert Ashby / Sustrans	
Connswater Greenway	Connswater Greenway	Sarah Mawhinney / Sustrans	
Foyle Valley Cycle Route	Third Bridge, Londonderry/Derry	Noah Rose / Sustrans	

345